OUTPUT DECLINE IN EASTERN EUROPE

International Studies in Economics and Econometrics

VOLUME 34

The titles published in this series are listed at the end of this volume.

Ouput Decline in Eastern Europe

Unavoidable, External Influence or Homemade?

edited by

Robert Holzmann
University of Saarland, Germany

János Gács
International Institute for Applied Systems Analysis, Austria

and

Georg Winckler
University of Vienna, Austria

Sponsored by

Ludwig Boltzmann Institute for Economic Analysis,
Vienna, Austria
International Institute for Applied Systems Analysis,
Laxenburg, Austria
European Institute, University of Saarland,
Saarbrücken, Germany

KLUWER ACADEMIC PUBLISHERS
DORDRECHT / BOSTON / LONDON

A C.I.P. Catalogue record for this book is available from the Library of Congress.

ISBN 0-7923-3285-7

Published by Kluwer Academic Publishers,
P.O. Box 17, 3300 AA Dordrecht, The Netherlands.

Kluwer Academic Publishers incorporates
the publishing programmes of
D. Reidel, Martinus Nijhoff, Dr W. Junk and MTP Press.

Sold and distributed in the U.S.A. and Canada
by Kluwer Academic Publishers,
101 Philip Drive, Norwell, MA 02061, U.S.A.

In all other countries, sold and distributed
by Kluwer Academic Publishers Group,
P.O. Box 322, 3300 AH Dordrecht, The Netherlands.

Printed on acid-free paper

Printed in the Netherlands

Contents

List of Figures

List of Tables

Contributors

Alberto F. Ades
Harvard University
Cambridge, MA, USA

János Árvay
Central Statistical Office
Budapest, Hungary

Andrew Berg
International Monetary Fund
Washington, DC, USA

Eduardo Borensztein
International Monetary Fund
Washington, DC, USA

Anne Bucher
Commission of the European Communities
Brussels, Belgium

Guillermo A. Calvo
Department of Economics
University of Maryland
College Park, MD, USA

Aleš Čapek
Institute of Economics
Czech National Bank
Prague, Czech Republic

Ke-young Chu
International Monetary Fund
Washington, DC, USA

Fabrizio Coricelli
Economics Department
University of Siena
Siena, Italy

Marek Dabrowski
Center for Social and Economic Research (CASE)
Warsaw, Poland

Daniel Daianu
National Bank of Romania
Bucharest, Romania

Bruno Dallago
Department of Economics
University of Trento
Trento, Italy

John S. Earle
Department of Economics
Central European University
Prague, Czech Republic; also
Department of Economics
Stanford University
Stanford, CA, USA

János Gács
International Institute for Applied Systems Analysis (IIASA)
Laxenburg, Austria; also
Institute for Economic and Market Research and Informatics
Budapest, Hungary

Stanislaw Gomulka
Department of Economics
London School of Economics
London, United Kingdom; also
Ministry of Finance
Warsaw, Poland

Daniel Gros
Centre for Economic Policy Studies
Brussels, Belgium

Robert Holzmann
Department of Economics
University of Saarland
Saarbrücken, Germany; also
Ludwig Boltzmann Institute for Economic Analysis
Vienna, Austria

Miguel A. Kiguel
The World Bank
Washington, DC, USA

Nissan Liviatan
Hebrew University
Jerusalem, Israel

Klaus Neusser
Department of Economics
European University Viadrina
Frankfurt (Oder), Germany

Ewald Nowotny
Institute of Economics
Economics University of Vienna
Vienna, Austria

Peter Nunnenkamp
Kiel Institute of World Economics
Kiel, Germany

Gábor Oblath
Institute for Economic and Market Research and Informatics
Budapest, Hungary

Jonathan D. Ostry
International Monetary Fund
Washington, DC, USA

Martin Raiser
Kiel Institute of World Economics
Kiel, Germany

Sándor Richter
Vienna Institute for Comparative Economic Studies (WIIW)
Vienna, Austria

Dariusz K. Rosati
United Nations Economic Commission for Europe
Geneva, Switzerland; also
Foreign Trade Research Institute
Warsaw, Poland

Richard Rose
Center for the Study of Public Policy
University of Strathclyde
Glasgow, Scotland

Jacek Rostowski
School of Slavonic and East European Studies
University of London
London, United Kingdom

Michal Rutkowski
The World Bank
Washington, DC, USA

Gerd Schwartz
International Monetary Fund
Washington, DC, USA

Ákos Valentinyi
Department of Economics
European University
Florence, Italy; also
Institute for Economic and Market Research and Informatics
Budapest, Hungary

John Williamson
Institute for International Economics
Washington, DC, USA

Georg Winckler
Department of Economics
University of Vienna
Vienna, Austria

Introduction and Overview

Robert Holzmann, János Gács, and Georg Winckler

In the countries of Central and Eastern Europe, as in other countries with a past of state socialism and central planning, the political revolutions of the late 1980s brought about dramatic and rapid changes in the economy. In allocating their resources, firms and households had to face the emergence of markets and challenges from foreign competitors. In financial institutions, the mono-banking system was broken up and replaced by Western-type central and commercial banks. Capital markets came into being. New fiscal structures, on the revenue as well as expenditure side, were introduced. Individual property rights were established, and mass-privatization efforts commenced. Simultaneously, macroeconomic stabilization was needed and external shocks – for example, the demise of the CMEA – had to be absorbed.

This transition of Central and East European countries to market economies has not been smooth. Despite all political efforts, and apparently unrelated to the specifically chosen sequence and speed of reform measures, an output decline set in, encompassing nearly all sectors of the economy.

Based on official estimates, the size of the decline in real GDP since 1989 looks discouraging (*Figure I.1*). Until 1993, average output for the Central and East European reform countries decreased by well over 20%. The fall in real industrial production was even stronger, and the average production level reached in 1993 corresponds to only some 60% of the 1989 figures (*Figure I.2*). As expected, the unemployment rate increased within four years from practically nil to levels experienced recently in many Western industrialized countries (*Figure I.3*).

In all reform countries, the reduction in industrial output was much stronger than in the overall economy, suggesting that important changes in the economic structure have already taken place. Particularly, since prior

R. Holzmann et al. (eds.), Output Decline in Eastern Europe, 1-12.

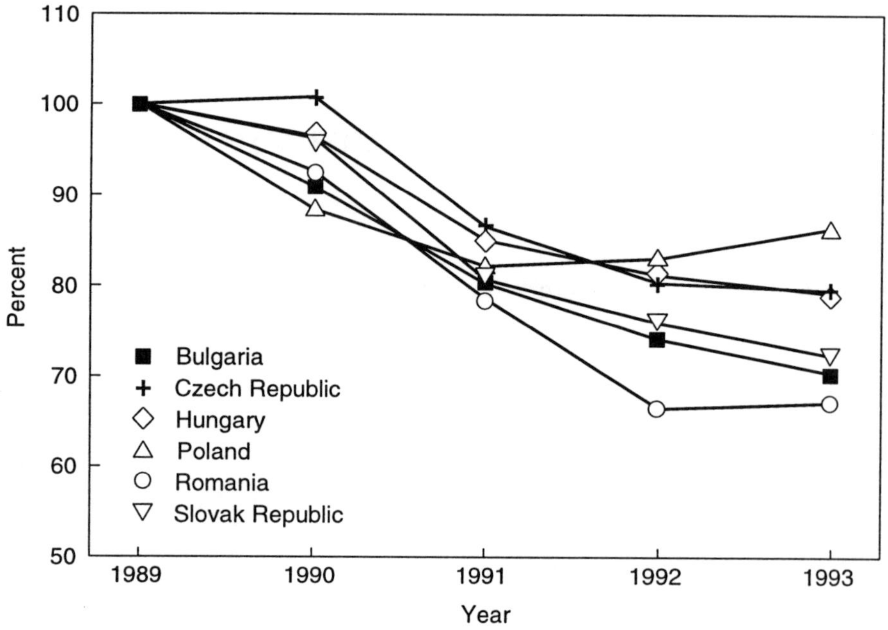

Figure I.1. Real GDP change from 1989 to 1993 (1989 = 100). Source: Statistical tables, *The Economics of Transition*, **1**(4) 1993; KOPINT-DATORG, 1994, *Konjunktúrajelentés* 1994/1 (Report on Business Tendencies 1994/1), Institute for Economic and Market Research and Informatics, Budapest, Hungary.

industrial output had to a large degree been associated with wasteful investments, military expenditures, large stock-building, and environmental problems, the fall may have had a smaller detrimental effect on actual consumption than the figures on output decline suggest.

Yet, despite these common trends, a mixed situation has evolved, with signals of both hope and dismay; as the reform process progresses, the economic performance has become less similar among reform countries. In a few countries, output decline has started to be reversed and growth is picking up (in Poland since 1992 and apparently in Albania, Romania, and Slovenia in 1993); in two other countries (Hungary and the Czech Republic) output decline seems to have been halted in 1993 and growth prospects are evident for 1994; the data for two further countries (Bulgaria and the Slovak Republic) indicate no bottoming out of output decline and gloomy prospects for a few more years.

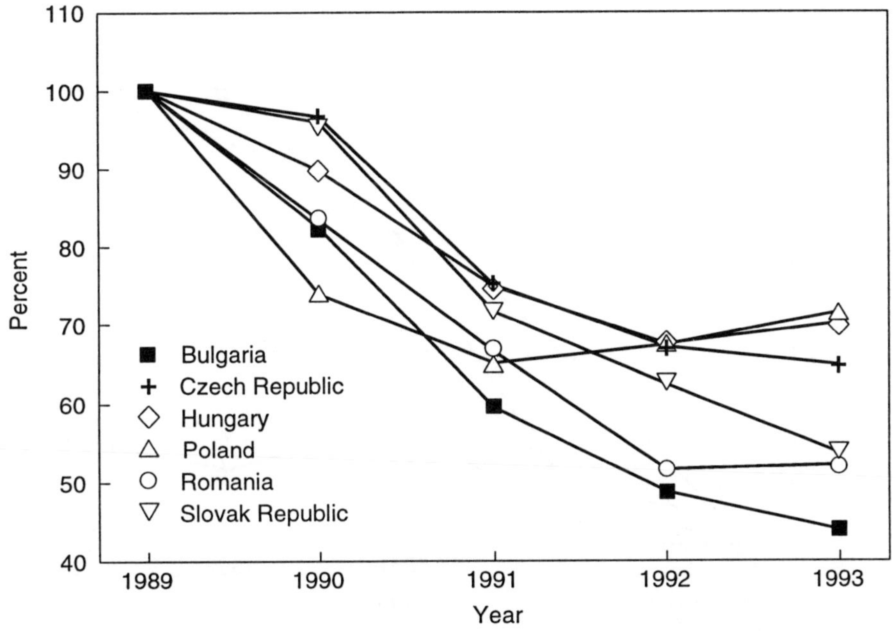

Figure I.2. Real industrial production change from 1989 to 1993 (1989 = 100). Source: Statistical tables, *The Economics of Transition*, **1**(4) 1993; KOPINT-DATORG, 1994, *Konjunktúrajelentés* 1994/1 (Report on Business Tendencies 1994/1), Institute for Economic and Market Research and Informatics, Budapest, Hungary.

The severe output fall seems to be at odds with the still moderate increases in unemployment rates, suggesting alternative interpretations of the scope of the adjustment process: either full structural adjustment may not yet have taken place in these economies and the traditional labor hoarding continues, the latter now as an inefficient device for providing social safety nets; or the registered rate of unemployment fully reflects the real level of economic activity, while the estimated GDP fails to do so.

Although output has undoubtedly declined, it is important to note that the extent of this decline is uncertain. Fundamental measurement problems result from distorted price indices. Besides, how useful are such output comparisons in the light of past wasteful buildup of capital and inventories? Official statistics also largely fail to take into account the shadow economy whose growth is encouraged by new conditions where tax evasion may be a major source of income. One can conclude from all these reasons that the true rate of output decline has been overestimated.

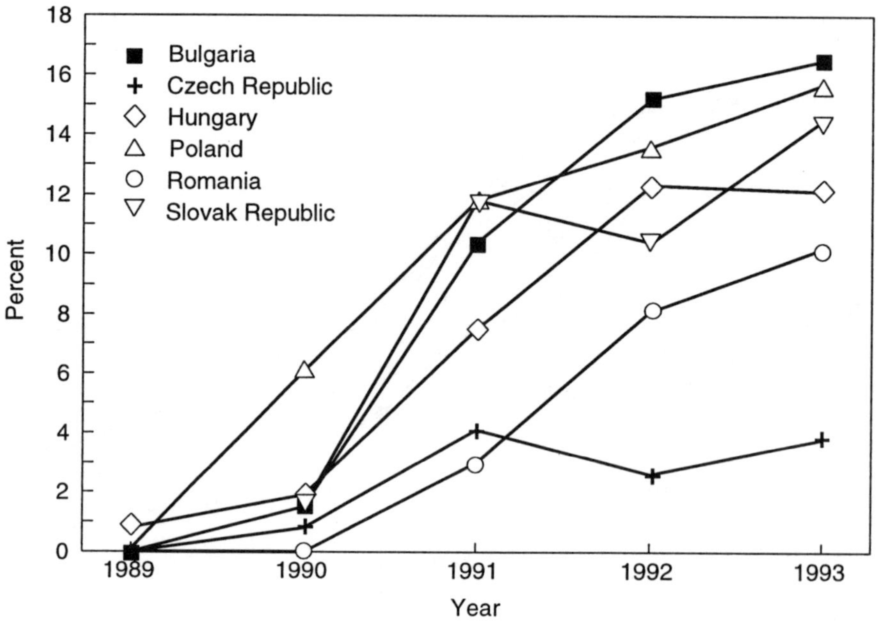

Figure I.3. Unemployment rates from 1989 to 1993 (1989 = 100). Source: Statistical tables, *The Economics of Transition*, **1**(4) 1993; KOPINT-DATORG, 1994, *Konjunktúrajelentés* 1994/1 (Report on Business Tendencies 1994/1), Institute for Economic and Market Research and Informatics, Budapest, Hungary.

But even given these more moderate rates, why has an output decline occurred, despite the initial optimism raised by most experts in the East and West? Various hypotheses have been advanced. Credit or fiscal policies may have been too tight. The collapse of the CMEA and the USSR was not foreseen. Individual incentives did not match existing institutions – for example, uncertainty about ownership rights in the pre-privatization period may have contributed to underperformance at the firm level. Changes in the composition of demand may have contributed to output decline, too, since domestic producers were neither experienced nor flexible enough to swiftly shift output to the new patterns of demand or new requirements of customers. In addition, output may have fallen simply because in the pre-transition days large inventories were accumulated, yet, when the transition started, the costs of holding inventories became striking. As a consequence, the initially huge inventories were depleted during the transition period, thus negatively affecting the level of production.

The unraveling of the output decline and the search for satisfactory explanations, as well as for understanding how the output decline has shaped the prospects for recovery, emerged as the central issue of the first phase of transition of centrally planned systems to market economies. Evidently, during this first phase, roads to fast growth could not be found. In hindsight, it seems obvious that market institutions did not quickly spring into existence as some had expected or hoped; time and efforts are needed to organize them. In the meantime, output decline will continue.

Acknowledging the scholarly and political importance of this decisive issue of the first phase of transition, the editors of this book organized the Conference on Output Decline in Eastern Europe: Prospects for Recovery?, which took place in Laxenburg, Austria, on 18–20 November 1993. The Ludwig Boltzmann Institute for Economic Analysis, the European Community (EC), the International Institute for Applied Systems Analysis (IIASA), the Austrian Federal Chamber of Commerce, as well as the University of Vienna cosponsored the event. Experts from universities and from international organizations (International Monetary Fund, World Bank, Organisation for Economic Co-operation and Development, European Bank for Reconstruction and Development, and the EC), having theoretical or practical expertise in this field, contributed to the Conference. Former ministers, deputy ministers, and advisers to governments in the East and West also participated.

Of the 24 papers and presentations given at the Conference, the editors of the book had to leave out several, otherwise valuable, contributions in order to keep the volume at a reasonable length and make it compact. Naturally, at one conference, and even less in one book, not all issues and topics on output decline can be addressed. However, the editors are confident that the book constitutes a unique presentation of this most puzzling problem. The editors did not tie the loose ends together and did not try to eliminate inconsistencies between arguments or even data presented by different authors. The puzzle remains with the reader and with future research.

Part I: Measurement of Output Decline

The book starts by analyzing the measurement of output decline. The most important measurement issues concern (1) whether the output decline is an artifact of adjustment in the systems of national accounts (the shift from the material product system to the system of national accounts), (2) the influence of distorted price indices, and (3) the difficulties of measuring output in the informal sector. These issues are treated in the first part of the volume.

János Árvay in Chapter 1 addresses the question of whether the output decline is a statistical artifact of measurement problems due to historically different systems of national accounts. In the former centrally planned economies, the material product system (MPS) was used rather than the system of national accounts (SNA) applied in the West. While surveying historical and current experience of transition economies, and raising a few methodological questions, Árvay concludes that different schemes of measuring growth may account for little of the output decline. The distortions in growth rates experienced in all transition countries are caused by other factors.

Bruno Dallago in Chapter 2 acknowledges that irregular activities were widespread even before transition. The systemic changes brought a restructuring in the irregular economy: shortage-related activities disappeared quickly and many formerly unregistered activities started to function as normal registered business. Transition, however, also contributed to the growth of some kinds of irregular activities, especially those that aim at circumventing increasing financial discipline (tax evasion) and those that provide employment for workers who have become redundant in the regular economy. Using data on Hungary, Dallago substantiates that the irregular economy has increased rapidly since transition; but he also points out that the capability of official statistics to measure it has increased substantially. As a combined effect of these two developments, whereas earlier official GDP in Hungary underestimated the total (i.e., official and irregular) GDP by approximately 11%–12%, by 1992 this ratio of underestimation may have increased to 15%–16%. These results are only modestly indicative for other countries since both the irregular economy and statistical practice may substantially vary from country to country.

Both **Richard Rose**, as a commentator, and **John S. Earle**, who provides an additional methodological note in Chapter 3, question the usefulness of looking primarily at the aggregate measure of GDP. They stress the importance of investigating disaggregated developments and the pattern of resource reallocation. One valuable source of this kind of information is surveys: they provide a more comprehensive view of the adjustment process in the firms and households, and also help to reappraise the official macroeconomic indices.

Part II: Causes of Output Decline

Part II presents nine papers, each analyzing the potential causes of output decline from a different viewpoint and providing alternative or complementary explanations. The topics investigated cover macroeconomic and microeconomic hypotheses, ranging from the issues of demand or supply shock, to the importance of the trade shock brought about by the demise of the CMEA (and the former Soviet Union), and to the issues of inter-enterprise arrears, bad debt, budget expenditures, and the changes in ownership structure.

Eduardo Borensztein and **Jonathan D. Ostry** in Chapter 4 investigate to what extent output decline is due to structural adjustment to a new set of relative prices, on the one hand, and to macroeconomic forces, including stringent financial policies and supply shocks, the latter associated with the energy price increase in an environment of tight credit, on the other. The authors have disaggregated data at the industrial level for the CSFR, Hungary, and Poland and decomposed the variance of output into factors that were common to a given industry in different countries (structural factors) and factors that were common to all industries in a particular economy (macroeconomic factors). Their findings suggest that most of the variance of output can be attributed to national or macroeconomic factors. There was little evidence in the early phase of reform that much structural adjustment had taken place. They investigate the importance of demand-side and supply-side forces in Poland in a simple supply–demand model of industrial output and conclude that demand-side factors were predominant in accounting for the output decline.

The topic of supply and demand factors causing the output decline in Central and Eastern Europe is also taken up by **Andrew Berg** who analyzes the development in Poland in Chapter 5. He concludes that the decline of industrial output in the socialized sector in early 1990, and hence in total GDP for the year, was due primarily to declines in demand. Berg asks, How important are the factors that fit under the rubric of "supply and demand" in comparison with other potential reasons for the output decline, especially adjustment away from the Soviet-style economic system? Investigating this point he emphasizes structural adjustment, rather than supply and demand factors, in explaining the transition in Poland. He sees that the explanation to this apparent contradiction is in the dynamics. The initial decline seems to have been due to a combination of aggregate demand shocks associated with the stabilization, declines in inventory investment caused by the transition from a shortage economy and perhaps by the credit crunch, and shifts in demand away from the socialized sector of industry toward other sectors of the economy. Subsequent developments have been dominated by the CMEA shock in 1991 and the steady and rapid growth of the private sector, both in services and in industry.

Dariusz K. Rosati in Chapter 6 examines the significance of the so-called Soviet trade shock on Central and East European economies based on price–volume comparisons. The analysis involves two steps: first, the terms-of-trade effects of replacing the CMEA trading rules by market rules is estimated; second, the impact of the loss of export markets in the former Soviet Union is assessed. His results from estimating the terms-of-trade effects for Hungary and Poland show that the income losses in 1990–1991 amount to 3.5% and 0.6% of GDP, respectively, and hence are less substantial than commonly believed. Estimates for the output effects of market losses in the former Soviet Union indicate that the collapse of exports in 1991 may have been responsible for less than one-third of the officially reported GDP fall in both the CSFR and Poland and for more than half of the fall in both Bulgaria and Hungary; the impact of CMEA-induced export fall was smaller.

János Gács in Chapter 7 estimates the output effects of the demise of the CMEA and the USSR in Hungary. Based on an input–output analysis, he estimates the direct impact of CMEA market losses on Hungarian output at 4%, out of 18% of decline registered in gross output from 1988 to 1992; the total (direct and indirect) effects amounted to 8%. He compares this loss with positive direct and total effects of Hungary's export expansion in Western markets on output, estimated at 2.9% and 5.6%, respectively. This result highlights reorientation from East to West, on the one hand, and the phasing out of certain export activities formerly directed to the East and the introduction of new exports to the West, on the other. Reorientation is found to be responsible for 19% of the shift of exports from the East to the West. The 1991 price explosion of imported inputs – a supply shock – inhibited the activity of Hungarian firms only moderately, due to earlier realistic domestic prices. Expressed in terms-of-trade losses, however, Hungary experienced a loss of 26%, being equivalent to between US$1,400 million and $1,600 million, if the trade volume of 1990 had been repeated. Gács concludes that due to decreased trade volumes and because of earlier special tax arrangements, much of the burden of terms-of-trade losses had to be borne by the budget.

Guillermo A. Calvo and **Fabrizio Coricelli** analyze the importance and economic effects of inter-enterprise arrears in economies in transition in Chapter 8. The paper provides theoretical and empirical support for the notion that inter-enterprise arrears in the reform countries do not simply reflect a situation in which the winners make transfers to the losers but, rather, reflect a situation in which winning firms cannot comply with their contractual obligations because other firms fail to do so. The simple model outlined in the paper suggests that policy should aim at modifying the present set of incentives, in particular, attacking arrears before they start to grow. They conclude that once there is a chain of arrears, there is little the policy maker can do. Under those conditions, even sound polices such as tighter bank credit may have no positive effect. Their analysis also suggests that the reform countries are no homogeneous group, implying that macroeconomic policy must pay close attention to institutional characteristics. In particular, they argue that when credit markets are dysfunctional, a credit crunch could have long-lasting consequences.

The contribution by **Stanislaw Gomulka** investigates the size and structure of bad debt of Polish enterprises. His analysis is based on enterprise data, collected by the Polish Central Statistical Office. The main findings are that bad debt constitutes a large proportion of total debt, to both banks and enterprises, but that the debtors are highly concentrated in a small segment of the enterprise sector. Some 90% of the enterprise sector is almost debt-free. The highly indebted enterprises form the "black hole" of the Polish economy. As regards the implications for monetary and fiscal policies, he argues that the large bad debt increases the interest rate spread and via the specificities of transition economies also results in higher nominal and real interest rates, altogether not conducive to economic recovery. In order to address the bad debt problem, he briefly surveys the main policy options and suggests an evolutionary strategy.

Ke-young Chu and **Gerd Schwartz** in Chapter 10 discuss the role of government expenditure policies in the decline in aggregate output in European transition economies. They argue that there is little evidence for the hypothesis that more expansionary expenditure policies would have helped to mitigate the output decline. While measurement problems only allow for very preliminary conclusions, it appears that government expenditures were, generally, not a binding constraint for output. In those cases where it could be argued that government expenditures were a binding constraint, they were usually not the only one. Current government expenditure levels remain on the high side, at least when compared with European market-based economies, and few reasons exist for pursuing expansionary expenditure policies to lift European transition economies out of the "transitional recession." While raising expenditure levels, *per se*, is an unappealing policy choice, a further reordering of expenditure priorities is desirable. In particular, increases in the share of government expenditures on capital – human and physical – are needed to improve long-run output potential.

Ákos Valentinyi in Chapter 11 analyzes micro data for several tens of thousands of Hungarian enterprises to investigate whether state-owned and private firms showed significantly different behavioral patterns during the process of a general aggregate output decline. While he admits that some unsolved methodological problems prevent him from arriving at a firm conclusion, he clearly states that both output and employment in the private sector grew rapidly between 1989 and 1992. One reason for the strikingly different performance between the private and the state sectors is related to the different sectoral composition of these sectors, as a consequence of which the private sector, mainly concentrating in trade, services, and construction, was less affected by the structural and demand shocks in 1990 and 1991. Valentinyi also finds evidence for the impact of another difference, namely, that enterprises in the private sector that had to face the same kind of shocks as their counterparts in the state sector adjusted faster to the shocks than the non-private enterprises.

Aleš Čapek looks for answers to similar questions that were considered by Valentinyi but on the basis of Czech enterprise data. He finds that private firms, especially small private firms and those under full foreign ownership, are superior in terms of growth performance and adjustment to the shocks. He singles out the group of state-owned enterprises belonging to the second largest size class as special trouble spots. In this class, unlike in the first largest size class, the pre-privatization rigidity is not alleviated either by the inherited more-advanced technology and generous capital allowance or by special efforts of the central authorities to restructure them. Taking into account several indicators Čapek does not find the future of the small private firms especially bright either. The reason for this is the spillover of the problem of bad debt from the state sector and the strictness of the credit policy. Čapek acknowledges the peculiar feature of output decline in the Czech Republic, namely, the tardy decline of employment as compared with decline in production; but unlike many other analysts, he considers it less a virtue of the Czech economic policy or enterprise management but more a transitory phenomenon that cannot be maintained for a long time period.

Part III: Policy Issues of Output Decline

The papers in Part III of the book address a few selected policy issues and measures for recovery. The three papers investigate the role of proper incentives for economic activity, the current restrictions on and the future possibilities of export-oriented growth (especially with respect to EC markets), and the lessons from stabilization programs in other parts of the world.

The chapter by **Martin Raiser** and **Peter Nunnenkamp** stresses the institutional void characterizing the early phase of economic transformation as a central factor in a comprehensive interpretation of output decline in

Central and Eastern Europe. In their view, the legacy and persistence of soft budget constraint for state-owned enterprises perpetuates a perverse incentive structure within the public sector, causing serious adjustment inertia. The paper compares policy responses to institutional problems in the Czech and Slovak republics, Hungary, and Poland. It is asserted that adjustment incentives depend critically on institutional arrangements and policy interventions that encourage discipline in the financial sector, shape the process of wage formation, and prevent a persistent struggle over the distribution of property rights. Their findings suggest that the Czech Republic has intervened most effectively, leaving it in a relatively favorable position for sustained economic growth.

Anne Bucher in Chapter 14 discusses the opening of Western markets as the response of the European Community to the economic and political reforms in Central and Eastern Europe. The paper surveys the steps undertaken by the EC to provide market access to products from the reform countries, the initial extension of the general system of preferences scheme, the conclusion of the Europe Agreements with the six countries of the region, and the additional decisions taken at the Copenhagen Summit in June 1993. She acknowledges the remaining restrictions – in particular on textiles, agriculture, steel, and coal sectors – and admits that the Community must do more to remove deadlocks in the sensitive sectors. The chapter also stresses the non-trade components of the Europe Agreements, which should improve the climate of cooperation and reduce trade disputes.

Alberto F. Ades, **Miguel A. Kiguel**, and **Nissan Liviatan** contribute to the debate on output decline by discussing experiences from regions outside Central and Eastern Europe. Their first piece of evidence is that, paradoxically, exchange-rate-based stabilization (ERBS) programs in Latin America were associated with an initial expansion in output. These episodes correspond to programs that used the exchange rate as the nominal anchor in chronic high-inflation economies. The second piece of evidence refers to experiences with money-based stabilization (MBS). While MBSs were few and sparse in Latin America, the facts strongly indicate that, in contrast to ERBS programs, they were clearly recessionary. The third piece of evidence comes from Western Europe, where the phenomenon of expansionary exchange-rate-based stabilization might not be confined to high-inflation economies. For example, an ERBS program launched in Denmark in the early 1980s generated outcomes similar to those in Latin America. The paper concludes with a discussion of how expectations of the possible success or failure of the program affect outcomes.

The **Summary** by **John Williamson** captures in an admirable way the main conclusions emerging from the Conference but also indicates areas for further investigation. At the economic policy level, he reminds us that the initial postwar recovery in Western Europe was much longer and more painful than had been generally expected in 1945, and only in 1950 were policy makers beginning to recognize that those trying years had been well-spent, building the base for a long boom. He concludes that the difficult counsel that we need to offer today to Central and Eastern Europe is to combine patience and resolution to get the fundamentals right and to avoid false panaceas with a ceaseless search for policy changes.

Saarbrücken/Laxenburg/Vienna
September 1994

Part I

Measurement of Output Decline

Chapter 1

The Impact of National Accounting Systems on Growth Rates

János Árvay

During the past four decades there have been widespread views among economic researchers and politicians that the growth rates of the former socialist countries were greatly distorted. The distorting effect was usually attributed to the application of the material product system (MPS) that provided the generally accepted international guidelines for the compilation of the national income and the other major macroeconomic aggregates in these countries. The MPS is a counterpart of the system of national accounts (SNA) recommended by the United Nations and applied in all market economies. It is true that the central aggregate used for indicating the level and growth rate of economic development is defined differently in these two systems. A major objective of this study is to determine whether the use of the MPS in the former socialist countries is solely responsible, or guilty, for the distortions of macroeconomic statistics as has been suggested for several years by Western economists. The answer given in this chapter is a definite NO!

The paper demonstrates that, as a general tendency, the gross domestic product (GDP), which is the main indicator of the SNA, shows a higher growth rate in the long run than the net material product (NMP), which is the key indicator of the MPS. This tendency is valid for any country independent of its socioeconomic system. In the chapter it is also pointed out that growth rates, measured on the basis of these two indicators, tend

R. Holzmann et al. (eds.), Output Decline in Eastern Europe, 15-29.

to move in opposite directions in periods of extraordinary rapid economic development or in periods of economic crises when the economy drastically shrinks. This chapter presents other factors causing rather considerable and tendentious overestimations of the indicators that have been used for demonstrating the fast development of the socialist economy.

However, before going into the substantive discussion of these two major topics, a short historical overview of the conceptual differences between the SNA and MPS is necessary for a better understanding of the issues.

1.1 Differences between the SNA and MPS

Shortly after World War II the United Nations recommended that the "system of national accounts" should be used nationally and internationally (UN, 1952). This system was successively introduced in almost all countries of the world, except in the centrally planned economies. In this latter group the "basic principles of the system of balances of the national economy" (UN, 1971) were adopted. This system (MPS) was fundamentally identical with the accounting system developed in the early 1920s in the USSR. In 1969, the system was documented and recommended by the Council for Mutual Economic Assistance (CMEA), and published by the UN in 1971 as one of the international standards. The two systems deviate from each other in one fundamental concept and in several small, but technical, details.

The one fundamental conceptual difference between the two international systems, however, effects almost all components and aggregates, and is reflected through the entire system. This difference is the narrow definition of the "productive activities" in the MPS according to which new value is created in the sphere of production of material goods only. In contrast, in the SNA both the production of material goods and the rendering of services in an institutionally organized way are considered value-generating activities. (Services provided within households for their members are excluded from the production boundary in both the MPS and the SNA.)

There are three other major differences between the MPS and the SNA:

1. The sphere of material production in the MPS covers not only the genuine output of material goods but also activities carried out to bring the goods from the producers to the consumers, namely, transport and trade of goods. These activities are called *material services*.
2. The so-called *nonmaterial services*, which are classified as nonproductive activities in the MPS (for example, education, health, finance, and general administration), are not entirely excluded from the system. The

material goods and the consumption of fixed assets used in these institutions are part of the net material product, because they are produced in the material sphere and are treated not as intermediate but as final products. "Only" the *value-added* components, which constitute the most substantial elements of these services, are excluded.

3. It is often misunderstood that all differences between the two *privileged* major aggregates (that is, GDP and NMP) originate in the differences in the production boundary. From a theoretical point of view not the value of GDP but the value of the national income at market prices in the SNA should be contrasted with the value of net material product in the MPS (in both cases net factor incomes from abroad are considered negligible). The deviating treatment of the depreciation in the two systems is mainly of a technical rather than of a theoretical character. *Figure 1.1* shows the relationship between GDP, national income (in SNA), and NMP (in MPS). In the figure three "main" aggregates are compared to demonstrate clearly the differences between the systems. The magnitude of these fundamental three concepts are illustrated by the actual data for Hungary in 1988.

The figure is self-explanatory; however, two interesting points deserve attention. First, in the 1960s, when the comparison of the two systems was initiated by the UN, the 1952 version of the SNA was in force in which "national income at factor costs" was defined as the central and final indicator of economic performance. Among others, this indicator was used for compilation of UN membership fees. As shown in *Figure 1.1* this amount for Hungary (Ft 971 billion) is smaller than the net material product of the MPS (Ft 1153 billion) (in the MPS the net material product is also called "national income"). Second, it is usually difficult to explain the inclusion of the value of nonmaterial services (Ft 64 billion) purchased by the enterprises producing material goods in the NMP. This value is not deducted as intermediate consumption from gross output of the material sphere because, based on the logic of the MPS, these services are not produced, so they cannot be included in the intermediate material consumption. Therefore, this component extends the scope of the NMP in relation to the GDP.

It should be mentioned that some further technical types of differences are of relatively small importance, and their effects to a certain extent cancel out each other.

When comparing the main aggregates of the two systems at a disaggregated level, several additional deviations can be observed. The following factors are of primary interest:

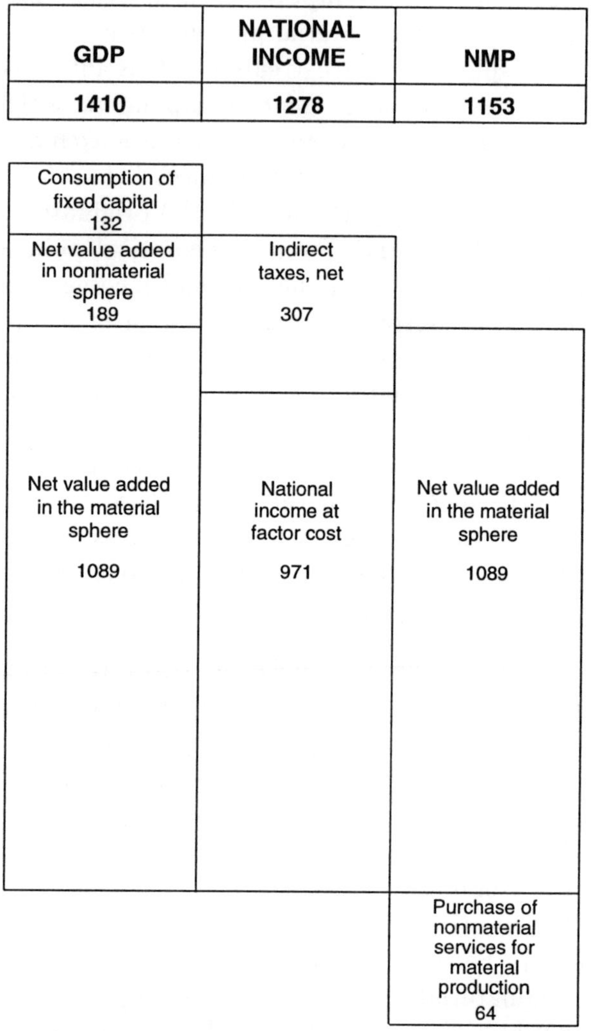

Figure 1.1. Relationship between GDP, national income (in SNA), and NMP (in MPS). Data for Hungary in 1988 in billion forints. Source: Hungarian Central Statistical Office, 1990.

1. *Industrial origin.* While in the SNA the International Standard Industrial Classification (ISIC) is used for this purpose, in the MPS the classification is based on the Classification of the Branches of the National Economy (CBNE); the two classifications differ from each other in many respects.

2. *Final uses.* The most important deviation is in the treatment of unfinished construction, on the one hand, and consumption expenditures on health, educational, and social services, on the other.
3. *Primary income distribution.* Differences in classifying the contribution of employers to social-security systems and the income of self-employed persons are of the greatest importance.

It should be noted that during the recently completed revision of the SNA and the MPS, some of the above differences were removed.

1.2 Impact of the Accounting System on the Measurement of the Level, Structure, and Growth of the Economy

1.2.1 Impact on level and structure

The scope of productive activity is much wider in the SNA than in the MPS. Therefore, it is evident that the global level of the main economic aggregates, first of all GDP, is considerably higher than the value of its counterpart in the MPS. The size of the differences for Hungary in 1988 is shown in *Figure 1.1*; however, this difference is considerably higher in the more developed countries.

These differences are of fundamental importance for international comparisons; therefore, adjustments must be made in one way or another when international organizations intend to rank or qualify countries using different accounting systems. For example, before an MPS-using country joins the UN International Comparison Project (ICP), it must first convert its NMP into GDP. The UN also requests that countries supply an estimated aggregate that can be used to determine membership fees. The World Bank and the International Monetary Fund require that the new members from Eastern Europe provide regular statistical information according to the rules of the SNA, even if they continue to apply the MPS domestically.

The SNA comprehensively covers all kinds of economic activities, while the MPS covers only a part of these activities. The latter system provides greatly distorted information on indicators such as the structure of output, the ratio between consumption and capital formation, the share of labor income to taxes, the ratio of profits and capital, and the composition of final consumption. There is also a large imbalance between output and various types of inputs (labor, capital stock) if the ratio is calculated using the MPS concepts.

These shortcomings were the main reasons why in 1970 Hungary introduced an accounting system that provided all major accounts of the SNA, but still preserved the fundamental concepts of the MPS. This system presented basic indicators as GDP, disposable national income, total compensation of employees, total consumption of goods and services, and savings (the system is described in Árvay, 1973).

1.2.2 Impact on growth rates in market economies

As indicated in the introduction, the view is widely held that the MPS-based growth rates are, in any period and in any country, systematically higher than the SNA-based growth rates. This conjecture cannot be proved, and just the opposite tendency can be observed for a relatively long period of time in the majority of countries. This trend follows from the character of the overall economic development that is driven by such factors as technological progress, the continuous division of labor in the production process, and the shift in demand from material goods to services. In normal periods of development these factors result in a shift of employment from the material to the nonmaterial sphere and, therefore, even if productivity of services increases at a slower rate than in the material branches (or simply cannot be properly measured), the volume indices of the nonmaterial services are regularly higher than those of the material production. *Table 1.1* shows the validity of this tendency in selected market economies over a 20-year period, comparing the volume indices of the material sphere, the nonmaterial sphere, and total GDP. Because the available information did not allow the derivation of net material product (only that of gross material product, GMP, which also covers the value of depreciation in this sphere), the last column shows the changes in the share of depreciation during this period. This share increased in all countries, with the exception of Belgium. So, it can be concluded that the volume indices of NMP would be even smaller in most countries than that of GMP.

The table convincingly demonstrates that, *ceteris paribus*, the SNA-based growth rates are in most cases, but not always, higher than the MPS-based growth rates. In the USA and Japan the GDP shows somewhat slower growth than the GMP. In Canada the two indices are practically identical. It should be mentioned that the uncertainties in the measurement of the constant price values for nonmaterial services are large in any country, and that the small differences in these three countries can be considered well within the margins of error.

Table 1.1. Growth rates of GDP and GMP in selected countries, 1970–1990.

	Volume indices (%)			
	GDP[a]	Nonmaterial[b] services	GMP[c]	Change in share of depreciation[d]
Austria	182	255	163	0.5
Belgium	170	192	159	-0.3
Finland	193	234	178	1.9
France	181	216	163	2.2
Germany (West)	163	212	143	2.4
Canada	208	208	209	0.1
USA	164	161	166	1.6
Japan	262	255	265	1.4
Hungary	178	221	172 (164[e])	[f]

[a]GDP at basic prices.
[b]Total of financial, insurance, real estate, community, social and personal services, and government and other producers.
[c]GMP is the difference between GDP and the value added of nonmaterial services.
[d]Difference in percentage points of the shares of consumption of fixed capital in GDP between 1970 and 1990 at current prices.
[e]If depreciation is excluded from GMP then index (164) shows the development of NMP.
[f]Not comparable.
Sources: OECD, 1992; for Hungary, Hungarian Central Statistical Office, 1993.

1.2.3 Impact on growth rates in former centrally planned economies

The Pre-transition Period

Before 1989, only Hungary regularly published official data on both NMP and GDP. In 1989, however, the Central Statistical Office of the USSR started to publish in its official statistical yearbook (Goskomstat, 1990) the absolute values and growth rates of GNP (which in practice were identical with those of GDP) and the traditional aggregates of the MPS. Following this signal, all other centrally planned economies in Europe carried out similar estimates, going back as far as 1980. So, it is now possible to compare the growth rates of GDP and NMP for these countries. *Table 1.2* shows the volume indices for the period between 1980 and 1990, which can be considered the pre-transition period. (*Table 1.4* shows the corresponding indices for years of transition.) The differences between the two indicators in the early 1990s are discussed in the next subsection.

Table 1.2. Growth rate of NMP and GDP in selected transition countries, 1980–1990.

	Volume indices in 1990: 1980 = 100	
	NMP	GDP
Bulgaria	126	120
Czechoslovakia (1989 to 1980)	110	112
GDR (1989 to 1980)	141	140
Hungary	106	111
Poland	95	97
Romania	98	105
USSR	125	132

Source: UN ECE, 1993.

In these countries the nonmaterial sphere developed at a faster rate than the sphere of material production during the decade before transition (*Table 1.2*). There are two exceptions. In Bulgaria the slower rate is most likely due to the fact that the two indices were taken from two different sources and it is not clear whether both indicators reflect the revisions made recently. Data for the former GDR in *Table 1.2* reflect a phase of growth when the relation between the two indicators tended not to follow the general rule. Hungary experienced a similar situation during the 1960–1970 period when the official volume index of NMP was 170%, while the volume index of GDP was "only" 168%. Therefore, it can be stated that in periods of very fast economic development of manufacture (and industry as a whole) the growth rate of NMP is most likely somewhat higher than that of GDP. In other "normal" periods the opposite tendency is the rule.

The Transition Period: 1990–1992

The comparison of growth rates for the two indicators in transition countries has been hindered by several factors in recent years. One of them is that in most transition economies the compilation of MPS data ceased in 1991, and since then only SNA-type aggregates have been published. (The replacement of the MPS by the SNA in transition countries was unanimously accepted at the Paris Conference of the OECD on Statistics in Transition Economies, September 1990.) Another important shortcoming of macro-statistics is due to the deterioration of the quality and timeliness of primary data.

Nevertheless, all available information clearly indicates the extraordinarily large and long-lasting decline in economic performance during the transition period. The economic branches most affected by the crises

Table 1.3. Changes in employment by main sectors in selected transition countries, 1990–1992, in percent.

	Total	Agricultural	Industry	Services
Bulgaria	−28.7	−31.2	−37.1	−16.8
Czech Republic	−8.8	−29.5	−14.2	2.7
Hungary	−12.1	−34.3	−17.7	−0.5
Poland	−12.6	−13.3	−20.4	−5.7
Romania	−4.5	12.9	−21.4	5.8
Russia	−4.2	−3.7	−6.9	−1.7
Slovak Republic	−13.5	−27.5	−22.6	1.8

Source: UN ECE, 1994.

accompanying the transition are manufacturing, construction, and agriculture, the fundamental areas of the material sphere. The large blocks of nonmaterial services, such as education, health, and administration, are much less touched by the collapse of the CMEA market or by the drastic decrease of domestic demand.

Table 1.3 clearly shows that during 1990–1992 the employment in the service sector increased in some countries and decreased at a modest rate in other countries while the number of employees in agriculture and industry decreased dramatically (except Romania).

It should be noted that the services sector also covers the changes in employment of the so-called material services, including freight transport and trade, which to some extent follow the changes in production of material goods. Consequently, employment change in nonmaterial services was even more favorable. For example, the employment in Poland in the financial service sector was 21% higher in 1992 than it was in 1989; in the Czech and Slovak republics the employment in this sector increased by 46% between 1989 and 1991.

Under these circumstances it is quite evident that the GDP shows a much smaller decline than the global value added in the material branches. The limited data available confirm this tendency (*Table 1.4*).

There are two exceptions to the overall tendency of these data. In countries of the Commonwealth of Independent States (CIS) in 1992, the decline of GDP was larger than that of NMP (UN ECE, 1993, pp. 3–5). This decline can be the result of either statistical inconsistencies or the drastic disarmament that occurred in this year. The other conflicting figures are found in Bulgaria for 1991 where the extraordinary fall in material production (25.7%) should indicate a much larger decrease of GDP than shown in

Table 1.4. Annual change in NMP and GDP in selected transition countries in the early 1990s, in percent.

	Year	NMP	GDP
Bulgaria	1990	−11.5	−9.1
	1991	−25.7	−11.7
CIS	1992	−18.5	−20.0
CSFR	1990	−1.5	−1.4
	1991	−19.2	−15.9
Hungary	1990	−5.4	−3.8
	1991	−13.2	−11.9
	1992	−7.4	−4.7
Poland	1990	−14.9	−11.6
Romania	1990	−9.9	−7.6
Slovenia	1990	−8.3	−3.4
	1991	−12.7	−9.3

Source: UN ECE, 1993.

Table 1.4 (11.7%). Similar inconsistencies were also found for Bulgaria in *Table 1.2*.

To conclude, during crisis periods of shrinking economic activity, the decline in the rate of the net material product is much larger than in the rate of GDP. In other words, nonmaterial services, especially nonmarket services, suffer less than industrial and agricultural output; therefore the development of GDP is usually (but not always and not in all countries) more balanced and smoother than the growth of NMP.

1.3 Factors of Distortions in Macro-statistics in the Former Socialist Countries

The discussion of the impact of the accounting systems on the growth rates in Section 1.2 tried to explain why the use of MPS-type macroeconomic aggregates alone is not responsible for the overreporting of growth rates in the former socialist countries during the previous four decades. Because the existence of distortions has been proved by many researchers, and the size of overreporting was sometimes extraordinarily large, it is worthwhile to discuss at least the main factors causing these deviations between the officially published and the alternatively estimated growth rates. The most well-known critical analyses of the official growth rates were made by Abram Bergson (1961, 1989) for the USSR and by Thad Alton *et al.* (1990) for the "small" centrally planned economies. According to their estimates the "true" growth rates were two to three times lower than the official rates in the USSR, Bulgaria, and Romania. The growth rates in Hungary and Czechoslovakia were also lower but to a much smaller extent. For example, the compound volume index between 1950 and 1988 of the official NMP was 1,000, 1,640, and 2,088% for the former three countries mentioned, while the estimated alternative volume index of GDP was 400, 488, and 585%, respectively. The official NMP indices were 525% in Hungary and 594% in Czechoslovakia, while the GDP estimates published by Alton were 311% and 313%, respectively.

In my view, these alternative estimates of Bergson and Alton *et al.* greatly exaggerate the size of the actual distortion; nevertheless, the overreporting of the growth rate of economic development cannot be questioned. The truth lies somewhere between the official and the quoted alternative estimates. Before identifying the main factors of the distortions in the official growth rates, it should be clearly emphasized that the magnitude of upward biases was considerably different between countries, even within countries during certain periods, and between the various aggregates of NMP. For example, the upward bias was much smaller for agricultural output than for industrial output, and it was smaller for final consumption than for capital formation.

Three major factors caused these biases in the volume indices of official net material product and its main components: distorted prices, hidden price increases, and the hidden economy.

1.3.1 Distorted prices

Due to the inherent nature of central planning, the prices of most intermediate, final, and capital goods were centrally regulated. They arbitrarily deviated from actual costs or from market-clearing price levels and were kept fixed for relatively long periods of time, even if drastic internal or external economic changes occurred. Prices of products or groups of products, such as beverages, consumer durables, and household appliances, showing above-average growth were relatively highly taxed and therefore their prices were usually high compared with their actual costs. In contrast, the commodities and services with below-average production growth, for example, food, housing, and cultural and social services, were highly subsidized and therefore had relatively low prices. It is evident that using such price ratios as constant weights for compiling overall volume indices would lead to an upward bias of the average indices.

It is not correct to state (as has been done many times) that the former socialist countries used very outdated price ratios for the Laspeyres-type volume indices for a long period of time. In most countries the weights were updated in five- to eight-year intervals. It is, however, true that with a few exception (e.g., Hungary), the introduction of the new weights had no retrospective effect: the old time series were chained with the new time series by using a single year's data.

1.3.2 Hidden price increases

For many years prices were declared by the government in "price lists" in most former socialist countries. Changes in the prices were declared in amendments or complementary price lists. No genuine price statistics existed in these countries. Instead, the statistical offices accepted the changes in prices as indicated in the amendments.

According to the ideological and theoretical dogmas the increases of prices were in contradiction with the basic law of the socialist system; therefore, enterprises could modify their prices only with the permission of the central organs and in most cases only as a result of hard bargaining. They were forced to find easier and more efficient ways to increase prices, which later became rather generally applied practices even for maintaining inefficient and loss-making activities. The enterprises, whenever possible, did not ask permission for price changes, but they asked for permission to include in the price lists new prices for "new" goods or for goods with substantially improved quality. In many cases small changes in shape, color, and size were sufficient for presenting the goods as new products. Free scope of manipulation was especially apparent in such product groups as machinery, equipment, construction, furniture, clothing, and household appliances.

Under these circumstances the statistical offices had no real means and tools for separating the changes in the "new" prices into a "pure" quality and a "pure" price component. The most simple way was to accept the "official" interpretation of the enterprises, which was also in line with the interest of the supervising ministries and even the central authorities: the prices did not increase! Consequently, using the deflators compiled from these prices, the production plans defined at constant prices of the base year were fulfilled or surpassed, the real wages increased to the same extent as nominal wages, and so on. Naturally, gross and net output of the economy developed at a fast rate, especially if the nominal (current price) value of these aggregates was considerably increased by hidden price increases.

There is an overall agreement among researchers and statisticians that this factor had the greatest impact on the upward biases of growth rates. It is, however, very difficult to estimate retrospectively the effect of the hidden price increases on the growth rates.

In Hungary in 1969 and in Poland and Czechoslovakia some years later "genuine" price surveys were introduced based on observation of prices for narrowly specified representative commodities quoted in actual market transactions. These price surveys were introduced in other transition countries only in the last two to three years.

The underestimated inflation rate in former socialist countries was due not only to neglect or underrating of the effect of hidden price increases but also to disregard of such factors as shortages, queuing, and forced substitution of goods in short supply. These phenomena were permanent concomitants of the central planning system. The correct numerical measurement of these factors, however, has not been properly solved in market economies either.

1.3.3 Hidden economy

The adjective "hidden" used to describe an economy has many synonyms: black, gray, unregistered, illegal, irregular. These terms denote activities and incomes which are not reported to statistical offices or not declared to tax authorities. The size of the hidden economy is considerably higher in the former socialist countries than in market economies and its share is increasing. During the past two to three decades of the pre-transition period the ratio between the hidden and documented economy changed only modestly; the various types of the hidden activities grew in parallel with the officially measured activities.

The situation has drastically changed during the transition period in all countries under discussion; however, it is of greatest significance in countries where the privatization of the economy has reached an advanced stage. There are several economists in both Western and Eastern countries convinced that the officially measured performance of the economy, irrespective of whether it reflects the level and growth of GDP or NMP, is largely underestimated because it does not reflect the growing contribution of the hidden economy. Some analysts even declare that the decline in the regular economy is to a great extent, or perhaps completely, compensated by the increase of the nonmeasured activities of private firms and by other hidden activities.

Table 1.5. Summary of major statistical factors affecting the growth rates of the economy.

Factors dependent on the accounting system	Factors not dependent on the accounting system
1. Value added of nonmaterial services.	1. Distorted prices.
2. Consumption of fixed capital.	2. Hidden price increases not reflected in the deflators.
3. Purchase of nonmaterial services for material production.	3. Hidden economy.

A recent paper by Árvay and Vértes (1994) attempts to calculate the ratio between the hidden economy and the official economy in Hungary. The main results of that study are given in Chapter 2 by Bruno Dallago.

1.4 Summary

The various statistical factors influencing the official growth rate of economies in transition can be classified into two major groups, each consisting of three components.

The first group consists of factors originating in the MPS indicator (NMP) that was used in the transition countries to measure final results of all economic activities. The size and sign of values of growth indicators depend on the cumulative effect of the faster or slower rate of growth of the three components shown on the left-hand side of *Table 1.5*.

The second major group consists of factors that are not dependent on the accounting system. The three main components are listed on the right-hand side of *Table 1.5*. If these factors were effective the growth rates of the transition countries would have been biased upward in the pre-transition period even if the SNA had been applied and the growth rates had been measured by the increase of GDP at constant prices.

Of course, it could be argued that if the UN accounting system had been used instead of the CMEA-recommended system, the distortions listed on the right-hand side of the table would not have occurred. This type of speculation, however, has no scientific logic or basis. In several market economies the growth of GDP is rather greatly influenced by the distorted price ratios or the hidden economy. In Hungary, where the basic aggregates of the SNA were officially compiled for the past 30 years, the factors in question had a considerable effect on the SNA-type indicators. It should be added that the distortion in Hungary was smaller than in most other transition countries. Other factors not discussed here also influence the statistical measurement of growth rates. However, the factors identified in this paper are extremely important, and deserved to be studied separately.

References

Alton, T.P., *et al.*, 1990, *Selected Charts of Economic Performance in Eastern Europe*, Occasional Paper 114, L.W. International Financial Research, Inc., Washington, DC, USA.

Árvay, J., 1973, *National Product – National Income – National Wealth: The System of National Accounting in Hungary*, Közgazdasági ès Jogi Könyuáiadó, Budapest, Hungary [in Hungarian].

Árvay, J., and Vértes, A., 1994, *The Share of the Private Sector and Hidden Economy in Hungary, 1980–1992*, Hungarian GKI Economic Research Co., Budapest, Hungary.

Bergson, A., 1961, *The Real National Income of Soviet Russia since 1928*, Harvard University Press, Cambridge, MA, USA.

Bergson, A., 1989, *Planning and Performance in Socialist Economies: The USSR and Eastern Europe*, Unwin Hynan, Boston, MA, USA.

Goskomstat, 1990, *National Economy of USSR in 1989*, Publishing House of Finance and Statistics, Moscow, Russia [in Russian].

Hungarian Central Statistical Office, 1990, *Main Indicators of Economic Developments in 1988*, Budapest, Hungary.

Hungarian Central Statistical Office, 1993, *National Accounts: Hungary 1991*, Budapest, Hungary.

OECD, 1992, *National Accounts*, Vol. 2: *1978–1990*, Organisation for Economic Co-operation and Development, Paris, France.

UN, 1952, *System of National Accounts and Supporting Tables*, Studies in Methods, Series F, No. 2. United Nations, New York, NY, USA.

UN, 1971, *Basic Principles of the System of Balances of the National Economy*, Studies in Methods, Series F, No. 17, United Nations, New York, NY, USA; originally published in Russian by the Council for Mutual Economic Assistance in 1969.

UN, 1977, *Comparison of the System of National Account and the System of Balances of the National Economy*, Part I: *Conceptual Relations*, Studies in Methods, Series F, No. 20, United Nations, New York, NY, USA.

UN, 1981, *Comparison of the System of National Account and the System of Balances of the National Economy*, Part II: *The Transformation of SNA Aggregates into MPS Aggregates and Vice-versa in Selected Countries*, United Nations, New York, NY, USA.

UN ECE, 1993, *Economic Survey of Europe in 1992–1993*, United Nations, New York, NY, USA.

UN ECE, 1994, *Economic Survey of Europe in 1993–1994*, Geneva, Switzerland.

Chapter 2

The Irregular Economy in Transition: Features, Measurement, and Scope

Bruno Dallago

In this chapter the term "irregular economy" indicates the social phenomena and activities that are undertaken for economic ends that share the characteristic of being deliberate attempts to evade or avoid the rules (laws, regulations, central plans, administrative orders, contracts, agreements, and related costs) that apply to a particular context; the purpose is to achieve a goal that is permitted, tolerated, or at any rate not explicitly condemned in the economic system concerned. The irregular economy, therefore, displays a discrepancy between economic goals – which are permitted – and the so-called rule-breaking instruments and means used to achieve them.[1]

Agents in the irregular economy of a market economy,[2] similar to free riders, escape private costs while enjoying public benefits. However, they do it to increase their private benefits; therefore, they should be more correctly defined as profiteers.

While free riding leads to the impossibility of establishing a market price, agents in the irregular economy produce and exchange private goods.

Research on which this paper is based has been supported by the University of Trento. The author gratefully acknowledges comments and suggestions from János Árvay, Richard Rose, and the participants in the Laxenburg Conference. This paper is dedicated to Gregory Grossman to whom I am greatly indebted for his constant intellectual stimulus and help.

R. Holzmann et al. (eds.), Output Decline in Eastern Europe, 31-60.

However, by partially escaping production costs, irregular agents turn out to distort market prices via market segmentation.[3]

The open acknowledgment of the existence and the relevance of a wide sector of the economy that escapes the rules and obligations typical of any social activity dates back at least to the early days of the political economy.[4] It seems, therefore, that the irregular economy is congenital in any socially organized economy. The same observation holds true for Soviet-type economies, where the disclosure of the existence of an "informal organization" of enterprises dates back to the early 1950s (Berliner, 1952, 1957). However, the systematic study of the characteristics of the "second economy"[5] and the first attempts to measure some of its components in Central and East European economies started in the 1970s. Since then it has been considered an organic and relevant component of the Soviet-type system, deriving from its fundamental features.

Many observers attributed the existence of a widespread irregular economy to the nonrational and bureaucratic nature of the Soviet-type system. As a consequence, one could expect that with the transition to a market economy the irregular economy should disappear. The events that have occurred since the beginning of transition have not met this expectation. However, one can observe that a rapid restructuring of the sector has taken place. The present irregular economy displays some features of the "old" (Soviet-type) irregular economy, but has also taken on new features.

A substantial part of the fall in the performance in transition economies has recently been called a statistical illusion because a relevant share of economic activity – the irregular economy – escapes registration. According to this interpretation, the actual (regular plus irregular) economic performance is substantially higher than what has been registered by statistics and the depression of those economies is in the worst case substantially milder than commonly thought.

Considering the deep and wide transformation occurring within the economies and the great relevance of their actual performance during transition an attempt must be made to assess correctly the role and weight of the irregular economy. One can distinguish at least three different areas where the irregular economy has a relevant impact. First, it has a great impact on institutions. To have a clear picture of the behavior and attitudes of economic agents and of alternative solutions available, one has to consider the kind of opportunities and constraints that the irregular economy offers and imposes. Second, it has a substantial impact on the level of aggregates and as a consequence on the structure of the economy. These indicators provide short-term economic information, on which decision-making is based.

Third, it strongly influences the growth and development of the economy, particularly in periods of great and rapid change. Disregarding the irregular economy may leave the actual situation of the economy unexplained and may lead to the implementation of wrong transformation and development strategies. The second and the third issues are relevant for statistics.

Indeed, the irregular economy and statistical recording of it concern two different issues, but these two concepts are often confused. Consequently, it is preferable to distinguish between the irregular economy and the unrecorded economy, although they largely overlap. Apart from errors in measurement and calculation, *per se*, statistical underestimation derives from the inadequacy of the methods and tools used in surveys and in quantitative estimates, as well as from the characteristics of statistical conventions. The gross domestic product calculated on the basis of the European system of economic accounts (SEC) and the United Nations system of national accounting (SNA) should include all regular and irregular activities plus a part of the informal and criminal economy; it should exclude, by convention, only domestic production, "do-it-yourself" and unpaid voluntary work, and various criminal activities. All statistical offices adopt various solutions to capture a substantial part of the irregular economy (see UN ECE, 1992, 1993; Rey, 1985; Siesto, 1987). That part of economic activity excluded by definition from national accounting is, therefore, limited to part of the criminal economy and the informal economy. Added to these activities (because of the above-mentioned weakness of the methods of survey and of calculation) is that part of the irregular economy not estimated by the national statistical apparatuses and not included under the headings of "errors and omissions" in the economic accounts, as well as possible underestimates of regular activities.

A brief discussion of the irregular economy's general features is given in Section 2.1. A fundamental understanding of the correct assessments of the features and transformation of the irregular economy is necessary to comprehend the actual situation of the economy and the working of the economic system; this is provided in Section 2.2. Once this aspect is clear, it is useful to try to assess the absolute and relative relevance of the irregular economy from existing evidence, which is presented in Section 2.3. The actual meaning of existing evidence greatly depends on the reliability of the estimation methods that were utilized; the method used in this study is briefly discussed in Section 2.4. Finally, Section 2.5 attempts to answer a fundamental question: Was the official level and structure of the national income and its growth rates underestimated or distorted because of the irregular economy? We use the case of Hungary to answer this question.

2.1 The Basic Features

From research projects conducted on various countries belonging to different economic systems it clearly appears that the irregular economy is not a homogeneous sector; this produces a (segmented) irregular economy within a segmented economy as explained in the introduction. In reality, the irregular economy comprises activities that are extremely dissimilar to one another.

It is frequently held that cost-cutting occurs through irregular activities (in particular, avoidance of taxes and social contributions, red tape, costs for controls to protect workers and consumers from physical hazards). Also, these activities are supposed to make use of greater flexibility, and therefore would be free of institutional and organizational constraints ("rigidity") compared with regular activities. Although irregular activities manage to overcome the barriers and constraints inherent in regular activities and to avoid or attenuate the impact of the cost elements also typical of these, they have several disadvantages and structural limitations. For this reason the capital present in a country does not come to be wholly invested in irregular activities and labor is not entirely employed in the irregular economy. Irregular activities have to meet supplementary costs, deal with constraints and specific rigidities which increase particularly transaction costs, and face a higher degree of risk and uncertainty than regular activities. Additional risk and uncertainty derive from the repressive action of the state and from the impossibility to act in a fully legal context that implies that irregular activities have to renounce to the control by the state over contract implementation and the state defence of independent economic activity. As a consequence, regular financial organizations are generally unwilling to lend to irregular agents or they impose upon them high collateral requirements, usually in the form of real estate and other physical wealth independent of the production activity of the agent.

All this means that irregular economic activities cannot utilize all the opportunities available, and in particular they may be prevented from taking advantage of possible economies of scale. The availability of labor, moreover, is not unlimited, since most workers – and in any case primary workers – prefer to find employment in the regular economy because of the greater certainty and rights they enjoy and the significant long-term advantages it offers. Only a marginal amount of working time remains for irregular activities. Therefore, the irregular economy has to count, for the most part, on marginal workers who are often intent on finding a steady job in the regular economy or who are prepared to commit themselves only for a limited period of time.

If risks and uncertainty of irregular activities are to be reduced, then measures must be taken to pay for supplementary costs like those incurred in the protection of the irregular activity against repression by the authorities or against the possible attentions of criminal organizations. In particular, these costs derive from the frequent necessity to corrupt public officials, to pay protection money, and to hide irregular activities behind a façade of regularity. This last practice is also necessary to justify the high earnings and therefore the consumption patterns of irregular entrepreneurs, capitalists, and workers, and requires camouflage techniques which end up complicating the life of the irregular economic agents and depriving them of additional flexibility.

Irregular activities, therefore, come up against substantial transaction costs and constraints. These costs rapidly increase when irregular agents seek to expand beyond a certain limit. As a consequence, productive irregular activities are necessarily limited to sectors where economies of scale are not significant. Their potential size, bearing in mind the risks involved, also depends on their capacity for corruption. The size of irregular enterprises that are subsuppliers to one or more regular enterprises is also governed by demands from the latter.

Research performed in different economic systems in the past suggests that there is no clear-cut separation between the four different components of the economic system: the regular, the irregular, the informal, and the criminal. In fact, individual activities can move from one subsystem to the other, following changes in economic institutions and rules (such as laws and contracts), the situation of the economy, the level of demand, relative prices, the nature of technology, and so on. For instance, when the price of certain services (e.g., plumbing services) increases, the supply can (in part) move to the irregular economy and, if the development of technology permits (e.g., through the production of cheap and easy-to-use tools), to the informal economy. In general, the increase of taxes provides an incentive to the irregular economy, while the prohibition of individual activities provides incentive for the criminal economy.

When the economy is in a depression and competition is strong, irregular economy activities may survive more easily than regular enterprises because their flexibility and ability to cut certain costs become more useful and advantageous in those circumstances (see, for example, Ricci, 1978, 1981). When the economy starts to expand again the irregular economy may shrink in relative and also absolute terms.

When an institutional and organizational transformation takes place in a country compliance with laws, rules, and contracts may be reduced, and this situation creates a temporary vacuum in institutional and legal order. Irregularities typically increase during periods of war and social unrest, deep political crisis, and disruption of the economic system. They decrease, however, when order is restored and improved in the economy, the government, and social and legal activities.

For example, empirical research on the irregular economy in Poland during the 1980s shows that some factors were particularly relevant in explaining the rapid growth of the irregular economy in the early 1980s: economic disequilibrium, accelerating inflation, decreasing real wages and a decreasing standard of living, and above all an increase in monetary overhang, which could act as a "lubricant" for the irregular economy (see Brus and Laski, 1985; Colijn, 1987; Górski, 1991, pp. 23–27; Wisniewski, 1986a, 1986b). The growth of the irregular economy was particularly fast in 1982 (by 1.7 to 3.5 times the 1981 level, depending on the estimate method used), when it counterbalanced the rapid decrease in real wages caused by high inflation.

The role of the irregular economy, together with the private sector, was quite important during the political and economic crisis that began in 1980. It provided people, particularly urban residents, with many goods and services after the collapse of the socialized sector: its role was fundamental in the production and distribution of basic foodstuff, although at higher prices and sometimes also for convertible currency. In this way, it helped to keep the crisis within manageable proportions and rendered official price increases less dramatic.

The transition process in Central and East European countries offers an opportunity to reassess the conclusions reached in different contexts. In spite of the disappearance of many of the conditions that produced the widespread irregular economy in many Soviet-type economies, during the transition the irregular economy may expand for at least two reasons. First, impoverished people will patronize the cheaper, irregular goods market and will supply marginal labor on the irregular labor market. Second, in a situation where private profit is becoming the main motivation for production, competition is increasing, and the budget constraints of the enterprises are becoming harder, enterprises may try to take advantage of the irregular economy to cut costs, increase flexibility, avoid regulation, pocket profits that belong to the state, and redistribute income from the state to the irregular private businesses via tax evasion. The first type of behavior is basically a defensive one, while the latter is an aggressive one. However, both can be seen as adaptive behavior deriving from the radical change, that is, the disruption of the old system and the lack of a new order. However, this same behavior can easily prepare the ground for a permanent change in institutions; the final result of the transition may be the distortion of the officially declared goal of a modern market economy, with relevant and possibly undesired economic, social, and political consequences.

2.2 The Irregular Economy in Transition

Sir John R. Hicks (1963) once noted, "Capitalist enterprise is the child of evasion; and on the long road from ancient smuggler to modern industrialist, the entrepreneur has learned more tricks than are easily reckoned with." The same observation is supported by many other scholars and researchers. Therefore, with the transition to a market economy and the development of private enterprises, new reasons for the irregular economy also arise.

The transition to a market economy was implemented in various countries under a situation of macroeconomic disequilibrium and after some years of economic stagnation. This situation made the process difficult because resources to finance the necessary transformation were very limited. With the beginning of transition, the old economic organization was disrupted, the productive structure started to change, and a new structure of foreign trade had to be implemented in a short time to overcome the collapse of traditional markets. Price liberalization, the rapid reduction of state subsidies to enterprises and to consumer prices, the introduction of a new tax system, the opening to foreign competition, and the implementation of bankruptcies led to hardening the budget constraint for both enterprises and consumers. As a consequence, demand collapsed much more than supply in both the goods and the labor markets, leading to the rapid disappearance of shortages and the appearance of substantial unemployment and underutilization of resources. The fight for survival became a primary goal of organizations and individuals, and this goal was also pursued through the irregular economy. These conditions constitute the pull effect (demand) of the irregular economy. Economic agents joining the irregular economy attempt to decrease costs through tax evasion and through the employment of irregular and cheaper inputs and to increase flexibility through the violation of laws, rules, and contracts.

The transition process has also created a push effect (supply) for the irregular economy. The dramatic fall of demand in the economy has left many resources unused and underused. In particular unemployed workers are willing to find employment in the irregular economy even if the wages are lower than in a regular economy. The irregular solution may be the only opportunity if the worker wants to keep unemployment benefits. A further push effect derives from the rapid increase in distributive disparities in personal incomes. In this case a demonstration effect acts that pushes the owners of resources to find a supplementary utilization of their resources, for instance, by taking on a second job. Other factors act in the same way: the uncertainty about the future (e.g., the fear of losing one's regular job); the decreasing relevance of the social-security net which may induce people to continue participating in the irregular economy to reduce risk and uncertainty and to gain the income necessary to meet extraordinary expenses (e.g., for medical treatment or to supplement one's pension); substantially increased prices which lead to a decrease of real wages and the spread of poverty; the possibility of buying luxury goods; the lack of laws and rules; and the lack of controls which provides an opportunity for pursuing illicit extraordinary income.

Relevant and far-reaching institutional changes have taken place which may constitute a favorable hothouse for the irregular economy. The most relevant institutional change for the irregular economy is undoubtedly the privatization of state ownership. In fact, this may involve such irregularities as corruption, the sale of assets at a price well below the market price to favor certain people, and the utilization of illicit capital.

The role of the state during transition has undergone a substantial change. This process temporarily decreases the state's capacity to control and ensure that the law, rules, and contracts are obeyed. This situation may increase the practice of irregular activities.

Transition to a market economy has also brought a fundamental change in the motivations of irregular economic activities. However, changes need time to be accepted, and they never involve the entire economy. Therefore, irregular activities of different types exist side by side. Three groups of irregular activities have been identified.

- The traditional irregular sector includes shortage-led redistributive activities and activities fostered by administrative limits on the private sector (such as the black market, speculation on goods in short supply, corruption, the utilization of stolen inputs, multiple job-holding where the primary job is in the socialized sector and the second irregular job is in the private sector), completely underground (unregistered) production activities (underground firms, artisans), activities living in symbiosis with the state sector ("crypto-private"), and traditional mismanagement of state ownership. This group also includes production activities existing only on paper and performed to cheat the state ("fictitious economy"). These activities are disappearing at different speeds in each country, depending on the implementation of the new institutional and legal framework, the liberalization of private activities, the effectiveness of the state in implementing its new role, and the success of stabilization.

- Transition irregularities typically occur during periods characterized by major and prolonged changes of institutions and organization of the economy. The main factors promoting irregularities are the disruption of the old institutions and organizations, the lack or insufficient development of the new ones, and the lack of controls and regulation. The most typical component during transition is the mismanagement of the state ownership and the unlawful gains obtained through the privatization of state assets.[6]
- Irregular market activities are mostly registered. Furthermore, only few of the features of these registered irregular activities are in fact irregular. Examples include tax evasion and black labor (irregularities in employment), such as the employment of people officially unemployed and wishing to keep unemployment benefits, and multiple job-holders with a specialization in high demand. On some occasions irregularities are utilized to increase demand; a typical example is the corruption of public officials to obtain state contracts. With the progress of transition, this group becomes the most relevant.

Overall, the size of the irregular economy has probably increased since transition started (see Dallago, 1992; Ékes, 1993). At the same time, a drastic restructuring of the irregular economy has occurred. Many activities in the shortage economy have disappeared or have greatly been reduced – for example, black market of convertible currencies, underground production, and secondary black market of goods in shortage. However, large-scale tax evasion[7] and other irregular activities have begun, often induced by the impoverishment of many people, such as the irregular employment of workers (black labor). Also irregularities on the border of the state and private sectors appear to have substantially increased, particularly in the privatization process. Finally, one of the most important feature of transition within the irregular economy is that today, unlike in the past, most enterprises are probably irregular only in part: they register, but keep part of their activities unregistered. For instance, they understate production or overstate expenses.

During transition there are more motivations for families to be involved in the irregular economy as workers, as consumers, and as suppliers of capital: the enhanced role of material incentives, growing unemployment, increasing disparities in incomes distribution and the spread of poverty, the greater availability of consumption goods for higher prices, and the possibility of lending savings outside the official financial system for a higher interest rate. Because of these developments, measurement of the irregular economy and of its contribution to the national income will remain highly problematic.

It therefore appears that a fundamental change has taken place during the transition period. In the past, irregular activities coexisted with regular ones on the output side but had to compete on the input side, because they operated in a situation of general shortage. Now, during the transition period the macroeconomic situation is increasingly characterized by deficient demand and unemployment. As a consequence, irregular activities compete with regular ones on the output side, but coexist (and may even cooperate) on the input side.

If one is convinced that the present difficult situation of economies in transition is temporary and new laws and rules are rapidly being established, one can suppose that after the completion of successful transition, in a situation characterized by a stable development path and a relatively high per capita income, two basic patterns are possible. On the one hand, in periods of expansion there should be a surge toward regularizing the positions of irregular workers and firms. Simultaneously, because of the system of progressive taxation, the resulting increase in regular incomes strengthens motives for tax evasion. Consequently, the marginal subjects of the previous period should be replaced by others who decide to resort to the irregular economy because it is more advantageous. On the other hand, in periods of recession the irregular economy should take on the role of protecting the levels of income that had previously been achieved and during the firms' infancy it should make available the resources necessary to accelerate technical progress and to become competitive with well-established firms.

However, an irregular sector also has many negative impacts on such factors as income distribution, employment, consumption, and the state budget (for a general survey see Ékes, 1993, pp. 80–102). In the transition period one of the most relevant impacts is exerted on the inflow of the much-needed foreign capital. Rose (1992), for instance, concludes from a 1991 survey of five countries (Poland, the CSFR, Hungary, Romania, and Bulgaria) that the spread of irregularities decreases the inflow of foreign capital. In fact, foreign investors are afraid of investing big sums in enterprises where property rights are uncertain and gains derive from irregular sources. At the same time, the spread of the irregular economy attracts capital from organized crime, a fact that has serious consequences on the development of the market and the economy, let alone on society and democracy.

2.3 The Measurement Question

The emergence of formerly irregular activities as regular ones (due to changes in legislation, improved expectations, and changes in relative prices), the development of new ones (due to the attempt to evade newly introduced taxes, to find employment for unemployed people or for illicit capital), and the "submersion" of previously regular activities (for instance, some officially bankrupt or interrupted private businesses) are likely to distort information and measurement of the economy.

In general, national statistics appear to be underestimated because the irregular economy's activities seek to avoid registration. But even more important is the structural distortion it creates in statistics; costs, incomes, and employment may not appear as they really are. Also the measurement of economic growth may appear distorted if the irregular economy is expanding or shrinking relative to the regular economy. Therefore, during transition, changes in statistical aggregates may be due to the irregular economy's inner movement and transformation and not solely to changes in the economic performance. This makes intertemporal comparisons difficult. As a consequence, correct assessment of the economy during transition requires a careful analysis of the irregular economy's structure and dynamics.

One relevant problem in assessing the quantitative relevance of the irregular economy derives from the great diversity of definitions used in different countries which is apparent in official publications. Often, this diversity concerns different official institutions within the same country (for a discussion on Hungary see Dallago, 1992).

A further difficulty comes from the worsening of statistics as a consequence of transition; the quality of new data may be worse than previous data and more time may be needed before they are available. There are various reasons for this. Often, many of the old officials have been replaced by new but inexperienced people. Furthermore, because of the difficult economic situation, resources have usually been decreased for the statistical apparatus in a time of increasing requirements. Central statistical offices were restructured to better respond to the new demands, but a period of time is required before the new organization starts to work efficiently. A transition from the old MPS-based national accounting to the new SNA-based method is under way. In particular, a growing number of small and medium-size enterprises are asking for a change from direct to indirect measurement methods. This task requires time. A further difficulty comes from the dynamism of the changes, in particular concerning the private sector; the situation changes daily, and this increases the difficulty for those in charge of measurement.

Finally, much of the basic information (in particular, registration of private enterprises) is unreliable because of the attitudes of the private enterprises themselves. A substantial part of registrations is falsified, and enterprises do not operate or operate on an intermittent basis (part-time or seasonally). In addition, firms are reluctant to provide information. Only a small number of the questionnaires sent out by the central statistical offices have been returned. This lack of response is generally attributed to the great mistrust among private business executives concerning any official requirement. However, lacking specific information and incentives to behave in a different way and under direct or indirect pressure to show a dramatic increase of the private sector, statisticians may take for granted that nonrespondents simply do not want to answer; in addition, they may not consider that some businesses may not be operating. As a consequence, the measurement of the private sector may result in overestimations. This effect is counterbalanced by the number of completely unregistered private businesses and by those underestimating their production. However, no sufficiently reliable data exist to assess the balance between these two groups. If one supposes that the registered but inactive group of enterprises is a rather stable share of private enterprises as is the irregular economy, the growth rate of the private sector should remain reasonably unaffected. However, we are left with an unclear picture of the structure of the economy, which can have substantial consequences on the economic policy, and in particular on taxation.

In spite of the above-mentioned difficulties, statistical offices are gradually drawing on new and improved sources for data collection and new methods of estimate (see Árvay, 1993; Dallago, 1992). These new sources are business registers, and the improved sources are sample surveys; household surveys; documents from customs officials, banks, financial agencies, and tax authorities; criminal statistics; reports from insurance companies; and the registers of professions characterized by large irregular extra earnings.

However, one should also consider that official statistics already comprise a relevant part of the irregular economy. Therefore, the underestimation depends on the capability of central statistical offices to capture the contribution of irregular activities in the economic process that are different from the activities in production. Usually this measurement is possible because irregular activities make use of regularly registered inputs and generate incomes that are at least partially spent on the regular market. Irregular activities can be divided into activities already included in official GDP, goods and services missing from official GDP, value differences on goods and services, and redistributive invisible incomes affecting not the level of GDP, but only its distribution.

These observations have important consequences on statistics. Before a conclusion can be reached, it is important to answers the following questions:

1. Did the old official statistics correctly take into account the irregular economy ("inclusion propensity")?
2. Do the new official statistics correctly take into account the irregular economy?
3. Is the irregular economy increasing or decreasing during the transition?
4. Do the new official statistics include the irregular economy in a better way than the old ones?

Given the elusive nature of the phenomenon, the answers attempted here can only be considered tentative.

First question. Considering the approach utilized to calculate official statistics, one can easily conclude that old statistics largely disregarded the irregular economy. Therefore, their inclusion propensity was very modest. In fact, direct methods based on responses directly given by enterprises were utilized, generally on the production side, to measure the contribution to the national income. This left irregular activities largely untouched, because they were by nature elusive both within and outside the state sector. This fact leads to the conclusion that official statistics were grossly underestimated because of the irregular economy, even if they included good estimates of the private sector's contribution to the national income.

However, one should re-examine this conclusion considering the role of the fictitious economy. This situation largely varied from country to country, but can be considered a structural feature of the Soviet-type system. In fact, enterprises were eager to overstate their production in order to obtain higher bonuses and premiums. Because of the direct estimate methods utilized, it was more difficult for statistical offices to remove this "production." The final result depended on the relevance of these two components acting in opposite directions. As a result, official statistics were probably somewhat better than usually considered, although this was so only by chance.

Second question. With transition, changes in prices and the disappearance of the enterprises' interest to overstate their performance made the work of statistical offices easier. However, new obstacles have appeared: enterprises are now interested in underestimating their net income to evade taxes, a tendency which could also be reflected in statistics; and the statistical apparatus, information gathering, and methodologies used are undergoing a

Table 2.1. Classification of the irregular economy.

		T_1	T_2	T_3
Income	Transactors	Registered transactors[a]	Unregistered transactors[b]	Illegal transactors[c]
I_1 (=)	Production usually included in official income.[d]	Construction of new dwellings. Small-scale agricultural production for the market.	Construction of new dwellings. Wages for work in small-scale agricultural farms.	Theft of inputs used in registered private units. Unauthorized use of goods and services of enterprises. Production and transactions controlled by organized crime.
I_2 (+)	Unregistered irregular income.[e]	Unreported wages. Unreported profit and rent. Final consumption recorded as intermediate consumption. Underreported leasing of dwellings. Barter in trade and production of goods and services. Benign plan violation and unrecorded transactions among state-owned enterprises (profit only). Unregistered (or registered as intermediate consumption) premiums granted by employers to employees. Tips and honoraria to employees. Extra payments for obtaining articles in short supply. Creation of unlawful funds via foreign trade (e.g., overinvoicing import prices) or to finance political parties or to reimport in the country as foreign capital.	Earnings from other households for maintenance and repair of dwellings, installations, and consumer durables. Production of other goods and services by unregistered firms. Unregistered leasing of dwellings, rooms. Paid household work. Childcare, teaching of languages, music, etc. Projecting, typing, drawing. Trade margin on goods sold in the streets, houses, etc. Counterfeiting of protected goods. Underrecorded output or overrecorded input to finance political parties, accumulate income to use in privatization, corrupt politicians, etc.	Production of alcohol, drugs. Prostitution, illegal abortion. Gambling. Theft of inputs used in underground and crypto-private enterprises. Theft of consumer goods from economic units. Unpaid use of phone, mail at work places. Unpaid use of TV, electricity, water, transport, etc., by consumers. Margin of smuggling for private gain. Margin on trading stolen goods. Margin on selling and buying foreign currencies by unauthorized persons. Usury (margin over market interest rates).

I_3 (=)	Registered irregular income.[f]	As for I_2.	As for I_2.	As for I_2.
I_4 (=)	Redistributive unlawful incomes.[g]	Purchase of fixed assets and stocks from public property at unlawful low prices. Unlawful capital gains in privatization. Tax and social-security payment evasion and unlawful avoidance.		Theft of cars, durables, and other valuables. Insurance fraud. Corruption, bribery, embezzlement, mismanagement. Racketeering, extortion. Cheating of customers in shops and restaurants.
I_5 (−)	Nonexistent production included in official statistics.[h]	Statistical consequences of fake registration of private businesses. Fictitious production (enterprises).		

[a] Economic units are registered, but their production is underreported or reported in such a way as to avoid taxation and other payments.

[b] Economic units and their production are not registered and form the so-called underground economy. Official statistics capture this production indirectly, usually starting from the consumption of inputs.

[c] Economic units and their production are not registered or are registered in a way that hides their true nature. Income produced is usually captured in official statistics, but is attributed to the wrong ownership sector or its true nature remains hidden.

[d] Production is usually included in official income (supposing that output is properly estimated) or can be easily included on the basis of production norms. However, it may be wrongly attributed to one sector (e.g., to the private sector) and not (at least in part) to a different one (e.g., to the state sector, when production was obtained by using stolen inputs).

[e] Irregular income produced is not included in registered official income. It leads to underestimation of official income and to the distortion of its branch breakup.

[f] Irregular income is already included in registered official income.

[g] These activities give rise to unlawful and unregistered income distribution with the aim of increasing personal incomes or financing organizations (e.g., political parties) in an unlawful way.

[h] Economic units and production do not operate or do not exist, but they are registered in official statistics and lead to the overestimation of official income.

deep restructuring and reorganization. Also, many new irregular activities have begun. However, methods used to calculate national statistics have become better suited to measuring a relevant part of the irregular economy. In particular, the increased use of indirect measurement methods and of comparisons of estimates on both the production side and the consumption side has been an important step in this direction. However, as noted above, another factor acts in the opposite direction: many registered private enterprises do not actually operate (fake registration) while others operate only on a part-time basis; but, also for political reasons, statistical offices often consider them operating on a full-time basis. This usually leads to an overestimate of the relevance of the private sector. The latter factor is probably less relevant than the former. Therefore, one could conclude that during transition official statistics are able to capture a relatively larger share of the irregular economy than before.

Third question. As was discussed above, evidence shows that during transition the irregular economy has substantially expanded. While some irregular activities have disappeared or become regular, new irregular activities have risen, and some old ones have survived or even expanded because of the weakening controls and institutional vacuum. These factors result in greater underestimation of national income during transition compared with before transition, leading to an underestimation of growth rates.

Fourth question. The preceding three questions and answers should be considered jointly to conclude whether or not new official statistics include the irregular economy in a better way than the old ones. To summarize, new statistics are probably better able than old ones to capture a greater share of irregularly produced income, but the irregular economy has greatly expanded. As a consequence, they are likely better in relative terms (the share of the irregular economy which is disregarded by national accounts is now smaller than before), but not necessarily in absolute terms (the total amount of the irregular economy which remains unregistered is probably greater now).

Table 2.1 presents a possible classification of the irregular activities. In the table transactors (T) refer to the agents of the irregular economy: T_1 transactors are registered but partially evade payments and underreport their activities; T_2 transactors are not registered, completely evade direct payments (direct taxes and the like), and do not report their activities; and T_3 transactors are illegal although not criminal, therefore, they are not registered, evade totally direct payments, and do not report their activities.

Following the definition given in the introduction, the irregular economy is defined as follows:

$$
\begin{aligned}
T_1 + T_2 + T_3 &= \text{Irregular economy.} \\
T_1 + T_2 &= \text{Legal irregular economy.} \\
T_3 &= \text{Illegal (underground) economy.}
\end{aligned}
$$

From the viewpoint of national accounts, the situation is as follows:

$I_1 + I_3$ = Irregular economy already comprised in the official income.

$I_2 - I_5$ = Irregular economy which is missing from official income.

I_4 = Redistributive irregular economy.

I_r = Income produced in the regular economy.

I_i = Income produced in the irregular economy.

I_d = Purely (re)distributive irregular activities.

I_o = Officially registered income (as reported in official statistics).

I_t = Total income produced in the regular economy and the irregular economy.

Therefore,

$$
\begin{aligned}
I_i &= I_1 + I_2 + I_3 - I_5 \ . \\
I_d &= I_4 \ . \\
I_o &= I_r + I_1 + I_3 \ . \\
I_t &= I_o + I_2 - I_5 \ .
\end{aligned}
$$

I_o is already registered. If we suppose that this is perfectly estimated, to reach a good measurement of the total (regular plus irregular) income from the viewpoint of the irregular economy, that part of the irregular economy which is still missing must be added to the official income and the income "produced" by those activities which actually exist only on paper must be subtracted.

However, a more precise conclusion can only be reached by performing the calculations on an individual economy. In Section 2.5 we calculate the data on Hungary.

2.4 The Case of Hungary

Since transition began, some traditional components of the irregular economy have faded away while new ones have arisen and expanded. Among the latter, tax evasion has become increasingly significant. Taxes and social-security charges appear rather high for business in its initial phase and deductions for starting ventures are rather insignificant and occasional (during the first three years new businesses are exempted only from profit taxes, whose rate is 40%). At the same time, tax evasion possibilities are numerous because they are easy to take advantage of and punishment is relatively insignificant. This situation has been well documented by data on tax returns in 1990. Entrepreneurs paid, on average, less personal income tax than state employees, and, although the number of ventures increased rapidly, official personal income from private business decreased to only 4.8% of the total (see Ékes, 1993). This situation has persisted since then.

Another typical component of a market-type irregular economy, namely, the irregular employment of people officially living on unemployment benefits (black labor), is expanding with the increase of unemployment. The black market and the illegal leasing of houses and country cottages are also increasing. Tips, on the other hand, are decreasing presumably because of decreasing real incomes.

As in other countries, in Hungary the irregular economy is concentrated mainly in the private sector.[8] As a consequence, the way in which private activities are estimated is very relevant when trying to officially measure irregular activities.[9] Until 1989 the Hungarian Central Statistical Office (HCSO) included only handicraft industry, private retail trade, and farmers in the private sector. It reported the number of artisans, their employees, their apprentices, and the volume of gross production, and distinguished between types of activity. Employment was divided among full-time, part-time, and employment of retired people, and material production was separated from supply of services (e.g., building maintenance). Production was subdivided between production for household consumption and other ends. Before 1989 the HCSO used normative values to estimate output and inputs of artisans and retail traders. The values were established separately for each activity and branch by a group of experts established by the association of private artisans and retailers on the basis of their direct experience.

Price indices for household services and data on employment and production of shopkeepers were also published. As for agriculture, the HCSO reported the number and output of small-scale agricultural units. Revenue obtained by households from the sale to the state of agricultural produce was registered in households' income, and total income of the population also included the consumption of self-produced goods. During this period the quality of statistics on the private sector, and even more so on auxiliary activities, was rather reliable due in part to the lack of dynamism and to the prevailing homogeneity of private activities.

The HCSO also reported various data on economic organizations such as joint stock companies, limited liability and partnerships companies, joint ventures, civil rights companies (PJT), and economic partnerships (GMK). Various data were published on enterprise labor partnerships (VGMK) and specialized groups of cooperatives until 1988, when VGMKs were abolished. Data included the number of organizations, number of members and employees, and production. The number of limited and share companies and joint ventures was available by economic sectors as well. Data concerning joint ventures also included the volume of capital and the share of foreign capital in it. Figures of GDP produced by enterprises included only private ventures with legal entity. GDP produced by small ventures consisted of three parts:

1. Small private units and individual ventures with full responsibility.
2. Private associations without legal entity (such as limited partnerships and general partnerships).
3. Household farms and unregistered housing construction.

The aggregate socialist sector category was removed from the statistics at the end of 1989. All the previous so-called auxiliary activities (basically, household agricultural plots) were included in the private sector. The rapid increase of mixed organizations during the late 1980s induced the HCSO to stop to calculate the classification of economic units according to the form of ownership starting from the beginning of 1990. In fact, the HCSO did not have any information concerning the structure of ownership in these mixed companies, and since then the situation has not change.

Since the late 1980s, the rapid expansion of the private sector and the slow development of the tax system have led to a rapid increase in tax evasion. Therefore, using tax declarations to measure the income produced by the private sector would result in a gross underestimate.

The tax system has often been modified and small ventures have rapidly adapted to these changes to take advantage of the new opportunities. When conditions change, they liquidate their business. If this is impossible because of liabilities, capital is taken from the old firm and used to open a new one in a sector favored by the new legislation. When this occurs the old firm only exists on paper. Moreover, some private units are only registered but do not operate either because they are waiting for better opportunities or simply because they were established to provide owners with credits and tax facilities on goods and services that are actually for consumption (usually houses, cars, and vacations). As a consequence, measurement based on business registers leads to an overstatement of income produced by the private sector. However, some of the artisans and enterprises that have not been dropped from the register in spite of the liquidation of their activity or that are registered but do not officially operate (they do not file a tax form) may actually be active in the irregular economy. As a consequence, measurement of private activity based on the business register may also indirectly capture a part of the irregular economy.[10]

A further factor has the opposite effect: because of the rapid increase in the number of new businesses – substantially more than the number of businesses closing down – if registers are not updated rapidly the number of registered businesses is likely to be underestimated. It also appears that many businesses declare fewer employees than they actually employ.

The HCSO has continued to use normative values applied to figures taken from business registers after 1989. These data are broken down by profession, branch, and region. The results are adjusted to take into account the consequences of inflation, changes in professional structure, and consequences of technical progress on productivity. Data obtained in this way on the production side are also compared, whenever possible, with the data obtained on the consumption side (for example, surveys on household consumption or the number of dwellings built or repaired with the help of private artisans and enterprises).

The Hungarian Central Statistical Office has traditionally made efforts to capture unregistered, informal activities (such as consumption of self-produced agricultural goods and self-help home improvements) as well as irregular activities (such as tax evasion). It has also included in the national income a usually prudent estimate of the income earned from households by people ("nonregistered persons") like doctors and teachers working privately.

An estimate of the irregular economy within the private sector was performed by Dallago (1989, 1992) in terms of full-time equivalent jobs in 1986 and 1990.[11] An adjusted building-block approach was used. Adjustments were made on the estimated amount of work performed by unregistered employees of artisans, work involved in room leasing, and work performed in agriculture. In 1986 the overall number of full-time jobs performed by unlicensed artisans and by moonlighters in other occupations (house-cleaning, typing, teaching, baby-sitting, etc.) amounted to between 230,000 and 255,000 and was performed by between 640,000 and 690,000 people.[12] This corresponded to 4.9% of the overall number of regular employees in the country. The corresponding figures in 1990 for full-time jobs were 346,500 or 7.2%. It should be noted that this relatively low level of the irregular economy derives from the fact that most jobs were part-time and that in Hungary many private activities were legal by 1990.[13]

The income derived from moonlighting and other types of "invisible incomes" such as tips was estimated by Ékes. She arrived at a global estimate of from Ft 65 billion to Ft 82 billion in early 1980s. These figures corresponded to between 11% and 14% of the population's total income or 9% and 12% of the national income. Ékes (1993) also prepared a survey based on a sample of 2,000 families taken in 1992. The results obtained from the survey show that "invisible incomes" (based on the definitions given in *Table 2.1*) amount to from Ft 204 billion and Ft 210 billion corresponding to 9% of the GDP. In addition, between Ft 339 billion and Ft 349 billion (15% of GDP) represent purely redistributive incomes (tax evasion, corruption, bribery, speculation, cheating of customers).

The consequences of the irregular economy for national accounts can clearly be shown on the basis of estimates recently produced on behalf of the Blue Ribbon Commission and the OECD by a group of Hungarian experts (see Árvay and Vértes, 1993a, 1993b; major results are summarized in Árvay and Vértes, 1994). These figures were obtained from various *ad hoc* investigations[14] on the unregistered income of five groups of economic agents: private corporate entities, registered individual entrepreneurs, unregistered private persons, organizations in public ownership, and companies controlled by foreigners.[15] These figures were compared with the estimated irregular income included in the official GDP to arrive to an estimate of the unregistered irregular income. The fundamental results are given in *Table 2.2*. The figures in the table show that the irregular economy developed fast during the period considered, but its dynamics has been particularly relevant since the beginning of transition.[16] However, the capability of official statistics to measure the irregular economy ($I_1 + I_3$) has dramatically improved. In fact, in 1980 only 13% of the overall irregular economy was included in official statistics [$(I_1 + I_3)/I_i$]. By 1992 the same share was at 40%.

As a consequence, the underestimation of the official GDP (I_t/I_o) basically remained constant during the 1980s, but has increased since the beginning of the transition. However, this increase is rather modest, due to efforts to improve the collection of data. In fact, between 1989 and 1992 the underestimation share [(I_t/I_o)] increased by approximately 4%. This means that the official growth rate of GDP during transition was underestimated by less than 1.5% per year because of the unregistered irregular economy, compared with actual growth rate. If we consider that during this three-year period official GDP declined by approximately 20%, it clearly appears

Table 2.2. The relation between registered GDP and total GDP in Hungary between 1980 and 1992 at current basic prices (factor costs).

		1980	1985	1989	1990	1991	1992
	In billion forints						
I_r	1. Regular economy	634	904	1442	1677	1874	2194
	2. Irregular economy						
$I_1 + I_3$	a. Comprised in official GDP	11	27	56	110	165	257
$I_2 - I_5$	b. Not comprised in official GDP	72	103	177	225	300	393
I_i	c. Irregular economy, total	83	130	233	335	465	650
I_o	3. Official GDP (1+2a)	645	931	1498	1787	2039	2451
I_t	4. Total GDP (1+2c)	717	1034	1675	2012	2339	2844
	In % of regular GDP						
I_r	1. Regular economy	100	100	100	100	100	100
	2. Irregular economy						
$I_1 + I_3$	a. Comprised in official GDP	2	3	4	7	9	12
$I_2 - I_5$	b. Not comprised in official GDP	12	11	12	15	16	18
I_i	c. Irregular economy, total	14	14	16	22	25	30
I_o	3. Official GDP (1+2a)	102	103	104	107	109	112
I_t	4. Total GDP (1+2c)	114	114	116	122	125	130
I_t/I_o	5. Total GDP in % of official GDP	111	111	112	113	115	116

Source: Árvay and Vértes, 1993b, p. 71 (with changes in terminology: the original source uses the term "hidden economy" to refer to what is termed here "irregular economy").

Table 2.3. Share of different ownership sectors within the official GDP and total GDP (comprising also the irregular economy).

	1980	1985	1989	1990	1991	1992
In official GDP						
Public sector	90	85	80	76	70	56
Private sector	10	15	20	23	27	36
Foreign sector	0	0	0	1	3	8
Total	100	100	100	100	100	100
In total GDP						
Public sector	83	79	74	70	63	50
Private sector	17	21	26	29	34	42
Foreign sector	0	0	0	1	3	8
Total	100	100	100	100	100	100

Source: Árvay and Vértes, 1993a, p. 50 (with changes as in *Table 2.2*).

that even taking into account the unregistered irregular economy the general trend of the economy would not change appreciably.

A further important conclusion to be drawn from the inclusion of the unregistered irregular economy in statistics concerns the share of the different ownership sectors within the total GDP (see *Table 2.3*). It is easy to infer that, because irregular activities are mostly private, they substantially increase the share of the private sector in the economy. However, because the present inclusion propensity is greater today than before the transition, the growth rate of the private sector turns out to be slower when irregular activities are properly included in statistics.[17]

2.5 Conclusion

The irregular economy has changed its structure during transition. Traditional, irregular activities have progressively been reduced; others which were previously irregular have become legal; and new irregular activities have emerged. In the sectors where transition has been successful in eliminating shortages and destroying the centrally planned system, the irregular activities typical of a shortage economy (such as speculation on goods in shortage and "benign plan violation") have disappeared almost overnight. In some cases previously irregular businesses have decided to register and have become fully (or more probably only partly) legal. Other traditional activities (such as tips and under-the-counter sales) have greatly been reduced.

Nevertheless, growing evidence shows that part of the irregular economy which is connected with increasing financial discipline and with increasing unemployment is rapidly growing. For example, tax evasion and unregistered employment have been increasing. However, most of these new activities are only partly irregular.

Three relevant questions should be raised at this point: Have old irregular activities been a good basis for the emergence of the new private entrepreneurs and are these entrepreneurs of the Smith–Hicksian type, namely, do they utilize the irregular economy as a weapon to establish themselves in market competition? Can the new (market) irregular economy become an engine of economic growth and a strategic factor in the new development strategy? Are statistical aggregates underestimated because of the irregular economy? An early and partial answer for each question can be attempted based on the existing, albeit scarce, evidence.

We begin with the first question. In effect, the idea that the irregular economy is a good basis for the development of a market economy is quite widespread in all countries. According to this approach, most irregular activities operate in a market environment and follow a market logic and behavior, even in Soviet-type economies. Legalization of these activities greatly helps the transition process. However, for the time being this process is far from being completed. Because of the institutional and legal vacuum and the weakness of the state apparatus in implementing laws, many traditional irregular activities have survived and have even increased. Unfortunately, this conclusion cannot be generalized. It appears easier to play such a role for those irregular activities which were dynamic already in the old system either because they operated in a partially competitive environment or because they operated under rapidly changing conditions.

The answer to the second question depends on various factors which are not yet clear. However, such a development model could be successful in Hungary and maybe also in Poland and some former Soviet republics (such as Armenia and Georgia) once the situation has stabilized. The most important factors are probably the attitude of irregular entrepreneurs who see irregularities as a way of overcoming barriers to entry into new markets and to new resources to invest until their businesses can successfully afford the competition of already established larger enterprises. Fundamental in this strategy is the entrepreneurs' willingness to reinvest the returns from their irregular activities in their businesses to implement technical progress. Instead, if irregularities such as tax evasion and unregistered employment are seen as a way to ensure survival of the business or higher consumption, it is likely that the irregular economy will be unable to play a directly positive role in the development strategy.

The above-mentioned positive event depends on the reaction of society to the situations during the transition and on government policy. It is important that society reacts positively and actively to the consequences of transition, even to unfavorable ones like growing unemployment. For instance, it is important that unemployed people do not wait for new opportunities, but create them by looking for an irregular job or start an irregular activity themselves, however small, if it is impossible or too difficult to start a legal one. It is also important that many skilled people seek to undertake a business, even irregular, on their own.[18]

A further important question consists in the relationship between the legal private sector and irregular economy. The latter could prevent the former from developing if the advantages to becoming irregular are too great, particularly in a situation characterized by low demand and unemployment. Beyond legal, social, and moral factors, the government's policy is of fundamental importance. Only if the legal private sector is substantially supported through a favorable credit and tax policy and the relevant services (for example, consultancy) are available at a cheap price can the danger of an unbearable competition by the irregular economy be overcome.

As was observed above, there are reasons for maintaining that official statistics have underestimated and overestimated the economic performance. As already explained, only a part of the irregular economy is not captured by official statistics (provided they are reasonably good) and another part only redistributes registered income. Therefore, the national income is not underestimated by the same amount of the irregular economy. In a similar fashion, one can notice that there are also reasons for believing that official statistics are overreported.

On the basis of the figures presented in the previous section one can conclude that the irregular economy in Hungary is an important component of the overall economy. It increased rapidly since transition started and now corresponds to approximately 30% of the regular economy. However, it was substantial even before the beginning of transition.

Official statistics have been able to capture the acceleration of the phenomenon. As a consequence, official statistics have not worsened substantially. The official GDP now appears to underestimate the total (actual) GDP by approximately 15% or 16% compared with 11% or 12% during the 1980s. This increase is important to measure the level of aggregate and per capita GDP. However, the consideration of the unregistered irregular economy does not appear to have dramatically changed the picture of the transitional depression.

The results may vary substantially from country to country depending on the answers given to the four questions discussed in Section 2.3. From existing evidence (Dallago, 1992) it appears that the situation of Hungary is favorable. In the other transition countries, possibly with the exception of the Czech Republic, the irregular economy has increased even more rapidly while the inclusion propensity has improved less than it has in Hungary. If this hypothesis is verified, one should conclude not only that national income and the share of the private sector both before and after transition in those countries is substantially underregistered, but also that GDP growth rates are underestimated in a somewhat larger extent than in Hungary. However, even in the other transition countries it is hard to believe that actual growth rates would be changed by the inclusion of the unregistered irregular economy to such an extent to invert the fundamental trends of the recent years.

Notes

[1] The irregular economy does not cover particular (reciprocity) relations, which are those existing within the family or among relatives (kinship relations) or friends, neighbors, and the like. I define the activities taking place within this context as the *informal economy*, which comprises activities for self-consumption or for persons directly associated with the agent (relatives, friends, acquaintances). Unlike the irregular economy, the informal economy activities do not involve material obligations (payment) but (often) moral obligations of reciprocity. In this context I define the *criminal economy* as comprising activities where both means and ends are against the rules and illegal.

[2] That is, the economy characterized by a quasi-hard budget constraint as opposed to an economy with quasi-soft budget constraint as in Kornai's definition (see Kornai, 1980). In fact, the latter gives rise to shortages. The irregular economy presents completely different features.

[3] This is provided that decreased production costs are transferred to consumers via lower prices. If decreased costs are pocketed by the irregular agent via higher than normal profit (extra profit), the market is in equilibrium (nonsegmented). Irregular agents consume or invest their extra profit. If they invest it in the same sector, and if the old price is an equilibrium price for the regular sector, then segmentation of the market or the disappearance of the regular supply (supposing that production techniques remain unchanged) occurs.

[4] Adam Smith's *Wealth of Nations* contains various references to irregular and illegal activities, such as tax evasion and smuggling. His basic explanation of such irregularities and illegalities is contained in a famous quotation:

> People of the same trade seldom meet together, even for merriment and diversion, but the conversation ends in a conspiracy against the public, or in some contrivance to raise prices. It is impossible indeed to prevent such meetings, by any law which either could be executed, or would be consistent with liberty and justice. But though the law cannot hinder people of the same trade from sometimes assembling together, it ought to do nothing to facilitate such assemblies; much less to render them necessary. [Smith, 1776, p. 128]

[5] "Second economy" is the term most often used to indicate activities in Soviet-type economies that escape the direct control of the state. The use of the term has mainly been due to the work of Grossman (1977, p. 25):

> The standard Western image of the Soviet "command economy" is one of a state-owned, hierarchically organized, centrally planned and managed, price-controlled, and otherwise regimented system, rigidly geared to the goals and priorities of the Soviet leadership, and operating in compliance with a myriad of state-imposed laws, regulations, and directives. However valid this image might be – and, while greatly oversimplified, it is not entirely incorrect – there is another, very significant side to Soviet economic reality, where production and exchange often take place for

direct private gain and just as often violate state law in some nontrivial respect.

[6] This component includes two groups of irregularities. One concerns the price at which assets are privatized, which is extremely uncertain because book values inherited from Soviet-type economies are unreliable in the establishment of market prices. The second group of irregularities derives from the fact that foreign capital involved in privatization may be treated in preferential terms, in particular they may enjoy substantial tax rebates. This stimulates domestic investors to export capital unlawfully and to reimport it as foreign capital or to establish fictitious joint ventures with foreign capital aimed at taking advantage of the different treatment of capital (see Ékes, 1993, pp. 74–77).

[7] For instance, according to Sergei Almazov, head of the Russian Federation's Department of the Tax Police, 25% of the firms audited by his agency in 1993 had failed to pay taxes. From January to September the department recovered R 400 billion, corresponding approximately to 1.5% of the latest planned revenues for the 1993 Russian state budget (see Radio Free Europe/Radio Liberty *Daily Report*, 11 November 1993).

[8] According to Árvay and Vértes (1993b, p. 52, English version) in Hungary 88.3% of the unregistered irregular economy originated in the domestic private sector in 1992. Another 1.8% should be added to this figure to account for (usually private) companies controlled by foreigners.

[9] The following presentation is based on Árvay (1993), Árvay and Vértes (1993b, pp. 41–42, 60, English version), and Ékes (1991, pp. 3, 42–46, 65). See also the answer given by the HCSO to a World Bank questionnaire in 1991 (in the files of the author).

[10] Based on preliminary calculations made by the HCSO for 1992, GDP produced by private entrepreneurs amounted to Ft 290 billion. According to experts within the HCSO this sum is likely to include value added produced by persons who were dropped from the business register and are thus not among those who filed a tax return. In such a way, the HCSO is likely to overestimate the GDP of the regular private sector (Árvay and Vértes, 1993b, pp. 41–42, 60, English version).

[11] It should be noted that data are not comparable with those reported in *Tables 2.2* and *2.3*. In fact, they do not comprise the entire irregular economy, but only the part included in the private sector. The estimate was part of an attempt to measure the real dimension of the non-socialized economy (i.e., not directly controlled by the state) in Hungary. Among the other quantitative estimates performed for Hungary see Révész (1986), who utilizes a methodology similar to Dallago (1989). See also Lackó (1992), who utilizes a monetary model based on a function of cash demand in the "illegal" economy derived from the well-known models worked out by Feige and Tanzi for Western economies.

[12] The value of the gross income produced amounted to approximately Ft 35 billion, or 6% of the population's total income.

[13] In fact, during this time legal private activities, in large part registered in official statistics, amounted to 2,106,000 full-time equivalent jobs (or 43.0% of the registered total) in 1986 and 2,361,800 in 1990.

[14] These consisted of monitoring the life-style of entrepreneurs and estimating the income of private firms; the views of interviewers on the reliability of the answers received in the life-style survey; the survey of 1,000 households on the frequency of purchases without receiving bills; the share of purchases from the private sector; surveys and assessment made by a taxation research team; the experiences of firm-registering, auditing, bookkeeping, and tax consulting firms; information on private businesses from banks; assessments based on the Financial Annual Reports of companies and enterprises; and consideration of the results of other researches and surveys (see Árvay and Vértes, 1993b).

[15] The largest part of unregistered income was from registered private entrepreneurs (36.9% of the total unregistered income), unregistered private individuals (27.7%), and corporate entities (23.7%). The remaining 11.6% was from corporate companies (6.6%), budgetary institutions (3.2%), and companies controlled by foreigners (see Árvay and Vértes, 1993b, p. 52, English version). It should be noted that a significant part of official GDP originates in the "supplementary economic activities of the population": here official figures are considered to reflect well the current situation and no underestimation of total income is included under this heading.

[16] The calculation was performed at current basic prices (at factor costs). However, since the transition a major change of prices has been introduced: market prices in the irregular economy – that previously were generally higher than official prices because of shortages – became lower than in the regular economy. As a consequence, one could consider that the irregular economy is actually larger than the figures given in the table and discussed here, if measured at the prices existing in the regular economy. However, prices of goods and services supplied in the irregular economy could be considered lower because they include a lower value added due to poorer conditions (for example, goods are offered in the streets rather than in more comfortable shops) or they discount lower production costs (for example, when taxes or social-security payments are evaded or when inputs are stolen). However, in other cases actual prices are higher than official ones either because they include payments necessary to reach the market-clearing level (e.g., in the case of tips and similar payments) or because they are similar to monopoly prices (e.g., when they include the price of corruption). As a consequence, the question of prices is very blurred and it appears wise to utilize actual prices in estimates.

[17] From the figures in the table it appears that the share of the private sector in official GDP in 1992 increased by 3.6 times compared with 1980 and 1.8 times compared with 1989. Therefore, between 1980 and 1989 it exactly doubled. The corresponding figures for the total GDP, including the irregular economy, are 2.5 and 1.6 times, respectively.

[18] The government's policy has an important role to play in this sense, both in a positive way and in a negative way. In a positive sense it should try to

support the new entrepreneurs giving priority to ground-up privatization over any other form, including privatization of the state sector. In a negative way, it could probably overlook some irregularities that will most likely lead to a sound development and concentrate on fighting against those that are the most harmful, such as organized economic crimality.

References

Alessandrini, S., and Dallago, B., 1987, eds., *The Unofficial Economy: Consequences and Perspectives in Different Economic Systems*, Gower, Aldershot, UK.

Árvay, J., 1993, Methods of Measuring the Hidden Economy in the Transition Countries, Paper presented at the Joint OECD/UNECE Meeting of National Accounts Experts, June 21–25, Paris, France.

Árvay, J., and Vértes, A., 1993a, A tulajdonosi szerkezet változása Magyarországon 1980–1992. között (The change of the ownership structure in Hungary between 1980–1992), Background document, Budapest, Hungary.

Árvay, J., and Vértes, A., 1993b, A rejtett gazdaság Magyarországon (The hidden economy in Hungary), Background document, Budapest, Hungary.

Árvay, J., and Vértes, A., 1994, *A magánszektor és a rejtett gazdaság súlya Magyarországon 1980–1992* (The weight of the private sector and the hidden economy in Hungary 1980–1992), GKI Gazdaságkutató Rt., Budapest, Hungary.

Berliner, J., 1952, The informal organization in the Soviet firm, *Quarterly Journal of Economics*, August: 342–365.

Berliner, J., 1957, *Factory and Manager in the USSR*, Harvard University Press, Cambridge, MA, USA.

Brus, W., and Laski, K., 1985, Repressed inflation and second economy under central planning, in W. Gärtner and A. Wenig, eds., *The Economics of the Shadow Economy*, Springer-Verlag, Berlin, Germany.

Colijn, L., 1987, Some proposed methodologies to quantify the influence of macroeconomic disequilibrium on the size of the second economy in Poland, in S. Alessandrini and B. Dallago, eds., *The Unofficial Economy: Consequences and Perspectives in Different Economic Systems*, Gower, Aldershot, UK.

Dallago, B., 1989, The non-socialized sector in Hungary: An attempt at estimation of its importance, in *Jahrbuch der Wirtschaft Osteuropas/Yearbook of East-European Economics*, **13**(2):67–92.

Dallago, B., 1992, The Private Sector in Historically Planned Economies: Conceptualization and Attempted Measurement, International Economics Department, Socio-Economic Data Division, August, World Bank, Washington, DC, USA [mimeo].

Ékes, I., 1991, Measurement of the Private Sector Contribution: Hungary, Paper prepared for the Research Project on Accounting for HPEs in Transition: System-Related Issues in Measuring Economic Performance, Socio-Economic Data Division, World Bank, Washington, DC, USA.

Ékes, I., 1993, *Rejtett Gazdaság – Láthatatlan jövedelmek, Tegnap és ma* (The hidden economy – Invisible incomes, Yesterday and today), Budapest, Hungary.

Gärtner, W., and Wenig, A., 1985, eds., *The Economics of the Shadow Economy*, Springer-Verlag, Berlin, Germany.

Górski, M., 1991, The Private Sector and the Second Economy in Poland, Paper prepared for the Research Project on Accounting for HPEs in Transition: System-Related Issues in Measuring Economic Performance, Socio-Economic Data Division, World Bank, Washington, DC, USA.

Grossman, G., 1977, The "second economy" of the USSR, *Problems of Communism*, **26**(Sept.–Oct.):25–40.

Hicks, J.R., 1963, *The Theory of Wages*, 2nd ed., Macmillan, London, UK.

Kornai, J., 1980, *The Economics of Shortage*, North–Holland, Amsterdam, the Netherlands.

Lackó, M., 1992, The extent of the illegal economy in Hungary between 1970 and 1989: A monetary model, *Acta Oeconomica*, **44**(1–2):161–190.

Rey, G.M., 1985, Influenza del sommerso sulla formazione del prodotto interno lordo, University of Rome, Italy [mimeo].

Révész, G., 1986, On the expansion and functioning of the direct market sector of the Hungarian economy, *Acta Oeconomica*, **36**(1–2):105–21.

Ricci, R., 1978, Alcune stime dell'evasione statistica nel ramo manifatturiero in Italia, *Rivista di economia e politica industriale*, Sept.–Dec.:389–405.

Ricci, R., 1981, Riflessioni sulla misurazione dell'economia sommersa, *Rivista di politica economica*, (5):591–610.

Rose, R., 1992, Eastern Europe's need for a civil economy, *AMEX Bank Review*, November.

Siesto, V., 1987, Statistiche macroeconomiche ed economia irregolare, Rome, Italy [mimeo].

Smith, A., 1776, *An Inquiry into the Nature and Causes of the Wealth of Nations*, The Modern Library, New York, NY, USA.

UN ECE, 1992, *Guide-Book to Statistics on the Hidden Economy*, Conference of European Statisticians, Economic Commission for Europe, Statistical Division, United Nations, Geneva, Switzerland.

UN ECE, 1993, *Inventory of National Practices in Estimating Hidden and Informal Economic Activities for National Accounts*, Conference of European Statisticians, Economic Commission for Europe, Statistical Division, United Nations, Geneva, Switzerland.

Wisniewski, M., 1986a, The sources and dimensions of the second economy in Poland, *Oeconomica Polona*, (2):247–276.

Wisniewski, M., 1986b, The economy and its shadow, *Eastern European Economics*, **24**(4):29–39.

Comments on the Papers by János Árvay and Bruno Dallago

Richard Rose

If understanding change in aggregate economic activity is the objective, then the starting point is a recognition that all the best variables are nominal, namely, conceptualization must precede quantification. What do we mean by economic activity? And what do we want to learn by measuring it? The standard approach is to define economic activity as *official statistics* about the national product, and to concentrate upon how it changes. In a normal market economy, typically this shows a growth rate of 1% to 3% a year. In post-Communist societies in transition, it can register an output decline of 5% to 15% in a year, and over several years a contraction of the official economy by 20% to 40%. Changes of such magnitude encourage skepticism, and this is reinforced by anecdotal evidence that official statistics leave out a lot. The conventional response is to make a plea for better statistics.

János Árvay's paper addresses the fundamental issue arising in trend analysis of official statistics. Is the baseline measure, the net material product (NMP) of a command economy, comparable with the system of national accounts (SNA) measure of market economies? He draws upon a wealth of experience as a master chef in the kitchens of a command economy to demonstrate in what ways the two sets of accounts, though overlapping, nonetheless differ substantially. This requires disaggregating global figures.

The first level of disaggregation (Árvay, *Figure 1.1*) tells us a lot: net material product omits most services, which account for a significant amount of value added in gross domestic product. Because advanced economies tend to grow more in the service sector, this omission is important. Also worth underscoring is the passing comment in his paper that "uncertainties in the measurement of the constant price values for nonmaterial services are large in any country" as to vitiate apparent differences found in most comparisons. Yet it is in just these fields, for example, health care and education, where enormous increases have taken place in both SNA and NMP systems in recent decades, and these fields are least likely to contract during transition. Berg's (1993, p. 42) study of Poland emphasizes the advantage of further disaggregation, for example, comparing data about output in private sector construction (down 7%) with data about employment in construction (up 4%).

Official estimates of national product in societies in transition have an important instrumental use: they provide a base for estimating tax capacity. Yet tax revenue cannot be properly estimated by applying tax rates to the official economy. It must be discounted substantially to take into account noncollection by tax collectors and nonpayment by those assessed, for the restructuring of the economy and of tax systems will cause a sharp fall in the actual collection of revenues due (cf. Casanegra de Jantscher *et al.*, 1992).

In economies in transition, state-controlled economic activity, the basis of official figures, must contract. Concurrently, officially unrecorded economic activities will increase, as there are more opportunities for individuals to engage in private enterprise openly or in the "shadows," and the state's capacity for routinely monitoring what is happening contracts with the end of the plan. If the object is to measure monetized economic activity the "irregular" economy examined by Bruno Dallago cannot be ignored. However, the abandonment of the pathologies of the irregular economy is a necessary condition of investment in capital-intensive, bureaucratized (and thus officially recorded) private enterprises needed to sustain a big economic boom.

The irregular economy is complex; Dallago's *Table 2.1* is a 16-cell matrix itemizing 39 different types of activity, ranging from registered units included in official statistics to illegal activities that ought to be prosecuted if officially cognized. Because irregular economic activity is highly disaggregated, understanding must be built up from the bottom. Dallago also shows that some irregular activities are integrally related to officially recorded activities, whereas others substitute for or are in addition to officially recorded economic activity. Attending to data about irregular as well as official monetized activities can explain such puzzles in household expenditure statistics as the increase in ownership of "hard money" goods such as color television sets and cars during a period of contraction in the official economy (see, e.g., Berg, 1993, Table 2).

If aggregate tax revenue is one's only concern, then the irregular economy can be dismissed as of secondary importance, a problem for tax administrators and law enforcement officials. Yet it is also an argument for a "least worst" theory of taxation in transition, such as a Franco-Italian tax system that emphasizes effectiveness in revenue collection, as against the prescription of measures that may be attractive in theory but ineffective in practice.

The IMF and the World Bank have joined microeconomists in focusing attention upon the living standards of households in societies in transition. Unfortunately, their aggregate official measures encourage the fallacy of drawing inferences about individuals from totals. If officially measured output declines by 25%, it does not follow that the average household suffers a decline of a quarter in living standards or that half the households suffer a 50% cut in living standards. To understand what is happening to people during transition we must consider economies in the original etymological sense of activities within the household. In transition societies, households depend upon *non-monetized as well as monetized* economic activities.

The mechanisms by which East Europeans are coping with the destabilization of the official economy, high and shifting rates of inflation, and uncertainties about employment or being paid by one's employer are by assembling portfolios that balance four different "economies," official and unofficial, monetized and non-monetized, legal, alegal, or illegal (Rose, 1993). In economies in transition, the majority of households do not rely solely upon the official economy for food and housing needs (see, e.g., Rose and Tikhomirov, 1993), the most important expenditure items in poor households in market economies.

If the objective of monitoring economic activity is to estimate what proportion of the population requires social protection because they cannot sustain themselves, we cannot rely upon aggregated official statistics, or even upon officially recorded statistics of household money income. Multivariate regression analysis of 1992 Russian survey data shows that there is no significant relationship between total money income from official and irregular sources and the capacity of a household to sustain itself, that is, get by without spending savings and/or borrowing (see Rose and McAllister, 1993). To assess household resources, we must think in terms of three types of activities: official and monetized; irregular and monetized; and non-monetized household production.

To dismiss data about household production as "soft" is to imply that currencies such as rubles are hard or that current money prices remain hard when converted by a series of heroic assumptions into "constant value" sums in a situation in which the economy is being transformed. To dismiss figures about the irregular economy as "only" estimates is to ignore Árvay's demonstration that summary figures about gross domestic product and net material product are themselves estimates, dependent upon specific accounting conventions that have been instrumental in some contexts but not others, and that should alter when the needs of policy makers alter.

The prudent conclusion is not that all three approaches can or should be summed in a single aggregate, but that measures differ in what they can tell us about systems in transition, *because* they differ in content and in their level of disaggregation (cf. Simon, 1969, pp. 73f, 99ff). In unconventional circumstances it is logical to look beyond conventional SNA measures to understand how economies in transition operate. Only after the transition is over can SNA data be sufficient as a measure of all the things that economic policy makers need to know today.

References

Berg, A., 1993, Measurement and mismeasurement of economic activity during transition to the market, in M. Blejer, G.A. Calvo, F. Coricelli, and A.H. Gelb, eds., *Eastern Europe in Transition: From Recession to Growth?* Discussion Paper No. 196, World Bank, Washington, DC, USA:39–63.

Casanegra de Jantscher, M., Silvani, C., and Vehorn, C.L., 1992, Modernizing tax administration, in V. Tanzi, ed., *Fiscal Policies in Economies in Transition*, International Monetary Fund, Washington, DC, USA:120–141.

Rose, R., 1993, Contradictions between micro- and macro-economic goals in post-Communist societies, *Europe-Asian Studies* (formerly *Soviet Studies*), **45**(3):419–444.

Rose, R., and McAllister, I., 1993, *Is Money the Measure of Welfare in Russia?* University of Strathclyde Studies in Public Policy No. 215, Glasgow, Scotland.

Rose, R., and Tikhomirov, Y., 1993, Who grows food in Russia and Eastern Europe? *Post-Soviet Geography*, **34**(2):111–126.

Simon, H.A., 1969, *The Sciences of the Artificial*, MIT Press, Cambridge, MA, USA.

Chapter 3

Interpreting the Decline of "Output" and the Prospects for "Recovery"

John S. Earle

> The primary aim of the government's economic policy has been to arrest the decline of aggregate output during the first half of 1993, so as to resume economic growth, if only modestly, this year.
>
> *Miso Negritoiu*
> Deputy Prime Minister, Romania
> *Leaders*, July–September 1993

Dramatic reports of collapsing production and skyrocketing inflation and unemployment have turned the attention of Western macroeconomists to recent events in the "transition" countries of Eastern Europe. By all reports this region should be fertile for macroeconomic exploration, with its enormous swings in almost every aggregate indicator. Largely conventional tools in the macroeconomists' kit are being brought to bear in an effort to account for these observations, and the statistical office announcements of standard macroeconomic indicators are eagerly awaited as signs of continued illness or renewed health in the transition economies.

I would like to thank Tanya Nemeth and Simona Spiridon for assistance. This research was supported by the National Council for Soviet and East European Research and the Research Program on Labor Markets in Transition of the Central European University Privatization Project.

R. Holzmann et al. (eds.), Output Decline in Eastern Europe, 65-72.

This chapter argues on the contrary, that the difficulties of measuring the relevant macroeconomic aggregates in Eastern Europe and the complexities of the goals of the transition process require even much more humility from macroeconomic analysis than usual. Not only are the ordinary irritations in defining and measuring output and price indices enormously exacerbated, but it is plausible that the nature of the transition process itself creates systematic measurement biases. And not only are there the routine obstacles to interpreting real GNP per capita, or some such statistic, as a social welfare index, but it is also possible that the objectives of the transition conflict directly with the implications of indicators of macroeconomic "performance."

It is second nature in the West to react to the news that country A's GNP is growing faster than country B's as equivalent to the proposition A is doing better than B. It is even second nature to well-educated economists who understand the difficulty of data gathering, the arbitrariness of index number construction and of aggregation, and the impossibility of value-free welfare measurement. The problems of this logical leap – those of false measurement, of omitted measurement, of distribution and equity, of converting quality into quantity, in short, of reducing all the variety and complexity of the world to a single number – are hardly novel.[1] In the West, these issues of measurement and interpretation usually receive at best brief acknowledgment before discussion passes on to the subject the macroeconomists find more interesting: the statistical behavior of their constructed aggregates. While this practice no doubt often conceals much of importance, it may be relatively venial as a simplifying assumption in stable economies which are not undergoing drastic structural change.

But in the transition context, there are many reasons to be even much more skeptical about macroeconomic reductionism. To start, the measurement problems are still more severe. Statistical offices accustomed to the socialist accounting conventions, the material product system (MPS), have had to adjust rapidly and with few resources to the very different system of national accounts (SNA). For this reason, the "initial conditions" of the transformation process are difficult to measure, and comparable time series are hard to construct. In some cases, the definitions have changed several years in a row, rendering impossible any year-to-year comparisons. Although some backward-looking estimates of the SNA categories, such as GDP, have been undertaken for several countries, some fundamental consistency problems remain.

One of the most crippling problems of consistent measurement is the question of which set of relative price weights to choose in a situation where prices are changing rapidly. The issue of index number relativity arose in earlier discussions of Soviet economic growth (see discussion in Gerschenkron, 1947; and Gregory and Stuart 1994) when it could decisively affect the evaluation of socialist versus capitalist "performance." But it is surely still more important to bear in mind when price liberalization allows massive changes in relative prices. Pre-liberalization prices lack the normative appeal of market prices, but in practice they are the ones typically used in constructing aggregate indices of real output.

Furthermore, the usual difficulties in distinguishing quality changes apply, *a fortiori*, in the transition. Anyone who has been served in a Central European restaurant before and after 1990 may attest to the importance of quality change, as can many company managers negotiating with suppliers. Technological change may be proceeding rapidly, but the cost-savings and product improvements may be impossible to quantify.[2]

Problems faced by East European statistical offices in measuring output are related to the fact that output growth seems to be occurring in sectors which they were not designed to monitor and which are, indeed, inherently difficult to monitor. To summarize, East European growth is taking place disproportionately in small firms, in private firms, and in the services sector. The MPS was applied to a stable set of large industrial state-owned enterprises and producer cooperatives. These firms are now mostly in decline, and increases are taking place in sectors that were de-emphasized, ignored, or nonexistent under the socialist regime. In every country of the region, hundreds of thousands of new legal entities have come into being, but, after an initial registration, their subsequent developments are largely unmonitored. It would be natural to expect, and there is some evidence to believe, that these start-ups experience significant volatility, further complicating the monitoring problem.

These problems do not disappear with the adoption of the SNA. The very definitions of the MPS reveal the socialist bias in that the aggregate net material product (NMP) excludes the so-called nonproductive sector, or most trade and services; thus, the ideological obsession with industrial development was well represented by the socialist aggregate system of accounts. But output indices in the West also tend to stress activity in the easier-to-measure goods-producing sectors. GDP purports to measure all output produced for the market, but the problems of measuring services output imply that movements in measured GDP are more likely to result from true movements in goods production than true movements in services.

The higher weight placed on goods production is also revealed by the tendency of economists to use industrial production as an aggregate output indicator. For instance, Figure 1 in Kornai's (1993) article on the transformational recession shows the "grave economic recession" in 11 countries. The measure of the recession, however, is industrial output. Although understandable for measurement reasons, this practice inevitably biases judgments about the "gravity" of the economic situation.

Moreover, this measurement bias takes on particular significance in the transition context of Eastern Europe. The extremely skewed allocation of capital and all resources toward industry, particularly heavy and military industry, much of which is productively and economically inefficient and environmentally hazardous, is a well documented characteristic of socialist economies that policy should seek to correct.[3] By the same token, it is hoped that the neglect of consumer goods and services will be remedied in response to the liberalization of economic activity and a more rational allocation of capital. Thus, in a successful transition, we should expect to see much downsizing of the favored industrial sector, while the neglected sectors grow rapidly.

In this light, it is not the least bit obvious that reversing the conventionally measured output decline *per se* should represent a short- or medium-term criterion for the success of policy. If industrial production is used, then perhaps a decline should even be applauded. Certainly the decline in the output of certain sectors – for instance, military hardware – is difficult to mourn. But the measurement biases in GDP imply that declines in this aggregate must also be interpreted guardedly.

I would argue that beginning the long process of reallocating resources to more efficient uses at all economic levels – international, macroeconomic, sectoral, occupational, individual – constitutes the primary current objective of the economic transition. No doubt that higher aggregate and individual incomes are greatly desired among East Europeans, but they should not be seen as short-term aims but rather as hoped-for long-run consequences. The allocational objective will not only take time, but likely impose "frictional" or "adjustment" costs, which may well lead to a short-run decline in observed performance. Paying too much attention to output decline, therefore, puts the cart before the horse and even carries the risk that policies may be enacted which retard the reallocation process and thus actually run counter to one of the transition's primary goals.

Evidence that such a bias in policy-making may present a real danger in Eastern Europe may be gained from a cursory look at some current policy proposals and discussions. "Stabilization" policies involving easier credits to enterprises, exchange rate subsidies (to finance imported inputs), and the like are often rationalized on the grounds that they are necessary to "arrest the decline in output," but the problem with them is not only that they are inflationary and financially unsound, but that they serve to prop up industrial dinosaurs that must disappear or be significantly downsized if resources are to be freed for more productive uses. "Structural adjustment policies," state-organized "restructuring of EIDs" ("enterprises in distress" termed by the International Financial Institution), and other forms of "industrial policy" are also often thinly disguised euphemisms for subsidies to certain sectors that drain resources from others. Disfavored sectors are squeezed, both through direct taxation and through the inflation tax, to support favored sectors, likely the same ones now as five years ago.

For the same reasons, the notion of looking for a "recovery" just now in Eastern Europe also seems to me to be somewhat misplaced, if often well intended. "Recovery" carries the connotation of returning to something prior and better, such as good health, or the reacquiring of something valuable. But it is far from obvious in the East European context that the people should be attempting to recover what they had before, difficult as the current period may be.

Thus, the current predicament in Eastern Europe should not be treated as a normal downswing in a typical business cycle. As Kornai argues:

> At the end of a capitalist trade cycle, the real structure of the economy has changed comparatively little since the beginning of the cycle, whereas it can be assumed (or rather hoped) that the situation after the transformational recession will be drastically altered.

Thus, the transition is supposed to accomplish something other than the recovery of the former growth path.

It is not the case, of course, that I oppose output growth in Eastern Europe; I wish only to argue that undue attention to the output variable alone may at least be profligate in neglecting variables which are more important, and it may even, indeed, have perverse effects on what the "transition" is supposed to be trying to accomplish: the movement of resources to new uses so that productivity and well-being may eventually be increased. Most importantly, economists should be cautious in attaching normative interpretations to reported changes in aggregate output. Some examples may strengthen the point.

According to the Economist Intelligence Unit (EIU), the highest growth rate of GDP in all of Europe in 1993 was registered in Albania, at 6%. Thus, a country never before considered a leader in Eastern Europe beat out Poland at 4%, Romania at 0%, and all the other countries, which were negative.[4] The figures reported by the European Bank for Reconstruction and Development (1993) in the *Annual Economic Outlook* differ somewhat:

Albania still leads the pack, but at an estimated 3.5% growth rate for 1993, followed by Poland at 2%, Czech Republic at 0, Hungary at –2, Bulgaria at –5, Slovakia at –8, and Romania at –9. *Business Central Europe* (April 1994) omits Albania, but provides the following figures: Poland at 4%, Romania at 1%, Czech Republic and Hungary at –1%, Slovakia at –4.1%, Bulgaria at –7.7%. The inconsistencies illustrate the difficulties of estimating these aggregates. But, even putting the inconsistencies aside, do any of these rankings correspond to our views of the order in which countries are handling the transition successfully?

Poland, the usual darling of the believers in "recovery," is a particularly interesting case. Although sources are again contradictory, it is often reported that, although both are positive, industrial output is growing faster than GDP.[5] For instance, the Economic Commission for Europe (1993) reports that in the first half of 1993, GDP was up 4%, but industrial production rose 9.3%. In 1992, the corresponding figures were 1% and 4.2%, respectively. Given that about 40% of Polish GDP originates in industry, this implies that nonindustrial sectors were stagnant in early 1993 and actually shrank in 1992! Even if there were some growth outside of industry, it would be the case that the structure of the Polish economy is shifting more toward industry and out of other sectors. But if, as I have argued, the transition is supposed to involve the restructuring and downsizing of industry, freeing resources to be used in other sectors, then the Polish record should be negatively rather than positively judged.[6]

This discussion brings up two important points with which I would like to conclude. First, since the transition is about structural change involving the reallocation of resources at all levels of the economy, then research should focus on inputs, not outputs, in the short run. Second, examination of the causes of the output decline, especially if it is disaggregated, can shed light on transition processes.

But the basic difficulty with such an assessment is that there are too many potential causes of output change. Aggregate demand may have shifted for various reasons including breakdown of the CMEA, harder budget constraints, and tightened monetary policy. Compositional changes in demand across sectors and reallocation of factors within and among sectors give rise to adjustment costs. Also critical to transition economies are coordination failures, not only in reallocation, but also in the breakdown of bureaucratic control before market institutions – supply and information networks and financial markets – are established. The coordination problems are aggravated by the prevalence of asset specificities, both between and within firms, and the resulting potential for holdup problems, and by the negotiation and enforcement costs associated with bilateral monopoly relationships. Other difficulties of adjustment are associated, for instance, with the locational maldistribution of employment opportunities.

All of these phenomena are interesting individually and important to consider, but I would like to argue that the aggregate output changes are much less so: this is a case where the total is much less than the sum of the parts; it obscures more than it reveals.

Notes

[1] There are problems both of definition and of measurement. If I spend time taking care of my children I am not contributing to conventionally defined national output, while if I hire a baby-sitter I am. On the other hand, if the sitter does not report the income, the production of this service will not be measured. A second extreme example is the possibility of a shift in the income distribution turning everyone into a pauper except for one individual, who becomes a trillionaire. GNP may be up, but no one I know would define this as an increase in welfare.

[2] Estimating the extent of quality change in computers has been quite important quantitatively in the USA, influencing, for instance, the measurement of productivity growth in the 1970s and 1980s. Much of the measured "productivity slowdown" was eliminated when improvements in computer technology were taken into account (see Baily and Gordon, 1988). It should be emphasized that quality changes are particularly difficult to qualify when they occur along several dimensions simultaneously.

[3] The importance of initial sectoral allocation for the transition is discussed by Berg and Sachs (1992) in the case of Poland; Earle *et al.* (1994) in the case of the Czech Republic; and Earle and Sapatoru (1993) in the case of Romania.

[4] I could find no estimates for GDP growth in the Czech and Slovak republics in the EIU's report.

[5] In most other countries, we observe a more rapid decline of industrial production than of GDP.

[6] János Gács has reminded me that another explanation for the difference could be that industrial production is measured as gross value added, while GDP is of course net. A rise in gross relative to net value added, however, also seems to provide little cause for celebration.

References

Baily, M., and Gordon, R., 1988, Measurement issues, the productivity slowdown, and the explosion of computer power, *Brookings Papers on Economic Activity*, **19**(2).

Berg, A., and Sachs, J., 1992, Structural adjustment and international trade in Eastern Europe: The case of Poland, *Economic Policy*, **14**.

Business Central Europe, 1994, Country indicators, April.

Earle, J.S., and Sapatoru, D., 1993, Privatization in a hypercentralized economy: The case of Romania, in J.S. Earle, R. Frydman, and A. Rapaczynski, eds., *Privatization in the Transition to a Market Economy*, Pinter Publishers, London, and St. Martin's Press, New York.

Earle, J.S., Frydman, R., Rapaczynski, A., and Turkewitz, J., 1994, *Small Privatization: The Transformation of Retail Trade and Consumer Services in the Czech Republic, Hungary, and Poland,* Central European University Press, London, UK.

Economic Commission for Europe, 1993 *Economic Bulletin for Europe*, **45.**

Economist Intelligence Unit, 1994, *Country Reports*, 1st quarter.

European Bank for Reconstruction and Development, 1993, *Annual Economic Outlook*, September, London, UK.

Gerschenkron, A., 1947, The Soviet indices of industrial production, *Review of Economics and Statistics*, **29**(4), November.

Gregory, P., and Stuart, R., 1994 *Soviet and Post-Soviet Economic Structure and Performance*, 5th ed., Harper-Collins, New York, NY, USA

Kornai, J., 1993, *Transformational Recession: A General Phenomenon Examined through the Example of Hungary's Development*, Discussion Paper, No. 1, Collegium Budapest, Hungary.

Part II

Causes of Output Decline

Chapter 4

Common Causes or Structural Adjustment? Output Decline in Eastern Europe and Poland

Eduardo Borensztein and Jonathan D. Ostry

There is no shortage of explanations for the output collapse in Eastern Europe, the extent of which took many observers (and official forecasters) by surprise. Some have argued that the magnitude of the decline has been overstated by official statistics, either because their coverage excludes all or part of the growing private sector (Berg and Sachs, 1991) or simply because, beginning from an initial situation of widespread shortages, standard price and quantity indices generally overstate the drop in output and the increase in the price level associated with price liberalization (Osband, 1992). Such explanations do not, however, claim that the decline in output is entirely an artifact of official statistics.

Some observers have viewed the output decline as being related to the price shock that followed economic liberalization. This "demand-side" view would argue that the decline in real wages, money, and credit associated with the (greater-than-expected) price increase depressed domestic absorption and thereby contributed to the decline in output. Other demand-side factors might include high real interest rates and, in 1991, the change in CMEA trading arrangements and the ensuing collapse in trade among the

The views expressed are exclusively those of the authors and should not be attributed to the International Monetary Fund.

R. Holzmann et al. (eds.), Output Decline in Eastern Europe, 75-96.

countries of the region (although this latter factor is not of course entirely exogenous). In contrast, a "supply-side" view would characterize the output decline as resulting from the increase in domestic energy prices which, because of overly tight credit ceilings imposed on state enterprises, did not allow firms to pay for their inputs, forcing them both to contract supply and to enter into arrears vis-à-vis their suppliers.

For a country that faces a new relative price structure – as was the case for the East European countries that engaged in reforms during the 1990–1991 period – one would expect that, over a period of time, resources would move toward sectors whose relative output prices had risen and away from the other sectors. Comparative advantage would imply that, if the country faced world market prices for its inputs and outputs, resources would flow toward those sectors where comparative costs were lowest, thereby gradually increasing the value of goods and services produced. A transitional period might, however, be required before factors were allocated to their efficient uses. During this period, the process of structural change might be associated with a decline in aggregate output, especially if, as seems likely, an expansion of activities that were profitable under the new relative price structure was delayed by the presence of significant adjustment costs and uncertainty. To the casual observer, the resulting decline in output would appear very similar to what would occur in a typical recession caused by macroeconomic factors such as fiscal and monetary austerity together with sharp increases in administered energy prices.

Disentangling the extent to which the output decline in Eastern Europe reflects either structural changes or adjustments, on the one hand, or macroeconomic forces (related to demand- or supply-side factors), on the other, constitutes the main issue for analysis in this paper. The issue is relevant for at least two reasons. First, if most of the observed output decline reflects macroeconomic rather than structural factors, then the shock associated with structural change has still to be faced in the future. In other words, output growth should be less robust during the period in which resources are being reallocated, for a given path of the macroeconomic factors. Second, if little of the output decline is a reflection of structural adjustment, then the argument that price and trade liberalization should have proceeded more slowly than was the case in a number of the "big bang" countries should be discounted. The chief reason for this, advanced by proponents of such a view, is that the output costs of transition can be reduced by adopting a slower pace of price liberalization, because under such a scenario the output costs of structural adjustment can be spread out over time.

To investigate this issue, in this chapter we collect data on sectoral developments (prices, output, and so on) in industry for a panel of East European countries. We adapt a methodology originally proposed by Stockman (1988) which allows us to decompose the variance of changes in output into factors that are industry-specific but common across countries (structural factors) and factors that are nation-specific but common across industries (macroeconomic factors). The idea that structural factors can be identified by industry-specific shocks is based on the assumption that the East European economies were fairly similar in terms of comparative advantage and systemic distortions prior to reform. Under these circumstances, the pattern of inter-sectoral resource reallocation following reform should be similar across countries. We choose the CSFR, Hungary, and Poland in part because they are in this respect a fairly homogeneous set of countries. Macroeconomic policies, in contrast, should affect all sectors within a country in a similar fashion, but there is little reason for them to affect output in other countries.

In addition to this central question of structural adjustment versus macroeconomic factors in the output decline, we also look in more detail at the composition of the macroeconomic forces at work, by examining the Polish experience in the first two years of its program of transition (for further details, see Borensztein and Ostry, 1992). Specifically, we estimate a simple supply–demand model for industrial output in Poland disaggregated by sector in order to decompose the source of output fluctuations between supply and demand factors in that country. In addition, the estimates shed some light on the relative importance of various macroeconomic factors (energy price increases, credit contraction, wage increases) in accounting for the output decline. The results suggest that the importance of various macroeconomic factors varies across sectors, but give some support to the view that both energy price increases and tight credit conditions may have influenced the behavior of industrial output in Poland during the two-year period since the initiation of reforms. Finally, we also look in detail at the Polish case to see whether there is any evidence at the national level (as opposed to the regional level) of structural change. We do this by examining the extent to which sectoral output and employment developments are correlated with estimates of comparative advantage (proxied by domestic resource cost which measure comparative costs at world, that is undistorted, prices).

The chapter is organized as follows. In Section 4.1, we explain the methodology used in disentangling common factors from structural change in the output decline in the East European countries, and we present the empirical results from using this methodology. In Section 4.2, we look at the Polish case in more detail – first by describing the behavior of some of the important variables in the aftermath of reform and then by presenting evidence on the type of macroeconomic shocks that were relevant in the output decline and on the extent to which structural change was correlated with comparative advantage. Section 4.3 summarizes the main conclusions of the analysis.

4.1 Structural Change or Common Causes?

Because the reform programs in Eastern Europe share a number of common features, including the removal of a number of distortions (for example, the subsidization of energy use) that were common across countries, it is to be expected that the resulting changes in the structure of industrial production might also be similar across countries. This hypothesis is strengthened to the extent that, in a global context, the countries of Eastern Europe share a similar pattern of comparative advantage. In this case, as relative price distortions come down, the resulting inter-sectoral resource shifts would tend to be similar across countries.

The strategy in this section involves decomposing the change in output in the industrial sectors of each country into factors that are common to all industries in a given country and factors that are common to all countries for a specific industry. The factors that are common to all industries in each country are associated with macroeconomic developments in that country, and are therefore not related to structural change. By contrast, factors that are common to a given industry in all countries are indicative of resource reallocation in production or structural change.

Our strategy, which follows Stockman (1988), is to estimate a regression of the rates of change of industrial output (disaggregated by branch) on a number of dummy variables that separate the different effects. Therefore, we stack data on the monthly rates of change of output in different industrial branches and countries in a variable $y(t)$, and we estimate the following regression:[1]

$$y(t) = m(i) + n(c,t) + u(i,c,t) \ , \qquad (4.1)$$

where the indices i, c, and t refer, respectively, to industry, country, and time in months since the initiation of reforms.[2] The vector $m(i)$ represents the product of the vector of dummy variables and the corresponding vector of coefficients that are industry specific (referred to as industry factors in *Table 4.1*). That is, each dummy variable in $m(i)$ takes a value of one for all the observations corresponding to a specific industry (say, the chemical industry), irrespective of the country or time period, and takes a value of zero otherwise. These variables are interpreted as representing shocks, such as a reduction in energy subsidies that was part of all the reform programs in the region, that are likely to have different effects in different industrial branches. The vector $n(c,t)$ represents the product of the vector of dummy variables and the corresponding vector of coefficients that single out countries indexed by c and time indexed by t (referred to as national factors in *Table 4.1*). That is, each dummy variable in $n(c,t)$ takes a value of one for all the observations that correspond to a given period and a given country (say, period one in Poland) across all the industrial branches in that country, and it takes a value of zero otherwise. Thus, this vector represents the factor that is common to all industries within a country, and might be identified with changes in national financial policies that exercised effects in one country that are different from its effects in the rest of the region. In this specification, we set the industry-specific shock to be independent of time (as might be justified, for example, by the fact that the largest reductions in energy subsidies and other price liberalization measures took place at the beginning of the reform programs), while the macroeconomic factor is specified to be time dependent (specifications presented below). Finally, the vector u represents the regression residuals.

Because the dummy variables are linearly dependent, a normalization is necessary to be able to identify the parameters. The normalization that is chosen involves excluding one industry from the set $m(i)$. This means that the resulting coefficients represent values *relative* to the excluded industry coefficient. The energy industry was chosen to be the "numeraire" sector in all countries, because it showed the least variability over the sample.

As shown in *Table 4.1*, the results from estimating equation (4.1) clearly indicate that most of the variance, or rather most of the explained variation in output, is accounted for by the national or macroeconomic factors.[3] Nearly all of the variance of output changes explained by the regressors is accounted for by the dummy variables that represent national or economy-wide factors. More formally, an F-test cannot reject the null hypothesis that the entire set of industry-specific dummies has no effect on the rate of change of output in these countries.

To allow for differences in the process of resource reallocation across countries, we introduce an additional set of variables. These variables represent country-specific industry shocks – that is, shocks that affect each specific industry in each country. In this way, we attempt to account for national

Table 4.1. Macro and structural factors in the output decline in industrial sectors in the CSFR, Hungary, and Poland.[a]

	F-Statistic	P-Value[b]	Percent of explained SS[c]
Regression 1 $y(t) = m(i) + n(c,t) + u(i,c,t)$			
$R^2 = 0.27$, DF = 522			
National factors	3.28	0.00	96.7
Industry factors	0.16	0.99	0.7
Regression 2 $y(t) = m(i) + n(c,t) + f(i,c) + u(i,c,t)$			
$R^2 = 0.28$, DF = 505			
National factors	3.32	0.00	90.0
Industry factors	0.05	1.00	0.6
National-specific industry factors	0.75	0.77	7.7
Regression 3 $y(t) = m(i,t) + n(c,t) + f(i,c) + u(i,c,t)$			
$R^2 = 0.56$, DF = 307			
National factors	2.51	0.00	35.9
Industry (time-varying) factors	0.91	0.65	50.4
National-specific industry factors	0.62	0.89	3.2

[a]The regressions were calculated on data from December 1989 to December 1991 for Hungary and Poland and from December 1990 to December 1991 for the CSFR.
[b]Marginal significance level.
[c]Percent of explained sum of squares attributable to orthogonal part of corresponding regressors.

differences in the process of resource reallocation. Therefore, the following modified version of equation (4.1) was also estimated:

$$y(t) = m(i) + n(c,t) + f(i,c) + u(i,c,t) \ , \tag{4.2}$$

where the additional set of dummies included in $f(i,c)$ identifies shocks that are specific to industry i in country c. Each of these dummy variables takes a value of one for all the observations corresponding to a given industry in a given country (say, the chemical industry in Poland), irrespective of time, and takes a value of zero otherwise. The inclusion of this additional set of regressors may be defended on the grounds that not all of the main liberalization measures were implemented in all countries of the region. To identify the parameters in (4.2), a further normalization is now required, and this involves the exclusion of the country-effect dummies in the last period.

As displayed in *Table 4.1*, the estimation of equation (4.2) produces similar results to those reported for equation (4.1). However, it should be noted that, as would be expected with the inclusion of another set of regressors, the fraction of the explained variation due to national factors now falls from 97% to 90%. Nevertheless, the overall picture – namely, that the country-specific macroeconomic effects are the most important ones in accounting for output developments – does not change. An F-test indeed finds that the joint effect of the industry effects $m(i)$ and the country-specific industry effects $f(i,c)$ is not statistically different from zero.

Finally, an even more general form of this equation,

$$y(t) = m(i,t) + n(c,t) + f(i,c) + u(i,c,t) \ , \tag{4.3}$$

was also estimated. Each dummy variable included in $m(i,t)$ now takes a value of one for each observation corresponding to a given industry *in a given period* (say, the chemical industry in period one) and it takes a value of zero otherwise. Thus, equation (4.3) allows for both time-dependent $[m(i,t)]$ and country-dependent $[f(i,c)]$ industry shocks. This specification, used in Stockman (1988), accommodates the idea of a real business cycle driven by industry-specific shocks. As a measure of structural change, however, this specification would make sense only if the signs of these shocks implied that the output changes due to industry-specific factors had consistently the same sign for each sector. That is, one would expect structural change factors to push for either an expansion or a contraction in the chemical industry, but not for a sequence of upward and downward shifts in this industry. This specification also has the property of geometrically increasing the number of dummy variables representing industry shocks which are common across countries. While this has the predictable effect of increasing the fraction of the variance explained by the industry factors, it only marginally improves the statistical significance of the industry factors. The F-statistic still cannot reject the null hypothesis that the whole set of coefficients on industry dummies is equal to zero (*Table 4.1*).[4] The evidence in favor of the view that macroeconomic shocks have been much more important than sector-specific shocks in accounting for the output decline thus appears to be robust.

An examination of the pattern of coefficients across the different industries can provide a sense of the implications of the regression estimates for the process of resource reallocation. In our formulation, a positive regression coefficient indicates that factors specific to that industry are expansionary (or less contractionary) in relative terms. In *Figure 4.1*, we plot the values of the industry factors (common across all three countries), derived from the estimates of equation (4.3), as deviations from their mean. The values

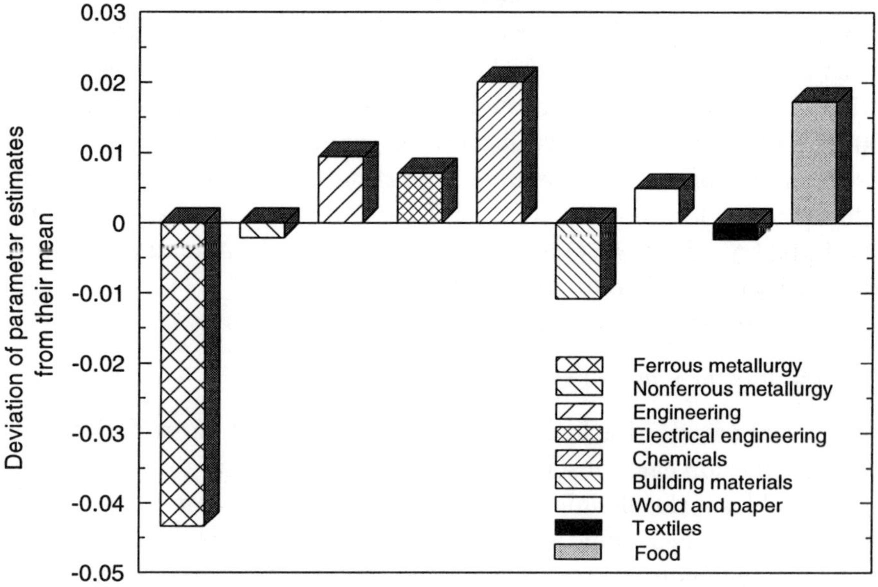

Figure 4.1. Decomposition of output decline, industry-specific factors for CSFR, Hungary, and Poland.

of the coefficients themselves are not meaningful because of the normalizations. The most salient feature is the relative uniformity of the coefficients with the exception of that of ferrous metallurgy, which has a large negative coefficient. The relative uniformity of coefficients is again an indication of little evidence of resource reallocation at this level of aggregation.

In *Figure 4.2* we present the results from the same exercise for the country-specific industry shocks. We calculate these shocks by taking the average of the time-dependent coefficients for each industry. In this case, we do find more variability across sectors; moreover, the patterns are not very similar across countries. It is striking that the chemical industry, which fared quite well in terms of shocks common across the three countries, displays a strong negative specific shock for Hungary and Poland. (The size of the country-specific coefficients is in fact much larger, implying a net negative specific shock for the chemical industry in Hungary and Poland.) It is also noticeable that ferrous metallurgy does not display a very negative factor at the country-specific level, as was the case at the regional level. The pattern depicted in the figures, however, is only suggestive since it is based on point estimates of coefficients that are not jointly (statistically) significantly different from zero.

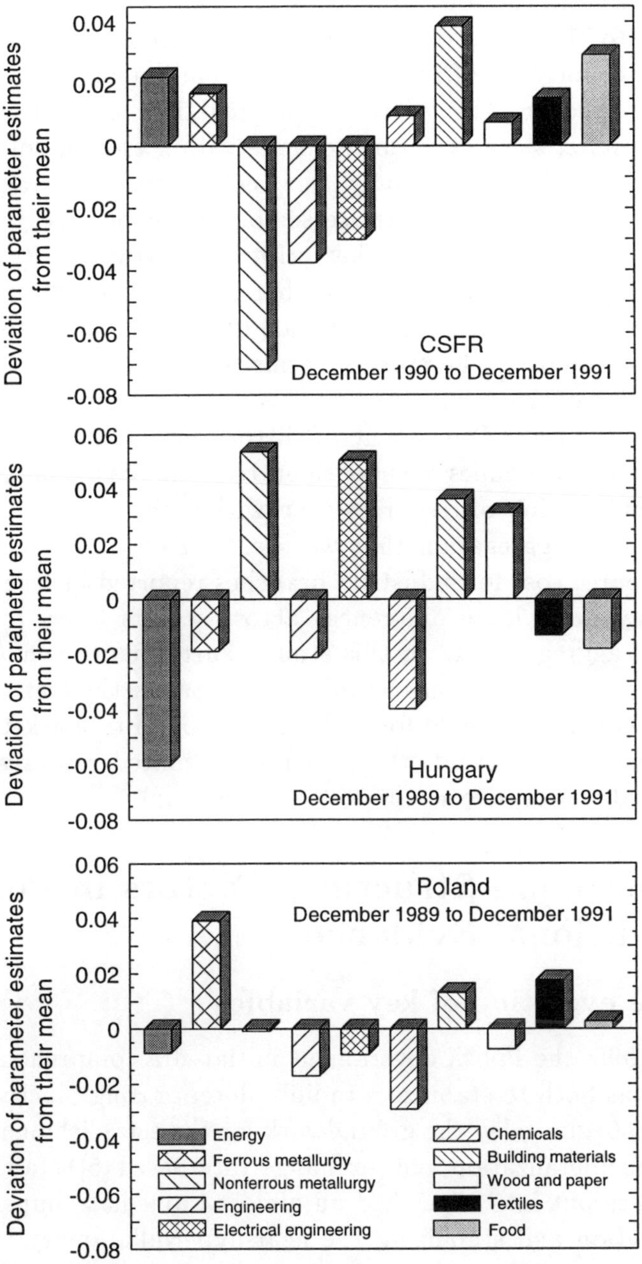

Figure 4.2. Decomposition of output decline, country-specific factors for CSFR, Hungary, and Poland.

Finally, despite the apparent robustness of the results, some limitations of the data used preclude us from drawing firm conclusions. First, the test applies only to the industrial sectors of these economies. Thus, it would not register reallocation of resources away from industry and into services, for example. Second, the level of disaggregation may have played some role in our results, since structural change within any one of our two-digit branches will not be picked up by our test. Third, coverage is, in most cases, limited to the state enterprise sector, either because of the scope of the available data or because other criteria for coverage (e.g., industrial enterprises employing a minimum number of workers) automatically select state enterprises. Therefore, a reallocation of resources from the state to the private sector would also be missed by our test.

The validity of the results, however, is not compromised by these shortcomings in the data. The extent of distortions in the centrally planned systems of these economies was considerable, and was responsible for considerable misallocation of resources even within the industrial sector taken at the level of disaggregation that we use. For example, the estimates of domestic resource cost for industrial branches reported in Hughes and Hare (1992) display quite large differences across sectors taken at roughly the same level of aggregation as in this study. Furthermore, while state enterprises may operate under considerable distortions in the transition phase, a hard budget constraint would force them to respond to market incentives in general terms. In any event, the evidence of limited resource reallocation within the state enterprise sector is itself significant.

4.2 Macro and Structural Factors in Poland: Additional Evidence

4.2.1 The evolution of key variables

In January 1990, the Polish government initiated a comprehensive program whose goal was both to stabilize a rapidly deteriorating macroeconomic situation and to begin to lay the groundwork for the establishment of a market economy. The liberalization and (exchange-rate-based [5]) stabilization measures that were put into effect had an almost immediate impact in sharply reducing inflation and stabilizing the near-hyperinflationary situation that existed at the end of 1989. However, there was an immediate and extremely serious deterioration in the real sector of the Polish economy that took many observers by surprise. We begin by describing the anatomy of the recession

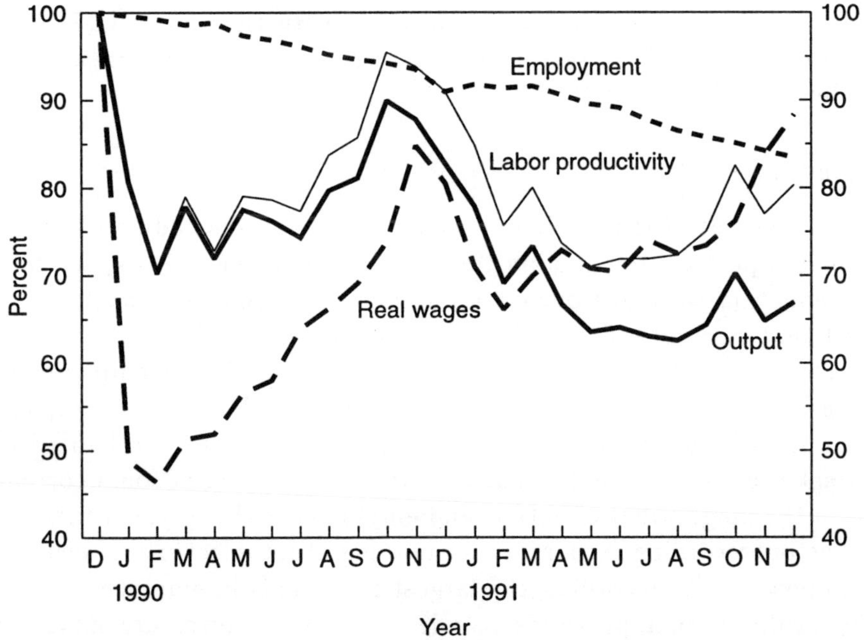

Figure 4.3. Developments in total industry in Poland.

in Poland. *Figure 4.3* plots monthly data on output, employment, productivity, and real product wages for the industrial sector for the two-year period beginning in December 1989, i.e., the month prior to the initiation of the Polish stabilization program.

Output

As far as output is concerned, there was a very steep fall in January 1990, stagnation until midyear, followed by a recovery (partially policy-induced) in the second half of 1990. At the beginning of 1991, there was another steep fall, a continuing downward trend until midyear, followed by a largely seasonal pickup in the closing months of 1991. Within the industrial sector, and particularly within manufacturing (which makes up the bulk of industry), there are some interesting subsectoral differences. For example, the change in output in January 1990 ranged from −32% in electro-engineering to 6% in the metallurgical sector, with the average for manufacturing as a whole being −19%. Similarly, after 12 months, the average decline in manufacturing was 17%, and the range was from −34% in the chemicals sector to 4% in the food sector. After two years, the cumulative decline in manufacturing was about

33%, with the largest decline (52%) being recorded in the electro-engineering sector (which is heavily dependent on trade with the former CMEA countries) and with the food sector actually recording a small increase relative to its level at the end of 1989.[6]

Employment

Given the extent of the decline in output, the very slow adjustment in employment is perhaps remarkable. While one would generally expect employment reduction to follow output reduction with some lag, the Polish data suggest that even after a period as long as two years, industrial employment has declined by only half as much as output. Moreover, the employment reduction has been very smooth, and there is little evidence, for example, that – following a large negative output shock – there was an accelerated effort to adjust the level of employment. Nevertheless, there is some correlation between the magnitudes of output and employment changes, with two of the three sectors recording the largest declines in output (electro-engineering and light industry) also recording the largest reductions in employment. There is also evidence that pressures to adjust the labor force are increased in enterprises with below-average profitability.[7] Finally, the relatively slow adjustment of employment to output changes may be taken as evidence of perceptions, on the part of enterprise managers, that the output decline is temporary. With adjustment costs, if managers feel that the output fall will be short-lived, they would reduce employment by only some fraction of the decline in sales. Obviously, if the output decline is viewed as temporary, it cannot at the same time be the result of structural change, which would presumably be viewed by managers as permanent.

Real Product Wages

Real wage developments for 1990 as a whole were broadly in line with program targets. To compensate for excessive (in light of productivity developments) real wage increases in the three years leading up to the program and the removal of the subsidy implicit in sharply negative real interest rates at the end of 1989, a downward adjustment in real wages of about one-third was thought necessary to maintain the viability of many state enterprises.[8] In 1991, however, both real wage and labor productivity were not consistent with the maintenance of enterprise profitability, as is attested to by the latter's continuing decline through the year. Real product wages (excluding premiums from profits) in industry have increased on average by about

18% in 1991 relative to their average level in 1990. Within manufacturing, the change in real product wages ranges from −5% in the fuel and power sector to over 20% in the electro-engineering, wood and paper, and mineral sectors and to over 30% in the light industry and metallurgical sectors.[9] In addition to the increase in real wages, labor productivity in industry has declined by an average of nearly 8% between 1990 and 1991, implying an increase in unit labor costs on the order of 25% over the same period. It would seem to follow therefore that, in addition to the shocks coming from the demand side (including the collapse in CMEA exports and the increase in import demand) and other supply-side factors (such as tight credit and continuing energy price increases), an increase in wage costs may have played some role in accounting for the continuing decline in output in 1991. This is in sharp contrast to developments in 1990 when producers were able to increase prices much more quickly than wages, thereby offsetting the impact of cost pressures coming, *inter alia*, from higher input prices and the move to positive real interest rates. In 1991, both the change in CMEA trading arrangements and the increase in labor costs are consistent with a view of the output decline being partially related to the emergence of a significant price/cost squeeze for firms operating in the tradable goods sector.[10]

4.2.2 Empirical findings

In this section we perform statistical analysis on monthly industrial production data disaggregated by branches for the period since the initiation of reforms in Poland, in an attempt to shed some light on the relative importance of different exogenous factors in accounting for the decline in output. Because the initiation of market reforms is a relatively recent phenomenon, the amount of data at our disposal is relatively modest, essentially covering two years in the case of Poland.[11] In the cross-sectional dimension, the sample covers about 20 industrial sectors (*Monthly Statistical Bulletin*, various issues, Polish Statistical Office). Nonetheless, the variance of estimators will tend to be high, and the sample may be too short to capture the proper lag structure of the adjustment to the economic shocks. Subject to these caveats, however, there is still important information that can be extracted from the data, particularly if the shocks that have affected the Polish economy are relatively large, as they appear to have been.

Our empirical work deals with two questions that may contribute to an explanation for the output decline. First, we try to see whether the type of structural adjustment that has taken place within the Polish economy has been correlated with estimates of comparative advantage. Second, within the macroeconomic forces at work, we try to assess the relative importance of demand-side and supply-side factors by estimating simple sectoral supply–demand models.

Structural Change and Domestic Resource Cost in Polish Output

To gauge the plausibility of the structural change view of the output decline in Poland, we examine the extent to which output and employment changes can be predicted on the basis of estimates of comparative advantage. For this purpose we make use of two studies that compute domestic resource costs (DRCs) for Poland prior to price and trade liberalizations (see de la Calle, 1990; Hughes and Hare, 1992). Domestic resource costs are defined as the ratio of value added at domestic prices to value added at international prices (that is, valuing products and inputs at their estimated domestic-currency equivalent of the world price). The lower the DRC, the more competitive a sector will be after price and trade liberalizations because the price of its output will rise more than the cost of its inputs.

It should be noted at the outset that the estimates of DRCs are highly tentative because of the large number of judgmental assumptions necessary to value products at world prices, including problems arising from the existence of non-traded goods, substantial quality differences, and peculiar exchange-rate arrangements in the CMEA area.[12] At a more fundamental level, DRCs are based on the assumption of a fixed coefficient technology and do not consider the possibility of different elasticities of substitution across sectors. As is well known, energy was generally the most underpriced input in many of the former CPEs. This implies that, according to the DRC methodology, sectors with high energy intensity will appear to be the least competitive. However, it might be that these sectors employed highly energy-intensive technologies because they had the highest elasticities of substitution between energy and other inputs (labor and capital). If this were the case, the DRCs would be misleading as far as providing a ranking of comparative advantage. Notwithstanding all these caveats, the DRC estimates are the only available measures of comparative advantage, and for this reason they cannot be overlooked.

To determine the extent to which output and employment changes are correlated with this measure of comparative advantage, we ran regressions of the cumulative output and employment change since the beginning of the reform program on (transformed) measures of DRC. The transformation is necessary because DRCs are not a monotonic measure: they are negative

Table 4.2. Output and employment changes and comparative advantage in Poland.[a]

	DRC[b]	DRC[c]
Output changes	–0.17 (1.50)	–0.19 (0.77)
R^2	0.13	0.04
Durbin–Watson	2.35	1.95
Employment changes	–0.11 (1.43)	–0.22 (0.16)
R^2	0.12	0.11
Durbin–Watson	2.04	1.71

[a]Cross-section regressions over 17 sectors of overall change in output and employment from December 1989 to December 1991. Figures in parentheses correspond to *t*-statistics (in absolute value).
[b]Inverse of domestic resource cost as calculated by de la Calle (1990).
[c]Inverse of domestic resource cost as computed by Hughes and Hare (1992, Table 2).

for those sectors that produce negative value added at world prices; when the DRC is positive, a higher DRC indicates a less competitive sector. To overcome this non-monotonicity, we applied the transformation suggested by Hughes and Hare (1992): for positive DRCs, we use the inverse of the DRC, while for negative DRCs we use the ratio of value added at international prices to the domestic price.

The results presented in *Table 4.2* do not provide much support for the structural change hypothesis since there is little evidence on the basis of the regressions that output or employment is moving in the direction dictated by the available estimates of comparative advantage.[13] As explained above, however, the construction of the DRC measures is subject to numerous pitfalls and the results may partly reflect the imperfections associated with this measure of competitiveness.

Macro Factors: Supply or Demand Shifts?

The issue of whether demand shocks or supply shocks have been predominant in accounting for the output decline is an important element in our understanding of developments in the early stages of reform in Poland. While it seems obvious that both types of shock have been present, it is not clear which has exerted the largest influence. The tight financial policies pursued to ensure domestic stabilization and a satisfactory balance of payments position, on the one hand, and the exogenous component of the drop in export demand from other former CMEA countries, on the other, certainly had a restraining effect on aggregate demand. But the increase in a number of administered prices – notably for energy – and liquidity restrictions affecting enterprises are also likely to have had a negative impact on aggregate supply.

To analyze these issues, we assume that demand in sector i is given by

$$\log D_t^i = \alpha_0^i + \alpha_1^i \log P_t^i + \alpha_2^i \log Y_t^i \ , \tag{4.4}$$

where P^i denotes a (relative) price index for sector i and Y is a scale variable that proxies aggregate spending (on a monthly basis).[14] Supply in sector i is given by

$$\log S_t^i = \beta_0^i + \beta_1^i \log P_t^i + \beta_2^i \log w_{t-1}^i + \beta_3^i \log P_t^E + \beta_4^i \log C_{t-1} \ , \tag{4.5}$$

where w^i is the real wage, P^E is an index of the price of energy input, and C is the real stock of bank credit to enterprises. That is, supply is a function of the price of the product and of the cost of the relevant inputs (labor and energy). All of these prices and the stock of credit are deflated by the overall industrial price index. We also incorporate the stock of bank credits to enterprises in real terms in order to proxy for the possible effect of an overall liquidity constraint that might have been relevant during this period (as argued by Calvo and Corricelli, 1992).[15]

Equations (4.4) and (4.5) were estimated using three-stage least squares – with the price of the product treated as an endogenous variable – for seven industrial subsectors (with data from the *Monthly Statistical Bulletin*, various issues, Polish Statistical Office). As can be seen from *Table 4.3*, the results are encouraging, since the vast majority of the coefficients have their theoretically predicted signs.[16] However, the relative price variable in the demand function and the (lagged) product wage variable in the supply function do not perform very well. As far as the former is concerned, the price elasticity of demand is usually estimated to be fairly small, with most of the estimated elasticities falling between 0.1 and 0.3. There are two possible interpretations of this result. One is that the demand functions are in fact highly inelastic. The other interpretation is that the demand equation is not well identified by the set of instrumental variables used in the estimation. As far as the finding that product wages do not seem to have played a substantial role over the estimation period is concerned, this may partly reflect the fact that firms did not believe that the very low real wages at the beginning of the program would be sustained. In this case, real product wages would underestimate the effective cost of labor over the relevant time horizon of firms and, therefore, firms would have been less likely to expand output on the basis of the very low wages at the beginning of the program, particularly if employment changes carried significant costs of adjustment.

Table 4.3. Demand and supply estimation results for Poland.[a]

	Metallurgy	Electro-engineering	Chemical	Wood & paper	Light industry	Food	Mineral industry
Demand							
Constant	−1.42	−3.82	−1.15	0.13	−3.49	5.94	−0.45
	(1.42)	(4.87)	(4.54)	(0.23)	(6.06)	(36.41)	(0.38)
Relative price	0.04	−0.09	−0.09	−0.42	−0.34	−0.07	−0.16
	(0.29)	(0.57)	(2.23)	(3.39)	(1.88)	(0.69)	(1.01)
Aggregate spending	1.29	1.74	1.15	0.90	1.66	0.52	0.91
	(5.83)	(9.95)	(20.48)	(7.06)	(13.37)	(7.96)	(4.07)
R^2	0.60	0.81	0.95	0.74	0.88	0.78	0.43
Durbin–Watson	0.63	0.87	1.54	0.74	1.43	1.66	0.73
Supply							
Constant	1.28	3.74	−5.74	−3.36	2.60	3.94	−28.67
	(1.08)	(2.58)	(1.13)	(0.54)	(3.85)	(12.34)	(0.16)
Relative price	1.84	4.53	9.51	7.53	4.25	1.75	24.90
	(4.00)	(2.41)	(1.91)	(1.21)	(4.45)	(3.70)	(0.19)
Real wage (−1)	−0.16	−1.85	3.23	−3.02	−0.61	0.26	−3.51
	(1.10)	(1.36)	(1.71)	(1.07)	(1.04)	(1.19)	(0.18)
Coal price	−1.10	−2.37	−5.37	−3.61	−1.37	−0.51	−12.90
	(4.78)	(2.49)	(1.98)	(1.29)	(4.75)	(2.68)	(0.19)
Real credit (−1)	0.78	1.70	4.56	4.14	1.12	0.03	9.90
	(2.50)	(1.31)	(1.85)	(1.16)	(2.30)	(0.17)	(0.18)
R^2	0.61	0.48	0.12	0.06	0.41	0.57	0.20
Durbin–Watson	0.83	0.49	0.77	1.26	0.66	1.11	0.57

[a]Estimation is by three-stage least squares. Sample period is from December 1989 to December 1991. Numbers in parentheses are *t*-statistics (in absolute value).

As mentioned previously, and notwithstanding these two shortcomings of the estimation, the model produces, on the whole, reasonable parameter estimates. As far as the supply regression is concerned, the results suggest that energy price increases were a significant determinant of output developments in five of the seven sectors, while the real credit variable turns out to be significant in three of the seven cases.

Using the above estimates, it is possible to decompose the total decline in output into a fraction caused by shifts in variables that affect the supply function and a fraction caused by shifts in variables that affect the demand function. Since the fit of the regressions is not perfect, there is a remainder,

Table 4.4. Decomposition of output decline for Poland.

	Total change	Supply shift	Supply-side change	Demand shift	Demand-side change	Error terms
1990[a]	–0.247	–0.846	–0.039	–0.251	–0.246	0.040
1990[b]	–0.263	–0.736	–0.028	–0.269	–0.264	0.030
1990	–0.199	–0.771	–0.031	–0.197	–0.193	0.024
1991	–0.185	–0.303	–0.008	–0.217	–0.213	0.044

[a]First quarter of 1990.
[b]First half of 1990.

which is explained by the random disturbances, and which cannot in general be allocated because the disturbances to the demand and supply equations are not independent. The output change in sector i caused by changes in the exogenous demand-side variables can be computed as

$$\Delta \log Q^i_{DS} = \left[\beta^i_1 / \left(\beta^i_1 - \alpha^i_1\right)\right] \left(\alpha^i_2 \Delta \log Y\right) \; , \tag{4.6}$$

where the operator Δ indicates the cumulative change in the variable. Similarly, the change due to supply-side shifts is

$$\begin{aligned} \Delta \log Q^i_{SS} &= \left[\alpha^i_1 / \left(\alpha^i_1 - \beta^i_1\right)\right] \\ &\quad \times \left[\beta^i_2 \Delta \log w^i + \beta^i_3 \Delta \log P^E + \beta^i_4 \Delta \log C\right] \; . \end{aligned} \tag{4.7}$$

Both the horizontal shifts in supply and demand functions (that is, evaluated at a constant price) as well as the equilibrium change in output due to those shifts [as given in equations (4.6) and (4.7)] were computed. We used the median value of the estimated coefficients and we estimated the shifts for the first quarter of the reform program in Poland (first quarter of 1990), for the first half of 1990, and for the full years 1990 and 1991 (relative to levels at the end of 1989 and 1990, respectively).[17] The results indicate very large supply shifts in the first quarter of 1990, but more moderate supply shifts over the rest of the period. Because our median estimate of the demand function is essentially completely inelastic, shifts in supply generate increases in price but little decline in output, as can be seen from the column identifying the change in output due to supply-side shifts in *Table 4.4*. However, as mentioned above, the inelasticity of demand functions may not be a robust finding.

It should be noted that, since the demand and supply shifts are not independent, there is no clear way of fully decomposing their effects. This is because, for example, an exogenous change in the price of energy may have some effect on aggregate demand, and thus would show up as both a demand-side shock and a supply-side shock. However, to the extent that the dependence between demand and supply shocks is characterized by a longer lag structure, the decomposition that we perform would still give reasonable results for short periods.

4.3 Conclusions

This paper has sought to investigate whether the output decline experienced by the East European countries in their move from plan to market was due to structural adjustments in response to a new set of relative prices or to macroeconomic forces, including stringent financial policies and supply shocks associated with energy price increases in an environment of tight credit. We collected disaggregated industrial-level data for the CSFR, Hungary, and Poland, and used a methodology (originally proposed by Stockman, 1988) to decompose the variance of output into factors that were common to a given industry in different countries (structural factors) and factors that were common to all industries in a particular country (macroeconomic factors). Our finding was that most of the variance of output that was explained by our model could be attributed to national or macroeconomic factors. There was little evidence that much structural adjustment had taken place in these countries in the early phase of transition.

The policy implication is that, to a large extent, the output shock associated with structural adjustment has still to be experienced in these countries, and that output growth will be lower than it might otherwise have been had deeper structural changes already taken place. Further, arguments in favor of more gradualism in implementing reforms lose some of their force because, to a large extent, they are based on the assumption that more gradualism spreads the output costs of structural adjustment over time. Since most of the output decline is attributable to macroeconomic factors, the cost of structural adjustment has already been pushed into the future.

We also examined, in some detail, the behavior of Poland's economy following the big bang at the beginning of 1990 to learn whether there was any evidence that the inter-sectoral variations in output that have been observed could be associated with measures of comparative advantage, as one would expect if resources were moving in response to the incentives created by the new relative price structure. The regression analysis revealed, however, that resource movements had little to do with comparative costs, again casting doubt on the structural change view of the output decline in that country. With most of the output decline in Poland attributable to macroeconomic factors, we then investigated whether demand-side or supply-side forces were the main contributors to output movements. We estimated a simple supply–demand model of Polish industrial output disaggregated by sector. The results indicated very large supply shifts at the beginning of 1990 (when energy prices were increased sharply), but more moderate shifts over the rest of the period. However, because demand was estimated to be relatively inelastic, most of the effect of supply shifts was on price rather than output, leaving demand-side factors as being predominant in accounting for the output decline.

Notes

[1] While Stockman (1988) estimates essentially the same regression for a set of industrial countries, he is testing for a different effect – namely, evidence of a "real business cycle" in the form of significant industry-specific shocks. There is, in fact, a small literature on the decomposition of output changes into industry-specific, regional, and national components. Stockman's methodology was applied in this study mainly because it imposes fewer structural assumptions on the data than some of the other papers in the literature.

[2] Specifically, January 1990 for Poland and Hungary and January 1991 for the CSFR.

[3] The estimation of equation (4.1) was carried out by pooling data from 10 industrial sectors for Poland, Hungary, and the CSFR, on samples that begin on the dates of each country's "big bang," defined with reference to the date of the first major price liberalization (January 1990 for Poland and Hungary and January 1991 for the CSFR). The sample ends December 1991. The sources of data are: for Poland, *Monthly Statistical Bulletin*, various issues, Polish Statistical Office (GUS); for Hungary, industrial statistical indices provided by the Central Statistical Office; for the CSFR, *Statistical Bulletin*, various issues, Federal Statistical Office.

[4] If one were to compare these results with those obtained by Stockman for the G-7 countries, one would see that the point estimates of the fractions of total variance accounted for by national versus industry factors are quite similar to those reported in *Table 4.1*. The difference, however, is that the standard errors associated with the industry factors are much higher for this group of countries than for the G-7. This results in the industry factors' statistical significance being much lower than that reported in Stockman's study.

[5] Wages were an additional nominal anchor in Poland, as elsewhere in Eastern Europe.

[6] While these differences may indicate the onset of a reallocation of resources across sectors, they may also simply reflect different sensitivities to business-cycle factors.

[7] Theoretically, of course, the correlation could go either way since low profitability might reflect lack of adjustment on the employment front. The data, however, seem to suggest that firms with subnormal profits have undertaken relatively more labor force adjustment.

[8] It should be noted, however, that the decline in labor productivity in 1990 was considerably larger than originally envisaged so that unit labor costs in 1990 would, other things equal, have been higher than foreseen under the program. One might therefore wish to think of the actual real wage in 1990 as being an upper bound on the market-clearing real wage.

[9] In sectors that benefited from trade under the "old" CMEA arrangements (for example, electro-engineering), a case could be made that the "equilibrium" product wage fell substantially between 1990 and 1991, owing to the negative terms of trade shocks experienced by such sectors. In this case, the increase in real product wages provides a (perhaps gross) lower bound of the magnitude by which real wage costs are currently out of line.

[10] An interesting parallel emerges here between Poland and eastern Germany following unification. Eastern German producer prices rose much more slowly than consumer prices (indeed they fell in some instances) in the period following unification, implying a much larger increase in product wages than in consumption wages and the emergence of significant pressures in both labor and product markets. Although Polish producer prices rose more quickly than consumer prices in 1990, alleviating pressures in labor and product markets, this trend was reversed in 1991, at which point significant parallels between the Polish and eastern German experience began to emerge. On the eastern German case, see Dornbusch and Wolf (1992).

[11] A change of methodology adopted by the Polish Statistical Office (GUS) at the beginning of 1992 also limited the sample size at our disposal.

[12] It should be mentioned that, for some sectors, the coverage in the Hughes and Hare study is more disaggregated than the one that was available to us. For comparability, in those cases (3 out of 17) a simple average was used to aggregate the data.

[13] Our transformation of the DRC is such that the higher the measure, the more competitive the sector.

[14] We use aggregate industrial production for all sectors except food (the demand for which is likely to come from final consumers rather than from firms) where total household consumption spending is used. It should be noted that, from the point of view of each subsector, aggregate industrial production is effectively exogenous.

[15] In the Calvo–Corricelli model, credit may be viewed as an input, like labor and energy, into the production process.

[16] In roughly 40% of the cases, however, the standard errors are large relative to the estimated coefficients.

[17] In interpreting the results, it should be borne in mind that Poland experienced a relative recovery in the second half of 1990.

References

Berg, A., and Sachs, J.D., 1991, Structural Adjustment and International Trade in Eastern Europe: The Case of Poland, Presented at the Economic Policy Panel, October, Prague, CSFR.

Borensztein, E., and Ostry, J.D., 1992, Structural and Macroeconomic Determinants of the Output Decline in Poland, International Monetary Fund, WP/92/86, Washington, DC, USA.

Calvo, G.A., and Coricelli, F., 1992, Stagflationary effects of stabilization programs in reforming socialist countries: Enterprise-side and household-side factors, *The World Bank Economic Review*, **6**(1):71–90.

de la Calle, L., 1990, Macroeconomic and Microeconomic Linkages of the Polish Reforms, IDP Report No. 77, October, World Bank, Washington, DC, USA.

Dornbusch, R., and Wolf, H., 1992, Economic transition in eastern Germany, *Brookings Papers on Economic Activity*, **1**:235–261.

Hughes, G., and Hare, P., 1992, Industrial Policy and Restructuring in Eastern Europe, Working Paper No. 653, March, Centre for Economic Policy Research, London, UK.

Osband, K., 1992, Index number biases during price liberalization, *IMF Staff Papers*, **39**(June):287–309.

Stockman, A.C., 1988, Sectoral and national aggregate disturbances to industrial output in seven European countries, *Journal of Monetary Economics*, **21**:387–409.

Comments on the Paper by Eduardo Borensztein and Jonathan D. Ostry

Klaus Neusser

I welcome very much the efforts by the authors to use econometric techniques and tools to disentangle the contributions of aggregate demand and supply, or macroeconomic factors and structural adjustments, to the observed decline in aggregate production. I have, however, my reservations whether the particular techniques used are well suited to capture the transformation process.

First, the method proposed by Stockman (1988) is only interpretable for economies whose outputs have reached their steady state distributions. During a phase of transition, the response of the system to shocks is not invariant over time but changes as the economy approaches its new steady state. Moreover, given the institutional changes experienced by these countries, the Lucas critique implies that the demand and supply relationships cannot be expected to remain constant. Thus it seems difficult to draw definite conclusions concerning the structural adjustment from these kind of exercises. Given these criticism, the results would therefore become more credible if they can be shown to be robust with respect to the sample period (dates of the big bang [1]), the specification of demand and supply (for example, change in bank credit instead of the level of bank credit, control of foreign developments), and the identifying restrictions. All relationships are static, although the Durbin–Watson statistics suggest positive autocorrelation. The inclusion of lagged output or prices seems appropriate. Efficiency of the estimates can be improved by constraining some coefficients to be the same across sectors.

Second, the disaggregation is probably much too crude to detect structural changes – especially, if one realizes that structural adjustment at this level of aggregation takes several years but that the sample period covers only one to two years. Moreover, the data are very noisy, particularly on a monthly basis.

Third, the paper concentrates only on manufacturing but overlooks services. This oversight is unfortunate because in most of these countries a reallocation toward services seems to have taken place. The results, therefore, underestimate the amount of adjustment.

Fourth, looking at manufacturing only, I think that the problem faced by these countries is not so much due to an inappropriate output mix, at least at the aggregation of the paper, but rather due to an outdated capital stock and extremely low efficiency levels. The common reaction, thus, would be to renew the capital stock and increase labor productivity. If, however, the adjustment costs are internal to the firm or the industry, such changes are necessarily accompanied by a reduction in production. As this type of problem is common across all industries in a given country, output declines simultaneously in all sectors. The speed and the amount of the decline, however, depend on the macroeconomic policy followed in each country. Thus the results provided by the authors are compatible with structural adjustment taking place.

Given these criticism, I would suggest that the authors deepen the investigation and look also at labor flows and labor productivity instead of output indicators. Alternatively, one might look at employment growth dispersion as proxies of labor reallocation.[2] This might bring about a broader picture of the structural changes in these countries.

Notes

[1] There may have been some reactions prior to the big bang for countries which started their reforms later.

[2] Lilien, D., 1982, Sectoral shifts and cyclical unemployment, *Journal of Political Economy*, **90**:777–92.

Chapter 5

Supply and Demand Factors in Output Decline in Central and Eastern Europe

Andrew Berg

What is the role of aggregate supply and demand factors in the output decline in Central and Eastern Europe? This question can have two interpretations:

1. What are the relative weights of supply and demand factors in generating the output declines observed in former centrally planned economies of Europe?
2. How important are the factors that fit under the rubric of "supply and demand" in comparison with other possible reasons for the output decline, especially adjustment away from the Soviet-style economic system?

The identification of supply or demand shocks as causes of output decline has little intrinsic interest. The question is important to the extent that it addresses underlying analytic or policy issues. In the US macroeconomic literature, for example, underlying the debate is the question of whether exogenous technological ("supply") shocks or macroeconomic policy ("demand") shocks drive the business cycle. The present context suggests two main motivations. First, we want to know how to design programs to avoid

I would like to thank Marek Dabrowski and conference participants for useful remarks. The views expressed in this paper are not necessarily those of the International Monetary Fund.

R. Holzmann et al. (eds.), Output Decline in Eastern Europe, 99-126.

problems in the states that have yet to go through the transition process. Policy-induced supply shocks, in particular, seem like a bad idea: they raise prices and lower output. Policy-induced demand shocks may, on the other hand, be a necessary tool for the reduction of inflation and the introduction of macroeconomic stability. Second, we want to know how to get a recovery going. If a fall in aggregate demand was the reason for the output decline, then perhaps an increase in aggregate demand would help spur growth.

Before going further, we need to clarify what we mean by supply and demand shocks. Perhaps the most common usage is a simple static model in price-output space in which the IS-LM model generates a downward-sloping aggregate demand curve while an expectations-based Phillips curve generates an upward-sloping supply curve.

The aggregate demand shocks that, in such a framework, may have affected output in Eastern Europe are not hard to identify. Beyond conventional ones, in particular the fiscal consolidation and the decrease in money growth central to the stabilization program, there are others specific to stabilization in this unusual type of economy. *Dis-hoarding*, not only of traditionally high inventories in Soviet-type economies but also of inventories accumulated in anticipation of price liberalization, might lead to a fall in sales and a further fall in production given sales. Unusually high uncertainty about what the future holds may lead workers to increase saving and firms to suspend investment plans. Despite the low exchange rate, the sudden availability of foreign goods might lead to a sharp increase in imports and a fall in domestic demand.

The problem with applying this model in Central and Eastern Europe is that it captures only some of the factors usually thought of as aggregate supply shocks. The increase in the price of imported raw material imports from the Soviet Union is one clear example of such a supply shock: like the oil price increases of the 1970s, it shifts the aggregate supply curve to the left. Another possibility is the appearance of widespread microeconomic supply constraints, as the reform program may have led to large dislocations in the distribution system, preventing inputs from going to firms or goods from getting to consumers. This would also lead to a leftward shift in the aggregate supply curve (see Gomulka, 1991).

Changes in domestic relative prices associated with the end of shortages and reduction in subsidies fit less well into this framework. The large reallocation of demand implied by the change in relative prices and the elimination of rationing could lead to a decline in aggregate output: sectors facing a decrease in effective demand would decline, while sectors facing an increase might be unable to respond so quickly. Similarly, the sectoral reallocation implied by rapid trade liberalization could cause net (transitional) output declines. The net shock is negative to the extent that adjustment implies cost and factors are unemployed during the transition.

In Chapter 4 of this book Borensztein and Ostry attempt to estimate supply and demand curves for a set of Polish industries in 1990 and 1991 and have derived estimates of the relative importance of supply and demand shocks. They regard demand shocks as being Keynesian aggregate demand shocks affecting the entire economy and supply-side effects as being sector-specific. As suggested by the above discussion, one problem with this approach is that it is difficult to find variables that shift the supply curve. Borensztein and Ostry include the (lagged) real wage, the (lagged) stock of real credit, and the price of coal. The coal price seems to capture well one potential source of relative price shocks driven from the cost side. The inclusion of the real wage is hard to justify as a cost shock, given that one component of wage payments is a profit distribution in Polish worker-controlled state enterprises.[1] This inclusion of real credit may capture part of what Calvo and Coricelli (1992) mean by the credit crunch, though as emphasized in Calvo and Coricelli (1993b), and as discussed below, this captures only a part of the impact of the credit crunch.

But what is missing is an instrument for the possible end of forced substitution and resulting switch in effective demand. Consider a two-sector economy with cost-plus pricing, where factors are allocated by the central planner. Unless these factor allocations happen to mimic a market allocation, one of the outputs will be in short supply given prices. If there is no saving, then income left over after the purchase of the scarce good will be spent on the other good. Thus, through forced substitution, all output will be purchased. Price liberalization in this economy would lead to a relative increase in effective demand in the shortage sector and a relative demand decrease in the surplus sector, without any change in subsidies or input costs. Depending on how factor markets and firms operate after liberalization, output would tend to decline in the surplus sector and increase in the shortage sector. The expansion is likely to be slower than the contraction, implying a transitional output decline. The point of this example is that coal prices or other input price instruments do not capture this effect.

Another approach to identifying supply and demand shocks in the macroeconomic literature derives from the idea that supply shocks represent technological shocks while demand shocks are largely cyclical. The implication, used for identification, is that demand shocks are temporary and supply shocks are permanent. A moment's reflection will demonstrate that this is not a useful strategy for reforming socialist economies. Supply shocks such as changes in the quantity of credit may be temporary, while demand shocks may well be permanent, if, for example, they come from changes in the CMEA trade regime or from the end of forced substitution in final demand.

These supply and demand factors are investigated in this chapter. Section 5.1 analyzes the relative weight of supply and demand factors in the output decline in Poland, including aggregate demand; the CMEA shock; sector-specific supply shocks such as input price increases; the credit crunch; and other identifiable supply-side disruptions. Section 5.2 addresses the importance of such supply and demand factors as a group compared with inter-sectoral adjustment. Section 5.3 concludes the chapter.

5.1 Supply and Demand Explanations of the Output Decline

The contraction in measured GDP in post-Soviet-style economies has been sharp in all the countries in question (see *Figure I.1* in the Introduction). This paper concentrates on Poland, where the output decline exhibits several salient characteristics.

- The decline took place largely in two steps, in early 1990 and early 1991. This suggests that what happened should be understood primarily in terms of two major events, liberalization and stabilization in January of 1990 and the CMEA shock in early 1991, and resulting endogenous dynamics.
- A decomposition of the decline into categories of final demand is complicated by the problem of measuring inventory investment during the hyperinflation, a point to which we return below. *Table 5.1* presents estimates that indicate that declines in inventory investment account for much of the total decline, though declines in fixed investment and consumption have also contributed. The trade surplus rose in 1990, though total imports and especially exports both increased, reducing the GDP decline (in an accounting sense).[2]
- The decline was concentrated in industrial production and in the state sector. Growth was immediate in services and in the private sector (see *Table 5.2* for an estimated decomposition of the 1990 change in GDP).[3] As the private sector has come to predominate, the whole economy has begun to grow. The state sector has not recovered, though the decline was halted in 1991.

Table 5.1. Real GDP growth in 1990 by final use in Poland.

	1989 share	Real change	Contribution to total
Private consumption	0.56	–4.8%	–2.7%
Investment	0.22		
Inventory			–6.2%
Fixed	0.21	–9.0%	–1.9%
Government	0.18	1.0%	0.2%
Exports (merchandise)	0.21		6.1%
CMEA	0.07	–13.2%	
Other	0.14	51.3%	
Imports (merchandise)	0.16		–0.5%
CME	0.05	–34.0%	
Other	0.11	20.4%	
Total			–4.9%

Source: Author's estimates.

Table 5.2. Real GDP growth in 1990 by sector of origin in Poland.

	1989 share	Real change	Contribution to total
Total	1.00	–8.7	
Industry total[a]	0.57	–17	–9.8
Manufacturing and mining			
Socialized	0.41	–21	–8.6
Private	0.03	5	0.2
Construction	0.08	–16	–1.3
Transportation	0.04	–14	–0.6
Agriculture	0.13	–2	–0.2
Services	0.31	6	1.7

[a]In this study industry includes construction and transportation, unlike GUS statistics.
Source: GUS data and author's calculations.

Most of the discussion of the output decline in Poland has focused on industry, and especially on state industry (except, e.g., Rostowski, 1993). This is partly because this is a major source of decline, as shown in the tables, but also because data are available on this sector.

- The drop in output in industry was steep. In the state sector – for which reliable monthly data are available – the decrease in sales was nearly instantaneous. Sales from industry were down by 20% in January and by 27% for the first quarter. The decrease was across the board: 93% of all three-digit branches had declines over the first quarter (see Berg and Blanchard, 1994). Within industries, the decrease was largest in consumer goods, and smallest in heavy manufacturing and mining. That there was also a large reallocation of demand is not in doubt. The standard deviation of sales changes across three-digit branches in industry in the first quarter of 1990 was 14%, a large number by Western standards. And the standard deviation of relative price changes was 23%. But the evidence from state industry suggests that the output drop was mostly due to a shift in aggregate demand.

5.1.1 Demand shock and finished goods inventories

Evidence from surveys of enterprise managers suggests that a decline in demand was the proximate cause of the output decline in early 1990.[4] Moreover, the fall in the markup in the first quarter is inconsistent with the view that supply bottlenecks were the dominant effect.[5] A cleaner test for a demand shock is provided by the behavior of finished goods inventories. If production bottlenecks were behind the decrease in output, one would have expected firms constrained in production to satisfy sales as much as possible out of inventories, thus inventory to be decumulated. But if demand contraction was the proximate cause of the output decline, one would have expected firms both to cut production and to accumulate inventories at the beginning. Thus when we look at both the aggregate and the cross-sectional evidence on inventories, two main conclusions emerge:

- While the evidence is ambiguous on the movement of inventories in trade at the beginning of the year, there clearly was a large increase in finished goods inventories in industry at the beginning of 1990, followed by decumulation later in the year (*Table 5.3*). Turning to the cross-sectional evidence, 90% of three-digit branches in industry had an increase in finished goods inventories in the first quarter. Those data are fraught with measurement problems, the main one being the issue of proper deflation of existing stocks. But partial data on physical inventories of durables (such as TVs, refrigerator, and washing machines) are in line with this observation (see Berg, 1994).
- A cross-section regression of changes in inventories on initial inventories and changes in sales shows a clear relation between sales declines and inventory accumulation. This suggests that decline in demand, and not difficulties with production, was the proximate cause of the fall in sales. The sector where the relation appears not to hold is the food-processing sector, where indeed anecdotal evidence suggests that there were serious distribution problems in early 1990.

Table 5.3. Finished goods inventories in 1989 and 1990 in Poland.

	$I/S_{1989-12}$[a]				$I_{1990-12}$[b]
	Dec. 1989	Jan. 1990	Mar. 1990	Dec. 1990	Dec. 1990
Industry					
$n = 1$	0.16	0.28	0.26	0.22	18.6
$n = 2$	0.17	0.36	0.24	0.22	18.9
Trade					
$n = 1$	1.15	0.72	0.79	0.78	31.8
$n = 2$	1.34	0.97	0.79	0.79	34.6
Total					
$n = 1$	0.60	0.53	0.54	0.50	50.4
$n = 2$	0.70	0.71	0.54	0.51	53.5

[a]The first four columns give inventories in a given month normalized by sales in 1989–12; n refers to the method of deflation of inventories; n indicates deflation by the average producer price index over the last n months, including the current month.
[b]The last column gives inventories in trillion zlotys in December 1990.

The question for the cross-section investigation is whether branches in industry that had larger declines in sales had, *ceteris paribus*, larger accumulation of finished goods inventories. We attempt to answer this question using data on sales and inventories of state firms for branches at the three-digit level for the last quarter of 1989 and the first quarter of 1990. The regression is specified as

$$\frac{I_{it} - I_{it-1}}{S_{it-1}} = a\frac{I_{it-1}}{S_{it-1}} + b\frac{S_{it} - S_{it-1}}{S_{it-1}} + \varepsilon_t \ . \tag{5.1}$$

In equation (5.1) I_{it} stands for inventories in branch i at the end of 1990–I and S_{it} for sales during 1990–I, both deflated by the price of the output of branch i at the end of 1990–I. The variables I_{it-1} and S_{it-1} stand for the same variables in 1989–IV. The specification allows for two effects. The first is the desire by firms to decrease inventories from their previous level due to the elimination of the pervasive excess inventories held in the pre-liberalization shortage economy of 1989 (see, for example, Kornai, 1992); we expect a to be negative. The second reflects the effects of sales on inventory accumulation. If firms were primarily affected by an adverse shift in demand, we expect a larger decrease in sales to lead to larger accumulation, thus b to be negative.[6] If firms were primarily affected by supply constraints, we expect tighter constraints to result in low sales and more decumulation, thus b to be positive. The results of estimation are given in *Table 5.4*.

Table 5.4. Results of regression estimations of sales, inventories, and credit in Poland.

	Constant	$\frac{I_{it-1}}{S_{it-1}}$	$\frac{S_{it}-S_{it-1}}{S_{it-1}}$	$\frac{C_{it}-C_{it-1}}{S_{it-1}}$	R^2
Dependent variable: $(I_{it}-I_{it-1})/S_{it-1}$					
OLS	0.07 (5.0)	−0.36 (−3.8)	−0.07 (−1.6)		0.14
OLS*	0.05 (3.8)	−0.03 (−0.2)	−0.10 (−2.4)		0.05
OLS	0.05 (4.9)	−0.09 (−1.0)	−0.08 (−2.1)	0.31 (5.9)	0.39
IV	0.06 (5.0)	−0.14 (−1.4)	−0.07 (−2.1)	0.26 (4.1)	0.38
Dependent variable: $(S_{it}-S_{it-1})/S_{it-1}$					
IV	−0.25 (−15.4)			0.21 (1.4)	0.00

The t-statistics are given in parentheses. Sample for all regressions except regression *: branches in industry, excluding coal, fuel, and electric power, with rates of change in sales between −60% and +50% from 1989–IV to 1990–I, and sales in excess of Zl 100 billion. There are 85 observations. Regression * further excludes food processing, and has 70 observations. The indices t and $t-1$ refer to the quarters 1990–I and 1989–IV, respectively. S_{it} is sales for branch i in quarter t, deflated by the average price of output of branch i during the quarter. I_{it} and C_{it} are inventories of finished goods and the stock of "working credit" (bank credit not associated with a particular investment project) for branch i at the end of quarter t, deflated by the price of output of branch i at the end of the fourth quarter of 1989. The IV regressions instrument the credit variable by the ratio of credit to sales at the end of 1989–IV.

The first regression in *Table 5.4* establishes the basic cross-sectional fact about inventory and sales, and offers support for the hypothesis that industries were primarily affected by an adverse shock in demand. It shows that larger sales declines were associated with inventory accumulation. The result holds across subsamples, except for the food-processing industries, where supply disruptions appear to have played a role, as both sales and inventories decreased. The second regression excludes food processing and shows a much more significant relation. Thus, from the data it may be interpreted that while firms wanted to decrease inventories (a is negative), the decline in sales was such as to lead, on net, to an increase. For the branches in the sample, the increase in real inventories from 1989–IV was equal on average to 12% of monthly sales, and more than 90% had an increase in inventories.

There is little evidence of supply shocks. The pattern between branches of industry defies explanation in terms of sectoral supply shocks. For example, if the initial price shock was cost-push, one would expect that the size of the price increase would help explain the output decline. But a measure of the initial price shock can be constructed using official price increases in January 1990 and an input–output matrix to calculate downstream cost effects. The resulting vector of shocks to each industry is not correlated to the output decline across industries, though it does explain a large part of the price increase in January of 1990. This is consistent with the results given by Borensztein and Ostry in Chapter 4 of this book. They show that the supply shocks mostly raised prices, while the demand shocks caused the output decline. This is another way of saying that output moved together across industries at the two-digit level.

5.1.2 Inventory investment and output decline

The conclusion that demand and not supply shocks caused the initial decline in state industrial output raises the question of the source of these demand shocks. There are many candidates, particularly given the inflation stabilization and associated fiscal and monetary contraction. This section focuses on the possibility, suggested in *Table 5.1*, that inventory decumulation was an important part of the decline in aggregate demand, in that demand for inputs (temporarily) declined sharply for a given level of production. There are several reasons to expect a large decline. In Soviet-style economies, firms were eager to accumulate essentially as much inventory as they could. The principal obstacle to increased production was a pervasive shortage of inputs, encouraging hoarding; interest rates were low or negative; and in any case costs could generally be passed on to buyers or consumers through prices.[7] Alternatively, a "credit crunch" of the Calvo and Coricelli (1992) variety could cause an attempted sell-off of inventories.

Sharp declines in inventory investment have been a macroeconomically significant feature of adjustment in Poland. Unfortunately, official data on inventory investment in 1989 and 1990 are highly problematic, as biases from changing rates of inflation probably amount to several points of GDP. It is nonetheless clear that much or all of the measured decline in GDP in 1990 can be accounted for by a decline in inventory investment. Official data suggest, moreover, that one-third of the decline of GDP in 1991 can be accounted for by a further decline in inventory investment.

The measurement of the change in inventory investment between 1989 and 1990 is tricky. There are two major problems in measuring inventory investment. First, there were no clear ground rules in Poland for cost accounting for inventories, so it is unclear how to measure real inventories based on the nominal inventory figures reported by enterprises. The contribution of inventory investment to nominal GDP until 1990 was measured by the statistical office (GUS) as the change in nominal stocks of inventories from the beginning to the end of the year. This greatly overstates real inventory investment in a hyperinflationary environment, as increases in the value of inventories due to inflation appear as positive real investment. GUS has recognized the potentially enormous errors implicit in its pre-1990 methodology but has not published corrected inventory investment data. I have thus made my own estimate of the contribution of inventory investment to GDP in 1989. It is similar to World Bank/IMF estimates and differs by some 10 percentage points of GDP from the published GUS estimates.

The estimates use the overall producer price index for industry as the price index for inventories and assume that firms use first-in first-out (FIFO) accounting. They also assume that inventories are held for five months, and, that at any time, the age of the inventory stock is uniformly distributed between one and five months. Based on these assumptions, they take as the inventory deflator a backward-looking five-month moving average of producer prices, with uniform weights on past months.[8]

The second problem is that there is virtually no information on inventory stocks held by small private firms. This is particularly distressing, since the big drop in measured inventories is in the trade sector, which is exactly the sector in which private firms are developing most rapidly. It was estimated that as early as 1989, the private sector accounted for less than 10% of retail outlets. By the end of 1990 private-sector employment accounted for some 80% of employment in trade. In view of the fact that tens of thousands of small shops in retail trade were privatized together with their inventory stocks, and in view of the fact that official inventory statistics cover the socialized sector, much of the drop in measured inventories might simply represent a transfer of inventory stocks to private firms. But it was not possible to find data to measure this effect. Certainly, new private establishments had inventory holdings not measured by GUS statistics.

The evidence is reported in *Table 5.5* and may be summarized as follows. In the non-trade socialized sector (mainly industry), inventories of materials tended to fall significantly while inventories of finished goods tended to fall slightly. This is consistent with the idea that industrial firms responded to

Table 5.5. Stocks of inventories in 1989 and 1990 in Poland.

	1989	1990
All socialized and private enterprises		
Total inventories		
Change as percent of GDP	–2.1	–6.2
All non-trade socialized enterprises		
Total inventories		
Percent of GDP	20.1	18.4
Months of sales	1.7	1.8
Change as percent of GDP	–4.1	–3.0
of which:		
Goods and finished products		
Percent of GDP	4.1	4.0
Months of sales	0.35	0.39
Change as percent of GDP	0.7	–0.4
Materials		
Percent of GDP	12.3	10.7
Months of sales	1.03	1.05
Change as percent of GDP	–4.1	–2.3
Socialized trade		
Total inventories		
Percent of GDP	11.2	5.3
Months of sales	2.22	1.32
Change as percent of GDP	1.6	–6.3
Trade inventories in private sector		
Change as percent of GDP	0.3	3.1

Sources: GUS data and author's calculations.

a cutback in final demand by using up their accumulated stocks of materials. There is direct evidence, marshaled by Schaffer (1992), that sales of industrial firms fell in advance of production, consistent with the idea that inventories of finished goods would tend to rise after the onset of the stabilization and liberalization program, and then be reduced afterward, following a cutback in production. The overall net change in non-trade inventories, taking into account both materials and finished goods, seems to be a fall of about 3% of GDP in 1990, following a fall of inventories of about 4% of GDP in 1989.

The situation in retail trade is more dramatic but more difficult to interpret. The estimate presented suggests that the unmeasured rise in inventories in the private sector amounted to some 3% of GDP, in other words, less than half of the measured decline in trade-sector inventories. Based on these guesstimates, I end up with an estimated overall drop in inventories between end-1989 and end-1990 of 6.2% of GDP.

Of course, the causal relationship between inventory investment and GDP is not obvious. Inventory declines could be a result of declines in GDP. But inventory investment seems to have declined by an unusual amount compared with other components of GDP. More importantly, there are good *a priori* reasons, mentioned above, to expect that the inventory decline was a causative factor.

5.1.3 The CMEA shock

All the countries of Central and Eastern Europe suffered large shocks associated with the end of the CMEA trading regime in 1991 (see also Chapter 6 by Dariusz Rosati and Chapter 7 by János Gács). This was an important cause of output decline. For current purposes, however, two points are worth making. First, the measured output decline in 1990 in Poland was not caused by changes in the CMEA trading regime. Similarly, the CMEA factor is unlikely to be the sole source of decline in other countries, where the timing does not easily permit this conclusion. Second, the channels through which the shock affected output in 1991 were both through demand, in the direct and indirect effects of the decrease in the value of exports to the CMEA, which was between 2% and 3% of GDP, and to a lesser extent through disruptions from the loss of or price increases for imports.

Support for these assertions comes from examining cross-section regression evidence on changes in sales, CMEA exports, and CMEA imports.[9] An industry's CMEA imports or exports, either the level in 1989 or the change between 1989 and 1990, do not seem to significantly influence its change in real sales in 1990. For 1991, the regressions yield three main findings. First, there are strong direct and indirect effects of the changes in CMEA exports on branch sales. Second, there is a negative but weak effect of CMEA imports, suggesting effects through the supply side, i.e., through the loss of crucial imports. And finally, in all cases the constant term in the regression, which captures the decline in output not explained by the export and import variables, is equal to 50% to 75% of the decline. There is no way to tell from these regressions whether the effect comes from multiplier effects from the loss of exports or from the effects of tighter monetary policy, for example.

5.1.4 The credit crunch

The remaining potential candidate for a supply-side cause of output decline is the "credit crunch" hypothesis, proposed for transition economies by Calvo and Coricelli (1992, 1993a, and 1993b). In a series of articles, they have argued that a credit crunch was responsible for a large part of the output decline in Eastern Europe, and that credit probably was too tight at the beginning of many of these programs. The potential policy relevance of their arguments justifies analysis of their claims. In this section, I review the Calvo and Coricelli propositions, place them in a slightly larger context, and confront the relevant evidence.

The argument, as presented in Calvo and Coricelli (1992), starts with the observation that there was a sharp contraction in the amount of real credit in January 1990. Real credit was well below IMF ceilings for the first quarter; although because of extremely high real interest rates, credit was not generally rationed. If the amount of real liquidity held by firms at the end of 1989 was that required for existing levels of production, then the production fall could have been caused by the decline in real credit.

The primitive nature of credit markets in Poland meant that firms had little scope for adapting to the decline in credit. Inventory reduction was limited by the lack of international tradability of much of the stock. Recourse to inter-enterprise borrowing was limited by the removal of National Bank of Poland guarantees on these loans and the general increase in their perceived riskiness. A reduction in wages, effectively borrowing from workers, was available, and indeed wage payments were well below those allowed by government wage controls in the first quarter of 1990.

When credit was tightened, the means of adjustment were generally inadequate, and for at least many firms liquidity was insufficient to allow the purchase of the inputs required to meet demand. Output fell as a result.

This "strong form" of the hypothesis is modeled in their paper. It implies a supply-constrained output decline traceable to a lack of liquidity in enterprises and resulting inability to buy inputs. Calvo and Coricelli also discuss a "weak form" of the hypothesis that reduced credit affects output (though they themselves do not make this distinction), pointing out that the methods mentioned above by which enterprises attempt to adapt to the fall in credit reduce demand for other enterprises' output. Inventory sell-offs, lower investment demand by firms, and lower wages of workers all tend to reduce overall aggregate demand.

The strong form would seem to imply that tight credit did not restrain the price level, since supply was constrained more than demand. Thus the initial credit contraction was stagflationary and presumably a mistake. The weak form, however, simply suggests the channels through which monetary policy lowered aggregate demand, as was the purpose of the policy. Whether aggregate demand was too restrictive is a question about the formation of expectations and the credibility of the program, here as with any stabilization program, and Calvo and Coricelli do not make clear how their somewhat different channel for the action of monetary policy modifies the traditional stabilization arguments (on the credit channel for monetary policy see Gertler and Gilchrist, 1992; Gertler, 1988).

Turning to the evidence, there is little support for the strong-form hypothesis – that is, that the December level of real credit was about right and that the reduction in credit reduced output by reducing firms' access to inputs. More plausible is the weak form, which holds that contractionary monetary policy acts directly through the amount of nominal credit, so that less nominal credit implies lower nominal aggregate demand. This interpretation constitutes no argument for looser credit in 1990.

Calvo and Coricelli (1993a) present aggregate data on real credit and real sales in the first quarter of the stabilization episodes in five East European countries, including Poland. They point out a correlation between the declines in real credit and the declines in output. They also note that liquidity from inventory sales appears to be able to cover only about half of the decline in credit and that inter-enterprise credit declined during the same period, at least in Poland.

This sort of evidence is inconclusive. For example, it does not distinguish between demand and supply of credit. As real interest rates went from being extremely negative to positive in early 1990, demand for credit (and inventories) could be expected to fall drastically, in an efficient response to the fact that credit now has an opportunity cost. Nor does it distinguish between any of the specific claims regarding the transmission mechanism for credit to affect output.

A potentially more fruitful approach, following Berg and Blanchard (1994), is to look at cross-industry regressions. Within the framework used to analyze inventory and sales behavior discussed above, one can examine the effects of other variables on both sales and inventory behavior. I thus construct a variable equal to the change in real working credit from 1989–IV to 1990–I, divided by sales in 1989–IV. From 1989–IV to 1990–I 80% of branches in the sample in industry had a decrease in real working credit so defined, and the average decrease as a proportion of initial sales was 3%.

The last three regressions in *Table 5.4* take up the role of credit factors. The last regression in *Table 5.4* relates the change in real sales to the change in real working credit, both as a share of initial sales. The change in working credit may be partly endogenous however; inventories may in part be used as collateral. Thus, I instrument the change in credit by the initial credit to sales ratio in 1989–IV. There is a positive, marginally significant relation between credit and sales. The effect is quantitatively small. The estimated coefficient implies that the 10% decline in working credit as a proportion of sales – the average for the sample of branches is 3% – leads to a 2% contribution to decrease in sales.

The third and fourth regressions in the table focus on the effects of working credit on inventories given sales. They regress changes in inventories on changes in sales and changes in working credit, each as a share of initial sales, with and without instrumenting the change in credit by the initial credit to sales ratio in 1989–IV. The evidence is that inventory changes are still negatively correlated with sales, but also positively correlated with the change in working credit. Thus, while there is little evidence that tight credit contributed much to the decrease in sales, there is stronger evidence that tight credit contributed to inventory decumulation, thus leading to a larger decline in production given that the decline in aggregate demand is much stronger. The adjustment to lower inventory levels and positive real interest rates should be seen as a necessary and ultimately positive feature of the adjustment to a market economy, despite the initial effect on output.

In sum, the evidence from these regressions is that credit has a weak direct effect on industrial sales but a stronger one on inventory holding of firms. Other sorts of evidence distinguish more clearly between the various hypotheses we have discussed. A variety of indications are that if credit matters, it is largely through demand, not supply. The survey responses from managers overwhelmingly suggest that the impulse for the output decline in January 1990 was a lack of demand, not a credit-constrained inability to purchase inputs. And industrial firms accumulated inventories of final goods in early 1990. While the evidence on inventories in trade is more mixed, even here the clearest data suggest an initial accumulation.

A way to avoid the problems of interpretation of aggregate inventory data is to formulate the Calvo and Coricelli strong-form hypothesis in terms of cross-industry inventory regressions. The results, presented in *Table 5.4*, demonstrate that in the industries where real sales declined the most, final goods inventories accumulated the most (or fell the least). This is a relatively powerful test versus the strong-form hypothesis, which would predict the opposite relation from that found in the data.

5.2 Supply and Demand Versus Structural Adjustment

This section addresses the question of whether supply and demand shocks together are a useful way of analyzing events in reforming Soviet-style economies. An alternative perspective emphasizes the structural adjustment characteristics of events since radical reforms. The starting point for this understanding of the events since the introduction of radical reforms in Poland, the CSFR, and Hungary is the pre-(radical) reform situation in the late 1980s. As described by many authors, the economies of Central and Eastern Europe were characterized by a profound misallocation of resources compared with Western economies (Kornai, 1992).

This initial misallocation had many dimensions. Among the most important were:

- The industrial sector was too large compared with the service sector. For instance, the share of services in total 1989 employment was 36% in Poland and 53% in a sample of eight poor OECD countries.
- There were too few small enterprises. Firms with fewer than 100 employees represented 1.4% of total 1989 industrial employment in Poland compared with 14% in West Germany and 32% in Italy.
- The particular goods produced at a very disaggregated level need not have been those called for by a market equilibrium. Little or no mechanism existed for producing the varieties and qualities of goods that would be most valued. For some countries the consumer goods market as a whole may have at times been in equilibrium, but generally speaking almost anything that was produced could be sold.
- Inventories, especially of inputs, were excessive compared with a market economy, as discussed above.
- A large fraction of foreign trade was conducted within the CMEA and involved a substantial part of the industrial sector providing substandard manufactured goods to the Soviet Union in exchange for raw materials.

A simple analytic two-sector model can illuminate the mechanisms that caused these misallocations (outlined in the Appendix). The "soft budget constraint" can be summarized as a situation in which the government sets prices as a fixed markup over costs.[10] Enterprise managers are given direct incentives to increase production. Each sector therefore has infinite demand for inputs at any price, since any increase in costs can be passed along in higher prices. In the resulting equilibrium, output is determined by the central authority's allocation of inputs in the two sectors. The center can thus control the quantities of real output in each of the two sectors by allocating inputs, confident that the inputs will be demanded if they are provided. There will be excess demand for one of the final goods. But with (by assumption) no possibility of savings, excess income beyond that spent on the "shortage good" will be spent on the surplus good. Thus, due to forced substitution all goods are consumed.

Most of the above-mentioned misallocations in Soviet-type economies have analogues in different definitions of the two "sectors" in the model. These may be thought of as industry and services since authorities channeled relatively large quantities of inputs into industry (and into large socialized sector firms), at the expense of services (and small firms). The two sectors may also be thought of at a more disaggregated level as different-sized firms or even different goods. There was no effective system to limit production of goods whose production resulted in relatively little (or even negative) value added per unit of input at shadow prices.[11] The proclivity to accumulate excess inventories can also be understood in terms of the simple model; it was a reflection of the "input hunger" and the fact that the costs of accumulating and holding inventories can be passed on through higher prices. Finally, the goods exported to CMEA countries, unlike those exported to the West, were not subject to any sort of market competition. As a result, they shared with domestic production the characteristic that there was little reason to assume that they would be demanded in a market.

Although there had been varying degrees of reform in Poland, Hungary, and Czechoslovakia, in 1989 the system still functioned essentially as described above. The key reform step, taken by all three countries in 1990–1991, was the elimination of the soft budget constraint. This involved price decontrol; the end of enterprise-specific taxes, tax relief, and subsidies; and some control over allocation of credit to the enterprises, including both a sharp rise in real interest rates and controls on the aggregate quantity of credit. In Poland, in addition, fiscal and monetary contractions were part of a macroeconomic stabilization program to stop hyperinflation. Finally, all three countries significantly liberalized foreign trade.

These dramatic programs obviously had a variety of large economic effects. Nonetheless, the complexity of the situation should not obscure the fact that much of what has happened can be understood in terms of the simple two-sector adjustment model, described above. When prices are liberalized, movement is toward a new equilibrium characterized by a decrease in effective demand for those goods produced in the "surplus sector" and an increase in effective demand for those goods in the previous shortage sector. The result is a movement of factors from the surplus to the shortage sector.

This is exactly what has happened: a dominant economic process since radical reform has been a reallocation of factors in more productive directions, as the large-scale state industry favored in the previous era gave way to small-scale private enterprise, at least initially concentrated in services. A series of factors can cause transitional output declines. For example, new jobs are not found without searching and it takes time to create new enterprises.

The most startling fact of economic transformation in Poland has been the speed of "privatization" of the economy through the decline of the public sector and expansion of new private businesses. As highlighted in *Table 5.6*, employment in public firms declined from 9.3 million (end-1989) to 6.4 million (mid-1993), but rose in the private sector, where recorded employment outside agriculture increased from 4.2 million (end-1989) to 5.3 million (mid-1993).

The second broad transformation in Poland, evidently related to the growth of the private sector, is the flow of resources out of industry, as shown in *Table 5.7*. Not surprisingly, labor and capital have flowed from industry into services and construction. This reallocation has slowed since the end of 1991, however, as private-sector growth has been relatively strong in industry. Also not surprisingly, given the concentration of private-sector activity in trade and services and the excessive industrial structure characteristic of centrally planned economies, most of the jobs have been created in very small businesses.

Most research on restructuring in Poland has focused on restructuring within industry (Borensztein *et al.*, 1993; and Hughes and Hare, 1991). This is partly because industry is the dominant sector of the economy and the source of the largest decline but more decisively because data are available on this sector. The pattern of output response across industries has not followed any clear pattern. Hughes and Hare (1991) have calculated the ratio of value added in domestic prices to value added at world prices (the so-called domestic resource cost or DRC) for different industries for several Central and East European countries. They and others have argued that efficiency-increasing structural adjustment should result in a relative increase in output in those industries which have the lowest DRC, because in these sectors the domestic resource cost of one dollar of export revenues is lowest. In fact, there is no such relation, at least through 1991, using the Hughes and Hare (1991) data (Borensztein *et al.*, 1993). The model in the Appendix can be used, however, to show that there is no necessary relationship between DRC and resource flow after liberalization. Pre-reform profit margins and relative wages, and hence value added, were determined by central authorities, and

Table 5.6. Employment by ownership type from 1989 to mid-1993 in Poland.

	1989	1990	1991	1992	1993–6
Millions of workers (end of year)					
Total	17.6	16.5	15.9	15.6	15.8
Nonagricultural	13.5	12.4	11.8	11.5	11.7
Public	9.3	8.2	7.0	6.6	6.4
Private	8.3	8.3	8.9	9.0	9.4
Agriculture	4.1	4.1	4.1	4.1	4.1
Cooperatives	0.3	0.3	0.2	0.2	n.a.
Other	3.8	3.8	3.9	3.9	n.a.
Nonagriculture	4.2	4.2	4.8	4.9	5.3
Cooperatives	2.2	1.6	1.5	1.1	n.a.
Other	2.1	2.6	3.3	3.8	n.a.
Share in total employment in percent					
Public	52.8	49.9	44.3	42.2	40.3
Private	47.2	50.1	55.7	57.8	59.7
Agriculture	23.3	24.8	25.8	26.3	25.9
Nonagriculture	23.9	25.3	29.9	31.6	33.8
Private noncooperatives	33.1	38.8	44.8	49.2	n.a.
Agriculture	21.4	23.3	24.3	25.0	n.a.
Nonagriculture	11.7	15.5	20.5	24.2	n.a.
Share in nonagricultural economy in percent					
Public	68.8	66.4	59.7	57.2	54.4
Private	31.2	33.6	40.3	42.8	45.6
Cooperatives	16.0	12.9	12.7	9.9	n.a.
Other	15.2	20.7	27.6	32.9	n.a.

Source: GUS.

did not necessarily measure actual factor use. The Appendix gives an example in which resources after liberalization flow into the sector that has a higher DRC as calculated by Hughes and Hare.

Another strand of research starts with the assumption that if changes in the composition of industrial output are related to comparative advantage, then these changes should be similar across similar Central and East European countries, as these countries were presumably similarly distorted before liberalization. Borensztein *et al.* (1993) show, however, that for a variety of Central and East European countries, including Poland, changes in real output in a given industry correlate more with own country macroeconomic factors than with real output changes in the same industry in the other

Table 5.7. Sectoral distribution of value added from 1989 to 1992 in percent.

	1989	1990	1991	1992
Industry	41.9	36.9	32.8	33.7
Construction	9.8	9.5	10.8	11.1
Agriculture	13.5	15.0	16.8	15.0
Transportation	5.4	5.4	4.6	4.4
Services	29.3	33.2	35.0	35.7
Trade	14.8	16.8	19.4	20.0
Other	14.5	16.4	15.6	15.8

Source: GUS.

Central and East European countries. This tendency suggests that there is no overall structural adaptation toward comparative advantage, which might be expected to be similar in the three countries.

This and other similar results suggest that the change in the composition of production within industry is not following a simple pattern. But this should not lead us to believe that the adjustment is not in the direction of comparative advantage. Several pieces of evidence suggest that firms within a given industry are extremely heterogeneous with respect to post-liberalization competitiveness, so that analysis of two-digit industrial data is not revealing.

- The private sector has expanded significantly in industry as well as elsewhere. As adjustment has proceeded, growth in the private sector has become more important in industry and in larger private firms. Fixed investment in large private firms was 48% higher in real terms in the third quarter of 1992 than in the third quarter of 1991, for example. Real investment in large state-sector firms was 3% higher over the same period. Essentially all the strong growth of aggregate industrial production since the end of 1991 has come from the private sector.
- The pattern of growth since mid-1991 is suggestive of the sorts of adjustment away from heavy and toward light industry that most analysts concluded were required.
- Anecdotal evidence suggests that state-owned enterprise in industry are still significant, and there is increasing heterogeneity in the way even state-owned enterprises are responding to the new environment (see, for example, Pinto *et al.*, 1993).

5.3 Conclusion

We now return to the questions with which we began. With regard to the relative weights of supply and demand factors in generating the output declines observed in reforming socialist economies of Central and Eastern Europe, the conclusion from Section 5.1 is that the decline in socialized-sector industrial output in early 1990 and hence in total GDP for the year was due primarily to declines in demand. How important are the factors that fit under the rubric of "supply and demand" in comparison with other potential reasons for the output decline, especially adjustment away from the Soviet-style economic system? Section 5.2 emphasizes structural adjustment, rather than supply and demand factors, in explaining the transition in Poland.

The resolution to this apparent contradiction lies in the dynamics. The initial decline seems to have been due to a combination of aggregate demand shocks associated with the stabilization, declines in inventory investment due to the transition from a shortage economy and perhaps to the credit crunch, and shifts in demand away from socialized-sector industry toward other sectors of the economy. Subsequent developments have been dominated by the CMEA shock in 1991 and the steady and rapid growth of the private sector, both in services and in industry.

The applicability of "one good" macroeconomics is limited in taking into account either the output decline or especially the subsequent growth in Poland. The decline and stagnation of industrial production in state-owned enterprises since January 1990 is not primarily due to declines in aggregate demand or supply but rather due to a decline in demand for particular outputs. This suggests that the usefulness of an aggregate demand expansion in returning output to previous levels would be limited. Lost output will not return to its old producers; rather resources are, over time, finding their way into the production of new output. And indeed, growth has come primarily from expansion in different sectors, such as services and residential construction, and in new enterprises, not from a recovery of demand for previously produced goods.

The most important item on the research agenda is the study of the inter-sectoral, inter-regional, inter-firm adjustment process, including the performance of factor markets. The dynamics deserve further examination. One possibility is that there are non-convexities in the economy that could lead to stagnant low-output equilibria. For example, if the declining sector falls so far that there is insufficient demand for the potentially expanding sector to take off, the economy could be stuck in the unfortunate transition stage. Another conjecture, suggested by a rough comparison of country experience in the region, is that the countries that adjust policies the most radically have the smallest cumulative declines; this clearly requires further analysis.

Notes

[1] This is obviously a simplification. See, for example, Dabrowski *et al.* (1991).

[2] The 4.9% estimated output decline is significantly lower than the official estimate of a 12% decline. The main source of the difference is that data from household surveys of physical units of consumption are used to estimate consumption. Official statistics, based as they were on the direct reporting of retail sales by trading organizations, are likely to be highly biased downward given the rapid privatization of retail and wholesale trade in 1990. See Berg (1993) for an extensive discussion of this and other measurement issues as well as an explanation of the derivation of the estimates in *Table 5.1* and *Table 5.2*. See also note [3].

[3] *Table 5.2* shows estimates of the output decline in 1990 from Berg and Sachs (1992). These estimates differ from official data in that they use employment as a proxy for output in private-sector industry and the Schaffer (1992) index of industrial production for the state sector. It should be noted that this lower estimate of the total output decline of 8.7% and the even lower estimate of 4.9% in *Table 5.1* are consistent with newer estimates from a GUS/Polish Academy of Sciences study of the change in national income between 1989 and 1992. Rajewski (1993) discusses a variety of problems with official statistics and tries to estimate directly the size of the unmeasured "second economy." He concludes, "If the second economy is taken into account the 1989–1992 fall in GDP was of the 5 to 10% magnitude."

[4] First, firms themselves perceived a sharp drop in demand. Surveys of several hundred state enterprises reported in Gorski *et al.* (1990) show that, whereas in November 1988, 87% of firms had perceived their market as being either balanced or in "excess demand," in February 1990, 97% perceived it as either balanced or in "excess supply," with 48% in the category of "state of relative surplus: relative lack of demand in relation to real possibilities of production; inventories being amassed; price discounts, etc." Only 9% indicated any inability to meet demand. Firms in a survey of about 700 industrial enterprises carried out every few weeks from 1989 to 1991 (Business Survey, 1990) stated that of the "factors limiting the growth of output in the enterprise," supply and employment shortages were the limiting factors in 62% of firms in October 1989; 37%, in January 1990; and 10%, by April. There is little qualitative evidence that inter-sectoral shocks or supply disruptions were a dominant factor: again from the same survey, there was no increase in the fraction of firms reporting increases in orders or supply constraints on output in January. Finally, in their study of nine Polish firms, Jorgensen *et al.* (1991) summarize

the managers' perceptions of the initial output drop as coming almost entirely from demand, with dislocations, credit, and other factors as "irritants."

[5] Had supply bottlenecks been prevalent, many firms would have operated along the vertical portion of their supply curve, and thus prices would have risen to clear markets. Given the observed real wage restraint, not only prices but markups of prices over costs should have gone up. Also, an increase in the exercise of monopoly power would of course have increased markups. It turns out that while prices were indeed sharply higher in January, the increase is more than accounted for by the increase in costs, and markups of prices over costs were sharply down. The average markup of prices over accounting costs for state firms was down from 40% in the last quarter of 1989 to 31% in the first quarter of 1990. And the markup was down in 66 out of 85 branches at the three-digit level.

[6] I am assuming here that the change in sales in early 1990 was unexpected by the enterprise managers. Surveys of Polish managers conducted in late 1989 and reported in the Business Survey (1990) indeed suggest that they expected no particular change in sales through the big bang.

[7] See Kornai (1992) for a discussion of inventory behavior under socialism and Winiecki (1991), who emphasizes the role of inventory decumulation after price liberalization and stabilization.

[8] GUS provides nominal end-of-year stocks of inventories as well as sales. The 1989 GDP, used to calculate changes as a share of GDP, comes from GUS estimates, except for inventory investment itself.

Inventory change as a percent of GDP and months of sales are calculated by deflating the end-of-period stocks by a five-month backward-moving average of the producer price index (where average prices in 1989 = 1), then compared with 1989 GDP and current year sales, respectively.

Trade inventories in the private sector result from assuming that the share of the private sector in trade at the end of the year is equal to the end-of-year share of the private sector in employment in trade. The private sector is assumed to hold 50% of the inventories per worker of the state sector.

[9] I look at the behavior of sales across branches in industry, first at the two-digit level because some of the variables can only be constructed at that level, and then at the three-digit level (see Berg and Blanchard, 1994, for a detailed presentation of the regressions discussed in the main text; see also Rodrik, 1994).

[10] It should be noted that this implies that profit rates and measured value added per worker carry no information about, for example, the return to capital. In practice, governments applied a variety of enterprise-specific taxes, tax reliefs, and subsidies to supplement cost-plus pricing in eliminating any effect of cost or demand factors on the enterprise, so that pre- and post-tax profit rates were largely uncorrelated, as described, for example, in Kornai (1992).

[11] See Winiecki (1991) for a discussion of these issue and Osband (1992) for a careful look at related measurement problems. McKinnon (1991) argues that virtually all manufactured output in Eastern Europe embodied negative value

added at world prices. Hughes and Hare (1991) present evidence that while this was not the case overall, it was the case for large parts of the industrial sector. Berg (1993) reviews many of the measurement issues mentioned in this section and concludes that at least for two-digit industries there is little evidence that the output decline is particularly high in "negative value-added" industries.

Appendix: Recession and structural adjustment in liberalizing a Soviet-style economy

Example A

The following example illustrates two points:

1. Price liberalization and the imposition of hard budget constraints in a Soviet-style economy results in the decline of one part of the economy and the expansion of the other. Adjustment costs can result in a transitional net decline.
2. Lack of profit-maximizing behavior in the declining sector does not stop or pervert this adjustment, though it tends to slow it down and may thereby reduce transitional unemployment.

1. Pre-liberalization Equilibrium

In this two-period general equilibrium example, there are two sectors. Sector one produces an "excess-demand" good, while sector two produces a "surplus" good. Both sectors use labor to produce goods at constant returns to scale, so

$$F \equiv [F_1, F_2] = [F_1(L_1), F_2(L_2)] = [L_1, L_2] \ . \tag{5.A1}$$

Firms follow cost-plus pricing, with a zero profit margin. The wage (w) is normalized to 1. Thus official prices are $P_1 = P_2 = 1$. Suppose there are two units of labor, and before liberalization $L_1 = 1$ and $L_2 = 1$, then from equation (5.A1) $Q_1 = 1$ and $Q_2 = 1$.

Turning to the consumers/workers, they have a utility function of the form

$$U(Q_1, Q_2) = 2 \ln Q_1 + \ln Q_2 \ . \tag{5.A2}$$

Each worker maximizes $U(Q_1, Q_2)$ subject to $P_1Q_1 + P_2Q_2 = Y$, where $Y = wL_1 + wL_2 = 2$. (We can solve for the two workers together by symmetry.) Pre-reform shadow prices are then

$$P^* = [4/3, 2/3] \ . \tag{5.A3}$$

This formulation of the pre-reform equilibrium captures the Kornai notion of pervasive shortage without reference to any "liquidity overhang." Here the soft budget constraint is due to the 100% marginal tax rate on profits that results from the fact that the government sets prices so that profits are zero. In practice the government applied a variety of enterprise-specific taxes and subsidies to supplement cost-plus pricing.

We can think of the government complementing this pricing policy with incentives for managers to maximize output. Excess demand for all inputs (Kornai's "input hunger") derives from the fact that managers can use any additional inputs, *at whatever price*, to increase output and can cover costs with price increases. Demand is guaranteed not by excess liquidity but by the implicit assumption that all income is spent each period, so that with forced substitution all output will be bought. It should be noted, however, that not all outputs will be in short supply. In this situation the government does not have to worry about prices, or what goes on inside the production function, as long as real output can be measured. It can control the structure of the economy by allocating (scarce) inputs.

2. Post-liberalization of Prices

Profit-maximizing firms. Consider now what happens after liberalization, taking first the case where there are no frictions associated with labor mobility and where firms act to maximize profits. In the post-price-liberalization equilibrium (indicated by prime $'$) the first-order conditions of utility maximization still imply that

$$P' = \left[\frac{4}{3Q_1}, \frac{2}{3Q_2}\right] . \tag{5.A4}$$

Profit maximization by firms in each sector implies that the price equals the wage in each sector, so that

$$Q' = [4/3, 2/3]$$
$$P' = [1, 1] . \tag{5.A5}$$

A constant second-period utility index shows a real output increase of 6%. Standard output indices, because they use official pre-reform prices, would show no output increase.

To the extent that labor could not move from sector two to sector one without costs, there may be transitional unemployment and output decline. If, for example, the labor that left sector two had to spend one period unemployed, output would fall in sector two but would not increase, initially, in sector one, and standard output indices would exaggerate this output decline. Or, if (relative) wages in sector two are rigid downward, then movement of labor from sector two to sector one would more likely proceed through unemployment, as workers would not be encouraged by wage differentials to find new jobs while still employed.

Nonprofit-maximizing firms. Of course, Polish state enterprises are not likely to have been profit maximizers. This section shows that while this would slow adjustment, it would not prevent it. Given the power of workers in Polish state enterprises in 1990, it may be more realistic to model managers in sector two, the declining sector, as maximizing profit per incumbent worker. It is easy to show that under these conditions, sector two neither hires nor fires workers. If sector one firms are profit-maximizing, they would like to expand by hiring more labor, but at least initially there is no unemployed labor as there are no firings in sector two.

Thus, quantities are unchanged from the pre-reform situation, and therefore post-reform output prices are equal to pre-reform shadow prices. Because its worker-controlled firms refuse to fire (by assumption), sector two's budget constraint forces wages to fall to maintain employment. Assuming a large number of firms and a perfect labor market within sector one, the wage in sector one is pushed up. Thus the post-liberalization equilibrium is characterized by

$$L' = [1, 1]$$

$$Q' = [1, 1]$$

$$P' = [4/3, 2/3]$$

$$W' = [4/3, 2/3] \ . \tag{5.A6}$$

The wage differential is not sustainable if sector one firms are profit-maximizing firms, as labor wants to move into sector one, pushing down the wage, and firms in sector one there will hire them. After this process is completed, and this presumably takes time for a variety of well-known reasons, the competitive equilibrium case, discussed above, is obtained.

The labor-adjustment process is of course not specified in this example, but this case has the property that labor adjustment is voluntary and is prompted by relative wage differentials.

Finally, it should be noted, that if firms in sector one also maximize value added per worker – if they are state enterprises, for example – then labor will not be able to move to sector one.

Example B

In the following example we show that the Hughes and Hare (1991) domestic resource cost (DRC) measure is not necessarily a reliable indicator of efficiency-increasing movements of factors after liberalization, because pre-reform value added does not necessarily indicate actual factor usage.

The pre-reform equilibrium is as in Example A, except that now the central authorities set profit rates other than zero for the two sectors. Specifically, suppose that the profit rate in sector two is still zero while the price in sector one is set so that the profit rate is 20%. (The difference in profit rates has to be large enough so that the pre-reform relative price of the shortage good is actually higher than the post-liberalization price.) Thus, the pre-reform equilibrium is characterized by

$$Q = L = [1, 1]$$

$$P = [1.2, 1]$$

$$VA = [1.2, 1] \ , \tag{5.A7}$$

where VA is measured value added (in domestic prices).

Suppose that world prices are $P^* = [1.1, 1]$. Thus value added at world prices is $VA^* = [1.1, 1]$. Suppose that price liberalization is combined with trade liberalization, so that post-reform prices are determined by world prices, $P^* = [1.1, 1]$. With free trade, post-liberalization production will be $Q' = L' = [2, 0]$. Thus resources flow into sector one.

DRC is calculated as $VA/VA^* = [1.1, 1]$. Thus according to the Hughes and Hare calculations efficiency-increasing structural adjustment would imply resource flow from sector one to sector two, which both does not and should not happen.

The reason the calculation breaks down is that it assumes that pre-reform value added is determined by actual factor usage. If, for example, the production of one unit of good A requires 1.2 units of labor, while the production of one unit of good B requires only one unit of labor, as suggested by VA, then post-liberalization resource flow should indeed be in the direction of sector two.

References

Berg, A., 1993, A critique of official data, in F. Coricelli, M. Blejer, G. Calvo, and A. Gelb, eds., *Eastern Europe in Transition: From Recession to Growth*, IMF/World Bank, Washington, DC, USA.

Berg, A., 1994, Supply and demand factors in the output decline in Eastern and Central Europe, *Empirica*, **21**(1):1–34,

Berg, A., and Blanchard, O., 1994, Stabilization and transition: Poland 1990–1991, in J. Sachs, O. Blanchard, and K. Froot, eds., *Transition in Eastern Europe*, University of Chicago Press, Chicago, IL, USA.

Berg, A., and Sachs, J., 1992, Structural adjustment and international trade in Eastern Europe: The case of Poland, *Economic Policy*, **14**(April):117–173.

Borensztein, E., Demetas, D.G., and Ostry, J.D., 1993, An empirical analysis of the output declines in three Eastern European countries, *IMF Staff Papers*, **40**(1):1–31.

Business Survey, 1990, *Center for Research on Economic Tendency and Markets*, Institute of Economic Development, Warsaw Central School of Planning and Statistics, Warsaw, Poland.

Calvo, G., and Coricelli, F., 1992, Stabilizing a previously centrally planned economy: Poland 1990, *Economic Policy*, **14**(April):176–226.

Calvo, G., and Coricelli, F., 1993a, Output collapse in Eastern Europe: The role of credit, in M. Blejer, G. Calvo, F. Coricelli, and A. Gelb, eds., *Eastern Europe in Transition: From Recession to Growth*, IMF/World Bank, Washington, DC, USA.

Calvo, G., and Coricelli, F., 1993b, Credit Market Imperfections and Output Response in Previously Centrally Planned Economies, May [mimeo].

Dabrowski, J., Federowicz, M., and Levitas, A., 1991, Polish state enterprises and the properties of performance: Stabilization, marketization, privatization, *Politics and Society*, **19**(4):100–101.

Gertler, M., 1988, Financial structure and aggregate economic activity: An overview, *Journal of Money, Credit and Banking*, **2559**(April):1–51.

Gertler, M., and Gilchrist, S., 1992, The Role of Credit Market Imperfections in The Monetary Transmission Mechanism: Arguments and Evidence, New York University, New York, NY, USA [mimeo].

Gomulka, S., 1991, The causes of recession following stabilization, *Comparative Economic Studies*, **32**(Summer):71–89.

Gorski, M. *et al.*, 1990, *Rownowaga na Rynkach Wyrobow Przemyslowych w Polsce* (Equilibrium on the Market for Industrial Goods in Poland), Report, May, East European Research Group, Warsaw, Poland.

Hughes, G., and Hare, P.G., 1991, Competitiveness and industrial restructuring in Czechoslovakia, Hungary and Poland, *European Economy*, Special Edition (2):83–110.

Jorgensen, E., Gelb, A., and Singh, I., 1991, Life after the Polish "Big Bang": Representative episodes of enterprise behavior, in V. Corbo, F. Coricelli, and J. Bossak, eds., *Reforming Central and Eastern European Economies: Initial Results and Challenges*, World Bank, Washington, DC, USA.

Kornai, J., 1992, *The Socialist System: The Political Economy of Communism*, Princeton University Press, Princeton, NJ, USA.

McKinnon, R.I., 1991, *The Order of Economic Liberalization: Financial Control in the Transition to a Market Economy*, Johns Hopkins University Press, Baltimore, MD, USA.

Osband, K., 1992, Index number biases during price liberalization, *IMF Staff Papers*, **39**(June):287–309.

Pinto, B., Belka, M., and Krajewski, S., 1993, Transforming State Enterprises in Poland, Policy Research Working Papers, February, World Bank, Washington, DC, USA.

Rajewski, Z., 1993, National income, in L. Ziekowski, eds., *Results of the Polish Economic Transformation*, GUS/Polish Academy of Sciences, Warsaw, Poland.

Rodrik, D., 1994, Foreign trade in Eastern Europe's transition: Early results, in O. Blanchard, K. Froot, and J. Sachs, eds., *Transition in Eastern Europe*, University of Chicago Press, Chicago, IL, USA.

Rostowski, J., 1993, The Implications of Very Rapid Private Sector Growth in Poland, University of London, London, UK [manuscript].

Schaffer, M., 1992, The Polish state-owned enterprise sector and the recession of 1990., *Comparative Economic Studies*, **34**(Spring):58–85.

Winiecki, J., 1991, The inevitability of a fall in output in the early stages of transition to the market: Theoretical underpinnings, *Soviet Studies*, **43**(4):669–676.

Comments on the Paper by Andrew Berg

Marek Dabrowski

Andrew Berg presents a comprehensive and solid study of existing hypotheses concerning the output decline in Poland. I am not a professional statistician, and it would be difficult for me to discuss technical details of the statistical methods adopted by Berg and the authors he discusses. I therefore concentrate on some general remarks and observations related to the topic covered by Berg.

First, I agree with Berg and the other authors that the scale of GDP decline in Poland was seriously overestimated by the official statistics. This fact should be considered more extensively by professionals, politicians, and the public; increased discussions should lead to a radical verification of the existing assessment of the positive and negative results of hitherto Polish transformation. I do not have sufficient knowledge to say if similar overestimations of the decline occurred in other former communist countries. However, some factors which led to the underestimation of GDP in Poland (for example, difficulties with recording the activity of the private sector) could also have taken place in other economies in transition.

Unfortunately, the Central Statistical Office in Poland still does not want to confirm this mistake and refuses to revise the 1988–1991 figures. In the meantime, many theoretical models, as well as many political assessments and recommendations were built on the basis of these mistaken statistical data.

Second, in his discussion of different factors influencing output decline, Berg misses one – the motivation crisis in state-owned enterprise. The management of state-owned enterprises in the typical centrally planned economy was administratively and politically stimulated to increase output, at any price.

In Poland in the 1980s this traditional system was significantly weakened but it still worked, at least to some extent. The collapse of what remained of the central control in 1989 created a kind of motivation vacuum. The profit motivation which is regarded as the standard incentive in a private market economy did not work at the beginning of the transition process, especially in state-owned enterprises.

Also the privatization process has complicated the incentive structure in state-owned firms and has seriously influenced their behavior. At least two factors have played an important role. First, one can observe the outflow of the best managers and employees (especially highly qualified accountants, lawyers, and engineers) to the private sector which limits the ability of state-owned enterprises to make necessary microeconomic adjustments to product, and cost structure, marketing, financial management, and so on. Second, the privatization process itself creates a very complicated game of interests, sometimes called "the end game" (Olivier Blanchard) or "privatization agony" (Pavel Mertlik). For example, management and employees can be interested in decreasing the market value of enterprise before privatization to make the insider buyout easier. It may lead to decreasing profit and output.

The motivation crisis, similarly to other typical microeconomic factors, is not explicitly discussed by Berg. However, this problem is hidden in that part of the chapter where he discusses the scale of output decline in 1990 and 1991 as the result of decrease in aggregate demand. The negative output reaction would probably have been smaller if more private firms had experience in the competitive market economy. The same hypothesis concerns the time lag between increasing demand for some goods and output response in the two-sector model analyzed by Berg.

Third, Berg's analysis of cross-industry statistics leads him to conclude that enterprises were influenced mainly by the fall of aggregate demand coming from stabilization itself as well as from decumulation of inventories caused by the elimination of a shortage economy. The shift in relative demand as the result of changes in relative prices does not play an important role in Berg's analysis. Such a conclusion seems to conflict with observations of day-to-day changes in the Polish economy in 1990 and 1991.

I suppose that the reason for this misunderstanding lies mainly in the inaccuracy of available research tools. It relates, in first instance, to the level of disaggregation adopted in Berg's analysis. On the one hand, the cross-sectoral analysis of industries even at the three-digit level is not detailed enough to illustrate the real shift in relative demand which often occurred only at the cross-product level (or are associated with the specific standard and quality of individual products). Berg seems to address this question when he discusses the export reorientation.

On the other hand, Berg's analysis is limited only to industry. One can observe a big change of GDP composition between industry (the share of which declined) and the trade/service sector (the share of which increased) which is strictly connected with changes in a relative demand structure.

Part of the problems may come from the implicit assumption that the output decline occurred in Poland only two times: in January 1990, after adopting the basic stabilization and liberalization package, and at the end of the first quarter of 1991, after a definite collapse of CMEA trade system. (This second shock contained three components: collapse of the CMEA market; the consequences of the trade embargo in relation to Iraq and Kuwait imposed by UN Security Council; and the demand contraction coming from the second stabilization package implemented in late 1990, after the relaxation of macroeconomic policy in mid-1990 which caused higher inflation.) If we analyze the phenomenon of the output decline at the aggregate level such an assumption can be justified. In reality, after January 1990 and April 1991 output in many firms continued to decline; however, this decline was offset by the output increase in other firms, mainly in the new private sector.

I agree that in January 1990 the first reaction of most enterprises was the same, namely, they decreased current sales meeting the demand barrier. However, evidence shows that in the next months the scale of output decline started to differ between individual enterprises and products.

Fourth, this observation is connected with the influence of import liberalization. Of course, import liberalization could not influence the initial output decline in January 1990 because at that time the level of protection was high due to relatively high tariffs (15%–20%) and due to a seriously undervalued exchange rate. Real import liberalization came later – in late 1990 – together with continuing real appreciation of the exchange rate as well as with temporary suspending and decreasing of some tariffs. Evidence indicates that some output was eliminated by competitive import, for example, in the computer industry or in light industry. At the same time trade liberalization stimulated strongly the GDP increase in the trade and service sectors. It seems that the relatively fast (in comparison with other former communist countries) output recovery in Poland has its roots both in spontaneous development of the new private sector and in the liberalization of foreign trade.

Finally, Berg's paper still does not answer the question, why have all the former communist countries experienced an output decline, despite very different transformation strategies that have been adopted by them? Moreover, the cumulative output decline has been even less severe in countries with more restrictive macroeconomic policies and more extensive liberalization strategies. This phenomenon seems to undermine the role of both the aggregate demand shock and the shift in relative demand as the key factors in determining the length and the scale of transformation recession.

Chapter 6

The Impact of the Soviet Trade Shock on Central and East European Economies

Dariusz K. Rosati

The unraveling of the Council for Mutual Economic Assistance (CMEA) in 1991 has commonly been considered one of the key factors behind the collapse of East European trade and the steep contraction of output in former CMEA member countries. Yet there have only been a few attempts to estimate the consequences of the CMEA dissolution for trade and output levels of member countries in a more systematic way.[1] While the negative impact of the CMEA dissolution on member countries' economies is obviously undisputed, the observed falls in output and trade levels have also been caused by other important factors, such as contraction of domestic demand caused by stabilization programs, reforms, and political upheavals in Central and East European countries (CEECs) in 1990 and 1991, and the disintegration of some federal states (most notably the USSR). The aim of this paper is to shed some light on this issue by analyzing the significance of the so-called Soviet trade shock on East European economies. Specifically, an attempt is made to disentangle CMEA-specific and other causes of the observed trade collapse, and to estimate their impact on trade and output levels in the CEECs. The analysis is limited to trade of CEECs with the

The author wishes to acknowledge helpful comments received on earlier drafts from Daniel Gros, Gábor Oblath, and Mica Panic. The views and opinions expressed in the paper are solely those of the author.

R. Holzmann et al. (eds.), Output Decline in Eastern Europe, 131-159.

former Soviet Union, chiefly because it has always been much more important than trade among CEECs themselves, but also because of difficulties in obtaining reliable trade statistics on former CMEA countries.

Empirical analyses of trade developments in Eastern Europe have been plagued for years by serious statistical and data problems (see, e.g., UN ECE, 1992). The difficulties were exacerbated in 1990–1991 when CEECs initiated the shift to a market system, thus changing the rules of trade flows valuation, classification, and reporting. The lack of important data on price and volume changes during the transition period, inconsistencies among data reported by different countries, and dubious and sometimes obscure techniques of obtaining aggregate trade figures have all imposed a number of limitations on the analysis. That being the case, the impact of the trade shock cannot be discussed to a similar degree of detail for every country, because the necessary data are not available for all the countries concerned. Moreover, in some cases it was virtually impossible to give quantitative results with any reasonable precision and, consequently, ranges of values had to be given instead of single numbers. Because the available data were most comprehensive for Hungary and Poland, these two countries receive relatively more attention in this discussion.

In Section 6.1 the implications for trade after the demise of the traditional CMEA system in 1991 are briefly recalled. Other, non CMEA-specific reasons for the trade collapse are also pointed out. In Section 6.2 the terms-of-trade effect is calculated for Hungary and Poland, based on a theoretical framework designed to measure the impact of CMEA price changes. In Section 6.3, the effect of the fall in CEECs' exports to the USSR is computed, with CMEA-specific and non-CMEA factors separated with a simple model of import change. Then, the impact on CEECs' GDP levels is estimated for alternative values of exchange rates. Conclusions are summarized in the last section.

6.1 Demise of the CMEA and the Collapse of the Soviet Market

6.1.1 The CMEA trading system and its reform in 1991

The system of trade among the CMEA countries, established in the late 1940s, remained, with few changes, in operation until 1990. It was based on barter-type bilateralism in mutual trade, with central government authorities determining detailed export and import flows in intergovernmental agreements and protocols. The role of market instruments (prices, exchange rates, tariffs) in the CMEA trade was marginal, and individual enterprises had practically no formal rights to undertake foreign trade transactions on their own.

When market reforms were initiated in the CEECs in 1989, the traditional CMEA system came under wholesale critique. Most countries agreed to abandon the system and to shift to market-based trade. It was widely expected that the change of the trade system in 1991 would immediately result in a sharp increase in the relative prices of commodities such as energy, fuels, and raw materials, and a sharp decline of trade in industrial goods within the CMEA. The Soviet Union, being the only large net exporter of commodities in the region, was expected to be the main (perhaps the only) beneficiary, with other countries incurring large trade deficits vis-à-vis the Soviet Union (for some early estimates of these costs for Poland and Hungary, see, respectively, Rosati *et al.*, 1990, and Oblath and Tarr, 1991). Of course, the economic rationale for the reform was that in the long run all countries involved were to gain from better allocation of resources and mutually beneficial trade based on principles of comparative advantage. In the short run, however, substantial transition costs were expected, raising serious concern about the ability of East European economies to adjust to the new external environment (see, e.g., van Brabant, 1993).

The trade reform introduced in January 1991 consisted essentially of three key elements:

1. Replacement of the artificial CMEA prices by world market prices.
2. Unraveling of the transferable ruble and adoption of convertible currencies as the only means of payments in all foreign trade transactions.
3. Abandonment of the detailed trade protocols concluded between governments, to be replaced with fairly general trade agreements of "indicative" character, with decision-making rights on concluding specific trade transactions transferred to individual, autonomous enterprises.

In fact, the changes were so fundamental that the CMEA as a system of state trading in practice ceased to exist in January 1991, although it was formally dissolved only several months later.

Each of the three elements of the reform exerted a strong influence on subsequent CMEA trade flows, though they worked through different mechanisms. The most important was perhaps the shift to world market prices, which resulted in a dramatic change in the countries' terms of trade. This was essentially a *Soviet-trade-specific* phenomenon, affecting mostly trade of the USSR with smaller CMEA countries, but with only marginal impact on trade among other East European countries. The shift to world market prices was expected to improve the terms of trade of net commodity exporters such as the USSR.

The abolition of the transferable ruble, together with the clearing system associated with it, is commonly believed to have sharply increased the demand for convertible currencies in the region (van Brabant, 1993). But the additional demand for transaction purposes (equivalent to one to two months of a country's total imports for the year) could in principle be met from foreign exchange reserves, with additional supply of foreign exchange proceeds from exports allowing for replenishment of the reserves fairly rapidly (perhaps except for countries with large initial trade deficits, such as Bulgaria). Also, the additional demand for precautionary purposes (to build up foreign reserves equivalent to three to four months' value of imports) was rather limited because of the sharp fall in overall import demand in the CEECs and the declining share of Eastern trade in their overall trade (again, Bulgaria stands out as an exception). What was then considered a "foreign exchange shortage" was rather a symptom of inability (or reluctance) to devalue the domestic currency sufficiently and to improve the allocation mechanism (this was the case with Romania). Poland, the CSFR, and Hungary, where a large measure of convertibility was established and the exchange rates were competitive, did not experience problems of immediate payments (although longer-term external balance position in some countries was indeed precarious because of substantial foreign debt service obligations).[2]

Liberalization and decentralization of foreign trade transactions have also led to some trade diversion from the East to the West. The elimination of the "soft" means of payments (namely, transferable ruble clearing) called for an immediate "rationalization" and restructuring of trade: nonessential trade flows have been cut back, with domestic producers and consumers shifting to Western markets in search of cheaper and more reliable sources of supplies. Although no systematic evidence is yet available, it seems that enterprises in the CMEA countries generally became less inclined to trade within the CMEA market than had been respective governments, which had done so largely for noneconomic reasons. Thus the shift in the supply and demand schedules of East European firms may have been a major factor behind the trade diversion effect, further diminishing the intra-CMEA trade levels. The trade diversion has generally been much stronger on the import side, leading to a further fall in demand for CMEA products, than on the export side, because the remarkable export growth in Poland and to a smaller extent in Hungary in 1990 was mostly the result of shifting sales away from the domestic market, and less so from CMEA markets.

6.1.2 The collapse of the Soviet market in 1991

When the CMEA reform was planned in 1990, trade analysts predicted that the shock would come mostly through the impact on the balance of payments of the increased hard-currency expenditure of the CEECs on their necessary imports of fuels and raw materials from the Soviet Union (see, e.g., UN ECE, 1991). It was also expected that the CEECs' economies would contract because they would be unable to cover their increased import bills with export earnings. Alternatively, they might be able to run large trade deficits vis-à-vis the USSR, provided that the latter would be willing to continue its deliveries to the region at the pre-1989 levels and on credit conditions. In that case, the contraction would be smaller.

As it turned out, the expected trade deficits did indeed emerge, but for somewhat different reasons. The hesitant pace of economic reforms in the USSR, the chaotic system of foreign exchange allocation, and the falling apart of central government controls over the economy due to precipitate disintegration of the Soviet state led to a sharp fall in Soviet output and trade in 1991. Soviet imports fell sharply, chiefly because of restricted access to foreign exchange, cuts in domestic absorption, and attempts to impose some measure of financial discipline on the enterprise sector. Most CEECs were able to cover the deficits in Eastern trade with the surpluses registered in their trade with the West. Thus, the trade shock proved to be more damaging on the CEECs' export side than on the import side, a result which had not been anticipated. The fall of exports arising from the collapse of the Soviet market proved to be much more painful for East European enterprises than the increase in import costs.

The collapse of trade between CEECs and the USSR in 1991 reflects therefore two distinct, albeit to some extent interdependent, developments. The first is the demise of the CMEA trading system which affected all trade in the region. The second is the domestic recession in the Soviet economy which affected only Soviet trade flows. Although both worked in the same direction, their separation for analytical purposes is important, because they imply different policy responses. Clearly, the issue of trade collapse should be addressed in a different way depending on the underlying causes: while in the first case there may be a scope for some multilateral arrangements for regional trade and payments, in the second the key issue is how to revitalize the post-Soviet economy and facilitate restructuring of the CEECs' trade.

Table 6.1. Changes in the territorial composition of trade, 1989–1991, shares in total trade, in percent.

	1989		1990		1991	
Country	USSR	Other CMEA	USSR	Other CMEA	USSR	Other CMEA
Bulgaria						
Exports	65.2	17.1	64.0	14.9	49.8	5.2
Imports	52.9	18.7	56.5	18.3	43.2	5.7
CSFR						
Exports	30.5	23.1	25.1	17.2	19.6	13.3
Imports	29.7	25.1	21.6	22.0	29.9	7.6
Hungary						
Exports	25.1	15.8	20.2	11.0	13.4	5.8
Imports	22.1	17.1	19.1	14.6	15.3	6.9
Poland						
Exports	20.8	14.0	13.1	8.3	11.0	5.8
Imports	18.1	14.0	15.4	6.8	14.1	4.9
Romania						
Exports	22.6	15.7	25.2	12.1	22.6	5.7
Imports	31.5	20.9	23.6	18.9	17.1	6.9

Total trade figures used for calculation of percentage shares were obtained through aggregation of ruble and non-ruble trade flows at national ruble/dollar cross rates.
Source: UN ECE data base, compiled from national trade statistics.

The need to separate factors which are specific to trade with the (former) Soviet Union is also justified by the much higher importance of the Soviet market as compared with other East European markets. This is illustrated in *Table 6.1*, where the territorial structure of exports and imports of the CEECs is shown for the period under review.

It is important to realize that the role of CMEA trade began to dwindle already in the late 1980s when the organization was still formally in operation. In particular, Poland and Hungary managed to reduce it substantially before the CMEA reform.[3] It can also be seen that in 1991 the share of CMEA trade fell sharply in all countries, roughly by between one-fourth (the CSFR, Poland, and Romania) and one-third (Bulgaria and Hungary). It may be observed that the fall of CMEA trade share was strongest in Bulgaria (by some 25 percentage points), while in other countries the adjustment was somewhat smaller: around 10 points for the CSFR, Romania, and Hungary; and 4 points for Poland. It should also be noted that the Soviet market had always been more important for the CEECs, its share being typically higher by half than that of the rest of CMEA. This domination was strengthened in 1991, with the share of other CMEA markets declining much faster than the share of the Soviet market. This may suggest that the proportion of "economically unjustified" trade flows was much higher in trade among the CEECs than in their trade with the USSR.

6.1.3 Two-step analysis of the Soviet trade shock: The terms-of-trade effect and the export fall effect

As is clear from the foregoing discussion, both the demise of the CMEA and the collapse of the Soviet market were bound to work strongly against Soviet trade with the CEECs. The sudden change in terms of trade would call for increased exports from the CEECs to finance necessary imports; but domestic recession, new possibilities of trading with the West, and relative scarcity of foreign exchange in the Soviet Union could be expected to reduce sharply effective Soviet demand for imports from CEECs. The impact of the Soviet trade shock on CEEC economies may therefore be examined in two steps. In the first step, one would focus on the impact of the terms-of-trade effect on trade volumes and values, in terms of increase of export revenues required to finance a given level of imports. In the second step, one can estimate the impact of the fall in export sales to the Soviet market on the CEECs' economies. These two steps are followed in the discussion in Section 6.2.

6.2 The Effect of Terms-of-Trade Change

6.2.1 The concept of terms-of-trade change

Under the traditional system, foreign trade prices in the CMEA were set by multiplying the average dollar price ($p_M^\$$ and $p_E^\$$) paid or received on international markets for one unit of a given commodity or its close substitute (the so-called comparator commodity) and the official CMEA or IBEC (International Bank of Economic Cooperation, the main financial institute of the CMEA) ruble/dollar rate (Φ^I). Thus, the "border" price of an imported good expressed in domestic currency (p_M) was equal to (see also Rodrik, 1992a):

$$p_M = p_M^\$ \cdot \Phi^I \cdot \Phi_R \ , \tag{6.1}$$

where Φ_R is the ruble rate in national currency. Correspondingly, the "border" price of an exported good (p_E) was equal to

$$p_E = p_E^{\$} \cdot \Phi^I \cdot \Phi_R \ . \tag{6.2}$$

Multiplying and dividing the right side of both equations by the national dollar rate ($\Phi_{\$}$) yields

$$p_M = p_M^{\$} \cdot \Phi^I / \Phi^N \cdot \Phi_{\$} \ , \tag{6.3}$$

$$p_E = p_E^{\$} \cdot \Phi^I / \Phi^N \cdot \Phi_{\$} \ , \tag{6.4}$$

where Φ^N is the national ruble/dollar cross rate.

Note, however, that prices *effectively* paid (or received) by domestic firms (users or sellers) were different from the "border" prices in equations (6.1) and (6.2), as they were typically adjusted with additional export and import taxes or subsidies.[4] Typically, a tax was imposed on imports of fuels and raw materials, and a subsidy was paid to exporters of industrial goods, thus reducing the differential between the dollar prices and the ruble prices (but in Hungary taxes were also applied on exports to the USSR). Generally, since in all CEECs the national ruble rate was lower than the IBEC rate – that is, the ratio Φ^I/Φ^N was less than one – the "border" prices were below the corresponding dollar prices converted into national currency at $\Phi_{\$}$. The ratio Φ^I/Φ^N, and consequently the national implicit dollar–ruble cross rate, was an *internal*, not external, policy instrument aimed at discouraging excessive ruble exports (above established limits) and the accumulation of ruble trade surpluses, as these were difficult to convert into additional imports under the traditional system.

In addition to the reforms in the trading rules between CMEA countries, introduced in 1991, all countries have substantially devalued their domestic currencies with respect to the dollar and introduced (partial) convertibility. Because of these changes, the new "border" prices paid (or received) in mutual trade since 1991 have differed substantially from the old "border" prices paid (received) prior to 1991. The index of change in "border" prices of exports and imports (from p to p') can be expressed analytically as follows:

$$\frac{p'_M}{p_M} = \frac{p_M^{\$'} \cdot \Phi'_{\$}}{p_M^{\$} \cdot \Phi^I / \Phi^N \cdot \Phi_{\$}} \tag{6.5}$$

and

$$\frac{p'_E}{p_E} = \frac{p_E^{\$'} \cdot \Phi'_{\$}}{p_E^{\$} \cdot \Phi^I / \Phi^N \cdot \Phi_{\$}} \ , \tag{6.6}$$

that is,

$$\frac{p'_M}{p_M} = \frac{p_M^{\$'}}{p_M^{\$}} \cdot \frac{\Phi'_{\$}}{\Phi_{\$}} \cdot \frac{\Phi^N}{\Phi^I} \tag{6.7}$$

and

$$\frac{p'_E}{p_E} = \frac{p_E^{\$'}}{p_E^{\$}} \cdot \frac{\Phi'_{\$}}{\Phi_{\$}} \cdot \frac{\Phi^N}{\Phi^I} \ . \tag{6.8}$$

As can be seen from equations (6.7) and (6.8), the overall change in the "border" prices paid by importers, or received by exporters, can be analyzed as the combination of three distinct effects (components):

1. The first effect is a result of the change in dollar prices from $p_{\$}$ to $p'_{\$}$, i.e., from the "reference" prices to freely negotiated prices for industrial goods, and from five-year moving-average prices to current market prices for fuels and raw materials. This is the "pure" price effect.
2. The second effect is the change in nominal exchange rate of national currencies against the dollar from $\Phi_{\$}$ to $\Phi'_{\$}$. An appreciation of the domestic currency reduces, *ceteris paribus*, profitability of exports and import substitution, while a depreciation has the opposite effect. This is the devaluation effect. It should be noted, however, that this effect has no direct relationship to the CMEA dissolution: national dollar exchange rates played no role in intra-CMEA trading (except in the Soviet Union), and devaluation is essentially a unilateral policy decision.
3. The third effect is the establishment of a uniform exchange rate for both the "internal" and the "external" use of the ruble in each country, reflecting the elimination of the (transferable) ruble from mutual settlements. It should be remembered that while the official IBEC rate (Φ^I) was used to set prices in mutual trade, domestic prices of imported goods were set using the national ruble rates, which were different in each country. Since the national ruble rates were as a rule lower than the IBEC rate, i.e., the ruble was domestically cheaper than in CMEA trade transactions, the unification of exchange rate in 1991 was regarded by some analysts (Rodrik, 1992a) to be equivalent to the elimination of an implicit tax on ruble exports and an implicit subsidy to ruble imports. It should be remembered, however, that these implicit taxes and subsidies were to a varying extent offset by explicit taxes and subsidies, applied – in the framework of various "price equalization schemes" (PES) – by East European governments to intra-CMEA exports and imports.[5]

This practice of the pre-1991 system was in a sense both "logical" and necessary, because the structure of CMEA trading prices was different from national relative prices and, therefore, firms had to be compensated for any losses that they incurred while effecting centrally planned export transactions; similarly, taxes were imposed to prevent windfalls in imports from being appropriated by importing firms. Thus, the "unification" of ruble exchange rates in each of the East European countries must have had a strong impact both on individual firms' effective payments (or receipts) and on government budgetary accounts. At the same time, it did not affect directly and *per se* the countries' position vis-à-vis each other, as all trade transactions among the CMEA members (excluding convertible currency transactions) were settled at the IBEC rate, not at the national ruble rates.

Thus, the total price effect on a former CMEA country's exports and imports is the combination of effect one and effect two, i.e., the sum of the "pure" price change and the exchange rate change, while the price effect of the CMEA dissolution is represented only by effect one, i.e., the "pure" price effect. This can easily be demonstrated if equations (6.7) and (6.8) are divided by each other to obtain the change in "barter" (external) terms of trade: both the exchange rate effect and the ruble elimination effect disappear, and the (external) terms-of-trade change is determined only by the ratio of relative dollar price changes in exports and imports, namely,

$$\frac{p'_M/p_M}{p'_E/p_E} = \frac{p^{\$'}_M/p^{\$}_M}{p^{\$'}_E/p^{\$}_E} \tag{6.9}$$

On the other hand, the impact on individual firms (exporters or importers) included not only the three effects identified above, but also the impact of any changes in the price equalization scheme which accompanied, or was induced by, the CMEA reform.

6.2.2 Estimating the terms-of-trade effect in Hungary and Poland

In this section, an attempt is made to estimate the income loss for Hungary and Poland arising from the deterioration of their terms of trade in the aftermath of the CMEA dissolution. The analysis provides a tentative answer to the following question: What would have been the gap in the trade balance of a given country under new market conditions, had the 1990 export and import volumes remained unchanged?

Changes in foreign trade prices, as reported by statistical authorities in both countries, incorporate both the change in dollar prices and the change

Table 6.2. Changes in prices for trade with CMEA trading partners in 1991 (1990 = 100) in Hungary and Poland.

Item	Hungary	Poland
A. Prices in CMEA trade[a]		
Export prices	155.1	159.6
Import prices	214.8	227.5
Terms of trade (CMEA)	72.2	70.2
B. Index of nominal dollar rate		
Exports	118.2	112.3
Imports	118.2	112.8
C. "Pure" price effect (A:B)		
Exports	131.2	142.1
Imports	181.7	201.7
D. "Pure" price effect in trade with the Soviet Union[b]		
Exports	131.2	142.1
Imports	226.5	261.3
E. Memorandum item		
GDP deflator	125.6	146.0

[a]Price indices for groups of countries: "countries in transition and nonmarket economies" for Hungary and "CMEA countries" for Poland.
[b]See note [7] for explanation.
Source: *Biuletyn Statystyczny* GUS, various issues, Warsaw, 1992; *Informacje Statystyczne - Handel Zagraniczny*, dane ostateczne, GUS, March 1992, Warsaw; *Statisztikai Èvkönyv*, 1992, Budapest.

in nominal dollar exchange rate. To estimate the change in "border" prices – for a country (and not for an individual firm) – the change in nominal dollar exchange rate has to be eliminated. For that purpose, tariffs and subsidies can be ignored, as they can be assumed to have no effect on the terms of trade.[6]

Unfortunately, official statistics do not show price indices for trade with the Soviet Union. The reported price indices for Hungary refer to trade with a group of countries, including all European and non-European CMEA countries, as well as non-CMEA socialist economies, while the price indices for Poland refer to all European CMEA countries. To estimate the relevant export and import price indices for the Soviet Union, the price indices for groups of countries were disaggregated with the assumption that price changes in trade with countries other than the Soviet Union were the same for exports and imports.[7] The relevant data for Hungary and Poland are given in *Table 6.2*.

An important inference from *Table 6.2* is that while the CMEA demise resulted in a sharp rise in foreign trade prices of exports and imports of both countries, the increase in import prices was much higher, which is consistent with the general perception that East European countries' terms of trade deteriorated vis-à-vis the former USSR. Oblath and Tarr (1991) predicted a deterioration in Hungarian terms of trade of 30% to 37% in 1991. Another interesting fact is that there was a real appreciation of both national currencies against the dollar in 1991, which probably dampened the impact of foreign price increase on domestic importers and exporters. Thus, the real exchange rate effect worked against exports and in favor of imports in both countries. This fact, disregarded by most analysts, may have exacerbated the negative impact of the collapse of import demand in the former USSR on revenues of CEECs' exporters.

The results reported in *Table 6.2* allow for the effect of terms-of-trade change in terms of income loss to be calculated, provided the initial value of CEECs' exports to the Soviet Union is known. Hungarian and Polish national statistics give the data on trade with the Soviet Union (prior to 1991) expressed in various combinations of rubles, dollars, and national currencies. These data are presented in *Table 6.3*. To calculate the income loss arising from the terms-of-trade change, the aggregate dollar values of trade in 1990 have to be compared with the corresponding dollar values for 1991. In principle, the 1990 values are difficult to obtain because of largely artificial transaction prices and distorted national dollar/ruble cross rates which are used for official conversion of ruble trade flows in dollars. However, the officially reported changes in export and import prices allow for calculating 1990 figures in 1991 dollars.

The procedure applied is as follows. The ruble component of Hungarian exports to the USSR in 1990 was worth Ft 113,173 million (see *Table 6.3*); but because export prices rose by 31.2% in 1991 (the "pure" price effect in exports – see *Table 6.2*), the value of 1990 exports in 1991 prices would be Ft 148,483 million (if the volume remained unchanged). The "implicit" dollar value of these exports would thus be $2,349 million (converted at the average official rate of Ft 63.2059/$1), and that should next be increased by the dollar component of Hungarian exports, i.e., $123 million (assuming constant dollar prices for 1990–1991). This gives the dollar value of total Hungarian exports to the Soviet Union in 1990 of $2,472 million, which can then be compared with the dollar value in 1991 – $1,369 million. Similarly, the forint value of the ruble component of Hungarian imports in 1990 is increased by the "pure" price effect in imports of 126.5%, and the dollar value of total imports for 1990 is obtained ($3,623 million). These results

Table 6.3. Hungarian and Polish trade with the Soviet Union in 1990 and 1991.

Item		1990	1991	1990 = 100
A. Hungary				
Exports, total	Ft mill.	120,947	102,276	
Ruble export:	R mill.	4,115	421	
	Ft mill.	113,173	11,580	
Dollar export:	$ mill.	123	1,200	
	Ft mill.	7,774	90,697	
Exports, total (at 1991 prices)	$ mill.	2,47	1,369	55.4
Imports, total	Ft mill.	106,187	131,261	
Ruble imports:	R mill.	3,530	375	
	Ft mill.	97,085	10,301	
Dollar imports:	$ mill.	144	1,590	
	Ft mill.	9,102	120,960	
Imports, total (at 1991 prices)	$ mill.	3,623	1,756	48.5
B. Poland				
Exports, total	Zl bill.	20,756[a]	17,312	
Ruble exports:	R mill.	6,632	—	
	Zl bill.	14,124	—	
Dollar exports:	$ mill.	698	—	
	Zl bill.	6,632	—	
Exports, total (at 1991 prices)	$ mill.	2,829	1,637	57.9
Imports, total	Zl bill.	17,947[b]	23,193	
Ruble imports:	R mill.	3,306	—	
	Zl bill.	7,066	—	
Dollar imports:	$ mill.	1,145	—	
	Zl bill.	10,881	—	
Imports, total (at 1991 prices)	$ mill.	3,131	2,208	70.5

[a]GUS-reported figure of Zl 19,768 billion covers only transactions registered on the basis of documents submitted directly by state enterprises to statistical offices (the so-called faktura-registered exports), and hence it had to be adjusted to take into account private-sector export transactions registered on the basis of customs declarations only. A factor of 0.05 has been applied, corresponding to the overall proportion of private-sector exports to state-sector (faktura-registered) exports in 1990.
[b]GUS-reported figure of Zl 15,370 billion worth of imports by state enterprises has been increased by a factor of 0.167 to take into account private-sector imports (see note *a*).
Source: Calculated from national statistics (see *Table 6.2*).

Table 6.4. The terms-of-trade effect in trade with the Soviet Union in 1991 in Hungary and Poland.

Item	Hungary	Poland
A. "Pure" price effect, exports		
In national currency [a]	35,310	5,946
In $ mill.	559	631
B. "Pure" price effect, imports		
In national currency [a]	122,813	11,431
In $ mill.	1,943	1,227
C. Terms-of-trade effect, $ mill.	1,384	596
D. Terms-of-trade effect, as percent of GDP [b]		
At official exchange rates	4.5	0.8
At PPP rates	2.6	0.4
At average rates	3.6	0.6

[a]In million forints for Hungary and in billion zlotys for Poland.
[b]Alternative GDP dollar estimates derived from converting 1991 GDP values expressed in domestic currency into US dollars at official exchange, at purchasing power parity (PPP) rates, and at the arithmetic average of the official and PPP rates.
Source: Based on data in *Table 6.3.*

are shown in *Table 6.3*. The same technique was applied to the Polish trade data, in which case the average exchange rates of Zl 9,420/$1 in exports, and Zl 9,313/$1 in imports were used.[8]

The procedure adopted allows one to calculate from the ruble component of trade the effective, "implicit" ruble–dollar cross rates based on effective price changes in each country. The "implicit" cross rate for Hungary is R 1.75/$1 for exports and R 1.02/$1 for imports, while the "implicit" cross rates for Poland are substantially higher, R 3.11/$1 and R 1.66/$1, respectively.[9]

Taking the "pure" price effects in exports and imports (for ruble components of trade only), the values given in *Table 6.4* are obtained for the terms-of-trade effect. The interpretation of the terms-of-trade effect reported in *Table 6.4*, line *C*, is as follows: had export and import volumes in trade with the Soviet Union in 1991 remained the same as in 1990, the CMEA price reform would have resulted in a net loss of $1,384 million for Hungary and $596 million for Poland. Of course, the assumption of constant trade volumes is hardly realistic, because price changes, as well as overall liberalization of trade regimes, have obviously also affected the levels and structure of trade between the Soviet Union and East European countries. Nevertheless, these two figures provide an interesting, although rough, indication of the terms-of-trade effects of the 1991 reforms on two former members of the CMEA.

The figure obtained for Hungary is somewhat lower than earlier predictions, but higher than more recent estimates, while the terms-of-trade loss for Poland is surprisingly low, both in absolute terms and as a proportion of GDP.[10]

The results for Poland can be, at least partly, explained by two facts. First, as 1990 has been taken as the base year, the exceptionally high level of Polish exports in that year obviously affected the calculations, reducing the increase in import costs relative to the increase of export earnings. To the extent that the level of Polish exports in 1990 could not be sustained in 1991, the terms-of-trade loss would be greater. Second, convertible currency payments for imports from the Soviet Union were already quite substantial in 1990, i.e., before the formal dissolution of the CMEA. In other words, the Polish economy had absorbed a large part of the terms-of-trade loss already in 1990. Some 30% of Polish exports and 60% of Polish imports from the Soviet Union in 1990 were conducted on non-ruble terms (mostly in convertible currencies), even though the CMEA was still formally in operation.

6.3 The Effect of the Fall in CEECs' Exports to the Soviet Union

In this section an attempt is made to answer two questions: Could the observed trade contraction be attributed to the demise of CMEA? To what extent has this contraction been a natural, and largely inevitable, outcome of various non-CMEA specific, domestic developments in the Soviet Union, such as stabilization programs, disintegration of the USSR, trade liberalization measures, and political changes? I begin by establishing a set of trade data to be used for all CEECs. Next, an attempt is made to distinguish in the Soviet trade shock between the relative importance of factors connected with the CMEA demise and those rooted in developments in the Soviet Union. Then, the effect of the Soviet market collapse on GDP of East European countries is estimated.

6.3.1 The data

As already mentioned, the analysis of changes in Eastern trade is seriously constrained by data problems. The difficulties concern the comparability

Table 6.5. Soviet foreign trade in 1990 and 1991, in million "commercial" (kommercheskich) rubles.[a]

Item	1990	1991	Index (1990=100)
Exports, total	119,838	81,419	67.9
Imports, total	137,628	79,230	57.6
Exports, non-CMEA	77,557	62,769	80.9
Imports, non-CMEA	87,404	59,780	68.4
Exports, CMEA[b]	42,281	18,650	44.1
Imports, CMEA[b]	50,224	19,450	38.7
Bulgaria			
Exports	7,492	2,244	30.0
Imports	9,908	3,741	37.8
Czechoslovakia			
Exports	8,804	5,082	57.7
Imports	10,031	4,198	41.8
Hungary			
Exports	6,927	3,032	43.8
Imports	7,126	2,312	32.4
Poland			
Exports	7,908	4,037	51.0
Imports	12,764	3,473	27.2
Romania			
Exports	4,731	1,718	36.3
Imports	1,784	1,571	88.1

[a]Convertible currency trade flows converted into rubles at the commercial rate: \$1 = R 1.7467 (trade-weighted average).
[b]Includes trade with non-European CMEA member countries (Mongolia, Cuba, and Vietnam).
Source: *Ekonomika i Zhizn'*, 13 March 1992, No. 13, pp. 14–15; author's calculations.

of data referring to various periods, on the one hand, and the various rules concerning statistical reporting on trade in individual countries, on the other.

To overcome these problems, it is necessary to have a consistent set of data on trade of the CEECs with the Soviet Union. Official statistics published by the CEECs do not obviously meet this condition because of different national cross rates. It was therefore decided to use the Soviet trade data for 1990 and 1991, because they offer the advantage of being obtained from recalculating different bilateral trade flows with a single uniform exchange rate, and hence may at least be used for estimating the change in the dollar value of trade. The Soviet trade data are shown in *Table 6.5*.

It should, however, be borne in mind that Soviet trade statistics for 1991 are still by no means reliable and should be interpreted with great caution. According to Goskomstat, the trade data for 1990 have been recalculated at the rate of R 1.7467/$1, to make them comparable with 1991 data. The operation implied a significant revaluation of nominal Soviet trade flows for 1990.[11] But it is not certain whether current dollar prices were used in all cases and, therefore, to what extent the data shown in *Table 6.5* reflect also the change in dollar prices. Moreover, it is not clear how barter transactions – which constituted a far from negligible part of Soviet trade with former CMEA countries in 1991 – have been accounted for.[12]

But the most important reservation with respect to the Soviet statistics is that the revaluation of trade figures for 1990 have made them largely inconsistent with the mirror statistics of East European countries. For instance, Polish sources reported exports to the former USSR in 1990 as amounting to Zl 19,768 billion, i.e., only $2,081 million at the official average exchange rate of Zl 9,500/$1, whereas the corresponding Soviet figure was $7,307 million. This and other differences in mirror statistics for 1990, which arose chiefly from diverging national ruble-dollar cross rates, imply that while the Soviet data may seriously overestimate the fall in intra-CMEA trade between 1990 and 1991 because of the "inflated" trade levels in 1990, the East European data may underestimate the fall in this trade because of excessively depreciated ruble trade values. This has to be kept in mind while interpreting the results of the calculations below.

According to *Table 6.5*, Soviet imports from the CEECs in 1991 generally fell more than exports, except for trade with Bulgaria and Romania, where domestic recession and the acute shortage of convertible currencies led to much larger cuts in their own imports than in other countries. The biggest losses in terms of relative changes in exports to the Soviet market (in Soviet imports) were incurred by Poland (down 72.8%), followed by Hungary (down 67.6%) and Bulgaria (down 62.2%). Poland's huge relative loss, however, partly reflects an inevitable decline from the unsustainably high export level attained in 1990. The CSFR seems to have been least affected by the trade volume changes, but nonetheless its total trade turnover with the former Soviet Union declined by half.

These results are dubious at best. Poland's loss seems to be largely overstated, and that of the CSFR probably understated, which is underscored by large discrepancies between the mirror trade data for these two countries. One possibility for making the results more realistic is to use the national effective "implicit" cross rates constructed in Section 6.2.2 for Hungary and

Poland to estimate the real dollar value of the CEECs' export decline in 1991.

As could be expected, if these national effective cross rates are used, the losses for Poland are significantly smaller ($3,293 million compared with $5,320 million), but the losses for Hungary are almost exactly the same, because the national effective rate (1.75) is practically the same as the Soviet "commercial" rate (1.7467).

6.3.2 Breakdown of the fall in Soviet imports from the CEECs: Domestic recession (DR), trade reduction (TR), and trade diversion (TD) effects

The sharp decline of GDP in CMEA countries from 1990 to 1991 is assumed to have affected the overall levels of import demand in these countries. This decline in import demand is not only an indication of the pure, or Keynesian, demand effect, connected with falling incomes. It also incorporates effects of some additional budget constraints, connected in some countries (the former USSR, Bulgaria, and Romania), with the shortage of foreign exchange and with the bureaucratic and inefficient system of foreign exchange allocation among importers. This is probably the reason why the rate of total import decline in the former USSR is much higher than the rate of its GDP decline (42.4% decline in import compared with 10.0% decline in GDP in 1991). It is, however, difficult to disentangle the demand effect and the (foreign exchange) shortage effect, so they will be lumped together into one category, being jointly held responsible for the *domestically induced* part of the fall in Soviet imports.

Theoretically, the domestic recession (DR) effect could in principle be measured by the fall in the country's total imports. However, such an assumption would be inappropriate because the fall in total imports reflects also the trade reduction (TR) effect, linked to the elimination of preferential trading with CMEA countries.[13] Nor can the fall in imports from non-CMEA markets be taken as a measure of the domestic recession effect because it was alleviated, at least partly, by the diversion of Soviet imports from CMEA countries to non-CMEA countries – the trade diversion (TD) effect. On the other hand, the fall of imports from the CMEA markets can be attributed to the combined effect of domestic developments (recession) *and* the dismantling of the CMEA trading system, which in turn resulted either in discontinuation of some trade flows or in diversion of some Soviet imports to the West. The overall effect was thus not only the absolute fall of Soviet imports from the CEECs, but also a heavy loss by these countries of the share in the Soviet market.

The impact of all three effects (domestic recession, trade reduction, and trade diversion) on Soviet imports from CMEA countries and from the West can be analytically investigated, under the assumption that income elasticities of imports from CMEA and from Western countries are equal,[14] within the following simple model:

$$M_{CMEA}(1 - DR) - TR - TD = M'_{CMEA} \tag{6.10}$$

$$M_{WEST}(1 - DR) + TD = M'_{WEST} \ . \tag{6.11}$$

For total imports (M), the trade diversion effect (TD) cancels out:

$$M(1 - DR) - TR = M' \ , \tag{6.12}$$

where prime ($'$) stands for import levels registered *after* the CMEA dissolution (i.e., M' refers to 1991 trade levels). It should be noted that in equations (6.10)–(6.12) DR is a fraction of the total imports, while TR and TD are expressed in terms of absolute values. As the system has three unknowns and only two equations (the third equation is simply a sum of the first two), it cannot be solved directly and some additional assumptions are necessary.

In the following, both TD and TR are assumed to take positive values, on the basis that the dissolution of the CMEA eliminated preferences for mutual trade and thus worked as a customs union mechanism *à rebours*. According to such interpretation, TD and TR would correspond to "negative," or reversed, trade diversion and trade creation effects, respectively.

Assuming $TD > 0$, and solving (6.11) for DR, the condition $DR >$ 31.6% is obtained; while assuming $TR > 0$, and solving (6.12) for DR, the condition $DR <$ 42.4% is obtained. Thus, for the trade diversion and trade reduction effects to take positive values, the value of DR has to meet the following condition: $31.6 < DR < 42.4$, that is, the domestic recession effect has to account for the fall of imports ranging between 31.6% and 42.4%. These limits correspond to possible values of TR falling within the range between Rb. 0 and Rb. 14,908 million, or between 0.0% and 10.8% of total Soviet imports in 1990.

However, the actual value of the trade reduction effect is probably closer to the lower limit than to the upper limit of the range, simply because the trade diversion effect in 1991 has definitely a positive value, as can readily be seen from *Table 6.5*. It may therefore be suggested that trade reduction arising from the CMEA dissolution was not as significant as commonly believed, and that the more-than-proportionate decline of imports from the CMEA can be attributed in large part to market share loss by CMEA exporters.

As a tentative hypothesis, the domestic recession effect will be assumed to take the mid-point value within the permissible range, namely, $DR = 0.370$ (or 37.0% of the import fall). Taking Soviet import values from *Table 6.5*, and substituting them into the three equations, the trade reduction and trade diversion effects for total CMEA-originating imports are easily obtained:

$$TR = \text{R } 7,476 \text{ million}$$

$$TD = \text{R } 4,715 \text{ million} \quad .$$

To calculate DR, TR, and TD values for individual CEECs, it has been assumed that $DR = 0.37$ and that for each country TR and TD remain in the same proportions as for the whole CMEA – that is, $TR/TD = 7476/4715$, or 37/63. The results are shown in *Table 6.6*.

The most important message from *Table 6.6* is that a substantial proportion of the Soviet import collapse has been caused by domestic developments. The CMEA-dissolution factor accounts in all cases for less than half of the total Soviet imports fall; nevertheless, according to this estimate, it is still responsible for some 40% of the exports fall in the CEECs. It should be noted that this result can change only marginally if different assumptions are adopted with respect to the shares of particular effects (see above). The impact of the CMEA-specific factors was the strongest in case of Poland in both absolute and relative terms (accounting for almost half of the Polish exports decline), and relatively mild for the CSFR. By contrast, Romania registered relative "gains" after the CMEA dissolution. According to the calculations, the total amount of export losses incurred by five East European CMEA countries has been estimated at \$6.3 billion (see totals in the lower-right corner of *Table 6.6*), the bulk of which (42%) was incurred by Poland.[15]

6.3.3 Impact on GDP

The impact of the collapse of Soviet trade on East European GDP levels can be estimated by taking the changes of individual countries' GDP in 1991, expressed in current dollars, and comparing them with total effect values computed earlier and presented in *Table 6.6*. There are at least two serious problems with this approach. First, the total effect values have been derived from Soviet statistics and in some cases (especially Poland) are

Table 6.6. The impact of the Soviet import decline on CEECs, in million rubles and million dollars.

Soviet imports from	DR effect mill. R	TR effect mill. R	TD effect mill. R	Total effect Million R	Total effect Million $	CMEA-induced effect[a] Million R	CMEA-induced effect[a] Million $	CMEA-induced effect[a] %
Bulgaria	3,666	1,534	967	6,167	3,531	2,501	1,432	40.6
CSFR	3,711	1,302	820	5,833	3,339	2,122	1,215	36.4
Hungary	2,636	1,336	842	4,814	2,756	2,178	1,247	45.2
Poland	4,723	2,803	1,766	9,292	5,320	4,569	2,616	49.2
Romania	660	−274	−173	213	122	−447	−256	—
CEECs-5	15,396	6,701	4,222	26,319	15,068	10,923	6,254	41.5

[a] TR and TD effects combined and as a proportion of total effect.

Table 6.7. Impact of the Soviet trade collapse on GDP of East European countries.

Item	Bulgaria	CSFR	Hungary	Poland	Romania
A. The data					
GDP change in 1991	–11.7%	–14.2%	–11.9%	–7.2%	–13.7%
GDP change in 1991, in mill. $, at "average" rates[a]	3,087	11,274	5,277	8,715	8,330
Export effect, in mill. $					
Total	3,531	3,339	2,756	5,320	122
CMEA-induced	1,432	1,215	1,247	2,616	–256
B. GDP change due to export fall effect, in percent of GDP					
"Average" rates[a] total	–13.4	–4.2	–5.8	–4.4 (–2.7)	–0.2
CMEA-induced	–5.4	–1.5	–2.6	–2.2 (–1.3)	0.4

[a]Arithmetic average of the official dollar rate and PPP dollar rate.
Source: GDP figures from national statistics; author's calculations.

clearly unrealistic. Second, the results depend very heavily on the exchange rates applied for converting GDP values in national currency into dollar values. Official exchange rates tend to underestimate the GDP values (and thus their changes) in 1991, because the nontraded part of the CEECs' GDP (nonmaterial services, rents, transport, construction) has typically higher real value than if converted at official rates.

Purchasing power parity (PPP) rates appear to be more realistic, but they are also open to criticism for not reflecting properly the position of a given country in international trade. In view of these all too familiar problems, the impact of the Soviet trade shock on GDP levels can only be estimated with some approximation.

In this section I apply the arithmetic average of the official exchange rates and the purchasing power parity rates. As simplistic as it is, the solution allows for the "appropriate" exchange rate to be considered a mid-range of the possible values within the upper and lower limits. The results of the calculations are shown in *Table 6.7*. As can be seen from this table, the proportion of each country's fall in GDP that can be attributed to the overall Soviet export shock varies from less than one-third for the CSFR to more than one for Bulgaria. The impact is negligible for Romania. The impact of CMEA-induced fall of exports is much smaller, and accounts for between 1.5% and 2.6% of GDP in the CSFR and Hungary, but for more than 5% of GDP in Bulgaria.

As already mentioned, export losses of some countries are probably overstated in Soviet statistics. National trade data of East European countries show a smaller fall of exports. An alternative estimate of the dollar value of the fall of Polish exports to the Soviet Union in 1991, as presented in Section 6.3.1, is $3,293 million, or some 60% of the loss reported in *Tables 6.6* and *6.7*. Since I find it more appropriate to take the lower figure into account, I assume that the fall of Poland's GDP attributable to "total" export shock is 2.7 percentage points from the total fall, and the CMEA-induced export shock may be held responsible for between 1.3% and 1.4% of GDP. These results, probably much closer to reality, are shown in parentheses in *Table 6.7*.

When interpreting the results obtained in this section and the previous section, important limitations and qualifications should not be ignored. First, possible errors may arise from the applied technique of GDP valuation at the "average" exchange rates. Second, the results obtained in this section refer to changes in the dollar *value* of Soviet imports from the CEECs, i.e., they incorporate the dollar price changes in the CEECs' exports, or the "pure" price effect, *and* the volume changes, which could not be directly estimated because of lack of data. The results, however, do not take into account changes in the national foreign exchange rates of individual countries. Third, the results show only the impact effect of exports decline, that is, they exclude possible multiplier effects. If the multiplier effects are taken into consideration, the figures shown in the bottom section of *Table 6.7* should be multiplied by a factor of between 2 and 2.5, and the entire cumulative effect of the export fall would probably be in the range of the GDP fall in most countries. However, it would be a mistake to attribute the entire GDP fall to the Soviet trade shock only, because this would imply a zero trade diversion, whereas it is clear that there has been an important redirection of exports to other markets, which partly offset the effect of the Soviet market collapse. Finally, if the "pure" price effect in imports from the Soviet Union is added to the export effect for Hungary and Poland (see *Table 6.4*, line *B*), the GDP losses would increase by 4.1% and by 1.6%, respectively.

6.3.4 Comparison with other results

Rodrik (1992b) estimates the impact of the Soviet trade shock to be 7.8% of GDP for Hungary and 3.5% for Poland. The results obtained in the present study are generally lower, but not by very much: the impact losses excluding the "pure" price effect in imports in 1991 are 5.8% of GDP for Hungary and 2.7% of GDP for Poland. Including the "pure" price effect in imports, the losses increase to 9.9% and 4.3%, respectively.

The differences arise partly from different assumptions underlying Rodrik's analysis, and partly reflect problems with statistical data. Rodrik compares GDP changes, converted from national currencies into dollars at the official exchange rates, with trade figures, converted from rubles into dollars at the IBEC rate. This procedure is clearly inappropriate because the same traded goods enter each of the aggregates at a different rate; hence, trade figures tend to be inflated relative to GDP figures. Second, it is not clear why the 1990 GDP falls are also included, even though the CMEA still existed, and Poland, for instance, actually registered some growth of exports to the Soviet Union. Third, trade figures for 1990 have been obtained by converting national trade data into dollars with the use of the IBEC rate, which is a rather doubtful procedure, as such figures do not represent any real trade values.

More importantly, however, some dubious assumptions have been used for the derivation of the analytical framework; subsequently the result is a very problematic interpretation of the three components of the Soviet trade shock. The reliance on the IBEC rate leads Rodrik to conclude that exports to Western markets fetched lower prices than exports to the Soviet market. This conclusion is incorrect, at least for Poland, because in reality exporters were compensated with special export subsidies for losses they incurred in exporting to the Soviet market. Microeconomic profitability of exports to Western markets was generally much higher, due to the deeply depreciated exchange rate.[16] Moreover, this approach leads to very dubious estimates of the three effects. The increase of export prices is clearly underestimated in Rodrik's terms-of-trade effect. The market-loss effect may, in fact, have been unimportant because, contrary to Rodrik's assumptions, Western market prices may not have been lower than Soviet market prices if converted into domestic currencies and adjusted for taxes and subsidies. Finally, the removal-of-subsidy effect cannot be calculated from Rodrik's analysis because the role of differential taxes and subsidies is ignored.

The existence of price equalization schemes makes the removal of "implicit subsidy" on imports by itself irrelevant, unless its impact is assessed together with the parallel changes in large-scale price equalization schemes.[17]

6.4 Conclusions

The significance of what is called the *Soviet trade shock* for selected Central and East European economies has been examined in this paper. The analysis involves two steps: first, the terms-of-trade effect of replacing the CMEA trading rules by market rules is estimated; second, the impact of the loss of export markets in the former Soviet Union is assessed. The analysis has been constrained by many critical assumptions, mostly dictated by unavailability of necessary data on trade and output changes in CEECs. These limitations notwithstanding, the results obtained offer some additional insights on the impact of the collapse of Eastern trade on transition countries.

The abrogation of the traditional CMEA trading rules between former CMEA partners in 1991 has led to a massive change in the "border" prices paid by importers or received by exporters in CEECs. This change was a combined effect of three distinct developments: the effect of change from "reference" dollar prices to freely negotiated dollar prices (or the "pure" price effect), the effect of the change in nominal dollar exchange rate (or the devaluation effect), and the effect of unification of national ruble rates in the CEECs. While at the firm level trade was necessarily affected by all three effects, and also by changes in national tax/subsidy rates, at the individual country level only the "pure" price effect matters, and thus determines the magnitude of the terms-of-trade effect.

The results of estimating the terms-of-trade effect for Hungary and Poland show that the income losses in 1991 may not have been as substantial as commonly believed (3.6% of GDP and 0.6% of GDP at the "average" dollar rates, respectively). The figure for Poland would be revised upward (to about 1% of GDP), if terms-of-trade losses incurred in 1990 are included.

The second part of the analysis has considered the losses arising from the collapse of CEECs' exports to the Soviet market. A decomposition into three distinct categories of the fall of total Soviet imports in 1991 reflects the impact of domestic recession, the reduction of trade with the former CMEA, and the diversion of imports from former CMEA to Western countries. While the first effect has no direct connection with the CMEA's dissolution, being essentially a result of domestic developments in the Soviet Union, the two other effects constitute direct outcomes of the dissolution. Using Soviet statistical data, all three effects are estimated for five Central and East European countries. The results demonstrate that the CMEA-induced part of the trade collapse accounts for from 36% to 49% of the total fall of exports to the Soviet Union by the CEECs (except Romania), with the impact of domestic recession being in all cases stronger than the CMEA dissolution effect.

An attempt has finally been made to estimate the impact of the Soviet trade shock on GDP levels in CEECs. While the results obtained should be treated with caution, they nevertheless indicate that the collapse of exports to the Soviet Union in 1991 may have been responsible for about one-third of the officially reported GDP fall in the CSFR and Poland, for more than half of the GDP fall in Hungary, and for more than the entire registered fall of GDP in Bulgaria. The impact of the CMEA-induced export fall was estimated at between 1.3% and 2.6% of GDP for the CSFR, Hungary, and Poland, and at 5.4% of GDP for Bulgaria. The impact of the Soviet trade shock on Romania was negligible. The results obtained suggest a smaller impact of the Soviet trade shock on Hungary and Poland than some other studies (Rodrik, 1992a, 1992b). The conclusions should, however, be taken with caution, because of many untested assumptions underlying the analysis.

Notes

[1] The most comprehensive attempt so far to quantify the effects of Soviet market collapse on East European output levels has been made by Rodrik (1992a, 1992b); but the methodology applied and the results obtained in his studies raise many questions which are discussed in this chapter. Tentative estimates can also be found in Berg and Sachs (1992), Klacek *et al.* (1992), and UN ECE (1992).

[2] An interesting aspect of the argument on the alleged "foreign exchange shortage" is that it was raised only in the context of Eastern trade, while there is no reason to assume that it would not affect Western trade as well.

[3] Both the high dependence on CMEA trade of Bulgaria and the low dependence of Poland in 1989–1990 are clearly exaggerated because of the distorted national ruble/dollar cross rates used for aggregating ruble trade flows.

[4] This important point is ignored in Rodrik's (1992a, 1992b) analysis.

[5] The analysis of official budget figures for Poland in 1990 leads Rodrik (1992a, 1992b) to believe that the "equalization taxes and subsidies had ... extremely limited effects" and thus they can be ignored altogether. He is obviously mistaken in doing so, because the price equalization account in Poland was separated from the official budget and operated as an independent extra-budgetary fund, called "Export Development Fund" or FRE. Official subsidies to Polish industrial exports to the USSR in 1990 paid out of this fund amounted to Zl 2.2 trillion or 11.8% of the value of industrial exports (Rosati, 1991b); in addition, large subsidies were paid for agricultural and service exports. The fund was financed by proceeds from customs duties and differential taxes on imports, the rates of which for some transactions (e.g., fuels) exceeded 500%. This was because domestic fuel prices in Poland in 1990 (but also in 1989) were much higher than the ruble price converted into domestic currency at the national ruble rate; they were in fact closer to world market prices. The same mechanism was in operation in Hungary (see Oblath, 1992).

[6] Tariffs do not affect terms of trade in this case, because East European countries are considered to be "small open economies," and demand for their exports may be assumed to be perfectly (price) elastic.

[7] It is plausible that in trade with countries other than the Soviet Union the price indices for exports and imports were roughly the same, because the commodity structure of this trade was similar in exports and imports; this implies of course that the entire terms-of-trade loss occurred in trade with the Soviet Union. Assuming that export prices to all CMEA countries, including the Soviet Union, and import prices from CMEA countries, excluding the Soviet Union, increased by the same margin – that is, by 31.2% in Hungary and by 42.1% in Poland (these numbers are taken from the export line of Section *C* in *Table 6.2*) – and taking the share of imports from the Soviet Union in 1990 from national statistics to be 53% of imports from "countries in transition and nonmarket economies" for Hungary and 50% of imports from the "CMEA countries" for Poland, the missing price index for imports from the Soviet Union for 1991 can be estimated as:

$100 + (81.7 - 0.47 \times 31.2)/0.53 = 226.5$ for Hungary and

$100 + (101.7 - 0.50 \times 42.1)/0.50 = 261.3$ for Poland.

[8] Polish statistics provide different exchange rates for exports and imports, with the difference arising chiefly from discrepancies in converting other currencies into dollars and different timing of import and export transactions.

[9] It should be clear that these effective implicit rates are more appropriate for estimating the real "dollar" value of ruble trade in 1990 than either the official IBEC rate as suggested by Rodrik (1992a, 1992b), or the national cross rates as used by Berg and Sachs (1992).

[10] Oblath and Tarr (1991) estimated the income loss for Hungary due to terms-of-trade deterioration at between $1,500 million and $1,900 million, while Rosati *et al.* (1990, p. 38) predicted a loss for Poland of $500 million for 1991. Rodrik (1992b, p. 80) gives an estimate of terms-of-trade loss at $1.86 billion for Poland and $0.96 billion for Hungary.

[11] Original figures for total Soviet exports and imports for 1990 were R 60,757 million and R 70,728 million, respectively (see, Narodnoye Khoziaystvo SSSR v 1990 g, Goskomstat, Moskva, 1991, p. 644), in other words they were slightly more than a half of the revised figures published in 1992 and shown in *Table 6.5*. Details of the recalculation of the 1990 data have not been published by Goskomstat. However, it may be assumed that the following technique was applied. Take oil exports as an example: under the traditional price-setting rules, the oil price was calculated as a five-year moving-average dollar price converted into rubles with the IBEC dollar rate. Then, if the "reference" dollar price for oil in 1990 was $164 per ton, it was exported to CMEA countries at R 97 per ton (the dollar price multiplied by the IBEC rate of R 0.59/$1), and was recorded in Soviet trade statistics at nominal ruble value. In 1991, due to the change in trading rules, oil was exported at the current dollar price of $140 per ton, and this price was converted into rubles at the "commercial" rate of R 1.7467/$1 (1991 average), thus yielding the statistical ruble value of R 245 per ton. Of course, the change from R 97 to R 245 has mainly been caused by the change in pricing rules (and partly by the change in underlying dollar price) and not by any volume change. Trade data for 1990 and 1991

would therefore be clearly inconsistent. To deal with this difficulty, 1990 data have been recalculated with the "commercial" rate of R 1.7467/$1: all ruble prices have been reconverted to dollars at the IBEC rate, and then translated into rubles at the "commercial" rate. Because the 1990 oil price of R 97 per ton corresponded to $164 per ton, the dollar price was multiplied by 1.7467 to obtain the comparable ruble price of R 286 per ton.

[12] A different treatment of barter transactions is probably one of the main reasons for the significant discrepancies existing between corresponding mirror trade data for 1991, as reported by other CMEA countries. For instance, in 1991 trade with the CSFR Goskomstat reports exports of $2,909 million and imports of $2,403 million, while according to CSFR statistics, the corresponding figures are $3,224 million and $2,153 million. In the case of Poland, these differences are slightly smaller ($2,311 million for exports and $1,988 million for imports are reported by Soviet data, as compared with $2,208 million and $1,637 million, according to Polish statistics).

[13] The reader should be aware that the term "preferential" does not mean that intra-CMEA trade transactions were necessarily characterized by better price conditions, as compared with non-CMEA trade transactions. They also reflected political preferences of respective governments.

[14] In other words, it is assumed that the DR coefficient is equal for both kinds of imports. In fact, this is a very conservative assumption, because the specific commodity structure of Soviet imports from the CMEA (relatively high share of capital goods) made it much more sensitive to output and investment falls in the USSR than other imports. If, however, income elasticity of CMEA-originating imports is higher than the overall elasticity, the proportion of the fall attributed to domestic recession would be larger than that attributed to the dismantling of the CMEA.

[15] As noted before, Soviet data seriously overstate Polish losses.

[16] This effect was also reflected in surveys of exporting enterprises. For the results of a survey of Polish exporters, see Danielewski (1991).

[17] Rodrik's study raises many other points, but it is not the purpose of this paper to discuss them in detail. Even if his estimates and those reported in this paper are not fundamentally different, it should be remembered that they may conceal larger errors working in opposite directions or canceling each other (which may, of course, be also the case in this paper). Besides, the published version of Rodrik's paper contains many printing errors which do not allow for a more elaborate analysis of his approach. For a critical assessment of Rodrik's analysis, see Oblath (1992).

References

Berg, A., and Sachs, J., 1992, Structural adjustment and international trade in Eastern Europe: The case of Poland, *Economic Policy*, **14**:117–174.

van Brabant, J.M., 1993, Economic recession in the East: The impact of changing external regimes, *Journal of International and Comparative Economics*, **2**(3):165–189.

Danielewski, J., 1991, Selected problems involved with introduction of new forms of settlement in trade with the USSR, in *Polish Foreign Trade in 1990*, Foreign Trade Research Institute, Warsaw, Poland.

Durka, B., 1991, *Polish–Soviet Economic Relations*, Discussion Paper, No. 21, Foreign Trade Research Institute, Warsaw, Poland.

The Economy of the USSR, 1990, A study prepared for the Houston Summit, EBRD–IBRD–IMF–OECD, Washington, DC, USA.

Klacek, J., *et al.*, 1992, Ekonomicka reforma v CSFR (prubezne hodnoceni), *Politicka ekonomie*, **9**(10):727.

Oblath, G., 1992, Comment, in M. Blejer, G.A. Calvo, F. Coricelli, and A.H. Gelb, eds., *Eastern Europe in Transition: From Recession to Growth?*, Discussion Papers, No. 196, World Bank, Washington, DC, USA.

Oblath, G., and Tarr, D., 1991, The Terms-of-Trade Effects from the Elimination of State Trading in Soviet-Hungarian Trade, Working Papers, WPS 690, May, World Bank, Washington, DC, USA.

PlanEcon, 1992, The Role of Exchange Rates in Western Investment Decisions in Eastern Europe, 7 May, New York, NY, USA.

Rodrik D., 1992a, Foreign Trade in Eastern Europe's Transition: Early Results, Stanford University, Stanford, CA, USA [mimeo].

Rodrik, D., 1992b, Making sense of the Soviet trade shock in Eastern Europe: A framework and some estimates, in M. Blejer, G.A. Calvo, F. Coricelli, and A.H. Gelb, eds., *Eastern Europe in Transition: From Recession to Growth?*, Discussion Paper, No. 196, World Bank, Washington, DC, USA.

Rosati, D., 1991a, *After the CMEA Collapse: Is a Central European Payments Union Really Necessary?*, Discussion Paper, No. 16, Foreign Trade Research Institute, Warsaw, Poland.

Rosati, D., 1991b, The Impact of the CMEA Demise on Polish Industrial Exports to the Soviet Union: An Initial Assessment, A study prepared for the World Bank, Washington, DC, USA[mimeo].

Rosati, D., *et al.*, 1990, Poland: Impact of Replacing CMEA Trade Regime by a Market Trade Regime, Foreign Trade Research Institute, Warsaw, Poland [mimeo].

UN ECE, 1992, *Economic Bulletin for Europe*, **43**.

Chapter 7

The Effects of the Demise of the CMEA and the USSR on Output in Hungary

János Gács

The need to reform intra-CMEA trade and the underlining pricing and settlements mechanisms were discussed quite early in Hungarian academic circles. Naturally, the dissolution of this international institution was an issue never touched upon during the discussions, but several possible options for a new mechanism were analyzed in the late 1980s (see, for example, Richter, 1988; Szamuely, 1989). One of these possible mechanisms of cooperation was the abolishment of state trading and the use of convertible currency payments instead of transferable ruble settlements, with the natural implication of the eventual application of world market prices in transactions. When evaluating the costs and benefits of the different options for new pricing and settlements (payments) mechanisms, several institutional questions remain unanswered. For instance, Who would make the decisions and sign contracts for transactions in the new system, especially for the still highly centralized socialist economies? What procedures could be used to enforce contracts? In 1989 and 1990 several calculations on the expected impact of a new settlement mechanism were carried out and official and semiofficial

This research was supported by the No. 701 Topic of the National Science Research Fund (OTKA), The Impact of Foreign Trade and Structural Adjustment in the Hungarian Economy in the 1990s.

R. Holzmann et al. (eds.), Output Decline in Eastern Europe, 161-184.

debates were organized in Hungary and in the Soviet Union about the different reform scenarios.[1] These debates helped to reinforce the commitment of Hungary's government and Communist party to initiate some changes within the framework of the CMEA. It would be difficult to trace the role of these deliberating activities on the process that led to the decision of the CMEA representatives in Sofia in early 1990 to change the system of pricing and settlements within the CMEA starting in January 1991.

However, it is important to note that the Hungarian administration (and the academic community) was not exposed to the changes of 1991 completely unprepared. Many administrators and academics were convinced that the replacement of the existing system would provide long-term benefits. Nevertheless, the calculations that were carried out in 1989 and 1990 could not take various factors into account. First of all, the collapse of the Soviet Union (Hungary's most important trading partner) and the ensuing deterioration of its economic situation were not considered. These events involved the unexpected decline of production and demand in the Soviet Union and later in the successor republics, on the one hand, and the increased chaos and uncertainty affecting trade, on the other. A further uncalculated factor was the simultaneous decline of economic activity in each of the trading partners within the CMEA due to, eventually, their transition to a market economy. The final demise of the CMEA was also not foreseen.

In fact, these previously unexpected factors must be the reason that we see very few *ex post* calculations on the effects of the change in the CMEA mechanism; but we have observed several *ex ante* calculations (see *ex ante* calculations for Hungary by Gács, 1989; Kenen, 1990; and Oblath and Tarr, 1992). Many analysts have realized that contrary to earlier expectations, it was much less the shift itself (namely, the replacement of transferable ruble settlements by convertible currency payments and the use of world market prices starting in early 1991) that subsequently influenced production and trade, and much more the demise of the CMEA, as well as the disintegration and collapse of the Soviet economy. Scholars and policy makers are more concerned with the consequences of the loss of markets in the former CMEA region and the hardships of securing payments for the remaining contracted exports that go to the successor republics of the Soviet Union than with the income losses stemming from the introduction of world market prices for trade with former CMEA economies, including the Soviet Union.

In this chapter some aspects of this complex topic are analyzed. After describing the background of output decline and trade in Hungary, the direct and the indirect impacts of the market loss in the CMEA region is examined for the period between 1988 and 1992. The following sections are devoted

Table 7.1. Growth rate of basic indicators, volume indices, in Hungary.

Period	GDP	Industrial production	Exports total	Imports total	Exports to CMEA	Exports to dev. market economies
	Average annual growth rates[a]					
1971–75	106.3	106.4	109.4	107.3	111.7	101.3
1976–80	103.3	103.2	106.6	103.5	105.9	107.6
1981–85	101.8	101.9	105.6	101.4	106.1	103.8
1986–88	101.8	101.9	102.6	101.6	100.0	109.9
1989–92	95.5	91.3	98.0	98.3	79.8	111.9
	1970 = 100					
1992	152.5	128.9	281.9	177.3	126.2	383.4
	1988 = 100					
1988	100.0	100.0	100.0	100.0	100.0	100.0
1989	100.4	99.0	100.3	101.1	93.1	108.9
1990	97.1	89.5	96.2	95.8	72.1	122.1
1991	87.2	76.9	91.5	101.1	40.8	148.5
1992	83.3	69.3	92.4	93.4	40.6	156.7

[a]Geometric average.
Source: See Appendix.

to analyses of the timing of the shock, the extent of trade reorientation, and the explanations for Hungary's surprising export performance in the West in recent years. Sections 7.6 and 7.7 deal with price impacts: the effect of price increases of imported inputs and the changes in terms of trade.

7.1 Trade and Growth: Background

The stagnation of output in Hungary did not start with the systemic changes during the late 1980s. A continuous, palpable growth of GDP has been absent since 1987. However, a clear decline only became visible as late as 1990 (see *Table 7.1*).

In a longer-time perspective, cumulative growth of exports exceeded the rate of growth of GDP, industrial production, and total imports by a substantial margin. The data in *Table 7.1* show that exports have acted as a catalyst in GDP growth since the beginning of the 1970s. The main reason, however, for such a speedy development of exports in this period has little relation to brighter export opportunities opening for Hungarian exporters, or especially strong export performance of the Hungarian economy. In effect, the country's terms-of-trade losses and the necessity to service mounting external debts forced the export volume to grow so rapidly, overtaking all other major macroeconomic variables. Hungarian analysts have stressed for many years that the foundation of that fast export growth was not sound, partly because much of the exports were oriented to distorted CMEA markets and partly because, even if oriented to the West, they were based on short-term incentives.[2]

This forced development of exports must be the reason that the 1992 level of exports was still very high in relation to past levels, the 1989–1991 decline in total exports notwithstanding: in the period 1975–1991 there were only four years when the export volume exceeded the level of 1992, whereas 14 years were characterized by a higher GDP than in 1992.

The 7% to 8% cumulative decline of total exports in the 1988–1992 period does not seem to be serious, especially if we take into account that exports grew by between 15 and 30 percentage points in previous periods of similar length. The structural rearrangement of the exports in terms of regions, countries, sectors, and partner firms, however, has been substantial. As *Table 7.1* indicates, there was a 60% shift within a relatively short period of four years in exports both to (former) CMEA countries and to developed market economies. This move from CMEA markets to the markets of developed market economies naturally had different impacts on the various sectors of the economy. *Figure 7.1* gives the development of sectoral exports to socialist and to nonsocialist countries; it is clear that the commodity group most significantly hit by the decline in CMEA exports was the machinery and transport equipment group.

7.2 Direct and Indirect Effects of Loss of Markets

To estimate the direct and indirect effects of the lost CMEA markets on aggregate Hungarian output we use a relatively straightforward method. Instead of GDP, we deal with gross output.[3] In the framework of input–output analysis export is one component of the final use (y) of output. If, as a result of exogenous changes, exports decline, output falls as a direct consequence by the same magnitude, but also indirectly through inter-sectoral relations. The familiar formula $\Delta o = (I - A)^{-1} \Delta x$ gives total (direct and indirect) change in gross output (Δo) as a consequence of change in exports (Δx), where small letters denote vectors and capital letters matrices, I is

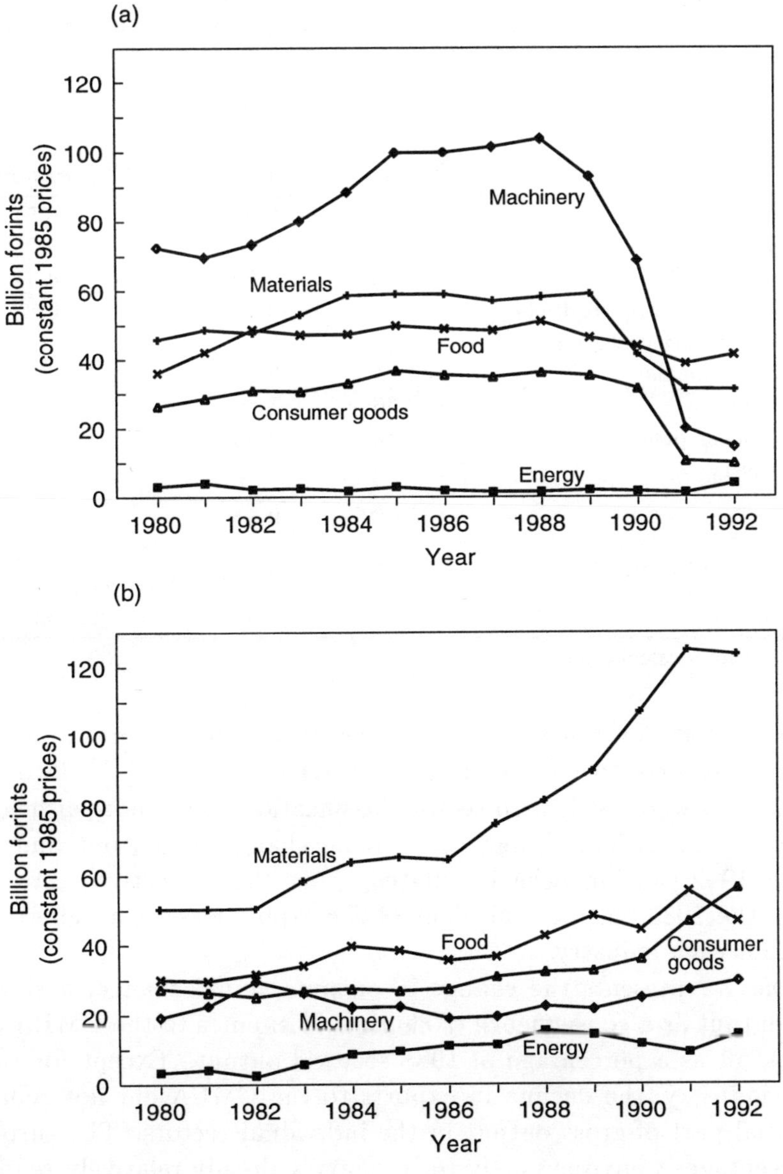

Figure 7.1. Exports to socialist (*a*) and nonsocialist (*b*) economies, commodity pattern.

the unit matrix, and A is the matrix of input–output coefficients. Similar calculations were carried out by Berg and Sachs (1992) for Poland.

Table 7.2. Changes in the volume of output, exports to CMEA and non-CMEA regions in 1988–1992 as a percentage of the 1988 sectoral output.

	Output change		
	Total	Due to change in exports to CMEA	Due to change in exports to non-CMEA
Mining	–38.28	–0.95	0.57
Electricity supply	–12.79	–0.20	0.00
Metallurgy	–56.35	–2.60	4.42
Manu. of engineering products	–49.96	–26.74	6.83
Manu. of building materials	–36.34	0.11	4.24
Manu. of chemicals	–34.04	–3.36	4.05
Light industry	–40.36	–8.56	21.76
Manu. of other products	–43.89	–3.53	16.09
Food industry	–16.86	–3.91	2.60
Total industry	–30.66	–9.31	6.92
Agriculture and forestry	–25.41	0.64	0.61
Total economy	–18.24	–4.06	2.90

Source: Author's calculation.

We started our calculation with the 1988 value of gross output and Hungary's exports to CMEA and non-CMEA countries.[4] Two sectoral classifications were used: a 10-sector classification and a more disaggregated 63-sector classification. Using the volume changes of output and exports for 1988–1992 (having been calculated using the respective sectoral price indices), the 1988 output equivalent of the export losses (or gains) was calculated for each industry.

Table 7.2 presents the change in output (actual change, first column) and in output as a consequence of changes in exports to the CMEA (second column), all as a percentage of 1988 sectoral output. Except for the engineering industry, the decline in exports to the CMEA did not represent a substantial part of gross output in the individual sectors. The surprisingly low percentages were due partly to Hungary's already relatively reduced exposure to CMEA trade in 1988 (43%) and partly to the gross nature of the measurement. In fact, only in the case of the engineering industry was the decline of exports to CMEA countries directly responsible for more than half of the output decline. The results of calculations on the more detailed classification (*Table 7.4* columns 1 and 2) obviously show industries with particularly high export-induced output decline both within the engineering

Table 7.3. Changes in the volume of output, exports to CMEA and non-CMEA regions in 1988–1992 as a percentage of the 1988 total output, direct and total (direct and indirect) impacts.

	Output change		
	Total	Due to change in exports to CMEA	Due to change in exports to non-CMEA
Direct impact			
Mining	–0.80	–0.03	0.00
Electricity supply	–0.38	–0.01	—
Metallurgy	–2.23	–0.10	0.17
Manu. of engineering products	–5.55	–2.96	0.76
Manu. of building materials	–0.50	0.00	0.06
Manu. of chemicals	–2.88	–0.28	0.34
Light industry	–2.38	–0.49	1.23
Manu. of other products	–0.17	–0.01	0.06
Food industry	–1.33	–0.29	0.19
Total industry	–16.22	–4.16	2.81
Agriculture and forestry	–3.96	0.10	0.09
Total economy	–18.24	–4.06	2.90
Total impact[a]		–7.91	5.57
Implicit multiplier		1.9478	1.9184

[a]Total impact calculated with aggregate input–output table for 1990.
Source: See Appendix and author's calculations.

industry and in other industries. Production of precision engineering equipment is an example of the former (52.5% of former output was lost due to the decline of exports to the CMEA, and almost all of the total 60.7% output decline in this sector was caused directly by these lost exports), and the wine industry is an example of the latter (47.0% decline and more than 100% of the total 41.3% output decline was caused by this export loss). Of the 63 industries, 9 suffered a more than 20% decline of output as a direct consequence of lost CMEA markets.

Table 7.3 also presents direct losses, but in terms of the 1988 total gross national output. As the numbers reveal, of the 18.24% output decline in the whole economy, 4.06% could be attributed directly to CMEA market losses, and of this 2.96% to the decline in engineering industry supplies to the CMEA countries. A further disaggregation of the data (not reproduced here) shows that two engineering industries (machinery and equipment production and motor vehicle manufacturing) made up more than 40% of the

Table 7.4. Changes in the volume of output in 1988–1992 as a consequence of changes in exports to CMEA countries, direct and total (direct and indirect) impact as a percentage of 1988 sectoral output.[a]

	Output change	Output change due to changes in exports to CMEA	
	total	Direct impact	Total impact[b]
Coal mining	–49.9	0.0	–4.6
Crude petroleum and nat. gas product.	–7.9	0.0	–6.1
Electric power generation	–12.8	–0.2	–6.2
Ferrous metallurgy	–58.6	–1.8	–15.9
Aluminum metallurgy	–47.1	–3.0	–11.4
Machinery and equipment production	–33.9	–28.1	–33.3
Motor vehicle manufacturing	–68.0	–36.4	–48.6
Electrical engineering	–50.8	–3.7	–13.7
Prod. of telecomm. and vacuum engineering	–48.0	–27.9	–35.9
Prod. of precision engineering products	–60.7	–52.5	–60.2
Fabricated metal products industries	–41.2	–4.0	–13.2
Crude petroleum processing industry	–19.7	1.2	–4.3
Gas production and gas distribution	–20.8	–0.5	–5.8
Organic and inorganic chemical industry	–36.9	–1.1	–7.4
Prod. of fertilizers and plant protectives	–64.9	–8.2	–13.7
Prod. of plastic mater. and chem. fibers	–33.2	2.9	–1.7
Synthetic material processing industry	–4.8	1.7	–3.3
Rubber products industry	–54.6	–6.7	–14.5
Pharmaceutical industry	–56.7	–14.8	–15.9
Furniture industry	–31.3	–2.3	–3.9
Paper industry	–29.2	–0.7	–8.7
Printing industry	–20.1	–1.1	–5.2
Cotton industry	–59.2	–10.6	–16.5
Hosiery	–54.7	–22.6	–26.3
Leather and fur industry	–53.8	–23.5	–30.5
Footwear industry	–51.6	–18.0	–19.7
Clothing industry	–28.0	–13.3	–15.8
Meat and meat products industry	–24.5	–7.0	–9.0
Poultry products industry	–40.7	–19.6	–20.1
Diary products industry	–18.4	0.9	0.4
Canned and preserved products industry	–28.3	–21.8	–23.5
Cereal grain flour industry	1.4	5.3	3.3
Bakery products industry	–29.7	–2.0	–2.4
Sugar industry	–5.7	10.8	10.1
Confectionery industry	–15.6	0.8	0.7
Vegetable oil industry	–16.8	9.4	7.9
Distillery products industry	–10.9	19.9	20.3
Wine industry	–41.3	–47.0	–57.9
Brewing industry	15.5	3.6	3.8
Total industry	–30.7	–9.3	–15.5
Agriculture and forestry	–25.4	0.6	–3.1
Total economy	–18.2	–4.1	–8.1

[a]Industries with negligible production and exports are omitted.
[b]Total impact calculated with disaggregated input–output table for 1986.
Source: See Appendix and author's calculations.

CMEA-induced output decline in the whole industry, and another 40% could be linked to six other industries (telecommunication equipments, precision engineering, pharmaceuticals, canned and preserved products, poultry products, and meat and meat products). The rest of the decline is widely scattered among the remaining industries.

The last column in *Tables 7.2* and *7.3* show the output equivalent of the expansion that Hungarian exports achieved in Western markets in 1988–1992. According to these results, export expansion to the West compensated for more than 70% of the direct output losses originating in lost CMEA trade. Since the 1991 changes in the accounting of international trade transactions in Hungarian statistics (see Appendix), our results for the output equivalent of the export expansion to the West may overvalue the actual changes (namely, exaggerate the effects of subcontracted processing or job work).

As for the calculation of the total (direct and indirect) impact of export decline, we used two of Hungary's latest available input–output tables: the aggregate table constructed for 1990 and the disaggregated table for 1986.[5] The 1990 table seems more appropriate for providing coefficients for our analysis for the period 1988–1992 than for 1986, since one could suspect that input–output coefficients changed substantially in the years of transition. This, however, is less the case for Hungary because of its earlier start in dismantling central planning.[6] The extremely small discrepancy between the results of the calculations with the two input–output tables verifies this conjecture. The results of calculations with the aggregate input–output table of 1990 are presented in the last two rows of *Table 7.3*, while those of the disaggregated table for 1986 can be seen in the third column of *Table 7.4*.

Given the usual homogeneity assumption of input–output tables, the indirect effects of changes in exports to CMEA and non-CMEA regions are different from each other only to the extent that their sectoral composition differs from each other. As the last row of *Table 7.3* shows, contrary to expectations (see Oblath, 1992), the implicit multiplier for exports to CMEA countries turns out to be only slightly higher than the multiplier for exports to the West.

According to the results in *Table 7.3* the total (direct and indirect) impact of the export decline to the CMEA (former CMEA) economies amounts to close to 8% in terms of 1988 output. This should be evaluated in comparison to the more than 18% of output decline. The output decline could have been higher, if 70% of the decline associated with exports to the CMEA had not been compensated by the growth of exports to the West.

Table 7.4 shows the more detailed version of the calculation for the first two columns in *Table 7.3*. In *Table 7.4*, however, output changes are expressed in 1988 sectoral outputs, and the results of detailed calculation for total (direct and indirect) impact of exports are also presented. The data show that only in few sectors was the total impact of the export decline responsible for all the sectoral output decline detected, but in quite a few industries the export decline was responsible for a high (20% to 25%) decline of sectoral gross production.

7.3 The Timing of the Shock

Conventional wisdom singles out the year 1991 as the time of the assault of the CMEA shock on small East European economies. This idea does have justification: 1991 was the year of both the shift to world market prices and the dissolution of the CMEA. However, some qualification is necessary. First, to some extent the shock could be sensed one to two years prior to 1991. For instance, Hungarian authorities had to introduce strict licensing of exports by Hungarian firms to the Soviet Union in early 1990, because of the apparent inability of the Soviet Union to pay for (or cover with supply of goods) the Hungarian export surplus. Also Hungarian trade liberalization, with its incentive to turn away from the CMEA, started as early as 1989. Second, one could assume that the shock was stretched beyond 1991 and had caused an impact with some lag. After all, the collapse of the Soviet Union and the payment difficulties related to the default of the Soviet Central Bank for Foreign Economic Affairs (Vneshekonombank) were more the result of events that occurred in 1992 than in 1991.

In *Table 7.5*, we calculate the approach of the shock by period. The table is the time-wise split of the changes displayed in *Table 7.3* (each section in *Table 7.5* corresponds to one column in *Table 7.3*). The results verify the importance of the year 1991 in output decline, and especially in trade flows. This table and more detailed data also support the view that a substantial decline in exports in all sectors preceded the shock of 1991. The lagged impact, namely, the shock of 1991 spreading over to 1992 or a further shock in 1992, however, seems to be relatively small.

7.4 Reorientation

Given the detailed data on changes in sectoral trade volumes we may attempt to answer the frequently posed questions: How much of recently lost CMEA exports were redirected to the West? In other words, what role was played by trade reorientation in the recent upswing of exports to non-CMEA

Table 7.5. Changes in the volume of output, exports to CMEA and non-CMEA regions in different periods in 1988–1993 as a percentage of the 1988 total output.

	Output change			
	1988–1990	1988–1991	1988–1992	1988–1993[a]
Total				
Total industry	–4.63	–10.31	–16.22	
Agriculture and forestry	–0.91	–2.11	–3.96	
Total economy	–2.82	–14.39	–18.24	
Due to change in exports to CMEA				
Total industry	–1.42	–3.84	–4.16	–3.47
Agriculture and forestry	–0.15	–0.19	0.10	–0.40
Total economy	–1.57	–4.03	–4.06	–3.88
Due to change in exports to non-CMEA				
Total industry	1.27	2.74	2.81	0.24
Agriculture and forestry	–0.06	0.24	0.09	–0.09
Total economy	1.21	2.98	2.90	0.14

[a]Forecast based on data from the first half of 1993.
Source: Author's calculations.

countries? Unfortunately, the concept of reorientation is not specifically defined in recent papers dealing with the subject. According to less precise delineations, one may speak about reorientation if the aggregate redirection of trade is achieved mainly through the redirection of trade within the individual sectors. We do not speak about reorientation if the general pattern is a decline in some sectors' exports to the East compensated by the growth of other sectors' exports to the West.

The extent (or rather the ratio) of reorientation is important from the viewpoint of the severity and durability of output decline, on the one hand, and of the foreseeable rate of long-term growth of exports, on the other. Instant reorientation is assumed to imply less cost of adjustment than the increase of exports from zero, or augmenting former export activities. If, however, increased Western exports originated in a further source, that is, switched from the dwindling domestic market, a future recovery would place in doubt the durability of these new export flows. Trade reorientation from East to West may turn out to be a once-and-for-all act, not showing much prospect for further export growth. Alas, given the immense extent of the loss of markets for some industries, a massive instant reorientation proper from East to West does not necessarily result in a sustained flow (maintained level) of exports, either. In 1991–1992 the necessity to use existing capacities to cover at least variable costs forced many firms to sell their marketable products in the West, even if they recovered only a part of their total costs. Because of the pervasiveness of this "distress export" the sustainability of this level of reoriented exports is questionable.

Partly on the basis of the considerations given above, analysts tend to see exports emerging from new opportunities as more prospective than those reoriented from domestic or Eastern markets.

Early analyses of trade reorientation (for example, Rodrik, 1991; Bruno, 1993) recorded negligible or no switch of exports from the CMEA to the West as, according to them, these "were largely goods that were not competitive at the new relative prices" (Bruno, 1993, p. 37). The discussion below tries to verify these statements.

Our approach is simple, straightforward, and mechanical. Only those sectors where both decline in export volumes to the East and increase of exports to the West could be recorded are taken into account, a total of 27 sectors (out of 63) for the period of 1988–1992. The other sectors did not show a loss-and-gain pattern; they either achieved gains in both markets (15 sectors) or losses (13 sectors). There was also some "negative" redirection of trade (from the West to the East), and some cases that could not be analyzed.[7]

In the clear cases where decline and growth took place in the general pattern (decline in the East and growth in the West) we distinguish between reorientation proper and "surpluses." The switch of trade can be characterized by Δx^e and Δx^w, where Δx^e is the volume change of exports to the East and Δx^w is the volume change of exports to the West. (According to our selection of sectors Δx^e is always negative and Δx^w is always positive.) We call the result of $(\Delta x^e + \Delta x^w)$ surplus, which is either negative or positive. The part of Δx^e that is matched by Δx^w is taken as reorientation proper. In fact, the whole concept of surplus and reorientation proper is analogous to the concept of inter-industry and intra-industry trade. The ratio of reorientation (with respect to the relevant sectors) is given by the familiar formula of intra-industry trade modified for our purpose:

$$1 - \frac{2\Sigma|(\Delta x^w + \Delta x^e)|}{\Sigma(\Delta x^w - \Delta x^e) + \Sigma|(\Delta x^w + \Delta x^e)|} \ . \tag{7.1}$$

The term following the minus sign represents the ratio of surplus to the sum of surplus and reorientation proper. The calculations resulted in a coefficient of 0.1893, which means that in the group of relevant sectors 19% of trade switching was reorientation proper. By looking at the two sides of trade flows separately, we may add that 28% of the losses in CMEA trade were reoriented, and 37% of the increases of exports to the West were attributable to reorientation from the East (all in the group of relevant sectors).

It is also worthwhile to look at the sectoral rate of reorientation. The sectors that were most prominent in trade reorientation in terms of *sectoral* output are the following (the percentage of 1988 sectoral output that was reoriented is in parentheses): hosiery (23%), footwear production (18%), haberdashery (18%), clothing industry (13%), and leather and fur industry (9%). The sectors that were most outstanding in trade reorientation in terms of *total* output are the following (the percentage of 1988 total output that was reoriented is in parentheses): motor vehicle manufacturing (0.20%), meat and meat products industry (0.11%), and machinery and equipment production, footwear industry, and clothing industry (0.09% each).

7.5 The Stunning Performance of Export to the West and its Reversal in 1992–1993

The striking export performance of the Hungarian economy in recent years up to the first half of 1992 induced a host of different explanations both during the upswing and especially following mid-1992 when Hungary experienced the reversal of this process. Exports to the West increased by 7%, 9%, and 20% in the years 1989, 1990, and 1991, respectively. In 1992 the growth was 1%, while in 1993 exports to the West fell by 27% (based on data for the first six months of the year).

The first group of explanations for the fast export expansion refers to institutional changes such as easier access to Western markets, deregulation of exports, and easier access to inputs for exports through the liberalization of imports. All observers accept the importance of these factors, but few attribute a substantial part of the export growth to them.

A general explanation accepted by most analysts puts the emphasis on the abrupt and significant decline in other components of the demand, namely, on domestic recession and the loss of markets in former CMEA countries.[8] Under pressure to utilize their idle capacities, Hungarian enterprises were driven to sell as much of their products in Western markets as they could. Many experts emphasized early that the spectacular export performance must have been achieved by increasing the share of the exports that did not carry profits for their producers. Moreover, a growing number of firms must have exported at a loss. Halpern (1994) finds in a sample of exporting firms making up 90% of Hungary's non-ruble exports that the average profitability of dollar exports declined from 9.8% in 1988 to 3.0% in 1991. He also shows that in 1991 already 43% of dollar exports were sold at a loss. Antalóczy (1993) and KOPINT-DATORG (1993, No. 1) arrive at similar, but even stronger, conclusions: in 1991 total industry and all major industrial sectors exported at losses.

Another explanation (see, for instance, Inotai, 1993) places the emphasis on the pull of the demand of the German economy. East Germany and West Germany combined traditionally accounted for between 16% and 17% of total Hungarian exports, which reached a spectacular 28% by 1992. Still, according to our analysis, the German mini-boom of 1988–1991 could not account directly for more than half of Hungary's export expansion to the West.

Many analyzers emphasize a specific feature of the "new exports": a very high share of these are subcontract processing for Western companies in labor-intensive industries such as clothing and footwear production. In 1991 as much as 60% of the increment of exports to the West originated in such outward processing or job work. The weak, defenseless position of Hungarian subcontractors resulted in Western partners cutting Hungarian supplies first in the course of deepening recession, causing about a $500 million loss in this single category of exports from the $10 billion total Hungarian exports within one year (see KOPINT-DATORG, 1993, No. 3).

The last column in *Table 7.5* shows trade flows as they can be forecasted on the basis of data from the first six months of 1993. As one can see, a small portion of markets in the former CMEA region is being regained. Even more important, and disappointing, is that the export successes in Western (mostly developed market) economies seem to vanish faster than they were achieved. More detailed data show an across-the-board pattern of being crowded out of Western markets, which proves that the West European recession has played a major role in the decrease in Hungarian exports. Light industries, however, show a special rapid drop of exports (responsible for half of the drop of exports in total industry), and this seems to verify the fragility of subcontract processing too.

One cannot exclude such patterns where the combination of losses in CMEA markets in 1991, the good performance in Western markets in 1992, and the collapse of Western exports in 1993 had a logical sequence at the firm level. Back in the 1980s, a group of enterprises was capable of selling products to both markets, and, in fact, did. According to the complicated system of profit equalization in that period, the group had a vested interest in putting all overhead costs on exports to the CMEA. With the switch-over and other abrupt changes, by 1991–1992 the Eastern markets either became as hard as the Western ones or simply disappeared. Now these Hungarian firms have redirected their exports to the West, but they should also cover their – proportionally even higher – overhead costs from these sales. Most of them have been unable to do so; therefore, following the redirection of exports they have been bound to cut back their Western exports.

7.6 The Effect of Price Increases of Imported Inputs

The massive terms-of-trade loss that Hungary suffered in connection with the conversion to world market prices was dramatically expressed in the price changes of imported inputs, especially of fuels and electric energy. The largest change was in 1991 when average import prices (accounted in forints) from the CMEA increased by 124.7%. Data for the five commodity groups show that energy sources experienced the greatest increase: fuels and electric energy prices increased by 165.2%, raw materials and semi-finished products by 127.3%, machinery and transport equipment by 84.3%, industrial consumer goods by 45.7%, and raw materials for the food industry and processed food products by 43.8% (*Yearbook of Economic Statistics 1991*).

Because much of the Hungarian economy used energy sources and raw materials imported from the CMEA (and primarily from the Soviet Union), the shock of the import price explosion could have had a particularly strong depressive impact. The reason that it did not have this impact is connected with the specific domestic price-setting system that had been in use in Hungary from 1980 until the liberalizations in 1989–1990. According to that system, domestic prices of fuels and raw materials were intended to be set at world market levels, and follow changes of world market prices according to a predetermined scheme. Enterprises paid world market prices for fuels and raw materials imported from the CMEA, while the difference between the cheap import price and the domestic price was collected by the state budget. *Table 7.6* gives information about energy and raw material price changes in imports and in the domestic economy in 1991–1992. From the table it can be seen that the change in the domestic sales price of energy lagged far behind the change in import prices. The reason for this is not that energy from domestic sources (48–50% of the consumption) would have been cheaper or extremely subsidized, but rather that producer prices of domestic energy were already somewhat calibrated to world market prices in 1990. Nevertheless, domestic energy prices increased by 20 percentage points more than the average of industrial prices. This reflects two factors: the earlier tuning

Table 7.6. Price indices[a] for fuels and electric energy and raw materials in Hungary, 1991–1992 (previous year = 100).

	1991	1992
Fuels and electric energy		
Prices of imports from CMEA countries	265.2	101.9
Prices of total imports	197.0	98.9
Domestic sales prices	151.0	109.6
Raw materials[b]		
Prices of imports from CMEA countries	227.3	106.2
Prices of total imports	134.1	112.5
Domestic sales prices	133.2	n.a.
Memorandum item		
Domestic prices for all industries	131.9	109.7

[a]At Hungarian forint prices. Import prices reflect the combined effect of price changes and exchange-rate changes.
[b]The category of raw materials is not completely identical in import and in domestic sales.
Sources: *Yearbook of Economic Statistics 1991, Statistical Yearbook of External Trade 1992, Statistical Pocket Book of Hungary 1992.*

of domestic prices to the world market level had not been complete; and in November 1990, envisaging the switch-over within the CMEA, Hungarian authorities increased domestic energy prices by an average of 42%–43%.

According to *Table 7.6* raw material import prices seem to have had even less impact on domestic price developments than energy import prices. Because of the limited effect of changes in import prices on domestic prices of inputs, we can reject, even on the basis of this simple analysis, the hypothesis that the output decline would have basically been supply induced, especially from the direction of input prices.

While Hungarian enterprises did not have to pay proportionally more for the higher price of imported inputs, someone had to pay the bill. The loss had to be covered by the budget in the form of net tax revenue losses. According to our *ex post* calculations, energy sources purchased by Hungary for transferable rubles in 1990 would have been equivalent to \$685 million. This calculation uses the (generally accepted as realistic) cross exchange rate between the US dollar and ruble that was valid in Hungary for foreign trade operations of enterprises. To ensure the same volume of net energy imports in 1991 as in 1990 Hungary should have spent \$1.385 billion to purchase energy. By decreasing the volume of imports by 18%, however, Hungary imported energy for only \$1.122 billion in 1991. Accordingly, the fictional and actual expenditure losses were \$700 million and \$437 million, respectively. These values fall very close to the $600 million to $700 million forecasted by KOPINT-DATORG (1990, No. 3).[9]

The impact of the switch-over on the budget had further components, such as the loss of tax revenues from other imported raw materials and the effects of taxes and subsidies related to ruble accounted exports. Altogether the effect of the switch-over made up one-third of the Ft 114 billion deficit of the 1991 budget (Antal–Riecke, 1993). This was equivalent to $500 million or 1.6% of the Hungarian GDP in 1991.

7.7 Terms-of-Trade Effects

Terms-of-trade effects reflect the combined impact of the switch-over on export and import prices, and they could eventually hit the Hungarian budget, businesses, consumers, or most probably, to some extent, all of them. Several calculations carried out in 1989 and 1990 tried to estimate these effects, particularly in Soviet–Hungarian trade.

Gács (1989) used the dollar export (and import) unit values of major Hungarian producers (customers) who exported to (or imported from) both ruble and dollar areas. Estimations were made for the dollar value of Hungary's ruble trade with the Soviet Union in 1988. According to these estimates Hungary would have suffered a terms-of-trade loss of 32% in the trade of a sample of products covering 80% of trade. The estimated loss in trade that was not balanced (the surplus of trade was Ft 15 billion, or 14%) was set between Ft 23.7 billion and Ft 61.3 billion, depending on the application of different correction schemes. These estimates corresponded to $470 million and $1,216 million at 1988 exchange rates.

Kenen (1990) used plausible price indices to analyze the effects of the shift in prices on Hungary's trade with its CMEA partners. These indices were based partly on the results of Marrese and Wittenberg (1989). For instance, fuel prices would have increased by 150%, while the prices of machinery and transport equipment would have decreased by 15%. As a consequence, taking 1989 trade volumes into account, Hungary would have experienced a terms-of-trade deterioration of 37% in trade with the CMEA area. The deterioration in the trade balance would have been $1.1 billion.

Oblath and Tarr (1992) used experts' estimates to obtain US dollar/transferable ruble price relatives for between 52% and 62% of Soviet–Hungarian trade, and calculated the expected income terms-of-trade losses on the basis of 1988 trade flows. According to their results the loss would

Table 7.7. Calculations for incomes terms-of-trade losses.

	1990		1990		1990		1990	
Calculation for 1990 volume	Exports to CMEA	Imports from CMEA	Balance	Balance	Exports to CMEA modified	Imports from CMEA modified	Balance modified	Balance modified
	Million forints	*Million forints*	*Million forints*	*Million dollars*	*Million forints*	*Million forints*	*Million forints*	*Million dollars*
At 1990 prices	190,949	184,929	6,020	95	187,891	187,891	0	0
At 1991 prices	300,554	388,859	−88,304	−1,397	295,741	395,086	−99,346	−1,572
	1991		1991					
Actual 1991 flow	Exports to CMEA	Imports from CMEA	Balance	Balance				
	Million forints	*Million forints*	*Million forints*	*Million dollars*				
At 1991 prices	149,882	203,792	−53,910	−721				

have stood between $800 million and $1,230 million, depending on how the 1988 trade surplus of Hungary could be redeemed.

Given the position that we now have the *ex post* forint price indices for Hungarian exports and imports for 1991, we recalculated the losses that were connected with the terms-of-trade changes. The result of the calculation shows that, on the basis of forint export and import price indices, Hungary suffered a 25.6% terms-of-trade loss in its trade with CMEA members from 1990 to 1991.[10]

By using the price indices and 1990 trade values for each sector we calculated how much should have been paid for imports and received for exports in 1990, if the 1991 prices used in CMEA markets had been applied to the flows (quantity) of 1990 trade. The method of Oblath and Tarr (1992) was followed. *Table 7.7* summarizes the result. Following the reasoning of Oblath and Tarr (1992), trade surpluses in 1990 could be dealt with in two ways: they are either redeemed in the future or they are lost. If it is impossible to recover them, the income terms-of-trade loss equals the trade deficit in column four in the upper block. If, however, we assume that they are fully redeemable, the deficit given in the last column of the top block of the table can be regarded as the terms-of-trade loss. To get this result, import and export vectors had to be increased and decreased, respectively, by the same proportion to obtain modified trade flows that do not produce a deficit on their original value. As the table shows, income terms-of-trade losses could have been between $1,397 million and $1,572 million had the volume of exports and imports of 1990 been repeated in 1991.

As actual data for 1991 show, forint values of both imports from and exports to the CMEA were approximately half of what they could have been had the 1990 volumes of trade been maintained. The extent of income losses envisaged were not realized in CMEA trade: part of them may have shifted to non-CMEA trade and another part could be prevented by structural adjustments or simply by the recession of the Hungarian economy.

7.8 Summary and Conclusions

Hungarian exports suffered a decline of between 7% and 8% in 1988–1992. The structural rearrangement of the exports in respect to regions, countries, sectors, and partner firms were much more substantial than this shift. There was a 60% decline in exports to former CMEA countries and a 60% increase in exports to developed market economies within four years. Among the commodity groups, machinery and transport equipment experienced the most painful shift, in fact an almost complete loss of traditional markets.

The calculation on the direct effects of market loss in the CMEA on Hungarian output shows that of the 18.2% decline registered in gross output between 1988 and 1992, 4.1% can be attributed to the fall in exports to the CMEA region. Given that in some important sectors with intensive inter-sectoral relations the losses suffered from reduced CMEA exports were between 50% and 100% of the output decline, one could expect that the total (direct and indirect) impact of export losses were responsible for a substantially higher ratio of total output decline than the direct one. The calculation carried out by the input–output inverse matrix puts the total CMEA-related output decline at 7.9% in terms of total 1988 output.

The analysis of trade-related output changes must also consider the impact of the expansion of Hungary's exports to Western markets. This increase of exports boosted output by 2.9%, if direct effects are taken into account, and by 5.6% if all (direct and indirect) impacts are calculated.

The analysis of the timing of the shock shows that 1991 was the year when most changes occurred; however the preceding period (1988–1990) also played a noticeable role in starting the process of eroding Hungary's trade relations with CMEA economies.

The analysis of reorientation using an index on the analogy of intra-industry trade brought results that are in conflict with common knowledge. The share of reorientation is not negligible – it may be responsible for as much as 19% of trade switching in the group of the relevant sectors.

The striking export performance of Hungary in the West in the period from 1989 to mid-1992 suffered a blow in late 1992 and in 1993. Exports declined by between 25% and 27% in the first half of 1993, almost eradicating the output gains that Hungary achieved through better performance in Western markets in 1988–1992. There is a host of explanations for both the success and failure of Hungarian firms regarding export. According to some explanations losses suffered in Western markets in 1993 can be the indirect consequences of the secular changes that took place in CMEA markets in 1991–1992.

The analysis of the price explosion of imported inputs shows that due to the specific system of price formation that was already in effect in the 1980s, the activity of Hungarian firms was only moderately inhibited by the growth of input prices in 1991 and 1992. Most of the cost of the price increases (about 1.6% of GDP) had to be covered by the budget.

The calculations for the terms-of-trade losses reveal a 26% terms-of-trade loss and income terms-of-trade losses between $1.400 billion and $1.600

billion. Since the level and the structure of the trade of Hungary with CMEA economies were substantially modified from 1990 to 1991, much smaller income losses must have accrued in Hungary's trade with CMEA countries than the calculations based on former trade volumes indicate.

The analyses carried out approach the issue of output decline and collapse of CMEA trade from different angles, using diverse methods. Clearly, a common framework is still missing. The input–output framework, for instance, is useful in tracing ramifications of shifts in final demand through inter-sectoral relations. In a time of turbulent changes like secular structural shifts, however, the benefits of input–output analysis are limited. In addition, tackling different components of final demand as exogenous and not interrelated prevents the analyst from taking into account, for instance, the impact of output decline on employment, consumption, and the ensuing further decline of output.[11]

While the lack of a comprehensive framework prevents a strong final conclusion from being drawn based on the result of the analysis, it is hoped that the partial conclusions, all supporting the importance of demand factors, help to clarify the real role of trade rearrangements in the development of output in Eastern Europe.

Notes

[1] Compare, for instance, the activities of a reform committee (of which I was a member) led by Rezső Nyers and of the KOPINT-DATORG Institute in 1988 and 1989 (see Köves, 1992, p. 75).

[2] These were mostly subsidies or other benefits attached to incremental exports.

[3] The reason is that industrial output data, as well as export and import data, are all gross concepts, and in addition the input–output tables that make use of gross output provide an acceptable base, as well as quantifiable data, for multiplier analysis.

[4] The choice of 1988 as the base year for the calculation was partly technical (detailed sectoral trade data for 1989 were not available) and partly substantive: Hungary's withdrawal from CMEA (and mostly Soviet) markets started earlier than 1991, the year of the change in and demise of the CMEA. In fact, the calculations for subperiods given in Section 7.3 reinforce our assumption that the usual focus on the year 1991 is misleading.

[5] See Central Statistical Office (1993). The more detailed tables were made available on diskette by the Department of Economic Models and Analyses of the Central Statistical Office of Hungary. I use this opportunity to thank them for their assistance.

[6] The changes in relative prices within the economy after 1989 and the ensuing restructuring in production and use of inputs were bound to be relatively

moderate in Hungary as compared with other East European economies, given the specific Hungarian system of price formation of the 1980s that had built substantially on the use of world market prices. The easier access to the world market in the late 1980s and the start of trade liberalization proper in 1989 meant much more for household consumption and less for the structure of production. Hence, there was no expectation for a very large impact on the input–output coefficients.

[7] Notably, zero export in the base period.

[8] Few analysts, however, change the direction of causality the way Bofinger (1993) does when questioning whether the loss of markets in the East was really an exogenous source of recent trade reorientation in transition economies or whether it was the consequence of more successful attempts at achieving better positions in the West.

[9] The forecast of KOPINT-DATORG was based on the calculations of Gábor Oblath.

[10] Statistical sources do not indicate whether the respective price indices refer to earlier ruble trade flows only or to all the trade flows carried out in 1990 and 1991. We assume the latter as most probable.

[11] Closing the model from the point of view of the household sector does not seem to resolve this problem.

Appendix: Statistical Data

Most of the data for sectoral trade (in value terms) have been taken from the data base of KOPINT–DATORG, Budapest. Because of a new classification of industries that was put into use in Hungary in 1992, some minor distortions may have occurred when sectors of the new classification were reclassified into the old ones. Throughout the paper the old classification was used.

In Hungary the collection and recording of foreign trade data were reorganized substantially in 1991. The two main changes were the following: (1) instead of direct reporting about transactions by foreign trading enterprises, data have been collected through customs declaration since 1991; (2) instead of recording direct trade until 1990, Hungarian authorities have recorded special trade since 1991. The first change has caused problems for a growing share of trade not covered by statistics, especially in 1991. The latest statistics attempt to compensate for this backlog. The second change has caused problems with trade flows connected with the import of products to be processed in Hungary with the aim of re-export (subcontract processing or job work). Earlier, these transactions were recorded at their net value, but since 1991 they have been taken into account at their total value. We could not correct the distortions that emerged from the above-mentioned rearrangements of foreign trade statistics. This applies also to taking into account the trade with East Germany in CMEA trade until 1990 and with non-CMEA trade since 1991.

Further foreign trade and other data come from the *Yearbook of Foreign Trade Statistics* (1989, 1990), Report on Foreign Trade Turnover January–December, Ministry of Trade (Ministry of Foreign Economic Relations, 1989, 1990, 1991, 1992), the *Annual Statistical Yearbook of Hungary* (1988, 1989, 1990, 1991), *Yearbook of Economic Statistics* (1990, 1991), the Hungarian National Bank's *Annual Report* (1990, 1992), *Statistical Pocket Book of Hungary* (1990, 1991, 1992), *Monthly Statistical Bulletin* (1993, No. 1), and *Price, Market, Competition* (various issues in 1990–1992).

In some cases the coherence of data could not be fully ensured. For instance, for the years 1989–1990 sectoral trade price indices of ruble and non-ruble trade were used, instead of (unavailable) indices for CMEA and non-CMEA trade. In some cases, because of inadequate data, indices for trade with socialist countries, trade with "European countries in transition" and trade with former CMEA countries had to be taken as equivalent.

Price indices were rarely available for all 63 industries, but they were regularly attainable for 10 industry groups. Therefore, the same price indices were applied to the industries within the 10 groups. In this respect, the poorest year is 1992: export price indices for only 5 groups of sectors were available, and they had to be used for 63 industries.

Volume indices for the gross output of agriculture and forestry, as well as the whole economy, were not available, so in these cases the respective GDP indices were used to fill the gap.

All initial values used for index calculations are in current forints. Price indices in trade refer to Hungarian forint prices and accordingly incorporate the changes in the exchange rate of the forint. As a consequence, volume changes are deflated from both export prices and exchange rate variations.

References

Antal, L., and Riecke, W., 1993, Hungary: Sound money, fiscal problems, in R. Portes, ed., *Economic Transformation in Central Europe: A Progress Report*, Centre for Economic Policy Research and European Communities, London and Luxembourg.

Antalóczy, K., 1993, Export efficiency in the period of transition, *Európa Fórum*, **3** [in Hungarian].

Berg, A., and Sachs, J., 1992, Structural adjustment and international trade in Eastern Europe: The case of Poland, *Economic Policy*, **14** April.

Bofinger, P., 1993, *The Output Decline in Central and Eastern Europe: A Classical Explanation,* Discussion Paper No. 786, Centre for Economic Policy Research, London, UK.

Bruno, M., 1993, Stabilization and reform in Eastern Europe: Preliminary evaluation, in M. Blejer *et al.* eds., *Eastern Europe in Transition: From Recession to Growth?*, Discussion Paper No. 196, World Bank, Washington, DC, USA.

Central Statistical Office, 1993, *The Mathematical Elaboration of Input–Output Tables, 1990*, Central Statistical Office, Budapest, Hungary.

Gács, J., 1989, *Calculation about the Changes Following the Introduction of Convertible Currency Settlements in Trade Between Hungary and the Soviet Union*,

KOPINT-DATORG Institute for Economic and Market Research and Informatics, Budapest, Hungary [in Hungarian].

Halpern, L., 1994, Factors and effects of trade reorientation in Hungary, in J. Gács, and G. Winckler, eds., *International Trade and Restructuring in Eastern Europe*, Physica-Verlag, Heidelberg, Germany.

Inotai, A., 1993, The European Communities and Central and Eastern Europe: A Critical Assessment of the Association Agreements in Strategic Perspective, Paper prepared for the Conference on Europe: What Next?, Vienna, Austria.

Kenen, P.B., 1990, Transitional Arrangements for Trade and Payments Among the CMEA Countries, Working Paper WP/90/79, International Monetary Fund, Washington, DC, USA.

KOPINT-DATORG (various issues), 1990–1993, *Report on Business Tendencies: The Position and Prospects of the World Economy and Hungary*, KOPINT-DATORG Institute for Economic and Market Research and Informatics, Budapest, Hungary [in Hungarian].

Köves, A., 1992, *Central and East European Economies in Transition: The International Dimension*, Westview Press, Boulder, CO, USA.

Marrese, M., and Wittenberg, L., 1989, Implicit Trade Subsidies Within the CMEA: A Hungarian Perspective, Northwestern University, Evanston, IL, USA [manuscript].

Oblath, G., 1992, External debt accumulation and the macroeconomic problems of debt management in Hungary, *Közgazdasági Szemle* (Economic Review), **7–8** and **9** [in Hungarian].

Oblath, G., and Tarr, D., 1992, The terms-of-trade effects of the elimination of state trading in Soviet Hungarian trade, *Journal of Comparative Economics*, **16**(1) March.

Richter, S., 1988, Some Thoughts on the Introduction of Convertible Currency Settlements in Hungary's Trade with CMEA Economies, Budapest, Hungary [in Hungarian, mimeo].

Rodrik, D., 1991, Foreign Trade in Eastern Europe's Transition: Early Results [mimeo].

Szamuely, L., ed., 1989, *Opening to the World Economy: Turn in the Economic Policy and the Reform of the Institutional Setup*, Summary publication of a reform committee led by Rezső Nyers, Közgazdasági és Jogi Könyvkiadó, Budapest, Hungary [in Hungarian].

Comments on the Papers by Dariusz Rosati and János Gács

Gábor Oblath

The papers by Dariusz Rosati and János Gács are very valuable contributions to the literature dealing with the implications of the demise of the CMEA (and the collapse of intra-regional trade) on the former member countries; their findings represent significant progress in this field of research. Therefore, I first briefly refer to the mainstream of this literature, and indicate where I see the importance of their contributions.

Two conflicting views prevail on this subject. According to one, the trade decline within the region is the main reason for the output decline in Eastern Europe. The other view maintains that the trade decline is not the cause, but the reflection (or the consequence) of the "transformational recession" in these countries.[1] Proponents of the latter view consider the collapse of intra-regional trade as "endogenous," i.e., the inevitable by-product of transformation. Naturally, the two views have rather different implications both regarding the interpretation of the recession that has hit these countries and in terms of policy prescriptions. However, neither interpretation is based on solid grounds. They rely on implicit and untested theories regarding the actual developments and/or on questionable assumptions and an analytical framework of the causes and consequences of the trade collapse. Moreover, both lack the necessary empirical underpinning. Therefore, the papers by Rosati and Gács are most welcome. They approach the topic without prejudices and, being aware of the complexity of the problems involved, with appealing intellectual modesty. Rather than try to prove some pre-established points, they raise several relevant questions concerning the reasons for and implications of the trade decline among the former CMEA countries. They clearly present the assumptions and the framework underlying their analyses, and attempt to answer the questions by relying on the available statistical data and other empirical information. They also indicate the limits of their analyses and findings.

Thus, both studies are empirically oriented, and try to make use of the available statistics. Rosati, however, is in a more difficult situation. While Gács focuses on one country, Hungary (for which both the availability and the quality of the statistics are generally better than for several other countries in transition), Rosati covers a group of countries (for many of which the necessary data are unavailable). Therefore, to be able to handle certain problems, in some cases he has had to use proxies. These may involve difficulties and raise questions; I shall return to some of these. However, I would like to stress that I find the papers correct and, keeping in mind the limitations of the data, their results convincing.[2]

Both studies find that the fall of the trade among former CMEA countries is to some extent responsible for the output decline in the countries concerned, albeit to a smaller degree than commonly believed. Since Gács considers the relation of exports to gross industrial output, while Rosati that between exports and GDP, their results are not directly comparable. However, the finding that the trade collapse did have a negative effect on the output in these countries, but that this factor cannot account for the total output fall is certainly reassuring: this is what one would intuitively expect.

The results for the income loss due to the deterioration of the terms of trade, calculated by both authors for Hungary, are, again, not directly comparable (Gács examines the terms-of-trade effect in the trade with "transition and nonmarket economies," while Rosati focuses on trade with the Soviet Union), but the similar magnitudes support Rosati's assumption of no terms-of-trade change in the non-Soviet component of Eastern trade. On the other hand, the large difference between Hungary and Poland in the calculated income loss is a clear indication that the results depend rather strongly on the incidental developments in the base period. The main reason why the income loss appears to be relatively small for Poland is that in the base period Poland had an extremely large trade surplus with respect to the Soviet Union (which surplus is implicitly considered by Rosati to have had no value). Poland, therefore, had a huge "buffer" to absorb the terms-of-trade loss, at least in the statistical sense. Still, the actual relevance of the measured "loss of income," which appears to be relatively small in the case of Poland and rather large in Hungary, is not altogether clear.

As Gács notes, it would be most useful to have an analytical framework that links the question of income loss and output loss, related to both price *and* volume changes, in trade among transition economies. Evidently, it was not simply the deterioration of the terms of trade, but also the decline in the volume of exports to the Soviet Union that had a negative effect on the level of *income* in Eastern Europe. Furthermore, the decline in the terms of trade, even if it had resulted in a loss of income, would not necessarily have caused a fall in *output*, had the demand for imports from Eastern Europe increased in the Soviet Union.[3] Both authors review the two issues – the income loss and the output decline – in separate sections; they do not attempt to discuss the potential and actual links between the two.

As I have no disagreement with the analysis and results presented by Gács, I turn to a few points related to Rosati's paper. A particularly interesting part of his analysis is devoted to the identification of factors that contributed to the fall of East European exports to the Soviet Union. This exercise is illuminating, the more so since he makes an attempt to quantify the impact of three different factors: domestic recession in the Soviet Union and trade reduction and trade diversion due to the dissolution of the CMEA. While, *within* the analytical framework applied, I find the methodology correct and the results convincing, I have some doubts about the actual (empirical) relevance of the three broad factors singled out by the author. For instance, in my view, a major reason for the sharp decline in Soviet imports from Eastern Europe is related to the fact that the Soviet authorities missed the opportunity to change the domestic regulation of their imports from the former CMEA countries so that it would have been in line with the change in the external framework of trade (e.g., former Soviet importers of East European products did not receive significant additional allocation of hard currency after the switch to hard-currency trade). This certainly led to trade reduction and trade diversion; it is also related to the dissolution of the CMEA. But the immediate cause of the decline in trade probably lies in the breakdown of government control in the Soviet economy, the inefficiencies of the system as well as in the foreign exchange shortage. How should one classify this factor: as one that is related to domestic (i.e., internal Soviet) reasons or to the dissolution of the CMEA? My answer would be that this is not the proper question, because it is related to both. Thus, when looking at some of the actual and direct causes of the trade collapse, it may turn out to be rather difficult to classify them into the broad categories proposed by Rosati.

When evaluating the impact of the decline in exports to the Soviet Union on the GDP of East European countries, Rosati uses the average of the official exchange rates and purchasing power parities (PPP) to convert national GDPs to dollars. His method is supported by the argument that the conversion at the official exchange rate understates the level of the GDP in the East European countries. This may well be the case; however, the method applied does not seem to solve the actual problem, which is the lack of foreign trade volume indices for most of the countries. The method applied in the paper is equivalent to using the average of the PPP and the official exchange rate, rather than the official exchange rate, for converting the change in the dollar value of exports into national currency in order to determine the impact of the export decline on the GDP (in national currency units). If put this way, it should become clear that the methodology applied does not offer a real solution to the problem of inadequate information on volume changes. To be sure, Rosati himself calls attention to the limitations of the methodology he was forced to apply. These remarks are meant to express my agreement: the limitations are indeed serious.

To sum up, the studies by Rosati and Gács are both instructive and represent significant progress in this field of research. However, I can only agree with János Gács that further work is necessary for integrating the various components of the research on the effects of the dissolution of the CMEA into a coherent analytical framework. Given the proposals, formulated both within and outside of the region, for re-establishing some kind of a regional framework for trade and economic cooperation, it should be very useful to clearly understand the reasons for and effects of the sharp decline in intra-regional trade in the early 1990s.

Notes

[1] For the first see Rodrik (1993); for the second, Brada (1993) and Kornai (1993). There is an interesting third interpretation, not directly related to the association between the trade and output decline. According to Bofinger (1993), as cited in the paper by Gács, the reason for the trade decline among East European countries is the reorientation of former intra-regional trade toward the West.

[2] It is worth mentioning that the importance of Rosati's paper is not only in the empirical findings, but also in the attempt to construct an empirically *relevant* analytical framework for handling the questions related to the effects of the trade decline among East European countries. While doing so, the author corrects and clarifies several confusions, empirical and conceptual misunderstandings on this issue, that have their origins in Rodrik's influential study (see Rodrik, 1993).

[3] This may have happened if the switch to world market prices had been combined with the adoption of some transitory clearing arrangement among the former CMEA countries. In this case the Soviet Union could have captured the gains from the improvement of its terms of trade in the form of a larger volume of imports from Eastern Europe. Eastern Europe would have suffered the same income loss as it actually did, but it wouldn't have experienced the output loss deriving from the collapse of exports to the Soviet Union. True, had this been the case, the "degree of reorientation," calculated by Gács, is likely to have been much lower.

References

Bofinger, P., 1993, *The Output Decline in Central and Eastern Europe: A Classical Explanation*, Centre for Economic Policy Research Discussion Paper, No. 786, London, UK.

Brada, J., 1993, Regional integration in Eastern Europe: Prospects for integration within the region and with the European Community, in J. De Melo and Arvind Panagariya, eds., *New Dimensions in Regional Integration*, Cambridge University Press, Cambridge, UK.

Kornai, J., 1993, *Transformational Recession: A General Phenomenon Examined Through the Example of Hungary's Development*, Collegium Budapest Discussion Papers, No. 1, Budapest, Hungary.

Rodrik, D., 1993, Making sense of the Soviet trade shock in Eastern Europe: A framework and some estimates, in M. Blejer, *et al.*, eds., *Eastern Europe in Transition: From Recession to Growth?*, Discussion Paper, No. 196, World Bank, Washington DC, USA.

Comments on the Papers by Dariusz Rosati and János Gács

Daniel Gros

These two papers deal with an important topic because there are few papers on the causes of output decline that do not mention the CMEA shock as one cause. The objective of these papers is to give us a numerical estimate of the importance of the demise of the CMEA.

The paper by Dariusz Rosati appears at first to be a careful attempt in this direction. Even before reading it, one is prepared to accept some inconsistencies in the data and some heroic assumptions. This is the price one has to pay for looking at the real world. I followed his paper in this spirit, trusting him to make the appropriate assumptions about old border prices, new border prices, commercial exchange rates, and so on.

However, my curiosity increased considerably when he mentions, rather *en passant*, that there are important discrepancies between Soviet data (on imports from Central Europe) and the corresponding export data from Poland and other sources. He acknowledges that the use of the Soviet data "may seriously overestimate" the decline in exports, but he proceeds nevertheless to use *only* this source. I do not understand why he does this. Since for me all Soviet statistics are inherently suspect[1] I turned to a classic Western source, namely, the Direction of Trade Statistics (DOT) of the IMF. When I did this the results changed so radically that I came to the conclusion that Rosati's results are as much as 90% an artifact of Soviet data. The data for the Polish case are summarized in the top panel of *Table C.1*; DOT data on USSR imports differ by only about 10% from Polish export data, which in turn are exactly equal to the Polish data Rosati gives (not surprising, since it must be same source). There is no reason not to believe the Polish data, which were recorded in zlotys, since that currency was already convertible at a market exchange rate in 1990. This implies that there is no reason to mistrust the Polish (or DOT) data in this case. However, both the USSR figures (as reported by DOT) and the Polish figures give a fall in Polish export to the USSR between 1990 and 1991 of only $400 million, whereas Rosati gives a decline of $5,320 million (*Table 6.7*) more than *twice* the level of 1990, which was about $2,000 million according to DOT. Since my priors are 10:1 that the Soviet data cannot be trusted I have come to the conclusion that the Polish exports to the USSR declined by about 25%, more or less in line with USSR activity. Moreover, total Polish exports actually increased in dollar terms between 1990 and 1991; the negative impact of the CMEA was thus offset by a positive shock to exports to the West (presumably most of it due to the German boom).

These observations show that one cannot draw conclusions from data that have been manipulated by various price indices and artificial exchange rates and assembled in a country on the brink of its own dissolution. The fall back position I recommend is to look at quantitites of the goods actual shipped (the number of machines, T-shirts, etc.); this should provide a rough cross-check of the DOT basis. Of course, this procedure also has the problem of how to aggregate across sectors.

Table C.1. Comparative trade data for Poland and Hungary in million US dollars.

POLAND				
	USSR imports from Poland	Polish exports to USSR	Polish exports total	Export drop from 1990 to 1991 as reported by Rosati
1989	3,094	2,813	13,533	
1990	2,289	2,081	13,627	
				5,320
1991	1,801	1,637	14,913	
1992	1,981	1,801	14,046	
HUNGARY				
	USSR imports from Hungary	Hungarian exports to USSR	Hungarian exports total	Export drop from 1990 to 1991 as reported by Rosati
1989	2,660	2,418	10,067	
1990	2,129	1,936	9,552	
				2,756
1991	1,320	1,200	10,183	
1992	1,545	1,404	10,705	

Source: Author's calculations based on *Direction of Trade Statistics Yearbook 1993*, IMF, Washington, DC, USA.

However, if the fall in production is roughly similar, this problem will not be too severe.

This brings me to the paper by János Gács on Hungary. His approach has the great advantage that it does not rely on dubious Soviet data. His results are also much easier to accept if one does a crude cross-check (see bottom panel of *Table C.1*): DOT reports imports of the USSR of $2,130 million in 1990 which fell by about $800 million to $1,320 million in 1991. This is about 2.7% of the GDP of Hungary at market exchange rates. Gács reports 4%, which is not too far off. Of course, if one were to apply the reasoning of Rosati that Hungary's exports should have declined anyway by about 30% because of the disorder in the USSR, a decline of $600 million would have been normal and the CMEA effect would be only $200 million, approximately 0.7% of the GDP of Hungary!

The paper by Gács attributes all actual changes in trade to the CMEA dissolution and thus does not follow the point made by Rosati that a significant reduction in trade was to be expected because of the decline of the USSR economy, but at least it brings out the output decline you can attribute to the actual changes in the quantity of exports which is found to be 8% of GDP. Since Rosati suggests that only half of the actual fall in exports to the USSR is a CMEA effect the total effect found by Gács should be halved from 8% to 4% of GDP. If you "subtract" from this the "Western" export shock, the "net" effect of the trade shock (East and West) must be minor.

Moreover there is "a dog that did not bark," namely, the fact that intra-Central European trade also declined, and much more than trade with the USSR. Why? One answer is that the old CMEA trade rules forced more "uneconomic" trade among the smaller Central European countries than with the USSR. But there is no reason why this should have been so. This subject was not addressed in either paper.

In a fundamental sense the dissolution of CMEA should be viewed just as the international aspect of liberalization in general. Under the old regime firms had to make deliveries according to plan regardless of profitability. Under the new market conditions some (perhaps many) of the old trade flows will disappear. However, new opportunities will also arise, and if firms could adjust instanteously there is no *a priori* reason to believe that output should decline. If one takes this broad view and, if one views overall external trade as one sector of the economy, adjustment has been remarkably quick in the sense that the *overall* export volume did not contract at all in Poland and by less than the GDP decline in other countries. Since some reduction in CMEA trade was unavoidable anyway because of the decline of activity in the USSR, as argued by Rosati, one is led to the conclusion that the dissolution of the CMEA cannot be considered a major cause of the output decline in Central Europe. The sharp economic decline of the former USSR was probably more important than the fact that the old CMEA regime was discontinued.

Note

[1] Moreover, I have been told that, in particular, 1991, the crucial year for Rosati, is a "black hole" in all Soviet statistics.

Chapter 8

Inter-enterprise Arrears in Economies in Transition

Guillermo A. Calvo and Fabrizio Coricelli

Most stabilization programs in previously centrally planned economies (PCPEs) have relied on a sharp tightening of credit policy. In addition to – or even more important than – the objective of curbing inflation typical of stabilization programs in market economies, the tightening of credit in PCPEs was meant to foster the restructuring of the economy, by forcing firms to adopt efficient methods of production and by filtering out of the system nonviable firms. In short, tight credit was a crucial instrument for imposing hard budget constraints. In previous works (Calvo and Coricelli, 1992, 1993) we have advanced the view that in the context of underdeveloped credit markets, with segmented financial circuits of households and firms, the contraction of bank credit likely played a significant role in the output collapse which accompanied the initial stages of most stabilization programs in PCPEs. However, it is often heard that even if tight credit partly contributed to the initial output decline it was nevertheless a key instrument for inducing a more efficient allocation of resources across firms and sectors. In this paper we raise doubts on the possibility of achieving such an efficient allocation in the context of underdeveloped financial markets. We focus on inter-enterprise credit, which effectively illustrates how a liquidity squeeze might be a major obstacle for an efficient selection of *bad* and *good* firms.

We provide evidence that inter-enterprise credit has developed mainly as a chain of arrears, which has linked good and bad firms. This network of arrears has perhaps softened the initial negative output effect of the credit

R. Holzmann et al. (eds.), Output Decline in Eastern Europe, 193-212.

crunch. However, in countries like Romania and Russia inter-enterprise arrears have become a major impediment for the recovery of the economy and, in fact, a stumbling block in the reform process.

According to some observers (for instance, Rostowski, 1993), arrears are simply a manifestation of continuing soft budget constraints, and thus they result from lax, rather than tight, credit policy. If governments could just credibly hold credit tight, arrears would cure themselves. An implication of this view is that arrears are mainly a channel for financing *bad*, nonviable firms, which are indeed kept alive by other firms upon expectation of a government bailout. Thus, we should expect to find a positive correlation between arrears and nonviable, loss-making firms, and, moreover, arrears should reflect large net debt positions.

The evidence presented in this paper does not support this view. Of course, the empirical evidence is still partial and incomplete, and thus inadequate for a robust test of different views. Nevertheless, the available evidence seems to support an alternative view, in which arrears are a systemic phenomenon, a sort of equilibrium response of the system to an initial liquidity crunch. Accordingly, in the context of the underdeveloped financial market characterizing PCPEs, a sharp contraction in enterprise liquidity may lead firms to settle on an equilibrium in which enterprise transactions become largely demonetized, with arrears becoming a norm, *ex post* tolerated by the system. This form of involuntary credit could be assimilated to stealing, and thus it is likely to have high social costs.

It is worth stressing at the outset that the implication of the paper is not that credit policy should be lax in PCPEs. More simply, the paper warns about the risks of an excessive contraction of liquidity at the beginning of stabilization programs in PCPEs. The paper emphasizes the trade-off between the attempt to enforce financial discipline and the need to provide sufficient liquidity for enterprises to operate. In fact, an excessive liquidity squeeze could throw the economy into a persistent state of low economic activity. After all, it was Adam Smith who argued that money is a fundamental instrument for fostering deeper division of labor and specialization in production and trade, key factors in the development of market economies. Lack of liquidity, indeed, is likely to consolidate the existing pattern of production and exchanges among enterprises.

The paper is organized as follows. Section 8.1 reviews some basic trends in inter-enterprise arrears and credit in several PCPEs, and it emphasizes the heterogeneity of country experiences. Section 8.2 outlines a simple framework of equilibrium with arrears, which shows the possibility of multiple equilibria with different levels of arrears and output. Section 8.3 contains a more detailed analysis based on the experience of Romania, for which we have a rich data set on enterprises. Section 8.4 contains some concluding remarks.

8.1 Some Basic Facts

As illustrated in Calvo and Coricelli (1993), all stabilization programs in PCPEs – with the exception of Hungary in 1990 – implied a sharp fall in the effective supply of bank credit. The fact that at the outset of stabilization programs inter-enterprise arrears invariably increased in relation to bank credit (*Table 8.1*) may be interpreted as an indication of the tightening of bank credit. Indeed, if the drop in real bank credit simply reflected the drop in output – caused by exogenous forces – one would have expected inter-enterprise credit to fall proportionally with respect to bank credit.

An interesting question is why the problem of inter-enterprise credit was neglected in designing stabilization programs in most PCPEs. The exception is the former Yugoslavia in 1990, where payment arrears beyond one month were supposed to trigger bankruptcy procedures. Arrears, however, were not a new phenomenon in several other PCPEs. Arrears grew sharply in Poland in 1989 (Calvo and Coricelli, 1992), compensating the decline in bank credit. Hungary experienced the same phenomenon in the 1980s, and even back in the 1970s. Although we can only speculate on this, most likely the problem of inter-enterprise credit was neglected in designing stabilization programs in PCPEs because of the perception that in the old regime inter-enterprise credit was simply a manifestation of soft budget constraints, and thus it would have disappeared in the new regime.

Figure 8.1 indicates that this may not have been the case. However, the country experiences were highly heterogeneous. This heterogeneity cannot be simply explained by different magnitudes of the initial contraction in bank credit.

In particular, after the launching of stabilization programs inter-enterprise arrears exploded in some countries, such as Romania and Russia, but not in other PCPEs, such as Poland and Hungary. Moreover, in both Romania and Russia the explosion of arrears was accompanied by a generalized bailout operation. Countries that experienced an explosion of arrears also experienced high and persistent inflation. The experience of the CSFR is atypical, as arrears grew rapidly despite a stable macroeconomic environment.

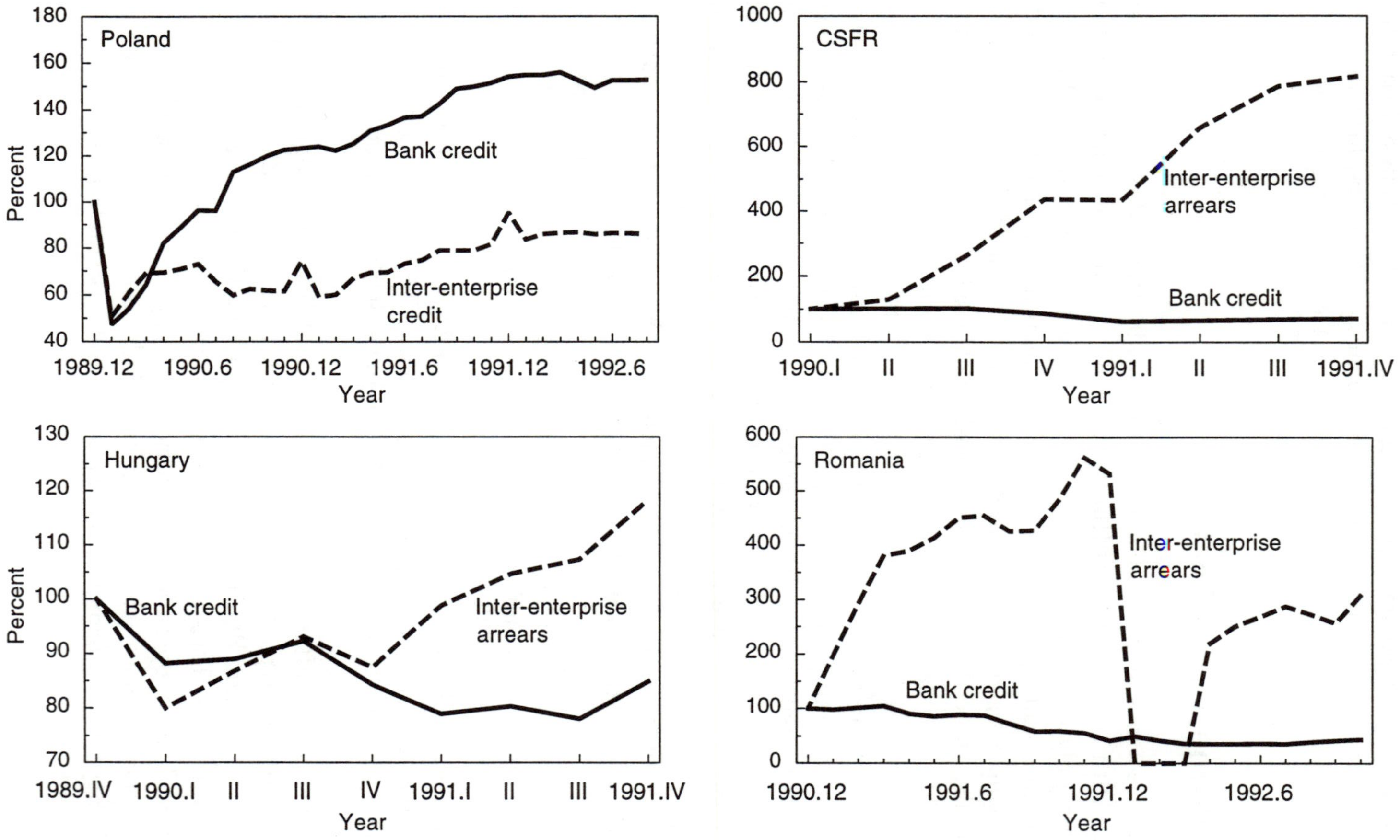

Figure 8.1. The development of bank credits and inter-enterprise arrears/credits, deflated by producer price indices; starting date figure = 100. Sources: Authors' calculations from central bank data for the CSFR, Poland, and Romania. For Hungary data were provided by István Ábel.

Table 8.1. Ratio of inter-enterprise arrears to bank credit.

	Poland[a]	Romania	Hungary	CSFR	Russia
1989. IV	1.6	n.a.	0.2	0.0	n.a.
1990. I	1.7	n.a.	0.1	0.0	n.a.
1990. II	1.2	n.a.	0.2	0.0	n.a.
1990. III	0.9	n.a.	0.2	0.1	n.a.
1990. IV	1.0	0.1	0.2	0.1	n.a.
1991. I	0.9	0.5	0.2	0.1	n.a.
1991. II	0.9	0.7	0.2	0.2	n.a.
1991. III	0.8	1.1	0.2	0.2	n.a.
1991. IV	1.0	1.9	0.2	0.2	0.0
1992. I	0.9	0.0[b]	n.a.	n.a.	0.9
1992. II	0.9	1.1	n.a.	n.a.	2.3
1992. III	n.a.	0.9	n.a.	n.a.	0.8[c]

[a]For Poland, the figures refer to inter-enterprise credit, while for the other countries the figures refer only to arrears, i.e., overdue credit.
[b]At the beginning of the year arrears were cleared through the Global Compensation Scheme.
[c]The figure is only for July. In July bank credit was injected into the system to clear the arrears.
Sources: Authors' calculations from central bank data for the CSFR, Poland, and Romania. For Hungary data were provided by István Ábel. For Russia data taken from *Russian Economic Trends*, various issues.

Important differences across countries relate not only to the magnitude of arrears, but also to their institutional characteristics. In Hungary and Poland, as in the former Yugoslavia, there was a system of trade credit even in the pre-reform period. Payment contracts were generally honored. Arrears were just the overdue proportion – estimated at about 30%, for instance, in Hungary – of this trade credit.[1]

By contrast, in Romania and Russia, a system of trade credit has not been developed. Arrears are the main, albeit special, form of involuntary trade credit. This difference points to the importance of institutional aspects concerning the development of private credit markets. While a failure in most aspects, the experience of partial reforms carried out in Hungary and Poland before 1990 may have proved important in laying down the basic structure of market institutions.

Another feature of inter-enterprise arrears is worth emphasizing. A large proportion of arrears is indeed associated with firms which have roughly similar payable and receivable arrears. In both the CSFR and Romania – the only countries for which information is available – net arrears account for only 30% of gross arrears (Hrnčíř, 1993, and authors' calculations on Ministry of Finance data for Romania). Thus, a large proportion of arrears do not imply any net transfer of liquidity among firms. It is worth noting that in the CSFR at the outset of reforms the ratio of net to gross arrears was much higher, in fact close to one in 1990. Over time the ratio declined, suggesting that a chain of arrears grew after reforms. In fact, while gross arrears registered a fivefold increase from 1990 to March 1992, net arrears increased by only 70%, a figure not far from the increase in prices. Therefore, the sharp real increase in gross arrears took place with practically no increase in real net debt positions of firms.

Finally, the comparison between the behavior of state and private firms in relation to the inter-enterprise credit market would shed some light on the role of microeconomic incentives. We have data only for Poland, which nevertheless point to the clearly different role played by inter-enterprise credit in the two types of firms. In particular, in 1992 the ratio of payables to sales in private firms was only one-third of that for state firms, 2.8% compared with 10% (data provided by GUS, the Central Statistical Office).

This brief overview raises three main sets of issues which any explanation of inter-enterprise credit in PCPEs should tackle. First, the experience shows a high degree of heterogeneity across countries. Thus, there are different possible outcomes of an initial credit squeeze, as arrears exploded only in Romania and Russia, but not in other countries. Second, one should be able to explain why a network of arrears can persist in a context of decentralized decisions by firms. Finally, one should be able to account for the fact that the network of arrears is highly "circular," with firms having similar amounts of arrears on both sides of their balance sheet. The next section tries to address these issues, sketching a simple analytical framework to analyze arrears.

8.2 A Simple Framework

Despite a superficial resemblance with trade credit – a fundamental form of credit in market economies – inter-enterprise arrears are a peculiar form of credit as they are involuntary. Inter-enterprise arrears occupy the place that stealing and shirking take in market economies. As a result, there are macroeconomic costs associated with them. It has been noted that this form of generalized debt contract failure (Hrnčíř, 1993) interferes with the proper functioning of markets, distorts signals, and delays restructuring. Even if they are a form of stealing, inter-enterprise arrears are nevertheless a source of financing of input purchases. By falling into arrears firms can economize in the use of money in their transactions. The link between inter-enterprise arrears and enterprise liquidity provides the channel through which credit and monetary policies affect arrears. To account for this channel, the model embeds inter-enterprise arrears in a model of liquidity-constrained firms. Having developed this model elsewhere (see Calvo and Coricelli, 1992, 1993), here we simply sketch the main behavioral rules and the equilibria of the model.

Consider a small open economy trading in both inputs and output at given world prices, which for convenience are set equal to one. Define x as real inputs and m as real monetary balances, both in terms of foreign exchange. Let us first outline the model in the absence of arrears. Firms face a liquidity-in-advance constraint. The exchange rate is fixed throughout. Their purchases of inputs at the beginning of the period require availability of cash, thus

$$x_t \leq m_t \ . \tag{8.1}$$

Assuming that wages (ω) are paid in cash, firms can accumulate cash over time through the accumulation of profits, according to the following expression

$$m_{t+1} - m_t = f(x_t) - x_t - \omega_t \ , \tag{8.2}$$

In equilibrium, the constraint (8.1) will hold as an equality and thus (8.2) becomes

$$m_{t+1} = f(m_t) - \omega_t \ . \tag{8.2'}$$

To account for the fact that the formal owner of firms (the state) has been largely an absent player, and thus firms have been controlled by the insiders, we assume that firms maximize the welfare of their workers, with r being the world interest rate, assumed constant for simplicity. Firms choose the path of labor income which maximizes the present discounted value of labor income, i.e.,

$$\sum_{t=0}^{\infty} \omega_t \left(\frac{1}{1+r}\right)^t \tag{8.3}$$

subject to (8.1), (8.2'), and the initial stock of liquidity m_0.[2] It can be noted from (8.3) and (8.2') that workers' utility depends only on the sequence of m_t. Assuming existence of a steady state, the optimal stationary level of real monetary balances m^* satisfies the following condition:

$$f'(m^*) = 1 + r \ . \tag{8.4}$$

The economic intuition behind (8.4) is straightforward, once it is recognized that r is the marginal return on money left in the hands of the workers and not invested in productive inputs, while $f'(m^*)$ is the marginal product of money used to purchase inputs (see Calvo and Coricelli, 1992, for a formal derivation and discussion). If an initial liquidity squeeze pushes real monetary balances below m^*, workers have an incentive in accumulating real monetary balances toward m^*. To this end they will set wages to the minimum acceptable level.[3] Thus, although an initial liquidity crunch may push the economy below its long-run output level, over time that level is recovered through the optimal adjustment of firms.[4]

The presence of arrears modifies significantly the above model. First, arrears "loosen" the liquidity-in-advance constraint (8.1). With positive arrears, (8.1) is replaced by

$$x_t \geq m_t \ , \tag{8.5}$$

which indicates that firms pay only a proportion of their purchases in cash. Let θ indicate such a proportion, which will be determined in equilibrium. Taking the extreme case in which arrears are expected never to be paid back, the competitive nominal price of inputs and outputs (recall that inputs and outputs are fully tradable and their foreign currency price is unity while, in the simplest model, the exchange rate is set equal to unity) must be $1/\theta$.

To put a natural break on arrears, we assume that arrears are costly, and that the present discounted value of the cost of additional arrears is proportional to the latter, where the factor of proportionality is denoted by $\kappa > 1$. Hence, focusing exclusively on firms that sell to other firms, the cash accumulation equation (8.2) in terms of foreign exchange now becomes[5]

$$\frac{\theta_t}{\theta_{t+1}} m_{t+1} = f(x_t)\theta_t - \kappa(x_t - m_t) - \omega_t\theta_t \ , \quad \text{for} \quad m_t \leq x_t \ . \tag{8.6}$$

The factor θ_t/θ_{t+1} accounts for the change in the price of input between t and $t+1$. The model now yields a multiplicity of long-run equilibria. The most interesting for our purposes are corner solutions, which yield two extreme stable equilibria.[6] In particular, if

$$\kappa < 1 + r \ , \tag{8.7}$$

then firms have incentives to economize on cash and instead accrue arrears. As a result, they will push the share of cash payments to the minimum possible, denoted by $\theta_{\min}$. This equilibrium can be defined as minimum liquidity equilibrium (MLE) and implies the maximum level of arrears. Given that arrears are costly, this equilibrium is associated with a low level of output.

At the other extreme, there is an equilibrium in which

$$\kappa > 1 + r \quad \text{then} \quad \theta = \theta_{\max} = 1 \ . \tag{8.8}$$

In this case the cost of running into arrears is larger than the benefits derived from economizing in the use of cash in the payment of inputs. Thus, firms will not fall into arrears, moving the economy back to the situation depicted above in the no-arrears equilibrium.

To keep the model simple we have assumed that both r and κ are exogenous. Besides reflecting the state of bankruptcy regulations and practices and the importance of reputation in credit markets, κ is likely to be affected by the aggregate amount of arrears. The larger the latter, the smaller the marginal direct cost of arrears is likely to be. As in stealing, the larger the number of "criminals," the lower the probability of being caught and punished. As a result, an initial increase in arrears due, for instance, to a bank credit squeeze, through its feedback on lowering the cost of arrears may force the economy into the high arrears–low output equilibrium. Similarly, the inequality in (8.7) is affected by the interest rate. For simplicity we assumed constant prices. However, in a more realistic model with inflation, the nominal rather than the real interest rate will appear in the inequality. Thus higher inflation raises the return on economizing in the use of money, and thus may push the system into the bad equilibrium (MLE). Moreover, the effective discount rate of enterprises can be affected by their horizon, which in turn is likely to depend on the prospects of privatization (see Calvo and Coricelli, 1993). In particular, the prospects of privatization and loss of control of the firms by their workers is likely to shorten the firms' horizon. This situation can be simply expressed by increasing the effective discount rate r. Thus, through this channel the probability of moving toward the bad equilibrium increases.

In sum, there is a host of microeconomic and macroeconomic factors at play. Their interaction determines whether a system converges toward good or bad equilibria. Unfortunately, a precise empirical measure of these factors is hard to identify, and thus a strict empirical test of the model is not feasible. However, the model highlights certain features of inter-enterprise arrears which can be verified empirically. First, the model indicates that arrears are consistent with the existence of firms that are viable and behave rationally, in contrast with the widespread view linking arrears to loss-making firms. Thus, one can check whether there is any correlation between arrears and loss-making firms. Second, the model suggests that arrears can be interpreted as an equilibrium phenomenon in which all firms settle on the use of a share of cash payments which is smaller than one. Therefore, one should expect a chain of arrears to develop, with firms affected by arrears on both sides of their balance sheet. Third, the model suggests a connection between liquidity and arrears, which can be tested empirically. Finally, although direct indicators of cost of arrears are not identifiable, one could look for indirect channels. For instance, firms with a larger exposure to international trade are likely to be less involved in the chain of arrears.

The next section tries to explore these empirical questions for the case of Romania.

8.3 A Closer Look at the Evidence: The Case of Romania

Romania, together with Russia, is the country in which inter-enterprise arrears have been at center stage after the launching of the reform program in 1991. Targets on arrears have even featured in the conditionality of IMF and World Bank programs. Moreover, Romania experienced a generalized attempt to clean up arrears at the end of 1991. However, our focus on Romania is determined also by the fact that Romania is the only country for which we have detailed information at the enterprise level.

Some caveats on this data set should be stressed at the outset. First, the data set is available only for 1992, thus for the period following the clean up, called global compensation (GC) scheme. Second, the data provide a snapshot of the situation in the first nine months of 1992, and not a time series. Despite these limitations, the data set permits an analysis of the main features of inter-enterprise arrears and of the correlation between enterprise characteristics and arrears.

First, it is useful to summarize the behavior of gross arrears since the start of reforms and relate them to bank credit. *Figure 8.1* shows that arrears grew rapidly after the launching of reforms in 1991, they accelerated sharply in the months preceding the implementation of the GC scheme, and they increased again after the cleanup, although they did not recover to pre-GC scheme levels. *Figure 8.2* indicates the negative correlation between the level of arrears, as a share of bank credit, and real bank credit to enterprises.

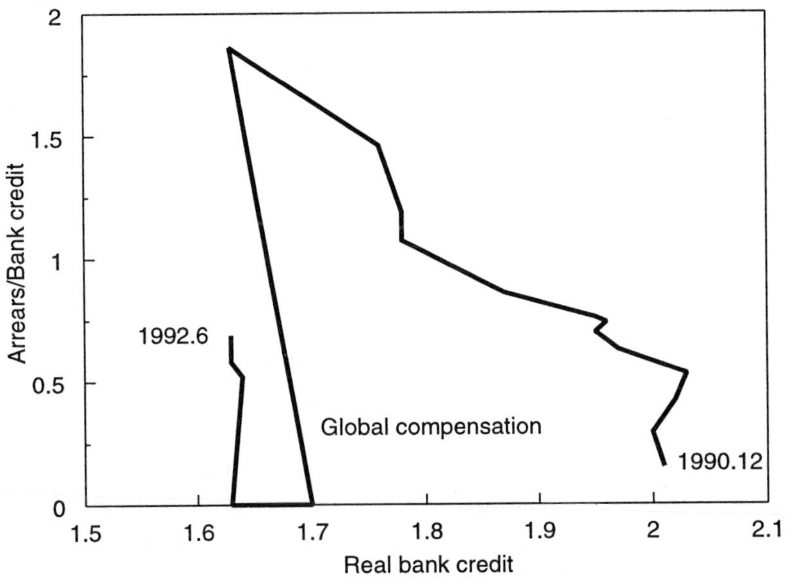

Figure 8.2. Arrears and bank credit in Romania, 1990–1992. Source: National Bank of Romania.

It is worth noting that the growth of arrears took place simultaneously with a sharp and continuous decline in production and high and persistent inflation.

The sharp initial contraction in real money and credit translated into a persistent phenomenon of "demonetization," or fall in money demand. Thus, *prima facie*, the case of Romania seems to correspond to the case of MLE identified in Section 8.2. Furthermore, the Romanian experience is an example of the limited efficacy of cleanup operations not supported by macroeconomic policies and microeconomic incentives.

Next we analyze in detail the characteristics of inter-enterprise arrears, using data on all state-owned industrial enterprises for the first three-quarters of 1992. These data permit one to analyze, first, the degree of "circularity" of the process, namely, how important are the debts of firms which have a roughly balanced debt-credit (payables and receivables) position, and, second, the role of loss-making firms in the network of arrears. Finally, we report some suggestive evidence from a small-scale enterprise survey (see World Bank, 1993) which provides qualitative answers on the features and determinants of arrears in Romania.

One simple measure of the degree of circularity is given by the ratio of total net arrears, defined as the sum of net debt positions of net debtor firms, to total gross arrears. This ratio has hovered between 25% and 30% during 1991 and 1992. This means that most arrears are a substitute for enterprise liquidity. Perhaps even more relevant is the number of firms involved in the network of arrears and the number of firms with significant net debt positions. For instance, in June 1992, out of 1,692 state industrial firms, 1,455 displayed arrears in payments to suppliers, while most net arrears were concentrated in a handful of firms.[7] Therefore, the vast majority of Romanian firms have both debts and credits of similar magnitudes, clearly illustrating the phenomenon of chain of arrears, while net arrears are not highly significant.

Regarding the importance of loss-making firms, only 200 firms, or 12% of the total number of firms, are loss-making, and they do not absorb a disproportionately large share of arrears – in relation to their sales, for instance. Their share in total gross arrears is about 15%, while their share in total sales is about 10%.[8] Although loss-making firms are important recipients of net arrears, they do not play a crucial role in the whole chain of arrears.

Another element supporting the view of inter-enterprise arrears as a systemic phenomenon, associated with specific incentives and penalties, is given by the lack of any correlation between inter-enterprise arrears and tax arrears. In fact, although not statistically significant, the coefficient of correlation between the two types of arrears is negative.

We now try to assess in a regression analysis the robustness of the facts we identified above on the basis of descriptive indicators. *Tables 8.2*, *8.3*, and *8.4* report results of a cross-section analysis on the sample of state-owned enterprises in 1992. Estimates are derived for payables, receivables, and their difference – namely, net arrears.[9]

The main objective of the regression analysis is to evaluate whether the idea of high degree of circularity of the phenomenon with arrears reflecting a widespread behavior in which all firms reduce the use of cash in their transactions is borne out by the data. This can simply be inferred by checking whether receivables and payables are positively correlated – once adjustment for scale factors are introduced – and whether receivables and payables add significantly to the explanation of each other in regressions including other possible factors affecting arrears, such as financial and technological variables.

The regression results seem to strongly support the view of a chain of arrears. Indeed, a main determinant of payables (receivables) are receivables (payables). The coefficients on these variables are statistically significant even when other "structural" variables, sectoral dummies, and legal-form dummies are included in the regressions. The export orientation of firms

Table 8.2. OLS regressions on inter-enterprise arrears in September 1992 on a sample of 1,655 firms in Romania.
Dependent variable: Arrears (payables)/Sales.

	Regression 1		Regression 2	
Variable	Coefficient	t-statistics	Coefficient	t-statistics
Constant	0.08	4.68	0.10	4.97
Material/Total costs	0.11	4.65	0.11	4.41
Profits/Sales	–0.45	–8.32		
Exports/Sales	–0.07	–2.62	–0.17	-5.77
Receivables/Sales	0.28	20.84		
Change in deposits/Sales			–0.02	–1.63
SD_1	–0.04	–1.18	–0.00	–0.06
SD_2	–0.06	–2.86	–0.07	–3.14
SD_3	–0.04	–1.07	–0.05	–1.36
SD_4	0.19	6.81	0.29	9.44
SD_5	0.07	3.33	0.11	4.90
SD_6	0.01	–0.35	0.02	0.79
SD_7	0.01	0.62	0.03	1.02
SD_8	0.07	3.72	0.09	4.20
SD_9	0.01	0.35	0.03	1.12
SD_{10}	0.05	2.24	0.07	2.96
SD_{11}	0.18	1.91	0.15	1.35
SD_{12}	0.16	2.72	0.15	2.26
FD_{11}	–0.02	–0.57	0.10	2.15
FD_{13}	–0.10	–1.80	–0.10	–1.60
FD_{21}	0.19	2.42	0.13	1.44
FD_{22}	0.12	3.11	0.04	0.96
Adjusted R^2	0.34		0.12	

SD_i denotes sectoral dummies.
FD_i denotes firm-type dummies.
Source: Authors' calculations from Ministry of Finance data.

is negatively correlated with both payables and receivables, indicating that linkages with foreign markets allow firms to escape the chain of arrears. This assumption seems consistent with Daianu (1993, p. 19), who argues that exports allow firms to "escape the 'network-trap' and build new chains of reliable suppliers and customers." The role of financial variables, in particular the liquidity conditions of firms, is less clear-cut. Profits – defined on an accrual basis – appear to have a highly significant and large negative impact on payables, while they are not significantly related to receivables. Given the extremely low level of the stock of enterprise money, profits may represent a good proxy for enterprise liquidity. The fact that profits affect

Table 8.3. OLS regressions on inter-enterprise arrears in September 1992 on a sample of 1,655 firms in Romania.
Dependent variable: Arrears (receivables)/Sales.

Variable	Coefficient	t-statistics
Constant	0.04	1.43
Profits/Sales	0.05	0.59
Exports/Sales	–0.09	–2.15
Payables/Sales	0.73	20.82
SD_1	0.12	2.31
SD_2	–0.01	–0.38
SD_3	–0.01	–0.23
SD_4	0.18	4.16
SD_5	0.12	3.88
SD_6	0.12	3.41
SD_7	0.05	1.45
SD_8	0.04	1.22
SD_9	0.08	1.94
SD_{10}	0.05	1.50
SD_{11}	–0.25	–1.62
SD_{12}	–0.01	–0.07
FD_{11}	0.41	5.93
FD_{13}	0.04	0.41
FD_{21}	–0.22	–1.72
FD_{22}	–0.11	–1.80
Adjusted R^2	0.29	

SD_i denotes sectoral dummies.
FD_i denotes firm-type dummies.
Source: Authors' calculations from Ministry of Finance data.

payables but not receivables suggests an asymmetric effect of enterprise liquidity on arrears. This is not surprising, as we are analyzing the phenomenon of arrears and not a regular trade credit market, in which liquidity is voluntarily transferred from "liquidity-rich" to "liquidity-poor" firms.

Using directly the change in bank deposits as a proxy for the liquidity conditions of firms, leads to less robust results. While a bivariate regression of payables on change in deposits yields a negative and significant coefficient (the coefficient is –0.02, with a t-statistics of –2.1), the introduction of the change in deposits in a multivariate regression yields a statistically insignificant, though still negative, coefficient (see Regression 2 in *Table 8.2*). Finally, several sectoral and legal-form dummies are significant, indicating the role of "structural" factors, related to the position of firms in the production and trade process.[10]

Table 8.4. OLS regressions on inter-enterprise arrears in September 1992 on a sample of 1,655 firms in Romania.
Dependent variable: Net Arrears (payables minus receivables)/Sales.

Variable	Coefficient	t-statistics
Constant	–0.02	–1.16
Profits/Sales	–0.20	1.01
Exports/Sales	0.06	0.75
Material/Total costs	0.08	2.16
SD_1	–0.12	–2.35
SD_2	–0.01	–0.52
SD_3	–0.00	–0.03
SD_4	–0.11	–2.68
SD_5	–0.09	–3.10
SD_6	–0.12	–3.30
SD_7	–0.05	–1.48
SD_8	–0.02	–0.70
SD_9	–0.07	–1.85
SD_{10}	–0.04	–1.10
SD_{11}	0.29	1.87
SD_{12}	0.07	0.57
FD_{11}	–0.37	–5.42
FD_{13}	–0.07	–0.67
FD_{21}	0.26	1.97
FD_{22}	0.15	1.94
Adjusted R^2	0.04	

SD_i denotes sectoral dummies.
FD_i denotes firm-type dummies.
Source: Authors' calculations from Ministry of Finance data.

The results on receivables are similar to those on payables (see *Table 8.3*). We already noted the insignificant coefficient on profitability, although it has the expected positive sign. The other two variables, export orientation and payables, are significant. The negative sign on the export variable seems to suggest that exports provide a more reliable source of cash for firms than domestic sales.

Results on net arrears are not easily interpretable. Indeed, net arrears are not an independent choice variable, at least within the approach outlined in the model in Section 8.2.[11] Since we did not use the same set of explanatory variables in the regressions on payables and receivables – as the ratio of material costs to total costs does not appear in the regression on receivables – the results on net arrears, namely, the difference between arrears on payables and arrears on receivables, cannot be mechanically inferred by

Table 8.5. Main causes of arrears in Romania.

Causes	Rating
Accumulation of overdue receivables	2.65
Increase in input over output prices	3.52
High interest rates	3.66
High profit tax	4.69
Loss of markets	5.38
Inventory accumulation	5.66
High turnover tax	5.66
Insufficient bank credit	5.76
High wage bill	7.86

On a scale of 1 to 10, 1 being the most important cause and 10 being the least important.
Source: World Bank, 1993.

subtracting coefficients of the two regressions. The results are in line with expectations, with technological factors such as the ratio of material costs to total costs, and sectoral dummies, affecting net arrears. In addition it is worth noting that the export orientation variable is positive, although not highly significant. Thus, exporters tend to be in a position of net debtors in the domestic market. This is consistent with the fact that they purchase inputs domestically, where arrears are tolerated and widespread, while they sell on foreign markets, where contracts tend to be enforced and thus payments must be carried out. Given the stronger effect of profitability – as a proxy for liquidity – on payables than on receivables, it should be expected that this variables will play a role as well on net arrears.

The main results of the above quantitative analysis seem to be supported by "qualitative" results obtained from a small-scale survey of Romanian industrial firms.[12]

Two outcomes of the survey stand out, because they strongly support the view of a chain of arrears determined by the low perceived cost of falling into arrears.

1. As reported in *Table 8.5*, the main cause of arrears is identified in the accumulation of overdue receivables, confirming the view of chain of arrears repeatedly stressed above. Factors affecting the enterprise cash flow, such as the relative price of inputs with respect to final output is a distant second, while profit tax comes fourth. The third factor is identified as high interest rates on bank loans, while availability of bank credit is not singled out as a main factor. Thus, credit constraints are

Table 8.6. Priorities of payments in Romania.

Payments to	Rating
Employees	1.45
Foreign suppliers	2.41
Banks	2.59
Budget	2.69
Domestic suppliers	3.28

On a scale of 1 to 10, 1 being the most important priority and 10 being the least important.
Source: World Bank, 1993.

felt more through the cost of credit than through credit rationing. Most firms perceived that the relative cost of arrears was much lower than the interest rate on bank credit, as they stated that no explicit, or implicit, interest rate was charged on arrears.[13]

2. Other important information on the perceived cost of arrears comes from the ranking on the priorities in payments by enterprises. *Table 8.6* displays the ranking, which clearly indicates as first priority the payments of wages and as last priority the payments to domestic suppliers. After wages, one finds foreign suppliers, banks, and the budget with similar ratings. In the context of the model in Section 8.2, the above ranking suggests that κ is lower than the return on using cash to pay wages. Interesting, additional information on this phenomenon is given by the fact that those firms that reported having fallen into arrears in wage payments (3 out of 29), stated that they resolved their problem by collecting their receivables.

8.4 Conclusions

Thc paper provides theoretical and empirical support for the notion that inter-enterprise arrears in PCPEs do not simply reflect a situation in which winners make transfers to losers but, rather, reflect a situation in which firms cannot comply with their contractual obligations, because other firms have faileded to do so. This chain-of-arrears situation complicates policy-making significantly. Straightforward solutions like starting bankruptcy procedures on firms that fall into arrears may, under these circumstances, have high social costs. Good firms may be forced into bankruptcy because their clients are unable or unwilling to pay their trade credit. On the other hand, massive inter-enterprise debt write-offs may give the wrong set of incentives. Even good firms may be induced to fall further into arrears in the expectation that they will eventually be bailed out.

The simple theory outlined in this paper suggests that policy should aim at modifying the present set of incentives. Arrears have to be attacked before they have a chance to grow. Thus, policies should aim at increasing the marginal cost of falling into arrears. If there is a chain of arrears, and arrears have had a chance to grow, there is little the policy maker can do. Under these conditions, even sound policies such as tighter bank credit may have no positive effect, given that firms may react by further falling into arrears with banks or the fiscal authority.

The analysis also suggests that PCPEs are not a homogeneous group. An explanation for this is that they come from widely different experiences with market institutions. Thus, an implication of the analysis is that macroeconomic policy must pay close attention to institutional characteristics. In particular, we argue that when credit markets are dysfunctional a credit crunch could have long-lasting consequences.

Notes

[1] Of course, even in Hungary and Poland the system may still be rudimentary. Nevertheless, there is a secondary market, a few banks are involved in factoring operations, bills of exchange are used, and, finally, information on creditworthiness and credit history of firms is published in specialized magazines.

[2] Equation (8.3) assumes that households have complete access to international capital markets, which justifies using the (constant) world interest rate as the relevant discount factor of household workers (see Calvo and Coricelli, 1992, 1993, for a full discussion). In addition, since our focus is not on labor market issues, labor is considered a fixed factor and its size normalized to one.

[3] As discussed in Calvo and Coricelli (1992), without a lower bound on wages the model would not have a well-specified solution. Interestingly, the lower bound on wages has the economic interpretation of a constraint on the possibility of firms to "borrow" from their workers in the form of negative wages.

[4] McKinnon (1991) has in fact argued that governments should aim at imposing such a self-financing constraint by closing completely the "faucet of credit."

[5] θ remains a factor in equation (8.6) because it is the relative price of *output in the firm* per unit of time to real cash balances, m. The presence of θ in equation (8.6) has nothing to do with the relative price of output with respect to input since, by previous considerations, the latter is always equal to unity.

[6] There is also an interior solution, characterized by the unlikely situation in which $\kappa = 1 + r$. It can be shown that this equilibrium is unstable (see Calvo and Coricelli, 1993).

[7] Indeed, 80% of net arrears were concentrated in 100 firms, accounting for 27% of sales, while the largest 10 debtors account for 50% of net arrears.

This implies that only for a small number of firms arrears involve a significant transfer of liquidity from other firms.

[8] The data refer to September 1992.

[9] As noted in studies of trade credit in market economies, the factors influencing payables and receivables can be quite different at the microeconomic level, where payables and receivables can differ one from the other (Nadiri, 1969). Moreover, since we focus on manufacturing firms, payables and receivables are not even identical in the aggregate, as the manufacturing sector is net creditor to other sectors, especially to the trade sector.

[10] The legal-form dummies indicate that the Regies Autonomes (large companies with high national interest, providing energy sources and other major inputs) tend to have lower payable arrears, with respect to the control variable, than commercial companies. This is interesting because usually the Regies Autonomes are singled out as the firms still working under soft budget constraints, benefiting from large explicit and implicit subsidies. The low ratios of arrears to sales in these firms are of course also due to the fact that they produce primary goods and energy. Nevertheless, the result is an additional indication of the fact that the phenomenon of arrears is not predominantly associated with "bad" firms.

[11] In the literature on trade credit in market economies there is a debate on the relevance of net and gross credit (Meltzer, 1960; Brechling and Lipsey, 1963). Those who see trade credit as a transfer of liquidity from liquidity-rich to liquidity-poor firms emphasize the role of net credit. By contrast, those who see trade credit as credit for transaction purposes, and a mechanism for the enterprise sector as a whole to economize in the use of money, emphasize gross credit (Ferris, 1981). Our view is closer to the latter approach.

[12] The survey was carried out at the end of 1992 by the World Bank, and it focused on questions of inter-enterprise arrears. The sample included 29 state-owned firms covering all the main industrial sectors. Given the non-representativeness of the sample, the survey provides mainly qualitative information on the phenomenon.

[13] It is worth noting that in 1992, when the survey was carried out, interest rates increased significantly with respect to 1991, and they were positive in real terms for several months (see World Bank, 1993).

References

Begg, D., and Portes, R., 1992, *Enterprise Debt and Economic Transformation: Financial Restructuring of the State Sector in Central and Eastern Europe*, Discussion Paper, No. 695, Centre for Economic Policy Research, London, UK.

Brechling, F.P.R., and Lipsey, R.G., 1963, Trade credit and monetary policy, *Economic Journal*, **73**:618–41, December.

Calvo, G., and Coricelli, F., 1992, Stabilizing a previously centrally planned economy: Poland 1990, *Economic Policy*, **14**.

Calvo, G., and Coricelli, F., 1993, Credit Market Imperfections and Output Response in Previously Centrally Planned Economies, May [mimeo].

Calvo, G., and Frenkel, J., 1991, From centrally planned to market economies: The road from CPE to PCPE, *International Monetary Fund Staff Papers*, **38**(2):268–299.

Clifton, E., and Khan, M., 1992, *Inter-enterprise Arrears in Transforming Economies: The Case of Romania*, IMF Paper on Policy Analysis and Assessment, International Monetary Fund, Washington, DC, USA.

Daianu, D., 1993, Arrears in Post-Command Economies: Thoughts from a Romanian Perspective [mimeo].

Ferris, S., 1981, A transactions theory of trade credit use, *The Quarterly Journal of Economics*, May.

Hrnčíř, M., 1993, *Financial Intermediation in the Czech Republic: Lessons and Progress Evaluation*, Discussion Paper on Economic Transition 9302, Department of Applied Economics, Cambridge University, Cambridge, UK.

Ickes, B., and Ryterman, R., 1992, The Inter-Enterprise Arrears Crisis in Russia [mimeo].

McKinnon, R., 1991, *The Order of Economic Liberalization*, Johns Hopkins University Press, Baltimore, MD, USA.

Meltzer, A.H., 1960, Mercantile credit, monetary policy and the size of the firm, *Review of Economics and Statistics*, **42**(2):429–97.

Nadiri, M.I., 1969, The determinants of trade credit in the US total manufacturing sector, *Econometrica*, **37**(2):408–423.

Rostowski, J., 1993, The Inter-Enterprise Debt Explosion in the Former Soviet Union: Causes, Consequences, Cures [mimeo].

World Bank, 1993, *Fiscal Study on Romania*, World Bank, Washington, DC, USA.

Comments on the Paper by Guillermo Calvo and Fabrizio Coricelli

Jacek Rostowski

The basic question regarding inter-enterprise debt (IED) in post-Communist economies is, What is it? Guillermo Calvo and Fabrizio Coricelli find that, at least in Romania, it is the "stealing" of liquidity by some firms from others. The costs of such stealing to the thief is the risk of being cut off from further supplies by one's suppliers (who are the victims of this theft). The greater the amount of "liquidity theft" in the economy, the greater the likelihood that the authorities will "validate" the theft by creating more money, and therefore the smaller the risk that the thief's suppliers will refuse to continue selling to him – i.e., the smaller the cost of the liquidity theft, the larger it is likely to be. As a result, Calvo and Coricelli suggest that once IED starts expanding (or exceeds a critical threshold),[1] it may grow in a self-sustaining manner. They see the source of the initial push which sets IED on its upward path[2] as a tightening of real bank credit, which "forces" firms to engage in liquidity theft. Tight credit policy can therefore be self-defeating.

Others, including myself, believe that IED is just a form of trade credit. In centrally planned economies trade credit was tightly administratively controlled. With the removal of such controls, it was bound to increase sharply, raising the velocity of circulation of money relative to GDP, i.e., V in MV = PY must increase once off.[3] In the absence of a tightening of monetary policy, prices must rise as the firm sector as a whole saves on money balances. This seems to be what happened in CSFR during 1990–1991. Qimiao Fan and Schaffer (1994) show that total enterprise receivables in the CSFR increased from 40.5% of GDP at the end of 1990 to 59.3% of GDP at the end of 1991. However, if monetary policy is lax, or if firms believe that it will subsequently become lax, then an IED bubble can occur in the short term, and IED expansion can become a part of the inflationary process in the long term.[4] A bubble can also occur if IED has not been administratively controlled, but inflation increases for some other reason. Poland in 1989 is an example of such a process.

If both buyers and suppliers underestimated inflation because they failed to take into account the effect of IED extension on prices, both sides will revise expected inflation and IED upward. The same real volume of transactions will be financed using IED, but the nominal stock of IED will increase. Higher expected inflation leads to higher IED, leading to higher inflation and higher expected inflation, so that an inflationary IED bubble may develop. The bubble must ultimately burst if the money supply is not increased, if only because the relative prices of intermediate and final goods become distorted (Rostowski, 1993). Nevertheless, the greater the volume of transactions which have been financed by IED, the greater the recession which will occur if the money supply is not increased. Actors may therefore expect that the money supply will indeed be increased, making them extend IED even more, giving a further thrust to the inflation-IED bubble.[5] If the money supply is increased sufficiently to avoid any recessionary effects, actors may come to believe that the authorities will not risk the recessionary effects of not satisfying inflationary expectations.[6] In that case, in the long-term IED expansion can become an integral part of the inflationary process, just as wage increases can in other contexts. Thus, if IED is trade credit, loose money rather than tight money can cause an IED explosion, and the sooner money is tightened to make clear to actors that the authorities will not allow money to depend on IED, the better. The example of Poland in 1990 shows that a credible stabilization will reduce IED, rather than increase it (Rostowski, 1993). Whether IED is "liquidity theft" or trade credit thus has great practical importance.

But what can the authorities do if an inflation-IED bubble occurs without any increase in the money supply, but just as a result of the removal of a ban on trade credit or as a result of the authorities having fed the inflation-IED bubble, so that the costs of bursting it have in fact increased? I have argued (Rostowski, 1993) that the least bad solution may be to make the IED tradable.[7] It may be almost as good to simply burst the bubble by tightening the money supply. A multilateral clearing would be definitely worse, but need not be a disaster as long as it happens sufficiently late to cause suppliers a real loss. Worst of all is validation through money creation. Such a sufficiently delayed multilateral clearing of IED seems to have happened in Russia in August 1992. As a result IED fell from 2.6 months' worth of industrial sales to 1.5 months' (Qimiao Fan and Schaffer, 1994).

A final question is whether IED is symmetrically distributed, or whether it is concentrated in "bad" firms. Calvo and Coricelli believe it is symmetrically distributed in Romania. From this they deduce that it is "systemic," i.e., due to all firms having an interest in "stealing liquidity" from others once a "bad equilibrium" (in which the costs of stealing are low) has been achieved. Those who believe that IED is essentially trade credit also think that, in equilibrium, it should *not* be concentrated in bad firms. How then to explain Gomulka's findings (see Chapter 9 in this book) that in Poland IED, like bank credit, is concentrated among bad borrowers. One possible explanation is that state enterprises (SOEs) conspired to thwart reformist governments' intentions, with the liquid and profitable enterprises subsidizing the bad ones through IED. If this were the case, one could deal with the problem by simply administratively liquidating enterprises with a high level of IED. Proposals to freeze the wages of SOEs with high IED are in the same spirit.

While one cannot be sure that the IED "black hole" in Poland was not originally due to such an SOE conspiracy, no one has suggested, to my knowledge, that the potential subsidizing of the bad by the good could have extended beyond the first year of the transition (i.e., 1990). In any event its dimensions remained quite limited, as real IED fell after the first quarter of 1990. Again, in Russia the ratio of IED to industrial production fell during the third quarter of 1992 (the first year of transition). In this context it is interesting that for Romania, Calvo and Coricelli find that IED is symmetrically distributed. Romania is one of the countries where reformists are particularly prone to believe in an SOE conspiracy against marketization. As regards Poland, it seems likely that IED concentration has the same source as the bank debt concentration in bad enterprises which accompanies it – that is, in mistakes made by lenders during the relative price shock caused by rapid liberalization and stabilization in early 1990.[8]

Notes

[1] Calvo and Coricelli are unclear on whether it is the rate of growth or the level of IED which could trigger such an explosion.

[2] So that either the rate of change or the level of IED exceeds its critical level.

[3] After which V returns to its previous level (Rostowski, 1993).

[4] Rational suppliers expecting monetary policy to be relaxed will extend credit to their customers, incorporating in the price a premium to compensate for the amount of time they expect to have to wait for payment (x days) and the rate of inflation during this period (y percent). If both sides have equal liquidity relative to their preferences, then the purchasers will accept the price proposed if they expect to be able to delay payment for longer than x days or if they expect inflation to be higher than y percent. If trade credit was previously banned, there will be a nonnegative number of cases on which supplier and customer can agree on the price of the good and an extension of trade credit, so that a positive level of IED will occur.

[5] This is a version of the Calvo and Coricelli mechanism described earlier, but introduced in a different context.

[6] Much the same can happen with workers' expectations revealed in wage claims in the context of an adjusted Phillips curve.

[7] This proposal was later embodied in a decree of the president of the Russian Federation.

[8] Qimiao Fan and Schaffer (1994) claim that perhaps one-third of IED in Poland is believed to be irrecoverable.

References

Qimiao Fan, and Schaffer, M.E., 1994, Government Financial Transfers and Enterprise Adjustments in Russia, with Comparisons to Central and Eastern Europe, CEP Working Paper, No. 394, February, Centre for Economic Performance, London, UK.

Rostowski, J., 1993, *The Inter-Enterprise Debt Explosion in the Former Soviet Union: Causes, Consequences, Cures*, CEP Discussion Paper, No. 142, April, Centre for Economic Performance, London, UK.

Chapter 9

The Financial Situation and Bad Debts of Enterprises in Poland

Stanislaw Gomulka

After the initial years of transition the problem of bad debts of enterprises emerged as a major obstacle to further evolution of the banking system and to the use of efficient ways to finance the enterprise sector. With the abolishment of central planning the banking system is bound to provide one of the crucial channels of reallocation of resources; as a result the danger is genuine that the bad debt problem may hinder both day-to-day operations and the much needed restructuring. The necessity for the banks to overextend credits to inefficient state-owned enterprises, the lack of credit or too-expensive credit available for efficient new private firms, and the threat on the viability of the banks themselves, all may contribute indirectly to the pervasive output decline. The study of the financial situation and bad debts of the enterprises may shed some light on the role of enterprise finances in current sluggish adjustment.

This is quite likely the first detailed study of enterprise finances in a transition country of Central and Eastern Europe. It is based on enterprise data collected monthly by the Polish Central Statistical Office (PCSO). Its primary purpose is to report on enterprise debt (particularly bad debt) to banks, other enterprises, and the government. The chapter analyzes the size of this debt, its distributions by sector of activity and type of ownership, and its evolution over time.

R. Holzmann et al. (eds.), Output Decline in Eastern Europe, 217-236.

The central findings are, firstly, that the bad debt is a large proportion of total debt to both banks and enterprises and, secondly, that this bad debt is highly concentrated. The study identifies enterprises, representing about a tenth of the whole enterprise sector in terms of sales (and possibly employment), whose debt in relation to the total income of these enterprises is particularly large. In terms of financial situation and the softness of the budget constraint, these enterprises have been distinctly different from most other enterprises, forming effectively a *black hole* in the economy. The Polish enterprise sector has thus been found to have, in 1992–1993, a dual structure: about 90% of the sector is almost debt-free, while the remaining 10% has accumulated large debts to banks, the government, and other enterprises.

The chapter also discusses the implications of these findings for the fiscal and monetary policies of the central authorities and for the lending policy of commercial banks.

9.1 Data

In 1992, the whole enterprise sector accounted for about 70% of the economy's total employment outside agriculture and for about 70% of the country's gross domestic product (GDP). The PCSO divides all enterprises (legal persons), irrespective of ownership, into three categories: large (L), medium (M), and small (S). Those in the L category employ 51 or more in industry and construction and 21 or more in other sectors (domestic and foreign trade, transport, communications, agricultural services, forestry, and communal housing services).

Enterprises in the M category employ between 6 and 50 in industry and construction and between 6 and 20 in all other sectors; those in the S category employ between 1 and 5. In 1992–1993, there were about 20,000 to 25,000 L-type enterprises, about 50,000 to 60,000 M-type enterprises, and some 1 million to 2 million businesses in the small category. Each month the PCSO collects key data from all enterprises in the L category (except state farms) and from a sample of 10% of those in the M category, using the so-called F0-1 form. We use this data set in this chapter.

9.2 Indicators of Financial Situation

We identify two indicators to describe the financial situation of each enterprise. One is the ratio of the stock of net financial assets, denoted by F, to quarterly gross sales and other income, S. The other is the ratio of a measure of gross profits, Z, to S, both on a quarterly basis. The stock of net financial assets is defined as follows:

$$F = \text{own money} + (\text{receivables} - \text{payables}) - (\text{credits} + \text{loans}) \ . \qquad (9.1)$$

Own money is either cash or, more often, deposits with banks. Receivables are payments due from customers, mainly other enterprises. Payables include tax obligations to central and local governments and to parabudgetary funds. However, most payables are payments due to other enterprises for goods and services. Credits represent borrowing from banks, while loans stand for borrowing from other sources (nonbank loans).

Until the beginning of 1993, there had been no automatic capitalization of the interest due but unpaid. The interest of this kind on "directed credit" (for example, to housing cooperatives and farms) was, and is, automatically capitalized. Until the beginning of 1993, the unpaid interest on any other credit was frequently not capitalized, but since then it has been capitalized. In 1992 the amount of interest payments involved were Zl 22.5 trillion and Zl 15.0 trillion for interests capitalized and not capitalized, respectively, according to internal data of the National Bank of Poland (NBP). These numbers may be compared with the GDP in 1992 of Zl 1,140 trillion and with the total bank debt of nonfinancial economic units at the end of 1992 of Zl 237 trillion.

In this paper we regard the entry "credits and loans" of the F0-1 form as a good approximation of the total bank debt. To obtain precise figures on bank debt, the data on "credits and loans" should be augmented by unpaid non-capitalized interest and reduced by nonbank loans. Given the magnitudes of the loans and unpaid interest, our procedure possibly underestimates somewhat the true debt position in 1992.

The financial situation (f) of an enterprise depends not on the amount of debt, but on the ability to meet its debt payments. We take the ratio

$$f = F/S \qquad (9.2)$$

as a measure of that ability, where S stands for an average quarterly gross income from the start of the year. We calculate f for each quarter. For example, to compute f for the second quarter of any year, we take F as it was at the end of the second quarter, while S is half of the gross income during the year's first two quarters.

The financial situation of an enterprise also depends on its ability to cover current production costs in the medium to long term. To measure the indicator of pofitability (z) we take the ratio

$$z = Z/S \ ,$$

where Z represents gross profits or the so-called gross financial result augmented by amortization (the depreciation allowance).[1]

Our intention is to divide the enterprise sector into groups characterized by similar values of f, and then subdivide each group further according to the value of z. The procedure aims, as a first step, to identify the enterprises which have both a highly negative f and a negative z.

9.3 The Distribution of Large Enterprises According to the f Indicator

Most enterprises, whatever the size, have an f indicator in the range between -1.5 and 1.5. We divide this range into 30 equal subranges, each 0.1 in length. A subgroup of enterprises corresponds to each subrange. The gross income of any such subgroup is then computed as a proportion of the gross income of the total population in the given category of enterprises. In this way we arrive at an income-weighted distribution of enterprises in terms of f; *Table 9.1* gives the distribution of different categories of large and medium-size enterprises. *Figure 9.1* shows these distributions for the third quarter in 1992 (not taking into account the ranges outside -1.5 and 1.5).

It turns out that the distribution for this period, and any other of the five quarters investigated, is bell-shaped, with a heavy concentration of enterprises near $f = 0$. Guided by this finding, and to facilitate analysis, we divide all enterprises into five groups according to their financial state as indicated by the value of f:

- Very bad: $f < -1.5$.
- Bad: $-1.5 < f < -0.5$.
- Satisfactory: $-0.5 < f < 0.5$.
- Good: $0.5 < f < 1.5$.
- Very good: $f > 1.5$.

The choice of f values separating these groups is essentially arbitrary. Nevertheless, the choice has been made to ensure that the central group, the one near $f = 0$, comprises enterprises accounting for about half of the gross income of the total population of our L enterprises. The division of the range of the f variable from -1.5 to 1.5 into three equal parts enables us to pinpoint such a central group.

Table 9.1. Distribution of sales and other incomes in terms of f for various types of enterprises in Poland at the end of September 1992, in percent.

f range	Large state	Large private	Lg. state industrial	Lg. priv. industrial	Medium state	Medium private
(Average f)	(−4.14)	(−5.73)	(−4.35)	(−3.85)	(−11.53)	(−3.77)
<−1.5	7.85	1.56	10.54	1.44	8.63	0.81
−1.5 to −1.4	0.44	0.14	0.62	0.41	1.03	0.12
−1.4 to −1.3	1.01	0.11	1.48	0.07	0.63	0.08
−1.3 to −1.2	1.00	0.17	1.48	0.37	0.00	0.15
−1.2 to −1.1	0.51	0.09	0.69	0.08	0.57	0.12
−1.1 to −1.0	2.11	0.31	2.67	0.62	0.00	0.24
−1.0 to −0.9	2.78	0.35	3.33	0.62	0.00	0.11
−0.9 to −0.8	1.24	0.22	1.79	0.30	0.32	0.29
−0.8 to −0.7	2.27	0.50	3.33	0.89	0.72	0.62
−0.7 to −0.6	1.42	1.01	2.02	2.18	1.40	0.62
−0.6 to −0.5	2.92	4.10	3.93	9.96	2.76	0.86
−0.5 to −0.4	5.21	2.67	2.94	3.20	2.96	1.79
−0.4 to −0.3	3.21	4.03	3.44	3.43	3.45	2.69
−0.3 to −0.2	3.40	8.55	4.23	6.45	4.57	4.95
−0.2 to −0.1	5.42	17.67	6.94	11.68	4.32	12.47
−0.1 to 0.0	16.83	32.23	10.13	31.37	13.62	39.94
0.0 to 0.1	15.81	17.54	16.59	20.74	5.66	24.20
0.1 to 0.2	6.46	5.22	7.46	3.91	7.70	7.34
0.2 to 0.3	4.28	1.86	4.48	1.22	8.26	1.62
0.3 to 0.4	4.37	0.76	4.16	0.65	4.77	0.50
0.4 to 0.5	2.16	0.57	2.17	0.01	4.06	0.15
0.5 to 0.6	1.78	0.14	1.42	0.09	3.96	0.16
0.6 to 0.7	1.98	0.04	0.94	0.05	1.64	0.06
0.7 to 0.8	1.10	0.01	0.82	0.00	2.89	0.00
0.8 to 0.9	0.90	0.05	0.70	0.12	1.57	0.00
0.9 to 1.0	0.56	0.02	0.38	0.00	1.25	0.02
1.0 to 1.1	0.47	0.00	0.50	0.01	0.41	0.01
1.1 to 1.2	0.09	0.00	0.05	0.01	0.36	0.00
1.2 to 1.3	0.22	0.03	0.16	0.09	4.92	0.00
1.3 to 1.4	0.36	0.00	0.09	0.04	3.25	0.05
1.4 to 1.5	0.06	0.00	0.00	0.00	0.24	0.00
> 1.5	1.76	0.06	0.52	0.02	4.08	0.03
(Average f)	(+2.10)	(+6.62)	(+1.94)	(+4.19)	(+6.18)	(+4.06)
No. of enterprises	6281	3853	3151	1817	2640	32600

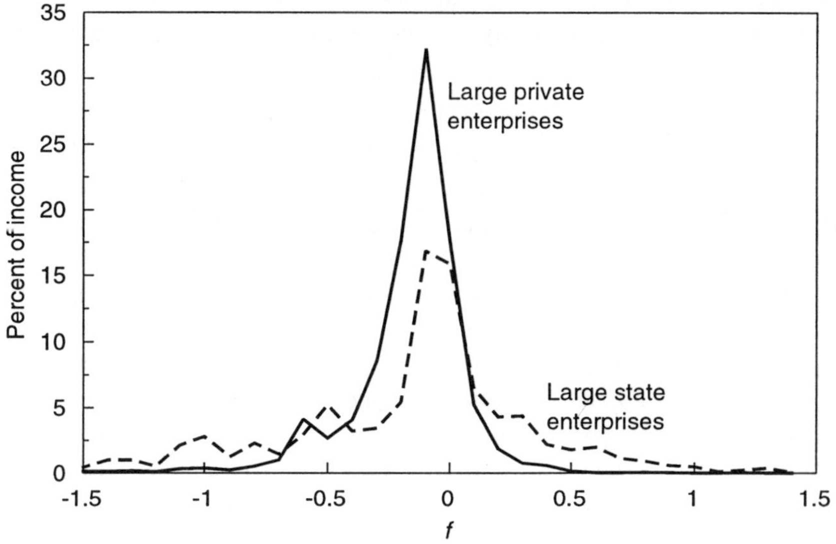

Figure 9.1. Distribution of sales and other incomes in large state and private enterprises in Poland at the end of September 1992, in percent of income.

All enterprises which fall outside the –1.5 to 1.5 range are regarded as outliers. They form the remaining two groups. Of particular interest in this study are enterprises in the *very bad* and *bad* categories.

9.4 Large Enterprises in the Very Bad Category

Tables 9.2 to *9.4* give the distributions of all L enterprises at the end of 1992 in terms of the five groups of financial state, by sector of activity and type of ownership. Similar tables have been compiled for the three earlier quarters of 1992 and the first quarter of 1993. This sequence of tables enables us to monitor the movement in all these distributions over the time period under study.

The first interesting feature of these data is that the very bad enterprises account for a smaller proportion of the total income of the enterprise sector than their proportion in the number of enterprises (see *Table 9.3*). A typical very bad enterprise is thus smaller than the average. One of the main reasons may be that the poor financial situation has been forcing many of them to contract.[2]

Table 9.2. Summary data for large enterprises in Poland, distribution by size of financial state (f) at the end of 1992.

	Total in trillion zlotys	Share in percent					
		Very bad	Bad	Satisfactory	Good	Very good	Total
Number of enterprises	21,824.0	14.2	13.6	59.2	10.5	2.4	100.0
Revenue per quarter	461.3	10.8	13.6	65.9	7.9	1.8	100.0
Credits and loans	186.6	61.6	15.3	21.4	1.4	0.6	100.0
Payables-receivables	109.3	98.2	31.4	0.0	–14.2	–15.4	100.0
Payables	410.7	38.0	18.4	33.2	7.1	3.3	100.0
Payables to government	71.8	42.9	20.8	30.9	3.1	2.3	100.0
Receivables	301.5	16.1	13.7	45.3	14.8	10.1	100.0
Own money	73.8	11.5	7.8	40.2	24.2	16.2	100.0
f average	–0.48	–4.29	–0.91	–0.03	0.85	3.29	

Table 9.3. Distribution of the number of enterprises (N) and of revenue (S) by size of financial state (f) across sectors in large enterprises in Poland at the end of 1992.

	Very bad		Bad		Satisfactory		Good		Very good		Total	
Sectors	N	S	N	S	N	S	N	S	N	S	N	S
Total	14.4	13.9	13.8	13.9	59.8	65.7	10.7	7.9	2.4	1.8	100.0	100.0
Industry	6.7	8.2	5.5	10.0	16.0	27.9	2.0	2.0	0.3	0.2	30.5	48.3
Construction	1.1	0.2	1.6	0.7	7.6	3.2	2.0	1.0	0.3	0.1	12.6	5.2
Agricultural services	0.9	0.0	1.1	0.1	4.9	0.4	1.2	0.1	0.2	0.0	8.3	0.6
Forestry	0.1	0.0	0.0	0.0	0.2	0.5	0.0	0.1	0.0	0.0	0.3	0.5
Transport	0.5	0.6	0.6	0.1	3.6	3.3	1.1	0.3	0.1	0.1	5.9	4.6
Communications	0.0	0.0	0.0	0.0	0.1	1.0	0.0	0.3	0.0	0.0	0.1	1.4
Communal services	0.1	0.2	0.2	0.0	3.1	1.6	1.3	0.6	0.2	0.1	4.9	2.3
Trade	1.8	3.5	3.5	2.2	17.9	20.7	0.7	1.6	0.3	0.6	24.2	25.6
Foreign trade	0.1	0.1	0.2	0.3	0.6	5.3	0.1	1.0	0.1	0.5	1.1	7.2
Other	3.1	1.1	1.1	0.5	5.8	1.9	2.3	0.8	0.9	0.2	13.2	4.5

Table 9.4. Distribution of number (N), revenue (S), and debt to banks (D) of large enterprises in Poland by type of ownership and f category at the end of 1992; N and S in percent and D in trillion zlotys.

	Total				Very bad				Bad			
Type of ownership	N	S	f	D	N	S	f	D	N	S	f	D
Total	100.0	100.0	–0.5	186.6	14.2	10.8	–4.3	115.0	13.6	13.6	–0.9	28.6
State	32.9	36.5	–0.5	105.2	5.8	8.1	–3.6	54.6	4.6	9.4	–0.9	20.2
Communal	4.4	1.5	0.2	1.2	0.2	0.0	–4.6	0.3	0.3	0.1	–0.8	0.1
Cooperatives	35.0	12.1	–1.0	40.9	4.5	1.2	–8.9	34.4	3.7	0.8	–0.8	1.8
Social organizations	0.8	0.1	0.2	0.0	0.0	0.0	–3.0	0.0	0.0	0.0	–0.8	0.0
Foreign	1.9	1.3	–0.6	2.7	0.3	0.1	–4.2	1.7	0.4	0.4	–0.9	0.8
Private domestic	18.4	8.9	–0.7	22.5	2.4	0.8	–4.8	16.9	3.7	1.9	–0.8	2.3
Mixed ownership	6.5	9.7	0.1	14.0	0.9	0.5	–4.4	7.1	0.9	1.1	–0.9	3.5

	Satisfactory				Good				Very good			
Type of ownership	N	S	f	D	N	S	f	D	N	S	f	D
Total	59.2	65.9	–0.0	39.4	10.5	7.9	0.8	2.5	2.4	1.8	3.3	1.1
State	16.5	42.4	–0.0	28.6	4.9	5.4	0.8	1.3	1.2	1.1	3.0	0.5
Communal	2.8	1.0	0.1	0.4	0.9	0.3	0.7	0.4	0.2	0.0	2.1	0.0
Cooperatives	23.5	9.6	–0.1	4.6	2.9	0.4	0.8	0.1	0.5	0.1	5.3	0.0
Social organizations	0.4	0.0	0.0	0.0	0.2	0.0	0.9	0.0	0.1	0.0	2.7	0.0
Foreign	1.0	0.8	–0.1	0.2	0.2	0.1	0.7	0.0	0.0	0.0	2.0	0.0
Private domestic	11.1	5.9	–0.1	3.2	1.0	0.3	0.8	–0.1	0.2	0.0	2.8	0.0
Mixed ownership	3.8	6.1	0.1	2.3	0.6	1.3	0.9	0.5	0.3	0.6	3.7	0.5

However, the most interesting feature of the data is the unusually large concentration of net debt in each category: to banks, to other enterprises, and to the government. In particular, by the end of 1992, the very bad group accounted for 61.6% of the bank debt of all the L enterprises (see *Table 9.4*). The group's combined net debt of all three categories equaled its gross income for about 13 months.

9.4.1 The distribution of very bad enterprises by financial result

We now use the z indicator of profitability to establish the viability of these very bad enterprises. We divide all enterprises into four groups according to their profitability, z, with ranges less than –0.1, between –0.1 and 0.0, between 0.0 and 0.1, and more than 0.1. We also have data which indicate the extent to which bank credits remain unserviced.

The cost of financial operations (line 4 of *Table 9.5*) is almost exclusively the interest paid on bank credits.[3] The bank credits of these very bad enterprises increased in the course of 1992 from about Zl 100 trillion to Zl 115 trillion. With interest rates typically ranging between 45% and 60%, the interest that would have been due under standard scheduling arrangements would probably have been about Zl 60 trillion. The interest actually paid by the group was, in 1992, about Zl 20 trillion, probably because of rescheduling arrangements. Since the group's bank credit represented about 50% of the total enterprise bank credit, about 33% or more of the total was effectively unserviced. The total amount of bad (unserviced) debt is somewhat greater still, as unserviced debt is also a part of the remaining 50% of the credit (see also Sections 9.7 and 9.8).

Table 9.5 also reveals that despite the large underpayment of interest, for most enterprises of the group the profitability indicator z was negative. It would thus appear that most of the very bad enterprises cannot stay in business for a long period of time unless they continue failing to service their debt and to accumulate tax obligations to the government and payments obligations to other enterprises. (In the case of housing cooperatives, continued survival depends largely on government subsidies; see Section 9.4.3.)

9.4.2 The distribution of very bad enterprises by sector of activity and type of ownership

It follows from *Table 9.3* that about half of the financially very bad enterprises were in the industrial sector. The sector "other" includes housing

Table 9.5. The distribution of large enterprises with $f < -1.5$ by profitability (z) at the end of 1992.[a]

Category	Total	$z < -0.1$	$-0.1 < z < 0$	$0 < z < 0.1$	$z > 0.1$
N in %	100.0	58.2	10.0	24.9	7.0
S [b]	49.8	24.4	8.7	11.1	5.7
Z [c]	-8.3	-9.6	-0.5	0.4	1.3
Cost of financial operations[c]	19.2	13.4	1.8	2.5	1.5
D	115.0	46.6	15.2	40.4	12.8
Average z [c]	−0.17	−0.4	−0.06	0.04	0.24
Average f [c]	−4.3	−4.2	−4.0	−5.4	−3.0
Receivables	48.6	28.4	6.1	8.8	5.3
Payables	156.0	86.1	26.7	31.8	11.3
Payables to government	30.8	21.4	3.5	4.0	1.8

[a]Except in rows 1, 6, and 7, the numbers denote trillion zlotys.
[b]Average quarterly income and other income in 1992.
[c]Annual 1992.
At the average official rate in 1992, Zl 1 trillion equaled $63.4 million. Official GDP in 1992 was, in current prices, Zl 1,140 trillion.

cooperatives, most of which belong to the group of enterprises in very bad financial state in terms of f. We also know that the two sectors account for the bulk of the bank credit of the group.

The distribution of the very bad enterprises by the type of ownership reveals in turn that, of their total bank credit, nearly half was owned by the state enterprises and an additional 30% by cooperatives.

9.4.3 Bank credit, enterprise size, and investment

This section is based on data pertaining to the third quarter of 1992. Of the 2,725 very bad enterprises, we select the largest 150 bank debtors. Their combined debt represented 62.5% of the group's total debt, by the end of September 1992. This suggests a considerable degree of concentration of bank debt within the very bad category. We divide this group of 150 into three subgroups: (a) the single highest debtor, now nearly extinct; (b) 58 housing cooperatives; and (c) the remaining 91 enterprises.

We can calculate how much variation in bank debt (D) can be explained by variation in size – measured by gross income (S) – and by the level of investment activity (I) in the first three quarters of 1992. In the following equations subscript i denotes individual enterprises, u_i is the error term, the numbers in parentheses are the standard errors, and N is the number of observations.

We combine subgroups (b) and (c):

$$\begin{aligned} D_i &= 0.156 + \underset{(0.092)}{0.876} S_i + \underset{(0.084)}{0.804} I_i + u_i \\ R^2 &= 0.904\,,\quad N = 149\ . \end{aligned} \tag{9.3}$$

Subgroup (b):

$$\begin{aligned} D_i &= 0.104 + \underset{(0.579)}{0.464} S_i + \underset{(0.207)}{1.019} I_i + u_i \\ R^2 &= 0.374\,,\quad N = 58\ . \end{aligned} \tag{9.4}$$

Subgroup (c):

$$\begin{aligned} D_i &= 0.191 + \underset{(0.125)}{0.783} S_i + \underset{(0.111)}{0.871} I_i + u_i \\ R^2 &= 0.908\,,\quad N = 91\ . \end{aligned} \tag{9.5}$$

In the case of housing cooperatives, subgroup (b), sales income is small and weakly correlated with bank debt. But these cooperatives have been para-budgetary units rather than typical enterprises. Hence the linear correlation (9.5) is more interesting. The relationship turns out to be exceptionally strong and the confidence intervals for the regression coefficients are sufficiently narrow.

The result of (9.5) would be satisfactory in explaining indebtedness of the very bad large enterprises if not for the fact that the magnitude of the constant term in (9.5) is large.

9.5 Large Enterprises in the Bad Category

The number and gross income of enterprises in the bad category are similar to those in the very bad category. However, their net financial debt equals approximately only a fourth of that for the latter group. *Table 9.3* shows that about one-third of the bad enterprises were industrial. State industrial enterprises tend to be large, and in 1992 they accounted for most of the group's bank debt.

Using data for the third quarter of 1992, we again select 150 enterprises with the largest bank debt, but this time from the bad category. This

Table 9.6. The distribution of large enterprises with $-1.5 < f < -0.5$ by profitability (z) at the end of 1992.[a]

Category	Total	$z < -0.1$	$-0.1 < z < 0$	$0 < z < 0.1$	$z > 0.1$
N, in %	100.0	26.5	27.1	34.5	11.9
S [b]	62.9	7.6	14.7	27.0	13.6
Z [c]	2.0	-1.4	-0.6	1.3	2.6
Cost of financial operations[c]	13.7	1.3	4.0	5.0	3.4
D	28.6	2.2	5.1	11.5	9.8
Average z [c]	0.03	-0.19	-0.04	0.05	0.19
Average f [c]	-0.9	-1.1	-0.9	-0.9	-0.9
Receivables	41.3	5.8	9.9	16.4	9.2
Payables	75.5	12.5	19.6	29.8	13.6
Payables to government	15.0	3.5	2.7	6.1	2.7

[a]Except in rows 1, 6, and 7, the numbers denote trillion zlotys.
[b]Average quarterly income and other income in 1992.
[c]Annual, 1992.
At the average official rate in 1992, Zl 1 trillion equaled \$63.4 million. Official GDP in 1992 was, in current prices, Zl 1,140 trillion.

subgroup accounted for 68% of the group's total bank debt, confirming a high concentration of the debt within the group. We then test the ability of the variables S and I to explain the debt. The regression is as follows:

$$
\begin{aligned}
D_i &= 0.061 + \underset{(0.022)}{0.254}S_i - \underset{(0.165)}{0.093}I_i + u_i \qquad (9.6)\\
R^2 &= 0.520\,, \quad N = 150\ .
\end{aligned}
$$

This time the correlation between D and I turns out to be insignificant.

We again use the z indicator of financial situation to determine the viability of these enterprises. We also try to establish the extent to which bank credits remain unserviced.

Since Z stands for gross financial result (profit) augmented by the depreciation allowance, a negative z indicates the potential for a cash-flow problem. Lines 1 and 2 of the *Table 9.6* show that the proportion of enterprises that were in an extremely poor financial position in terms of N and S is quite large.

Another potential problem is the serviceability of bank debt. The interest due in 1992 was about Zl 15 trillion, which is quite close to the cost of financial operations (line 4 in *Table 9.6*). We conclude therefore that most of the bank debt was, and possibly remains, serviced by the group.

In this respect there is thus a large difference between the group of enterprises in the bad category and enterprises in the very bad category.

9.6 Changes in the Financial Situation of Large Enterprises over Time

In this section we compare key enterprise financial data for the end of March 1992 with those for the end of March 1993. The period between the two dates was also the first year of post-reform recovery. The results of the comparison are displayed in *Table 9.7*.

For most financial variables changes in the distribution of enterprises across our five groups were relatively small during the year in question. The size of both outlier groups, very bad and very good, had increased. This may suggest a trend of increasing polarization in the fortunes of enterprises. Very good enterprises are free of bank debt and, although accounting for less than 2% of total sales, have accumulated nearly 20% of total cash deposits. Therefore these enterprises represent probably the highest growth area of the economy. Most members in the very bad group would be doing the opposite: contracting activity and, at some point, ceasing operations. The group is, however, constantly resupplied by failures from the bad and satisfactory groups. Consequently it may also expand, as it did in the period in question.

9.7 The Distribution of Medium Enterprises According to the f Indicator

In our study M-type enterprises are those which employed between 5 and 49 in industry and construction and between 5 and 19 elsewhere at the end of September 1992. Once again we divide the whole sample of enterprises into 32 classes using the indicator f and calculate the proportion of sales and other gross income for each class. The resulting f distribution also turns out to be bell-shaped, with the average f equal to –0.38 and a high concentration of enterprises ranging between –0.3 and 0.3. We classify the enterprises into five f categories. The main difference between the L and the M enterprises is that there is an even greater concentration of debt (to banks, to enterprises, and to the government) in the very bad category of the M enterprises.

Table 9.7. Distribution of financial assets and liabilities of large enterprises in Poland by f category at the end of March 1992 (A) and 1993 (B).

	Total absolute levels		In percent									
			Very bad		Bad		Satisfactory		Good		Very good	
Category	A	B	A	B	A	B	A	B	A	B	A	B
N (number of enterprises)	20130	18021	12.0	15.1	14.0	15.0	59.3	58.3	10.8	8.9	3.3	2.8
S (gross income)	388.6	496.9	6.9	11.2	15.6	12.9	68.6	67.0	7.6	7.3	1.3	1.6
D (bank debt)	169.7	195.3	60.9	62.3	17.4	13.7	19.6	22.2	1.4	1.2	0.7	0.6
Own cash	53.6	67.1	13.3	10.3	11.3	7.8	38.7	40.6	21.7	23.5	14.9	17.7
Receivables	275.1	310.2	10.7	17.2	16.1	12.6	47.9	49.1	16.7	11.6	8.5	9.5
Payables	304.6	420.5	24.2	38.8	23.9	17.6	38.8	35.2	10.4	5.0	2.8	3.3
Payables to government	48.8	82.2	26.9	45.5	32.3	19.1	34.5	30.2	4.9	3.3	1.4	1.9
Average f	–0.4	–0.5	–5.3	–4.0	–0.9	–0.9	0.0	0.0	0.8	0.8	4.2	3.3

The value unit of account is Zl 1 trillion. GDP in current prices was Zl 1,140 trillion in 1992 and about Zl 1,530 trillion in 1993.

For example, in the case of bank debt, the category accounted for 74% of the total, compared with 60% for the group of large enterprises, on 30 September 1992. If two-thirds of this 74% is unserviced, such bad debt would amount to about 5% of the total bank credit to the economy. The combined bad debt for both L and M enterprises would appear to be, by September 1992, about 38% of the total bank credit to the nonfinancial sector of the economy.

9.8 Estimation of the Total Bad Debt

To estimate the total stock of bad debt, one needs to know the quality of bank credits given to farms, both private and state, and to other small businesses employing up to five persons. This sector accounts for about 20% of the total bank credit. If the quality of that credit is not much different from that of the other 80%, the total of bad debt in 1992, and probably in 1993, ranged between 45% and 50% of total debt. An early internal audit of nine state commercial banks found the share of bad debts on 30 June 1991 to range between 9% and 79%, with 42% being the weighted average (Ministry of Finance, 1992b, p. 4). Audits conducted since then have shown that the shares have changed only slightly.

Aggregate NBP data on total capitalized interest (on credit directed according to set rules and as a result of rescheduling arrangements) and interest due but unpaid and not renegotiated show an increase during 1993 of about Zl 30 trillion. This is despite a direct budget subsidy to creditors of some Zl 10 trillion. The total midyear bank debt of nonfinancial economic units was Zl 286 trillion. These numbers allow one to estimate the share of bad debts. Given that the market interest rates range between 40% and 50% in 1993, the interest payments due ranged between Zl 115 trillion and Zl 143 trillion, the unpaid interests (Zl 40 trillion) thus representing some 28% to 35% of the total payments. This range is on the low side of the estimate given above. However, the interest rates offered by banks after renegotiations may be lower than the market rates. Hence the NBP data may underestimate the size of the problem.

9.9 Implications for Fiscal and Monetary Policies

The large size of bad bank debts appears to be a very serious problem for the banking sector. However, their heavy concentration in about one-tenth of the enterprise sector means that the remaining 90% of the enterprise sector is almost debt-free. This financial duality has implications for economic policies of the government, the National Bank of Poland, and the lending policy of commercial banks. It also has an influence on the pace of economic recovery.

The immediate effect is that banks have to maintain a wide interest spread, thus increasing the cost of borrowing to creditworthy enterprises and the government. With the increases in the cost of servicing public debt, we have one or more of the following situations: (i) a higher budget deficit, (ii) cuts in other public expenditures, or (iii) higher taxation. Option (i) is welcome by banks, as it offers them an opportunity for improving the quality of their assets. However, such a deficit also implies a higher inflation rate and, therefore, higher nominal interest rates and lower investment activity. The budget position is affected adversely also on the revenue side; the reason for this is deteriorating profits of banks, as provisions are made against bad debts. The provisions are built up gradually, and in Poland it will take several years before they are adequate.

During such a period, therefore, there is a tendency for changing the composition of demand for new bank credit: away from the economy and toward the government. The real interest rates during this period are too high for most good enterprises, and credit to most badly performing enterprises is blocked by the more cautious banks.

Because the velocity of money tends to be several times higher in transition economies than in developed market economies, a given budget deficit that is financed by credit expansion is also several times more inflationary. High nominal and high real interest rates are the result. The problem of a large bad debt is, therefore, that it contributes to creating an economic environment which, while perhaps not a major threat, is not at all conducive to recovery.

One should of course separate out the debt issue as an inherited macroeconomic problem affecting adversely good enterprises and taxpayers from the question of future viability of the debt-ridden enterprises. These enterprises need not be closed down, and those that would make a gross profit when not servicing the debt should not be closed down.

The separation is best achieved by adopting a shock therapy: cancellation of all bad debt and the issue of government paper to banks in the same amount (Begg and Portes, 1992). However, the therapy would have the effect of removing pressure from the very bad enterprises to meet at least some of the debt-servicing cost. Even more importantly, it would reduce the disciplining function of bad debts for banks in their credit policy. The bad debt problem could then reappear quickly.

Polish authorities have also rejected the standard, less radical approach to the banks' financial restructuring, which was, according to senior Ministry of Finance officials, advocated for Poland by international financial institutions (Kawalec *et al.*, 1993). This course proposes to transfer bad loans to a specially created loan-recovery institution and to replace them with interest-bearing treasury bonds. Given the circumstances of Central and Eastern Europe this second approach may, however, differ little from the first one. As Kawalec *et al.* (1993) explain:

> We did not believe that a centralised, government-sponsored agency can vigorously and effectively recover bad debts. We did not believe in our ability to create, within a reasonable time period, a strong institution in terms of high quality of its staff and internal organisation. Neither did we believe in the possibility of devising an adequate incentive system that would ensure that institution's active approach toward the indebted enterprises. We also did not believe that such an institution could be made to resist the political pressure.... By painlessly removing the burden of bad debt from the banks, the centralised approach creates a danger that the bad loan portfolio will re-emerge in a near future.

An evolutionary strategy seems, in this case, more appropriate. The government may recapitalize banks with its paper, and possibly cash, by a large fraction but not by the full amount of the bad debt. The level of recapitalization should be sufficient so that the banks are able to create just about adequate provisions against bad loans. But the banks should also be encouraged, through financial incentives and administrative means, to draw up financial and business restructuring plans for enterprises with bad debts. The Polish Law on Financial Restructuring of Enterprises and Banks envisages that conciliation procedures may take place between creditors holding at least 50% of the claims and debtors, leading to agreements about how to implement such plans. The agreements may imply a full or a partial recovery of the bank loan. They were to be reached before end of March 1994, but the deadline has been extended. If the agreements cannot be reached, one of the following is to take place: bankruptcy is declared by the court, liquidation of the debtor's business is initiated, or creditworthiness of the debtor is regained by servicing the debt for at least a three-month period. The banks also have the options of selling the debt on the market for cash or swapping it for equity. This decentralized approach to bad loans is expected to limit, somewhat, the magnitude of the direct call on state resources, while stimulating supply-side restructuring, privatization, and good banking management.

However, Polish authorities have probably underestimated the size of the bad debts and, therefore, the amount of recapitalization needed. This has been partly recognized already in the budget for 1994 by increasing this amount from Zl 23 trillion to Zl 39 trillion. The cost to the budget for operating the so-called subsidiary government intervention to help important enterprises is also likely to be high. Tax losses resulting from the obligation for banks to make increased provisions against bad debt will probably be much higher than initially anticipated.

Acknowledgments

All computations needed to compile the various tables were performed by the Computer Department of the Polish Ministry of Finance at the request and under the direction of the author. Econometric computations were performed by Joanna Gomulka, and diagrams were prepared by Gilles Alfandari. The paper benefited much from suggestions by Jacek Rostowski of the School of Slavonic and Eastern European Studies, London University, and Mark Schaffer of the Centre for Economic Performance at the London School of Economics. Skillful secretarial assistance was provided by Pat Nutt. The study was prepared when the author was Economic Adviser to Jerzy Osiatynski, the Polish Finance Minister. An earlier version was presented to a number of academic and policy-making groups in Poland, as well as at seminars held at the London School of Economics and Oxford University. The Warsaw-based Centre for Social and Economic Research distributed the paper as Working Paper No. 6 in its Studies and Analyses Series. A version of the paper appeared in *Economics of Transition*, **2**(2), 189–208, 1994.

Notes

[1] Cash flow equals $Z - \Delta$inventories $- \Delta$receivables $+ \Delta$payables, where Δ denotes change during the accounting period. If inventories and receivables do not increase, but payables continue to increase, the cash flow position is better than that indicated by Z.

[2] A primary example of this is a private company called Art B, which at one time employed about 15,000 people, but which is now a small business with an outstanding bank debt of hundreds of millions of US dollars.

[3] It also includes net purchases of stocks and securities, discounts on sold debts, the effects of changes in the exchange rate, and interests on bonds.

References

Begg, D., and Portes, R., 1992, Enterprise Debt and Economic Transformation: Financial Restructuring in Central and Eastern Europe [mimeo].

Kawalec, S., Sikora, S., and Rymaszewski, P., 1993, Dealing with Bad Debts: The Case of Poland, Presented at World Bank and IMF Conference on Building Sound Finance in Emerging Market Economies, 10–11 June, Washington, DC, USA.

Ministry of Finance, 1993, Intended Actions to Implement the Programme of Financial Restructuring of Enterprises and Banks, 19 March, Warsaw, Poland.

Ministry of Finance, 1992a, Explanations and Justifications of the Proposed Law on Financial Restructuring of Enterprises and Banks, 11 June, Warsaw, Poland.

Ministry of Finance, 1992b, Data Concerning Underperforming Assets of the Nine Commercial Banks in 1991 and Early 1992, 11 June, Warsaw, Poland.

Comments on the Paper by Stanislaw Gomulka

Daniel Daianu

The research under scrutiny is a "first detailed study of enterprise finances in a transition country of Central and Eastern Europe." Stanislaw Gomulka's endeavor is more than commendable if one bears in mind the difficulty encountered by many economists in entering the black box we call *enterprise* – with its behavioral patterns and routines – and figuring out the financial anatomy of different groups of enterprises. The results of the study confirm the seriousness of the bad debt problem in the frontrunner economies as well (see Calvo and Kumar, 1993) and provide additional evidence for making us even more attentive to the complexity of the transformation process. The study is also interesting for its goal to take a look at the evolution of bad debt in Poland.

The Polish experience shows that there is no way for substantial bad debt reproduction to be arrested unless wide-ranging restructuring of the economy takes place. Since massive restructuring cannot be but a lasting affair under the circumstances, the whole issue of bad debt becomes very much a dynamic story. The implicit warning contained in the chapter is worth stressing again: because of the legacy of extreme misallocation of resources (in a command economy), bad debt will haunt and daunt policy makers for years to come, with no clear solutions in sight. Therefore, Gomulka's preference for an evolutionary approach in dealing with this problem is understandable.

If one accepts "bad debt being a lasting affair" as a working assumption, then the dynamic story becomes the relevant issue to explore. Unfortunately, the author has not been able to deal more extensively with it. In my opinion future investigations would be very useful in this respect for at least two reasons: in spite of large bad debts and, consequently, high positive real interest rates and wide spreads practiced by banks – which, presumably, would impede growth – the Polish economy revealed the highest growth rate in Europe in 1993 (over 4%); high positive real interest rates are detrimental to many companies which, because of poor capitalization and a large stock of bad debts (not necessarily connected with the current status of their productive operations), appear financially unhealthy.

In my opinion, the growth resumption and the burgeoning private sector in Poland beg several questions. How can one explain the growth of this economy in spite of considerable bad debts and high positive real interest rates? Maybe this is related to the dynamics of bad debt, or perhaps the growth of the economy is only a temporary breakthrough. Another explanation could be linked to the reluctance of the private sector to resort to bank credit because of its cost. As Rostowski (1993) indicates this may be very much the case. Could the private sector continue relying on nonbank circuits for financing its operations and what are the conditions attached to this financing? What about that part of the economy that could be financially solvent if real interest rates were less burdensome? The answer to the last question is relevant to determine how the "balance of power" between the "black hole" (mentioned by Gomulka) and the healthy portion of the economy will unfold.

Does one witness the emergence of a "dual economy," made up of a financially insolvent sector (the black hole) and a financially healthy one, at unusually high positive real interest rates? To what extent would such a dual economy be a stable one?

Given this reasoning one comes to the issue of how to approach bad debt in order to improve the functioning of the whole economy. As Gomulka points out, bad debt in Poland is heavily concentrated – with the "black hole" constantly renewed by dropouts from the other categories. Nevertheless, one has to admit that there are dropouts that may not deserve such a fate. If this black hole is easily discernible, the idea of creating a *cordon sanitaire* around it should become very tempting. It is unquestionable that bad debt shapes banks' behavior as "passive creditors," as argued by Begg and Portes (1992). Therefore, if much of bad debt is concentrated in specific enterprises, it makes sense to think of a specialized institution that could deal with this issue – at least partially. In this way, banks would be relieved of much of the burden and would more likely undertake the task of restructuring as agents of change. Banks could get involved in restructuring under the hypostasis of strategic equity owners.

It is true that the jury is still out in the "universal vs. narrow banks" debate. But as Székely (1993) properly points out, in Central and Eastern Europe "the model issue is not an issue any longer" under the flow of events, and banks are asked to play a major role. Besides, as van Wijnbergen (1992, p. 14) said, "the objection that banks do not have the skills to do that right is less compelling than at first sight. The point is not that banks are good at doing this, but that they are likely to be better than anybody else." Consequently, any means that can help banks behave as active creditors should be more than welcome.

In this way banks would have more leeway in escaping the grip of the "power of structure" represented by the network of heavily indebted banks. Specialized institutions have been used in advanced market economies (in the USA, after the savings and loan association debacle, in Japan, and so on), and I do not see a solid reason for rejecting such a solution, out of hand, for transforming economies – especially when bad debt seems to be heavily concentrated.

I would conclude by emphasizing two transparent questions which are suggested in Gomulka's paper. Is growth sustainable under the current circumstances? If the government has underestimated the magnitude of the problem of bad debt, what would be the best way to tackle it? In my opinion, these two questions touch upon what I consider to be a major issue missing in the whole debate about transition: the magnitude of the required structural adjustment in a post-command economy – in an economy with a legacy of extreme misallocation of resources. Four years have passed since the start of structural reforms, and I am quite puzzled by the neglect of this issue. When I see Western governments tinkering on the fringes and deeply reluctant to undertake relatively minor adjustments, I consider it myopic not to talk about the size of the problem and its implications.

In this vein, dealing with bad debt in a pragmatic way (by combining a centralized approach with a decentralized one) makes sense if one understands the need for an industrial policy seen as a "damage control device" – an industrial policy aimed at mitigating the pains and costs of restructuring in a very fuzzy and volatile environment. Such an industrial policy would involve "picking losers among losers" in order to ensure a certain balance between exit and entry in the economy. The Enterprise and Bank Restructuring Program, the special fund meant to deal with *sensitive* enterprises and administered by the Industrial Development Agency, is a component of what can be defined as the Polish industrial policy.

References

Begg, D., and Portes, R., 1992, *Enterprise Debt and Economic Transformation: Financial Restructuring in Central and Eastern Europe*, Centre for Economic Policy Research, London, UK.

Calvo, G.A., and Kumar, M.S., 1993, Financial markets and intermediation, in *Financial Sector Reforms and Exchange Arrangements in Eastern Europe*, Occasional Paper, No. 102, International Monetary Fund, Washington, DC, USA.

Rostowski, J., 1993, *The Implementations of Rapid Private Sector Growth in Poland*, Discussion Paper, No. 159, Centre for Economic Policy Research, London, UK.

Székely, I., 1993, *Economic Transformation and the Reform of the Financial System in Central and Eastern Europe*, Discussion Paper, No. 816, Centre for Economic Policy Research, London, UK.

van Wijnbergen, S., 1992, *Enterprise Reform in Eastern Europe*, Discussion Paper, No. 738, Centre for Economic Policy Research, London, UK.

Chapter 10

Output Decline and Government Expenditures in European Transition Economies

Ke-young Chu and Gerd Schwartz

In recent discussions on government expenditures in transition economies, it has occasionally been suggested that a fiscal stimulus is needed to overcome the transition-induced recession. As a result, there has been a renewed interest in Keynesian demand policies that are advocated, however cautiously, as a remedy for overcoming the recession quickly (Kornai, 1993; WIIW, 1993). Indeed, it may be argued that some governments in European transition economies have already begun to make expansionary fiscal policies an explicit part of their policy agenda. For example, the current coalition government in Poland, at least in its rhetoric, sees a need for a "temporary and noninflationary" increase in the state budget deficit.

This paper tries to study three basic questions on expenditure policies in European transition economies. First, we ask whether actual changes in the level and composition of government expenditures in European transition economies were largely the result of expenditure policies or of broader

We gratefully acknowledge comments and suggestions by Ajai Chopra, Charalambos Christofides, Benedict Clements, Liam Ebrill, Dan Hewitt, Mark Lutz, Ewald Nowotny, and the Conference participants. The views and opinions expressed are strictly personal and do not necessarily reflect those of the International Monetary Fund.

R. Holzmann et al. (eds.), Output Decline in Eastern Europe, 241-261.

transition-induced exogenous factors. Second, we ask whether actual expenditure policies contributed significantly to the measured output decline, and, if so, whether this was attributable to specific expenditure components. Third, we ask whether there were more desirable alternatives to the policies that have been undertaken, and what the prospects for recovery would have been under these alternatives. The analyses can only be seen as a first step. A final answer to the questions raised will have to await more detailed analyses and careful evaluation of the available quantitative evidence.

For the purpose of this paper, the group of European transition economies comprises Bulgaria, former Czechoslovakia and its two successor republics, Hungary, Poland, and Romania. Section 10.1 provides an overview on the channels by which government expenditures may affect aggregate output, and discusses various problems related to measuring economic activity in transition economies. Section 10.2 describes recent changes in government expenditures in European transition economies, and reflects on the changes in the levels and composition of government expenditures as possible causes and contributing factors underlying the developments in output. Section 10.3 provides concluding observations.

10.1 Government Expenditures and Output: General Remarks

Table 10.1 summarizes the main channels through which government expenditures can *potentially* contribute to a decline in aggregate output.[1] In the short run, governments affect output through four main expenditure channels. First, the government produces goods and services, the factor costs of which are largely reflected in payments of wages and salaries and in interest payments. Second, the government provides producer subsidies. Third, the government has a direct demand that is reflected in purchases of goods and services and capital expenditures. Finally, the government makes payments with income transfer characteristics that influence household demand for goods and services, for example, consumer subsidies and social expenditures. In practice, a single expenditure may affect output through more than one channel. Transfers to finance unemployment compensation, for example, not only affect household demand, but may also affect the pace of enterprise restructuring. In the longer term, government expenditures affect potential aggregate output, investment, and employment, particularly via physical and human capital investments.

Table 10.1. Government expenditures and output decline in transition economies.

Short-term considerations

Government expenditures may adversely affect actual output via:

1. Reductions in factor income payments
   - wages and salaries for government employees
   - interest payments
2. Reductions in producer subsidies
3. Reductions in direct government demand
   - government purchases of goods and services
   - capital expenditures
4. Reductions in expenditures with income transfer characteristics
   - consumer subsidies
   - social expenditures

Longer-term considerations

Government expenditures may adversely affect potential future output via:

1. Reductions in physical capital spending
2. Reductions in human capital investments

The analysis of the effects of government expenditures on output is hampered by a number of factors. Measurement problems for both national income and fiscal accounts exist everywhere. However, these common measurement problems are compounded in transition economies because of a severely distorted structure of relative prices, sometimes high inflation, a growing private sector that is not adequately captured in the national statistics, and institutional arrangements that often do not clearly distinguish between the government and the rest of the public sector and, in addition, are undergoing rapid change.

Four examples may illustrate these problems. First, food prices in many centrally planned economies had been kept at artificially low levels through large consumer subsidies. Increases in relative food prices at the start of transition frequently reflected a reduction of consumer subsidies, not an increase in value added. Second, earlier there had been a proliferation of in-kind wages and benefits, and, as a result, monetary wages were low. Increases in wage expenditures frequently reflected a monetization of in-kind benefits rather than an increase in government value added. Third, there existed a distorted interest rate structure, with real interest rates that were substantially negative. Recent increases in interest payments frequently reflected financial market reforms that resulted in more market-oriented interest rates.

Finally, there was the problem of the quasi-fiscal operations of central banks. Increases in government expenditures in recent years frequently reflected a shifting of some of the central bank's quasi-fiscal operations to the fiscal accounts (where they belong), and did not necessarily imply that the actual extent of government intervention in the economy and its impact on output had increased.

The problem of measuring government expenditures in transition economies is also compounded by four other factors.

First, with high inflation and high nominal interest rates, a large share of interest payments represented amortization of government debt because it compensated creditors for the erosion in the real value of their assets. In theory, it is possible to remove this implicit inflation-induced amortization from the calculation of the fiscal deficit (Blejer and Cheasty, 1992). In practice, however, it may often not be clear to what extent domestic interest payments should be regarded as constituting amortization payments. This problem is particularly pronounced when real interest rates are sharply negative.

Second, many transition economies had a stock of explicit or implicit contingent liabilities, for example, in the areas of the environment, housing, and bank guarantees for loans to state-owned enterprises. Ignoring these contingent liabilities meant underestimating the current extent of the government's role in allocating resources in the economy and potential expenditure levels that, under current policies, may prevail in the future.

Third, during central planning it was not really meaningful to speak of "fiscal" policy and "public" finance since these concepts imply the existence of "private" finance, and thus a significant private sector (Tanzi, 1993). As part of the transition, the boundary lines between the government, the financial sector, state-owned enterprises, and the private sector needed to be redefined, and, as a result, large blocks of assets and liabilities tended to get reshuffled in the early years of transition. Privatization and government involvement in the problem of the banking system's bad debt were two of the most visible manifestations of this reshuffling.

Finally, sizable reforms of intragovernmental fiscal relations in many transition economies often led to a situation where various expenditures were removed from the state budget. As suggested by Bird and Wallich (1993), this was part of a strategy of pushing expenditure responsibilities to subnational (i.e., regional or municipal) or extra-budgetary levels in the hope that the necessary cost cutting would be done there. Generally, this tended to obscure the true fiscal policy stance.

10.2 Government Expenditures and Output in Transition Economies

This section elaborates on the three main questions posed in the introduction, using data for the 1988–1992 time period.

10.2.1 Expenditure levels

Governments in European transition economies moved relatively swiftly to establish market-oriented rules, including laws aimed at ensuring property rights, competition policies, and private economic activities. These reforms went hand in hand with a reordering of spending priorities.

All transition economies faced a two-pronged fiscal problem. To create room for private initiative, governments had to reduce the extent of state intervention in the economy. This meant reducing the size of government, raising revenues in a less distorted fashion, and improving the expenditure mix. At the same time, the fiscal deficit had to be kept within the limits that were compatible with macroeconomic stabilization objectives.

Accounting problems aside, transition economies showed a clear tendency of reducing the overall extent of government intervention. Given high starting levels, reducing government intervention was one of the basic premises for successfully establishing a market-based economy. Reductions in government intervention manifested themselves through changes in institutional arrangements, as well as through reduced shares of government output and employment, but not necessarily through reduced government expenditures and budget deficits. In this sense, it was not reductions in government expenditures, *per se*, but reductions in the extent of government intervention in the economy that, since it was not instantly and fully replaced by private-sector coordination, contributed to what Kornai (1993) has termed the "transitional recession."

Still, the behavior of government expenditures in European transition economies was not uniform. If 1990 is considered the first full year of transition, all economies experienced some initial expenditure reductions in this first year, with declines of 1 percentage point of GDP in Bulgaria, 4 in Romania and Hungary, 9 in Poland, and 10 in former Czechoslovakia (see *Table 10.2*). In general, expenditure reductions can only to a limited extent be interpreted to reflect fiscal "adjustment" or "tightening."

While simultaneous reductions in real GDP and the government expenditures to GDP ratio implied that real government expenditures declined

Table 10.2. Government expenditures and their components, in percent of GDP.

	1988	1989	1990	1991	1992
1. *Total government expenditures*					
Bulgaria	64	61	60	46	43
Former Czechoslovakia	72	72	62	55	56
Hungary	62	61	57	59	63
Poland[a]	48	49	40	48	50
Romania	39	43	39	41	48
2. *Factor incomes*					
Bulgaria	7	8	11	12	12
Former Czechoslovakia	7	7	7	n.a.	n.a.
Hungary	10	11	11	13	15
Poland	4	7	6	9	12
Romania	5	5	6	8	8
Wages and salaries					
Bulgaria	5	5	6	5	6
Former Czechoslovakia	7	7	7	n.a.	n.a.
Hungary	8	8	8	9	10
Poland	4	7	6	7	8
Romania	5	5	6	8	8
Interest payments[b]					
Bulgaria	2	3	5	7	6
Former Czechoslovakia	0	0	0	1	1
Hungary	2	2	3	4	5
Poland[c]	0	0	0	2	3
Romania	0	0	0	0	0
3. *Producer subsidies*					
Bulgaria	16	14	11	4	2
Former Czechoslovakia	n.a.	19	12	8	5
Hungary	8	5	4	3	3
Poland	6	5	3	2	1
Romania	2	2	5	5	n.a.

[a]General government data for Poland in 1992 includes, for the first time, the extra-budgetary units of the local authorities. On a consolidated basis, expenditures by these entities amounted to some 2.4% of GDP. Hence, if they were excluded, total government expenditures in Poland would have remained constant during 1991–1992.
[b]Not corrected for inflation (see Blejer and Cheasty, 1992).
[c]Before 1991, interest payments were part of other current noninterest expenditures.
[d]Defined as total expenditures of the three main social-security funds: the Social Insurance Fund, the Social Insurance Fund for Farmers, and the Labor Fund.
Sources: Data provided by the national authorities, and estimates by the authors.

Table 10.2. Continued.

	1988	1989	1990	1991	1992
4. *Direct government demand*					
Bulgaria	23	25	20	15	14
Former Czechoslovakia	27	26	25	n.a.	n.a.
Hungary	20	19	16	16	17
Poland	9	7	7	8	6
Romania	22	23	14	14	14
Purchases of goods and services					
Bulgaria	18	19	17	13	12
Former Czechoslovakia	17	18	18	n.a.	n.a.
Hungary	12	12	11	9	10
Poland	4	3	5	6	4
Romania	5	5	6	8	8
Capital expenditures					
Bulgaria	5	5	3	2	2
Former Czechoslovakia	10	8	7	6	7
Hungary	8	7	5	6	7
Poland	4	3	3	2	2
Romania	17	18	8	6	6
5. *Payments with income transfer characteristics*					
Bulgaria	12	12	16	14	13
Former Czechoslovakia	n.a.	20	18	16	16
Hungary	20	23	25	27	26
Poland	19	20	15	20	22
Romania	11	14	14	14	n.a.
Consumer subsidies					
Bulgaria	2	2	4	0	0
Former Czechoslovakia	4	7	4	0	0
Hungary	5	7	6	4	1
Poland	10	8	4	3	3
Romania	3	4	3	4	n.a.
Social expenditures					
Bulgaria	10	10	12	14	13
Former Czechoslovakia	n.a.	14	14	16	16
Hungary	15	16	20	23	25
Poland[d]	9	11	11	17	20
Romania	8	10	11	10	10
6. *Other*					
Bulgaria	6	3	2	1	3
Former Czechoslovakia	n.a.	1	0	3	4
Hungary	4	4	2	0	2
Poland	10	11	9	9	9
Romania	0	0	0	1	4

even more than GDP, traditional countercyclical policy considerations were ill-suited for transition economies: a transition is not a cyclical downturn within a regular business cycle and therefore requires different policy prescriptions. In particular, given high starting levels of government expenditures, it would be unreasonable to expect real government expenditures to increase during the transition from a centrally planned economy to a market-based economy, independent of the behavior of GDP.

For analytical purposes, European transition economies can be grouped into two categories. Countries in the first category, namely, Bulgaria and former Czechoslovakia, experienced at least two years of declining government expenditures during 1990–1992, and reduced, relative to GDP, government expenditures from their pre-transition levels. Countries in the second category, namely, Hungary, Poland, and Romania, experienced only one year of declining government expenditures during 1990–1992, and did not reduce, relative to GDP, government expenditures from their pre-transition levels.

In Bulgaria, general government expenditures declined from 61% of GDP in 1989 to 43% in 1992; in former Czechoslovakia, they declined from 72% to 60% of GDP over the same time period. While this drop was impressive, it was to some extent an inevitable part of the transition in these two economies; in particular, it did not primarily reflect fiscal tightening, but a correction in the degree of state interference in the state-owned enterprise sector, which was high even by the standards of other transition economies.

To a large extent, the drastic reductions in government expenditures in Bulgaria and former Czechoslovakia were due to strong reductions in producer subsidies. Budgeted subsidies were high in all European transition economies, but in Bulgaria and former Czechoslovakia the bulk of all subsidies were producer subsidies that went to state-owned enterprises, while in Hungary, Poland, and Romania, the bulk of all budgeted subsidies were consumer subsidies.[2] In 1989, budgeted producer subsidies amounted to 14% and 19% of GDP in Bulgaria and former Czechoslovakia, but only to 5% of GDP in Hungary and Poland, and 2% of GDP in Romania. A large part of producer subsidies were cross-subsidies. Cross-subsidies were funds provided predominantly to unprofitable state-owned enterprises, often on a discretionary basis, and simply constituted the counterpart to punitive taxes levied on their more profitable counterparts. The need for these cross-subsidies was particularly high in Bulgaria and former Czechoslovakia, where the share of value added produced in the state-owned sector amounted to over 90%, and significantly exceeded the levels of other European transition economies.

To establish a market-based economy, it was important to liberalize prices, impose a hard budget constraint on state-owned enterprises, and introduce a modern system of taxing enterprise profits. As soon as the transition got under way, both the scope and the need for cross-subsidies and profit remittances to the budget were reduced. Making changes was relatively easy for three principal reasons: first, at least from a long-run perspective, the system of cross-subsidies and punitive profit taxes was at best a zero-sum game; second, revoking these subsidies was not perceived as revoking entitlements; third, at least over the short run, some state-owned enterprises compensated for the reduction in producer subsidies by increasing tax arrears and/or inter-enterprise arrears. Hence, it should not come as a surprise that the two countries with by far the highest pre-transition level of general government expenditures, value added in the public sector, and producer subsidies were also the only ones that reduced government expenditures significantly during the transition.

In Hungary, Poland, and Romania, the level of government expenditures relative to GDP, after declining in 1990, increased during 1991–1992. The initial decline occurred for different reasons, but in all three countries they were closely associated with a surplus in the overall fiscal balance during that year. In Hungary, the reduction in government expenditures by 4 percentage points of GDP in 1990 reflected relatively even cuts in most expenditure categories, even though social expenditures increased by 4 percentage points of GDP, and interest payments by 1 percentage point.

In Poland, the reduction in government expenditures by 9 percentage points of GDP in 1990 was driven by a strong reduction in subsidies (6 percentage points of GDP), mostly consumer subsidies. With the freeing of most consumer prices in January 1990, the extensive system of subsidizing consumer products was no longer viable. The general government surplus of 3 percentage points of GDP was not only due to expenditure restraint but also due to an unexpected windfall in enterprise income taxes. These increased by 6 percentage points of GDP when historical cost accounting within the highly inflationary environment that characterized Poland in 1990 resulted in taxing paper profits.

In Romania, general government expenditures declined by 3 or 4 percentage points of GDP in 1990, largely as a result of reduction in capital expenditures, which fell by almost 10 percentage points of GDP. Virtually all other expenditures increased relative to GDP, notably producer subsidies (3 percentage points of GDP) and wages and salaries (1 or 2 percentage points of GDP). The strong increase in producer subsidies occurred for two main reasons: first, with little change in subsidization policies and GDP declining, subsidies naturally had to increase relative to GDP; second, some of the subsidies that were previously hidden were made explicit.

During 1991–1992, all three countries experienced increases in government expenditures relative to GDP. However, it is not clear to what extent these increases prevented further declines in real GDP. At least from a cross-country perspective the evidence is inconclusive: Poland, the country with the seemingly steepest increase in government expenditures during 1991–1992 (10 percentage points of GDP), also experienced the smallest decline in real GDP (-7%) during that period.[3] At the same time, Romania, which experienced a similarly steep increase in government expenditures during that time period (9 percentage points of GDP), was the country with the steepest drop in real GDP (-30%).

It is possible that these vastly different results for Poland and Romania reflected problems of measuring GDP and actual government expenditures. Another possibility is that the binding constraints in these two economies were very different. For example, during 1991–1992, credit constraints were probably much more severe in Romania than in Poland, as reflected in the massive increase in inter-enterprise arrears that occurred in Romania during 1991 (Clifton and Khan, 1993; and Chapter 8 in this book by Calvo and Coricelli). If it could be assumed that credit constraints were binding in Romania while they were not binding in Poland, the same overall increase in government expenditures could have had substantially different "multiplier" effects. Hence, changes in the level of budgeted government expenditures alone, without taking into consideration the binding constraints that existed in an economy, may not provide a forceful explanation for the behavior of aggregate output.

10.2.2 Expenditure composition

In this section we argue that changes in the composition of government expenditure had but a small effect on the decline in aggregate output in European transition economies, and that, generally, it was not government expenditure that constrained aggregate output or determined the magnitude of the output decline. Even in cases where it could be argued that government expenditure constraints were binding, they were usually not the only binding constraints. For example, sectors that experienced severe input constraints – such as those caused by the collapse of the CMEA – could not have responded to impulses from government demand. While it has been argued that credit tightening and the imposition of hard budget constraints for state-owned enterprises were brought about too rapidly, it is difficult to make a general case that a different set of expenditure policies, *per se*, would have mitigated the output decline. Indeed, evidence from Poland suggests, for example, that consistency in applying a hard budget constraint (i.e., maintaining a "no bailout" policy) helped to establish the credibility of Poland's reforms which in turn yielded improvements in manufacturing output, efficiency, and resource allocation (Pinto, 1993).

In addition, government expenditures in European transition economies still remain on the high side, at least compared with European market-based economies. As a result, few reasons exist for pursuing expansionary fiscal policies as a way to lift European transition economies out of the transitional recession, even when abstracting from possible adverse macroeconomic consequences. However, a further reordering of expenditure priorities is desirable. In particular, increases in the share of government expenditures on capital – human and physical – may be needed for improving long-run output potential.

The expenditure mix that was inherited by the governments of European transition economies was clearly inappropriate for the needs of a market-based environment, and therefore had to be changed. For analytical purposes, we continue to use the four main categories of government expenditures that were outlined above: factor income payments that constitute a part of GDP, producer subsidies, direct government demand, and expenditures with income transfer characteristics. *Table 10.2* shows magnitudes of these expenditure components in European transition economies.

Two major government expenditure items constitute *factor incomes*: wages and salaries, and interest payments. In all transition economies, with the exception of former Czechoslovakia, spending on factor incomes increased significantly relative to pre-transition levels, fueled by increases in both wages and salaries and interest expenditures. The increase during 1989–1992 was remarkably uniform across European transition economies, amounting to 4 percentage points of GDP everywhere, except in former Czechoslovakia, where no data are available. There were probably two main causes for these increases: first, government wage policies that had to be carried out to prevent a brain drain from the civil service and to mitigate the difficulties encountered with civil service reform in the light of rapidly increasing unemployment; second, financial reforms that resulted in market-oriented domestic interest rate policies and made real interest rates positive for the first time in recent history.

Although still low relative to GDP, at least when compared with Western industrial economies, wages and salaries in the government sectors of

European transition economies increased from 5%–8% of GDP in 1989 to 6%–10% in 1992. Particularly in Hungary and Poland, and, even though there are no data available, probably also in former Czechoslovakia, some real wage increases in the government sector were necessitated by increased competition for qualified labor by the enterprise sector.

Overall, only a small part of the increased wage expenditures reflected an increase in government consumption; much of it was simply a monetization of in-kind benefits that did not increase the government's actual value added. In general, wage expenditures are always difficult to reduce; in practice, it may even happen that reductions in the productivity of government employees and decreases in their value added coincide with increased wage expenditures.

In countries with low levels of domestic and foreign debt, such as former Czechoslovakia and Romania, interest payments were not a major expenditure item. In contrast, in Bulgaria, interest payments increased from 3% of GDP in 1989 to 6% of GDP in 1992. In Hungary and Poland, interest expenditures grew, reaching 5% and 3% of GDP in 1992, respectively.[4] In part, the observed increases in interest payments that occurred in all European transition economies reflected financial market reforms, requiring the government to offer competitive interest rates for its borrowing operations. Part of the increased interest payments could be considered amortization of debts rather than interest payments.[5]

As regards *producer subsidies*, some evidence indicates that reductions affected the output decline in European transition economies. In former Czechoslovakia, for example, annual declines in real GDP averaged a steep 8%–9% during 1990–1992. At the outset of transition, former Czechoslovakia was the country with the highest level of government expenditures, amounting to 72% of GDP in 1989. During the transition, total expenditures fell by 16 percentage points of GDP, reaching 56% in 1992, largely reflecting a steep reduction in producer subsidies, including cross-subsidies, which fell from 19% of GDP in 1989 to 5% in 1992. Similar conclusions hold for Bulgaria, which experienced average annual declines in real GDP of 9% during 1990–1992, and underwent a reduction in government expenditures of 18 percentage points of GDP during the same time period.

When comparing Bulgaria and former Czechoslovakia with Hungary, Poland, and Romania, the relationship between producer subsidy reductions and the decline in output is less obvious. In Romania during 1990–1992, real GDP and industrial output decreased more than in the other European transition economies. Yet, government expenditures actually increased, largely due to increases in producer subsidies. In fact, Romania was the only European transition economy where producer subsidies increased during 1990–1992, though much of this just reflected the fact that previously hidden expenditures were made explicit. Romania's government was not as determined as other governments to reduce these producer subsidies, and it is unlikely that the massive industrial output decline was brought about by fiscal constraints on industry. While the Romanian government's direct demand expenditures declined, and while the increase in producer subsidies gave enterprises little additional liquidity, Romanian enterprises faced a number of other constraints, as suggested by the massive increase in inter-enterprise arrears.

Leaving aside Romania, where measurement problems are quite severe, the two economies that already started with a significantly lower level of government redistribution through the state budget, Hungary and Poland, were also the ones where the output decline was somewhat smaller than in those economies that started out with a high degree of cross-subsidies, notably Bulgaria and former Czechoslovakia. This would suggest that the extent to which the budget was used as a redistributive instrument, particularly among state-owned enterprises, may have had some impact on the extent of the observed output decline. Still, even if this were true, it is not clear whether it was the withdrawal of producer subsidies, *per se*, or rather the coordination vacuum of "neither plan nor market," which came about with the reduction in government intervention, that was the instrumental factor in determining the size of the output decline.

However, it would be difficult to argue that the reduction in producer subsidies was completely inconsequential. Since the bulk of producer subsidies went to industrial enterprises, one would expect to see industrial output declines to be strongest in economies that experienced the most dramatic reductions in producer subsidies, namely, Bulgaria and former Czechoslovakia. In these two economies, both characterized by a high degree of cross-subsidization, annual declines in real industrial output during 1990–1992 averaged 13%. Producer subsidy reductions clearly had an adverse effect on the financial viability of many enterprises, and contributed to increased layoffs, cuts in production, and the curtailment of investment plans, while simultaneously resulting in increased tax and inter-enterprise arrears.

In contrast, in Hungary and Poland, where, starting from a much lower initial level, producer subsidies were reduced by only 2 and 4 percentage points of GDP, respectively, industrial output declines during 1990–1992 averaged only 8% and 10%, respectively. Also, some producer subsidies were rather resilient, particularly in agriculture. In some cases, such as fuel and fertilizer subsidies for agricultural producers in Poland, they even staged a comeback. Romania, again, does not fit this general picture: while explicit (budgeted) producer subsidies increased, industrial output still declined by an average of 18% during 1990–1992.

In general, it is likely that the cuts in producer subsidies reinforced other adverse factors that affected the supply side, including increases in wages and salaries, interest payments, raw materials, and energy. Also, they may have reinforced other domestic demand-side factors, such as reductions in government capital expenditures and purchases of goods and services, which came in addition to external factors, such as the collapse of the CMEA arrangements. This suggests that the reduction in producer subsidies was a likely contributor to the polarization of the enterprise sector, where "successful" and "unsuccessful" enterprises became apparent rather quickly. Nevertheless, it was clearly not the only determinant, and probably not even a major one.[6]

Subsidy-accounting is clearly an imperfect science, and, particularly in Romania, changes in budgeted producer subsidies may largely reflect changes in budgeting procedures rather than policy changes and the effects of economic transformation. But there are also other, more fundamental, doubts about the extent to which reductions in producer subsidies affected output. The reduction in producer subsidies itself may not have been a binding constraint if either low-cost credit was expanded or producer prices were liberalized. Clearly, while most producer prices were liberalized as part of the transition, credit conditions have often been fairly tight. It is likely that the reduction in subsidies had an adverse impact on production when it affected enterprises that operated with liberalized output prices, were not credit constrained, and were not impacted by the loss of CMEA markets. Still, to the extent that it affected enterprises that faced some or all of these other constraints, the reduction of producer subsidies alone probably did not have a significant impact on the magnitude of the output decline.

As regards government expenditure components that constitute *direct government demand*, i.e., purchases of goods and services, and capital spending,[7] there has been a decline in all European transition economies. The declines were most dramatic in Bulgaria and Romania, where, during 1990–1992, they amounted to 11 and 9 percentage points of GDP, respectively; in Hungary and Poland the declines amounted to only 2 and 1 percentage points of GDP, respectively. While direct government demand decreased everywhere, in Poland and Romania government spending on goods and services actually increased, even though the increases were relatively small, and did not exceed 3 percentage points of GDP during 1990–1992.

All European transition economies reduced capital spending. Reductions were particularly dramatic in Romania, where capital expenditures dropped from 18% of GDP in 1989 to 6% in 1992. These reductions may have had a dampening effect on production in various industries, particularly in capital-goods industries. Notwithstanding the general reductions in capital expenditures relative to current expenditures, there are also definitional problems: to some extent, the distinction between purchases of goods and services and capital expenditures remains fuzzy as anything can be called a "capital expenditure," and definitions across countries are not uniform.

As regards government *expenditures that have income transfer characteristics*, all European transition economies, with the exception of former Czechoslovakia, experienced increases. However, the two main components of income transfers – namely, consumer subsidies and social expenditures – behaved very differently.

Budgeted consumer subsidies were reduced everywhere, with Romania being the sole exception. In 1989, before the onset of the transition, consumer subsidies in former Czechoslovakia, Hungary, and Poland amounted to 7% or 8% of GDP. This was much higher than the levels observed in Bulgaria (2% of GDP) and Romania (4% of GDP). Before the transition, it was generally not money that was scarce, but goods that consumers were able and willing to purchase. In an environment with severe supply constraints, direct or indirect support of the purchasing power of consumers was of little use. In the late 1980s these supply constraints were probably more severe in Bulgaria and Romania, where consumer subsidies were accordingly lower.

When prices were liberalized, consumer subsidies were dramatically reduced in most transition economies. Still, a number of consumer subsidies continued in many European transition economies, including items like housing, utilities (e.g., heating and hot water), and basic consumer goods (e.g., bread and milk). Also, public transportation services usually continued to be subsidized, even though a pollution tax for private transportation might be a better policy option. Often, these remaining consumer subsidies were provided in the form of prices that were administered below market-clearing levels; this made them difficult to detect as their cost was not directly reflected in the budget. But they were not without cost: often, transport companies operating with administered output prices had significant tax arrears and required equity injections and other support by the state.

Both social expenditures and consumer subsidies transfer income to households. The experience of European transition economies suggests that, to some extent, consumer subsidies and social expenditures were substitutes:

everywhere but in Romania consumer subsidies were significantly reduced, while social expenditures increased substantially. The overall result was that, during 1990–1992, all these economies registered increases in income transfer payments, with the exception of former Czechoslovakia, which registered a decline.

It is surprising that social expenditures in "gradualist" Hungary and "shock-therapist" Poland increased much more rapidly than elsewhere: during 1990–1992, social expenditures increased by 9 percentage points of GDP in both Hungary and Poland, while increases amounted to 3 percentage points of GDP in both Bulgaria and former Czechoslovakia and 1 in Romania.

This suggests that social expenditures were an "automatic" stabilizer: as the transition got under way, social expenditures increased everywhere and, regardless of the speed of transition, helped to keep up private-sector demand. Given that much of the increase in social expenditures happened during 1991–1992, the quantitative importance of this stabilizer increased when reform efforts intensified and the social costs of transition became more apparent. Much of the increases in social expenditures resulted from increases in pension expenditures and newly introduced unemployment benefits. The increase in pensions and unemployment payments and the simultaneous reduction in consumer subsidies would also suggest that large parts of the transition-induced social costs were borne by permanent social security arrangements rather than by more temporary social assistance schemes. In Hungary, for example, budgeted consumer subsidies were reduced from 7% to 1% of GDP during 1990–1992, while during the same period social expenditures increased from 16% to 25% of GDP. In Poland, budgeted consumer subsidies were reduced from 8% to 3% of GDP during 1990–1992, while during the same period social expenditures benefits increased from 11% to 20% of GDP.

Even though, during 1989–1992, unemployment went from virtually zero to double digits in both Hungary and Poland, increases in unemployment benefit payments were surpassed by increases in pension payments, largely caused by a retirement "boom." Poland, for example, registered a 36% increase in old-age (including early retirement) pensions from December 1989 to December 1993 and a somewhat smaller, but still pronounced, increase in disability pensions (Maret and Schwartz, 1993). The public's expectations of universality die hard: even the government of former Czechoslovakia, probably the most outspokenly market-oriented government of all European transition economies, provided universal income support to compensate for the removal of retail subsidies on food in 1990 (Schwartz *et al.*, 1994).

While the process of transformation required creating new safeguards in the form of cost-effective social safety nets, these often came as additions to the old system, leaving the old system still in dire need for reform. The exact extent to which increases in transfers to households helped to maintain the demand for certain goods and services – and thus helped to maintain their production – was unclear. The increase in social expenditures counteracted declines in real wages (due to deteriorating economic conditions) and in income from consumer subsidies (due to price reform), and was probably spent largely on basic consumer goods (e.g., foodstuffs).

While some efforts were made to increase the cost-effectiveness of social expenditures, much of the reform remained piecemeal. This resulted in inefficiencies and waste, and, to the extent that benefits were regarded as long-term entitlements that could not be revoked, may have retarded incentives for household savings. Social expenditures in European transition economies continued to have much of the universal "from the cradle to the grave" characteristics of the former planned economies.

10.2.3 Longer-term considerations

In general, the transition from plan to market brought about drastic reductions in capital expenditures, for both physical capital and human capital. This may have affected potential future output levels.

Capital expenditures decreased in all transition economies, with the exception of Hungary. Large parts of the investment plans conceived under central planning were unsuitable for a market-based environment, and simply had to be scrapped. It has often been argued that the levels of capital expenditures that now prevail in many transition economies appear to be on the low side of what would be desirable from a long-run perspective, especially considering that private-sector responses may not be fast enough (Chu and Holzmann, 1992).

Since it takes time to conceive new investment plans, the declines in government capital formation may just be of temporary nature and should not be worrisome as such. Still, the reductions in capital expenditures included, *inter alia*, maintenance expenditures for basic infrastructure and expenditures on health and education. The impact of these declines was not immediately obvious, largely because the stocks of physical and human capital that were created before the outset of the transition were still being utilized, and because reductions in infrastructure spending usually affect aggregate output with a relatively long lag.

While it remains to be seen to what extent the reductions in capital spending during the past two to three years will affect long-run output, it seems likely that, without increases in capital expenditures during the next few years, a deterioration in economic infrastructure, as well as in the health and education systems, may lie ahead. This is likely to have a significant impact on private-sector productivity and output as well.

10.3 Summary and Conclusions

In this paper we have considered three main questions. First, we asked whether actual changes in the level and composition of government expenditures in European transition economies were largely the result of policies or of exogenous factors. Second, we asked whether expenditure policies contributed significantly to the measured output decline, and, if so, whether this was attributable to specific expenditure components. Third, we asked whether there were more desirable alternatives to the government expenditure policies that have been undertaken, and what the prospects for economic recovery would have been under these alternative policy scenarios.

In trying to address these questions, this paper has presented four main channels by which changes in the level and composition of government expenditures can affect aggregate output. First, aggregate output can decline because of reductions in factor income payments by the government. Second, it can decline through reductions in producer subsidies, which, other things being equal, can reinforce the supply-side effects of increases in input prices, including capital, energy, land, and labor. Third, it can decline through reductions in direct government demand. Finally, it can decline through reductions in expenditures that transfer income to households and thereby affect household demand. In addition, a reduction in government expenditures on physical and human capital can have negative implications for the economy's long-run output capacity and the productivity of the private sector.

As regards the first question, we note that all European transition economies showed a clear tendency to reduce the overall extent of government intervention in the economy, which, given high starting levels, was one of the basic premises for successfully establishing a market-based economy. These reductions in government intervention manifested themselves through changes in institutional arrangements and reductions in the share of government output and employment, but not necessarily through reductions in government expenditures and budget deficits. In this sense, it would appear plausible to assert that it was not government expenditures, *per se*, that contributed significantly to the transitional recession, but rather the reduction of government intervention and coordination in the economy, as it was not instantly and completely replaced by the private sector. We have argued that, to a large extent, changes in the levels and composition of government expenditures were an inevitable result of the transition. For example, reductions in producer subsidies and increases in transfers to households were inevitable once the transition to a market-oriented pricing system got under way. Still, generally, policy makers had various degrees of freedom for making expenditure policy choices and safeguarding fiscal sustainability.

As regards the second question, we have noted that various measurement problems only allow for conclusions of a preliminary nature. We found insufficient evidence for concluding that government expenditures accounted for but a small share of the decline in aggregate output. Overall, it seems plausible to conclude that changes in the level and composition of government expenditures acted to reinforce other factors through both supply and demand channels, but, generally, were not a binding constraint for output. Even in cases when they were binding, they were probably not the only binding constraint. For example, sectors that experienced severe input constraints – for example, through the collapse of the CMEA – could not have responded to increased government demand.

As regards the third question, we have argued that it is difficult to make a general case that a different set of government expenditure policies, *per se*, would have helped to mitigate the output decline. Government expenditures in European transition economies, generally, remained on the high side, at least compared with European market-based economies.

As for the future, there is little reason to believe that more expansionary fiscal policies would be needed to lift European transition economies out of the transitional recession. Indeed, recent proposals that advocate Keynesian demand policies have little merit as they would lead to a further deterioration of fiscal accounts, and, even when pursued on a temporary basis, run the serious risk of destabilizing the transition. Still, governments have various degrees of freedom, and should use these to further reorder expenditure priorities. In particular, increases in the share of capital expenditures – human and physical – are needed to improve long-run output potential and to promote efficiency.

While budget deficits in European transition economies have generally increased, they have not been spinning out of control. However, without further reform, current fiscal positions are not sustainable. Over the next few years, creating a sustainable fiscal position and a noninflationary financial environment are fundamental for enhancing the confidence of domestic and foreign private entrepreneurs and for making private-sector decisions more predictable. Private-sector investments and subsequent increases in production should offset the decline in production in state-owned enterprises. Government expenditure policies will be crucial for reinforcing a stable financial environment that it is hoped will eventually ensue. European transition economies have not yet arrived at this stage.

Notes

[1] The table abstracts from more indirect effects, for example, private-sector responses to changes in government expenditures and the role of expectations.

[2] In addition to budgeted subsidies, there were substantial subsidies that were not budgeted. These resulted from quasi-fiscal operations of central banks or were implicit, as, for example, in the case of excessive procurement prices or discretionary tax reliefs. For Romania in 1992, Blanchard *et al.* (1993) estimate that, even after various subsidies were made explicit, subsidies arising from quasi-fiscal operations alone still amounted to about 9 percentage points of GDP.

[3] It is possible that Poland's 1990 GDP is underestimated. If this is the case, the decline in GDP and the increase in government expenditures (relative to GDP) during 1991–1992 would in reality be less pronounced.

[4] In countries that have not been making full payments on their external debt, notably Poland and Bulgaria, interest payments are bound to increase significantly once the external debt restructuring exercises are completed.

[5] In general, the considerable interest payments that are to be made by various transition economies may be a constraining factor of growing importance for the expenditure choices the governments of these economies will be able to make.

[6] See Pinto *et al.* (1993) for microeconomic evidence on the importance of various factors that contributed to the successful adjustment of state-owned enterprises in Poland.

[7] The large disparities in the levels of direct government demand across countries that are shown in *Table 10.2*, reflect, to some extent, differences in the way these expenditures are classified. In Poland, for example, a part of "other" expenditures may also constitute direct government demand, particularly purchases of goods and services.

References

Bird, R., and Wallich, C., 1993, Fiscal Decentralization and Intergovernmental Fiscal Relations in Transition Economies: Toward A Systemic Framework of Analysis, Policy Research Working Paper, WPS 1122, World Bank, Washington, DC, USA.

Blanchard, O., Commander, S., and Coricelli, F., 1993, Unemployment and Restructuring in Eastern Europe, Paper prepared for the World Bank Conference on Unemployment, Restructuring, and the Labor Market in Eastern Europe and Russia, October 7–8, Washington, DC, USA.

Blejer, M., and Cheasty, A., 1992, How to measure the fiscal deficit, *Finance and Development*, **29**(3):40–42.

Chu, K., and R., Holzmann, 1992, Public expenditure: Policy aspects, in V. Tanzi, ed., *Fiscal Policies in Economies in Transition*, International Monetary Fund, Washington, DC, USA.

Clifton, E.V., and Khan, M.S., 1993, Inter-enterprise arrears in transforming economies, *IMF Staff Papers*, **40**(3):680–696.

Kornai, J., 1993, *Transformational Recession: A General Phenomenon Examined Through the Example of Hungary's Development*, Discussion Paper No. 1, Collegium Budapest, Institute for Advanced Study, Budapest, Hungary.

Maret, X., and Schwartz, G., 1993, Poland: The Social Safety Net During the Transition, WP/93/42, International Monetary Fund, Washington, DC, USA.

Pinto, B., 1993, Brian Pinto explains why Polish state firms are restructuring, *Transition*, **4**(7):4–5.

Pinto, B., Belka, M., and Krajewski, S., 1993, Transforming State Enterprises in Poland, WPS 1101, World Bank, Washington, DC, USA.

Schwartz, G., Stone, M., and van der Willigen, T., 1994, Beyond stabilization: The economic transformation of Czechoslovakia, Hungary, and Poland, *Communist Economies & Economic Transformation*, September.

Tanzi, V., 1993, The budget deficit in transition: A cautionary note, *IMF Staff Papers*, **40**(3):697–707.

WIIW (Vienna Institute for Comparative Economic Studies), 1993, *Transition from the Command to the Market System: What Went Wrong and What to Do Now?*, Vienna, Austria.

Comments on the Paper by Ke-young Chu and Gerd Schwartz

Ewald Nowotny

In their very interesting paper Ke-young Chu and Gerd Schwartz first discuss whether actual changes in the level and composition of government expenditures in transition economies were the result of policy choice decisions or of transition-induced exogenous factors. Chu and Schwartz argue that to a large extent expenditure changes were an inevitable result of the transition and not the outcome of a specific policy choice decision. To a large extent this obviously is true, because a move to a market system necessarily involves a different structure of public expenditures.

Even given the general need for structural adjustment, contrary to what the authors say, I see several fields of public expenditure where there were indeed degrees of freedom with regard to expenditure policies. One important example is housing production which – also in a West European context – relies heavily on direct and indirect public expenditures. Figures contained in a report by the Vienna Institute for Comparative Economic Studies (WIIW, 1993) demonstrate that there has been a dramatic decrease in annual housing construction in the transition countries: comparing the average of the 1980–1988 period with the 1992 average, construction of flats per 1000 inhabitants dropped in Bulgaria from 7.5 to 1.3, in the CSFR from 6.4 to 3.3, and in Hungary from 6.6 to 2.5. This indicates that in important sectors of the economy stabilization potentials have not been used.

The second question asked by Chu and Schwartz is whether expenditure policies contributed significantly to the measured output decline. Their basic answer is that government expenditure policies did not make more than a small contribution to the decline in aggregate output. It is undoubtedly correct to attribute the main responsibility for the output decline to external factors like the collapse of the CMEA and problems of structural change in industry. But in my view the interesting question remains whether government expenditure policies could have helped to reduce the decline in aggregate output.

From a methodological point of view I see a certain problem in the way Chu and Schwartz discuss these questions. Their approach is to compare government expenditures and its components all measured as a percentage of GDP. But if there is a decline in GDP a constant share of government expenditures means a real reduction of government expenditures and thus a destabilizing effect. What we would expect in a period of decline is an increase in the share of government expenditures.

So we have two elements to take into consideration: the long-run tendency to reduce the share of government expenditures inherent in the transition process and the short- and medium-run needs of the public sector to help in stabilizing demand. To my reading the figures by Chu and Schwartz on direct government demand demonstrate that these latter needs have not been fulfilled, as the authors show that especially direct government demand decreased everywhere in the transition economies, with particularly drastic reductions in capital expenditures.

The third question asked by Chu and Schwartz is whether more desirable alternatives to the expenditure policies have been undertaken. Their answer basically is negative, i.e., they do not consider current government expenditures levels as too low and therefore they see little rationale for expansionary fiscal policies. They advocate, however, a reordering of expenditure priorities, especially increases in expenditures on human and physical capital.

To take up this last point I basically agree, but I am afraid that the authors take a much too narrow view when speaking about human capital. When they criticize the still "from the cradle to the grave" characteristics of social expenditures in transition economies and hint that these are to a substantial extent waste, they seem to ignore that a certain social consensus – a social infrastructure – is needed to secure the political basis for a transition process. This does not exclude necessary reforms of the social systems with regard to better incentive structures and higher efficiency. But it would be a grave political error to expect that Central European countries with a certain tradition of social responsibility can be reduced to the social structures of Asian countries or the USA.

In my comments, I opted to concentrate on the "political economy" aspects. The recent election results in many of these countries underline the danger of underestimating the political, social, and psychological aspects of the difficult process of economic transition.

Chapter 11

Output and Employment in Private and Non-private Businesses in Hungary: 1990–1992

Ákos Valentinyi

Most East European countries are still in a deep recession due to the transformation process.[1] While Poland exhibited positive real growth in 1993, the recovery in the other countries did not occur. In some countries the development seemed at least contradictory. In 1993, for example, the industrial production seemed to recover in Hungary, while the trade balance and the current account heavily deteriorated.

Since the transition literature is lacking in empirical works, one could achieve more insight in the development process of the East European economies by conducting empirical investigations. In this chapter I present a brief analysis based on output and employment trends in the Hungarian economy. The data mainly refer to the 1990–1992 period. In the analysis I have used aggregate data structured by ownership classes and industries. Section 11.1 describes the data set and methods used to estimate the figures presented in the paper. Section 11.2 analyzes the output trends, while Section 11.3 examines the data on employment. Section 11.4 presents data on the profitability of the enterprises and conclusions.

I would like to express my thanks to my discussant at the IIASA Conference and to Kornélia Krajnyák for helpful comments.

R. Holzmann et al. (eds.), Output Decline in Eastern Europe, 265-284.

11.1 Methodological Remarks

In this section I describe the data set used in the analysis and how it relates to GDP and employment aggregates of Hungary. I also present the classification method of ownership categories and the data sources.

The analysis is based on year-end financial statements of individual Hungarian enterprises for the years between 1989 and 1992, provided by the Ministry of Finance and made available by the KOPINT-DATORG Institute in Budapest. This data set includes the balance sheets of all Hungarian enterprises that paid corporate tax at the end of the year (more than 14,000 enterprise 1989, more than 27,000 in 1990, more than 43,000 in 1991, and more than 57,000 in 1992). However, the data set does not include data on enterprises that went bankrupt during a given year. Moreover, the data on enterprises that have changed their legal form during the year consider only the interval between the date of the change in legal form and the end of the year. Therefore, if an enterprise changed its legal form on 1 December, its total output standing in the year-end financial statement was in fact produced only in December.

The data set is closely related to GDP aggregates reported by the Hungarian Central Statistical Office (HCSO), however, it is not sufficient to reproduce the HCSO's macro data. According to the Hungarian statistical classification, the total GDP at basic prices (net of commodity taxes) is produced by four kinds of economic organizations – namely, enterprises, small businesses, households, and institutions financed by the state budget. GDP produced by the economic organizations called "enterprises" in the Hungarian statistical terminology comprises of three components: (1) the value added by the enterprises that have paid corporate tax at the end of the year, (2) the value added by the enterprises that went bankrupt during the year, and (3) the value added that was produced by enterprises before they changed their legal form. The second and the third components were not significant in 1989 and 1990 but became significant in 1991 and especially in 1992. According to the estimation of the Ministry of Finance, the second and the third components amounted to one-fifth of the GDP produced by all enterprises in 1992. In addition to this problem, the data set available from the KOPINT–DATORG for 1989–1991 does not include all items that are necessary to compute the exact figure of the value added of the enterprises.

To use this data set to analyze issues related to ownership structure, one must classify the individual enterprises into ownership categories. I identified four classes: state-owned enterprises, cooperatives, private enterprises with foreign direct investment (FDI), and private enterprises without FDI. In this analysis the four categories are used only in the case of aggregate GDP and employment. For simplicity, in the analysis by industry the first and second categories are combined and called non-private enterprises while the third and fourth categories are called private enterprises. The sources of information used for the classification and the method applied are described below.

Information about the legal form of an enterprise is available in the data set for each year and can be used as the basis for classification. In addition, a code on the ownership form of each enterprise is available for 1989 in the data set. Moreover, the amount of the share capital owned by the state is available in the data set for 1992. Furthermore, the size of the foreign direct investment is available for each year. In addition to the information included in the data set, I have used external information from the State Property Agency on the enterprises controlled by the state in 1991.

The general method of classification is based on the following principles. The category of private enterprises with foreign direct investment is identified as the enterprises with a ratio of FDI to share capital that is larger than 25%. This classification dominates all the others. The cooperatives are identified according to their legal form. To identify state-owned enterprises, I have used the legal form of the enterprises, information available in the data set, and external information. In addition to the legal form, I classified an enterprise as state owned for 1992 if the share of the state in the share capital is larger than 50%. Moreover, I assumed that if an enterprise is state owned at a later date, it had to be state owned at an earlier date. In other words, if an enterprise was classified as state owned in 1992 and if it existed already in 1989, then it was classified as state owned also for 1989. The remaining enterprises were classified as private enterprises without foreign direct investment.

It is obvious that the classification into ownership categories can be criticized for several reasons. Nevertheless, I think that these categories can be used very efficiently in an analysis of output and employment trends by industry and by ownership.

The data on the Hungarian GDP by economic organizations were taken from the official publications of the Central Statistical Office of Hungary. The data set was extracted from financial statements for further disaggregation within the enterprise sector. The estimates of the distribution of the value added across industries and the four ownership classes are based on value added computed for individual enterprises. The estimates of the distribution of GDP produced by the enterprises are based on the estimated coefficient and GDP data from the HCSO.

The deflators for 1990 by industry are from a publication of the United Nations on national accounts. The deflators for 1992 by industries were provided by the Hungarian Central Statistical Office. Since the Hungarian system of industrial classification was adjusted to international standards in 1992 and the deflators for 1991 were published for the old industries only, I had to use the available deflators to estimate the deflators in the new industries.

The data set includes data on the annual average number of the employees in the 1990–1992 period. This information was used in the employment analysis. Using data aggregated from the data set, I have derived the figures on the wage rate by dividing the total wage expenses by the annual average number of employees. The figures on unit labor cost were computed by dividing the nominal wage expenses by the gross nominal output. In contrast to these data derived from the aggregates of the data set, the after-tax return on equity was computed individually for each enterprise. Because the data set is characterized by outliers, I have used the maximum likelihood estimation of Tukey to get reasonable mean values.[2] Moreover, because of computer limitations I have had to take a random sample of 2,500 enterprises for each year by ownership class to estimate after-tax returns (this applies to the calculation of values summarized later in *Tables 11.15* and *11.16*).

11.2 Changes in the Structure of Output

11.2.1 Development of the private sector in aggregates

Table 11.1 shows the distribution of GDP at current basic prices, and *Table 11.2* presents the real growth rate of GDP across economic organizations.[3] The private sector as a whole exhibited rapid real growth during the 1990–1992 period, while real GDP of the non-private sector declined.[4] The growth rate of the private sector even seems to accelerate during the period. The figures on the output shares show only a slightly different development – that is, unbroken, but not accelerating change in the share of the private sector in 1990–1992. As a consequence of these developments the Hungarian private sector produced more than 40% of the GDP in 1992 while it had produced less than 30% in 1989. However, it should be emphasized that not only growth within the given ownership class contributed to this development. The move of economic activity between ownership classes also played an important role in the process. Throughout the following analysis the effect of ownership restructuring on growth rates in the different ownership classes should be borne in mind.

Table 11.1. Distribution of GDP by economic organization.

	1989	1990	1991	1992
GDP total at basic prices	100.0	100.0	100.0	100.0
Enterprises	71.6	69.3	67.3	65.0
A. State-owned enterprises	46.8	42.6	38.1	33.3
B. Cooperatives	11.5	10.6	7.8	6.2
C. Private enterprises	13.2	16.1	21.4	25.6
Private enterprises with FDI	4.2	5.1	6.6	8.5
Private enterprises without FDI	9.0	11.0	14.8	17.1
D. Small businesses	7.5	8.7	9.7	11.8
E. Economic activity of households	6.7	6.6	6.3	5.7
F. Budgetary institutions	14.2	15.4	16.8	17.4
Private sector (C + D + E)	27.4	31.4	37.4	43.1
Non-private sector (A + B + F)	72.5	68.6	62.6	56.9

Source: *Statistical Yearbook of Hungary*, various issues, and author's calculations.

Table 11.2. Real growth rate of GDP by economic organization (previous year = 100).

	1990	1991	1992
GDP total at basic prices	96.4	90.2	95.7
Enterprises	95.0	84.5	93.1
State-owned enterprises	89.4	78.1	84.4
Cooperatives	93.7	76.3	77.0
Private enterprises	115.8	107.8	118.4
Private enterprises with FDI	117.6	108.1	126.4
Private enterprises without FDI	115.0	107.7	114.5
Small businesses	100.3	114.0	115.6
Economic activity of households	90.9	99.5	86.5
Budgetary institutions	100.2	98.2	98.5
Private sector	105.5	107.7	111.4
Non-private sector	92.2	82.1	86.9

Different organizations in the private sector developed differently. The class of enterprises with FDI exhibited a higher real growth rate than the group of enterprises without FDI. It should be noted, however, that in Hungary foreign capital plays a crucial role in the privatization of state-owned enterprises. Hence it is reasonable to say that without moving already existing production to the enterprises with FDI, the growth of these firms might have been lower. Nevertheless, at the end of 1992 these organizations still produced less than 10% of the GDP. Private enterprises without FDI also grew rapidly. These companies have the highest share in GDP within the private sector. By 1992 small businesses also produce already more than 10% of the GDP.[5] It is not surprising that the share of economic activity of households declined. One possible explanation for this fact might be that many activities in households were reclassified as small business. This allowed the households to economize on their tax payments.

The private sector as a whole grew at a higher rate than the non-private one, and the difference between the two growth rates has increased over time. However, the aggregate data also suggest that the output in private enterprises does not develop independently of the overall performance of the economy. In 1991 the real growth of output in private enterprises was smaller than in both the previous year and the following year. This result might be strongly related to the overall decline of GDP in 1991 brought about by several factors, but primarily by the external shock.

11.2.2 Development of private sector by industry

In this section GDP produced by enterprises is analyzed by industry and ownership class, while differentiating only between private and non-private enterprises. *Table 11.3* shows distribution of GDP by ownership class across industries. In 1989 the activity of the private enterprises was already high in the trade, construction, and community and personal services and very low in agriculture,[6] mining, electricity, and transport. This is not surprising since the last three industries had traditionally been dominated by a few large state-owned enterprises while agriculture was dominated by state farms (enterprises) and cooperatives both belonging to the group of non-private enterprises.

During this period private enterprises expanded their share in value added in all industries. The most important changes were probably those that could be recorded in manufacturing, on the one hand, and in finance and business services on the other. In both sectors private enterprises were already responsible for more than 40% of the value added produced in the sector. As *Table 11.3* indicates construction and trade maintained their distinction as being the sectors with the highest share of private activity.

Since the relative changes analyzed so far could be caused by both positive and negative, but different, real growth in the industries, the real growth rates should also be analyzed. *Table 11.4* shows that in each year private enterprises exhibited positive real growth rate in almost all industries. The non-private enterprises, however, grew at a negative rate in all industries with the exception of community and personal services in 1990. The

Table 11.3. Distribution of GDP by ownership class across industries.

	1989	1990	1991	1992
Total GDP	100.0	100.0	100.0	100.0
Private enterprises	18.5	23.3	31.9	39.3
Agriculture, hunting, forestry, fishing	1.9	2.6	2.8	9.2
Mining, quarrying	0.8	2.3	5.1	13.1
Manufacturing	19.6	23.7	30.9	41.2
Electricity, gas, water	0.1	0.3	1.5	3.8
Construction	38.6	48.3	59.3	70.9
Wholesale/retail trade, restaurants, hotels	33.8	44.7	60.4	65.9
Transport, storage, communication	4.2	7.1	11.1	12.9
Finance, insurance, real estate, business services	17.0	26.2	34.9	41.4
Community, social, personal services	31.6	29.6	31.8	38.2
Non-private enterprises	81.5	76.7	68.1	60.7
Agriculture, hunting, forestry, fishing	98.1	97.4	97.2	90.8
Mining, quarrying	99.2	97.7	94.9	86.9
Manufacturing	80.4	76.3	69.1	58.8
Electricity, gas, water	99.9	99.7	98.5	96.2
Construction	61.4	51.7	40.7	29.1
Wholesale/retail trade, restaurants, hotels	66.2	55.3	39.6	34.1
Transport, storage, communication	95.8	92.9	88.9	87.1
Finance, insurance, real estate, business services	83.0	73.8	65.1	58.6
Community, social, personal services	68.4	70.4	68.2	61.8

Source: Author's calculations.

figures suggest that the increase in the private enterprises' share in GDP was brought about partly by a drop in non-private activities and partly by the rapid growth of value added in the private enterprises.

Table 11.4 also provides some information on the relation between growth rates in ownership categories and in industries. The growth of non-private activities was, on average, the lowest in trade and in construction where private enterprises achieved the strongest position. One interpretation may be that the private enterprises drove out the non-private ones. But it is also possible that non-private activities were transformed most rapidly into private ones in these industries.

The conclusion of this brief analysis is that private enterprises expanded fast, while the non-private ones declined rapidly. There are two types of theoretical explanations for this. The first points to the fact that the operating environments of private enterprises are different from non-private ones. It may mean a different regulatory environment but also different industries.

Table 11.4. Real growth rate of GDP by ownership class across industries (previous year = 100).

	1990	1991	1992
Total GDP	95.0	84.5	93.1
Private enterprises	115.8	107.8	118.4
Agriculture, hunting, forestry, fishing	120.9	88.2	271.0
Mining, quarrying	260.1	192.7	213.2
Manufacturing	106.7	109.3	121.2
Electricity, gas, water	265.2	403.3	247.8
Construction	96.0	102.7	116.7
Wholesale, retail trade, restaurants, hotels	142.9	114.3	99.8
Transport, storage, communication	150.8	147.1	98.5
Finance, insurance, real estate, business services	163.0	122.8	125.7
Community, social, personal services	91.9	103.9	119.7
Non-private enterprises	90.3	77.7	82.9
Agriculture, hunting, forestry, fishing	91.7	79.4	78.0
Mining, quarrying	85.2	84.0	75.4
Manufacturing	83.7	76.0	77.2
Electricity, gas, water	97.6	87.3	94.5
Construction	64.7	65.9	69.5
Wholesale, retail trade, restaurants, hotels	90.5	60.7	78.6
Transport, storage, communication	87.0	89.8	82.4
Finance, insurance, real estate, business services	94.1	81.4	95.2
Community, social, personal services	101.1	93.6	90.3

Source: Author's calculations.

The second type of explanations is based on the reasoning that private enterprises always perform better than non-private ones. The first reasoning is supported – at least weakly – by the stylized facts presented above. In the late 1980s private activities were mainly concentrated in the service industries. These industries were only weakly affected by both the structural and demand shocks. Due to the overall underdevelopment of these industries there was excess demand for their activities rather than a collapse in demand. On the other hand, non-private enterprises produced mainly the output of industries which were affected by both the structural and demand shocks. Such differences, however, cannot be the only explanation why private enterprises performed better than non-private ones. For instance, one of the main fields of private activity, namely, construction, seems to be an exception in this respect. Despite the decline in productive investments and housing, private enterprises in the construction industry could increase their production after 1991 while non-private industries could not. Moreover, private firms played an important role in manufacturing which was affected by both structural and demand shocks. Despite these shocks, private activity in manufacturing grew each year. This implies that differences between efficiencies of enterprises with different ownership also had to contribute to the development described above.

11.3 Changes in Employment and Wages

11.3.1 Development of the private sector in aggregates

The trends in employment are similar to those observed in production: the share of private enterprises in respect to the number of employees increased between 1990 and 1992, while that of the non-private sector decreased (see *Table 11.5*). Moreover, the data in *Table 11.6* indicate that while in the whole enterprise sector the number of employees decreased, private enterprises managed to increase the number of workers employed.

Changes in the real wage rate shown in *Table 11.7* indicate differences between 1991 and 1992.[7] Whereas in 1991 the real wage rate decreased in each category of enterprise except for enterprises with FDI, in 1992 the increase of real wages was more common, the highest rate being achieved by the state-owned enterprises.

In addition to the development of real wages, the nominal wage rate (nominal wage per employee) and the unit labor cost also exhibited some special features. *Table 11.8* shows figures on the nominal wage rate across the different ownership classes. Whereas in 1990 and 1991 the wage rate in state-owned enterprises was lower than in private ones, by 1992 it had already reached the level characterizing private enterprises and exceeded the nominal wage rate paid in private enterprises without FDI. This wage development within the state sector resulted in increased unit labor costs as reported in *Table 11.9*. Not surprisingly, throughout the whole period cooperatives had the highest unit labor cost; however, by 1991 state-owned enterprises had the second highest unit labor cost.

The increasing real wages in state-owned enterprises were accompanied by increasing unit labor costs and nominal wages being leveled off with those of private enterprises. This evidence is also related to the sectoral differences between private and non-private enterprises, which are discussed in Section 11.3.2.

However, one of the explanations should be emphasized. The development of the unit labor cost may imply that private enterprises (both those

Table 11.5. Distribution of employees by ownership class in percent.

	1990	1991	1992
Total enterprises	100.0	100.0	100.0
Private enterprises	15.0	18.2	35.7
Private enterprises with FDI	4.8	7.6	11.3
Private enterprises without FDI	10.1	10.6	24.5
Non-private enterprises	85.0	81.8	64.3
State-owned enterprises	65.4	65.2	49.9
Cooperatives	19.6	16.6	14.3

Source: Author's calculations.

Table 11.6. Change in employment by economic organization in percent (previous year = 100).

	1991	1992
Total enterprises	84.6	83.9
Private enterprises	102.7	164.9
Private enterprises with FDI	132.1	125.1
Private enterprises without FDI	88.7	193.2
Non-private sector	81.4	65.9
State-owned enterprises	84.4	64.2
Cooperatives	71.5	72.6

Source: Author's calculations.

with FDI and those without FDI) have had to adjust to the overall macroeconomic situation while non-private ones have not. During the period of early transition (1989–1990), when the uncertainty about the future of the economy was high, unit labor cost decreased in private enterprises. It also declined in 1991 when the effect of demand and structural shocks resulted in the largest drop in real GDP. In 1992, however, several new regulations were enacted and the effect of the demand shock seemed to be over; private enterprises started to pay more wages than before. The adjustment of the private sector to the overall macroeconomic situation may not be the only explanation for the changes in the unit labor cost. The situation on the labor market may also have contributed to it. One can suppose that wages in private enterprises may have been formed by the effort to keep the difference between nominal wages paid in private and non-private enterprises small.

Having briefly analyzed the differences between private and non-private enterprises, we now turn to the dissimilarities within the group of private

Table 11.7. The growth of real wage rate by ownership class (previous year = 100).

	1991	1992
Total enterprises	92.7	107.7
Private enterprises	95.1	95.2
Private enterprises with FDI	112.3	108.0
Private enterprises without FDI	84.2	91.4
Non-private enterprises	91.4	109.2
State-owned enterprises	91.3	112.0
Cooperatives	88.5	99.6

Source: Author's calculations.

Table 11.8. Nominal wage rate by ownership class in thousand Hungarian forints.

	1990	1991	1992
Total enterprises	151.1	189.1	250.5
Private enterprises	175.5	225.2	263.6
Private enterprises with FDI	169.3	256.6	341.0
Private enterprises without FDI	178.4	202.9	228.0
Non-private enterprises	146.6	180.9	243.0
State-owned enterprises	154.7	190.6	262.5
Cooperatives	119.4	142.7	174.9

Source: Author's calculations.

enterprises. *Tables 11.5* through *11.9* indicate that there are some significant differences in this respect. Employment rose in enterprises with FDI in both 1991 and 1992. In contrast, in private enterprises without FDI employment decreased in 1991 *(Table 11.6)*. This fact might be interpreted if we take into account that, as shown in *Table 11.2*, the real growth of production in enterprises without FDI also lagged behind the growth in enterprises with FDI in that year. Because the largest drop in total GDP over the whole period occurred in 1991, this may imply that private enterprises without FDI suffered more from the structural and demand shocks than enterprises with FDI. Since private enterprises, in general, were concentrated in the industries not directly affected by the shocks, the data indicate that private enterprises without FDI – although indirectly – were influenced more by the shocks than private enterprises with FDI.

Table 11.9. Unit labor cost by ownership class in percent.

	1989	1990	1991	1992
Total enterprises	13.2	13.1	13.3	16.1
Private enterprises	13.9	11.4	9.6	13.8
Private enterprises with FDI	11.6	9.4	10.1	12.2
Private enterprises without FDI	14.5	12.6	9.2	15.2
Non-private enterprises	13.1	13.5	14.8	17.9
State-owned enterprises	12.2	12.7	14.2	17.2
Cooperatives	18.4	18.0	19.4	23.4

Source: Author's calculations.

However, the data also suggest that the private enterprises without FDI did in fact adjust to the shocks. Data in *Tables 11.2* and *11.6* show that these enterprises decreased the number of their employees considerably when they faced lower real growth rate (lower than a year before). But, in 1992 employment increased in this class of enterprises much more than real growth itself would have justified. However, as *Tables 11.8* and *11.9* show, these changes resulted in lower unit labor cost and lower nominal wage rate than was reached in state-owned enterprises.

11.3.2 Development of the private sector by industry

To get a more detailed picture of the development process of employment and wages this section analyzes the differences, by industry, between private and non-private enterprises. The distribution of employment across industries is similar to that observed of GDP. *Table 11.10* shows that the share of private enterprises in employment is the highest in construction, trade, and finance and business services.[8] It is also important to note that the private sector's share of GDP is higher than its share in employment. This indicates that the average productivity of labor is higher in the class of private enterprises than in that of non-private ones.

The changes in the employment in *Table 11.11* support the finding that private enterprises expanded rapidly. In some industries where the presence of private enterprises had been weak in the past, such as in agriculture, mining, and electricity, the growth of employment was very high. However, it should be noted that due to the low starting point, the high growth is not surprising.

Table 11.12 provides stronger evidence about the different developments of real wages in the private and non-private sectors. Real wages paid in

Table 11.10. Distribution of employees by ownership class across industries in percent.

	1990	1991	1992
Total enterprises	100.0	100.0	100.0
Private enterprises	15.0	18.2	35.7
Agriculture, hunting, forestry, fishing	1.0	1.7	7.4
Mining, quarrying	3.2	5.6	37.1
Manufacturing	19.5	24.0	44.5
Electricity, gas, water	0.2	0.2	12.6
Construction	32.9	35.0	58.5
Wholesale/retail trade, restaurants, hotels	17.6	18.7	48.0
Transport, storage, communication	3.1	5.0	7.8
Finance, insurance, real estate, business services	22.1	29.5	50.4
Community, social, personal services	17.7	21.4	36.6
Non-private enterprises	85.0	81.8	64.3
Agriculture, hunting, forestry, fishing	99.0	98.3	92.6
Mining, quarrying	96.8	94.4	62.9
Manufacturing	80.5	76.0	55.5
Electricity, gas, water	99.8	99.8	87.4
Construction	67.1	65.0	41.5
Wholesale/retail trade, restaurants, hotels	82.4	81.3	52.0
Transport, storage, communication	96.9	95.0	92.2
Finance, insurance, real estate, business services	77.9	70.5	49.6
Community, social, personal services	82.3	78.6	63.4

Source: Author's calculations.

private enterprises decreased more than real wages in non-private enterprises in almost all industries in both 1991 and 1992. In non-private enterprises the real wage rate increased in several industries in 1992: in manufacturing where private companies became more active and in construction, trade, and finance and business services where private enterprises were mainly concentrated. The increase in real wages resulted in equalizing the nominal wage between ownership classes not only at the aggregate level but in industries as well (*see Table 11.13*). The equalizing of nominal wage rates may imply that labor supply in private enterprises was already large enough to influence the allocation of the total labor force and hence the wage development.

While non-private enterprises paid increasing real wages in 1992, their efficiency measured by unit labor cost deteriorated considerably in almost all industries. The only exception was the electricity-generating industry which is highly monopolized. *Table 11.14* indicates that unit labor cost

Table 11.11. Change in employment by ownership class across industries in percent (previous year = 100).

	1991	1992
Total enterprises	84.6	83.9
Private enterprises	102.7	164.9
Agriculture, hunting, forestry, fishing	127.6	328.4
Mining, quarrying	73.7	409.8
Manufacturing	106.7	156.5
Electricity, gas, water	84.4	779.9
Construction	89.2	109.1
Wholesale/retail trade, restaurants, hotels	96.4	217.9
Transport, storage, communication	134.7	143.8
Finance, insurance, real estate, business services	115.0	163.4
Community, social, personal services	102.6	173.0
Non-private enterprises	81.4	65.9
Agriculture, hunting, forestry, fishing	77.4	71.0
Mining, quarrying	41.3	40.9
Manufacturing	82.1	61.6
Electricity, gas, water	95.8	96.6
Construction	81.2	41.7
Wholesale/retail trade, restaurants, hotels	89.7	54.3
Transport, storage, communication	82.2	88.7
Finance, insurance, real estate, business services	77.9	67.3
Community, social, personal services	80.9	81.7

Source: Author's calculations.

increased in non-private enterprises, especially in industries that face the most competition.[9] These industries are construction, trade, and finance and business services. For example, in construction, while unit labor cost increased in the non-private sector, it decreased in the private sector during most of the period.

In the analysis of aggregates I have argued that the data might indicate that private enterprises have adjusted to the external and structural shocks while non-private enterprises have not. This reasoning is supported by the analysis by industry. In the year 1991 when the Hungarian economy was the most heavily affected by shocks, private enterprises decreased their unit labor cost in all industries where private industries were concentrated. This was true even in the manufacturing industry. In contrast, the unit labor cost in non-private enterprises increased in 1991.

Table 11.12. Growth of real wage rate by ownership class across industries in percent (previous year = 100).

	1991	1992
Total enterprises	92.7	107.7
Private enterprises	95.1	95.2
Agriculture, hunting, forestry, fishing	75.9	90.8
Mining, quarrying	71.9	148.4
Manufacturing	96.9	94.1
Electricity, gas, water	127.0	78.8
Construction	93.2	96.1
Wholesale/retail trade, restaurants, hotels	89.6	89.1
Transport, storage, communication	92.8	102.2
Finance, insurance, real estate, business services	99.9	97.3
Community, social, personal services	91.7	96.2
Non-private enterprises	91.4	109.2
Agriculture, hunting, forestry, fishing	86.9	99.0
Mining, quarrying	102.8	96.4
Manufacturing	87.8	107.9
Electricity, gas, water	96.1	98.2
Construction	81.6	130.4
Wholesale/retail trade, restaurants, hotels	83.6	121.6
Transport, storage, communication	109.8	103.7
Finance, insurance, real estate, business services	107.1	111.4
Community, social, personal services	106.3	99.6

Source: Author's calculations.

11.4 Conclusion

The analysis presented in this paper has shown that the Hungarian private sector grew rapidly between 1990 and 1992. The increase of real output in the private sector partly offset the fall of output in the non-private sector. Private enterprises exhibited high real growth not only at the aggregate level but in almost all industries. Their activity was especially high in construction, trade, and the service industries. At the same time the non-private sector declined. It has to be emphasized, however, that the analysis does not provide an answer for the question of how closely the decline of the non-private sector is related to the rise of the private one. The total growth of the private sector could not have been divided into two components – namely, growth within the private sector and activity transfer between the two sectors.

Table 11.13. Nominal wage rate by ownership class across industries in thousand Hungarian forints.

	1990	1991	1992
Total enterprises	151.1	189.1	250.5
Private enterprises	175.5	225.2	263.6
Agriculture, hunting, forestry, fishing	180.8	185.2	206.8
Mining, quarrying	188.8	183.3	334.6
Manufacturing	154.4	201.9	233.5
Electricity, gas, water	196.9	337.6	327.3
Construction	165.9	208.7	246.6
Wholesale/retail trade, restaurants, hotels	194.3	235.0	257.6
Transport, storage, communication	180.6	226.2	284.5
Finance, insurance, real estate, business services	258.8	349.0	417.7
Community, social, personal services	210.2	260.2	307.9
Non-private enterprises	146.6	180.9	243.0
Agriculture, hunting, forestry, fishing	126.7	148.7	181.0
Mining, quarrying	203.4	282.2	334.8
Manufacturing	149.2	176.7	234.5
Electricity, gas, water	178.4	231.4	279.6
Construction	128.2	141.2	226.5
Wholesale/retail trade, restaurants, hotels	145.0	163.6	244.7
Transport, storage, communication	140.6	208.4	265.7
Finance, insurance, real estate, business services	187.9	271.6	372.2
Community, social,personal services	144.1	206.8	253.2

Source: Author's calculations.

The development in employment was similar to development in output. While the number of employees in the private sector decreased in some industries in 1991, it increased in 1992 in all industries. Real wages, in general, decreased in the private sector, whereas in non-private enterprises they increased in some industries in 1991 and in almost all industries in 1992. On the one hand, this resulted in the equalization of nominal wage rates between the ownership classes within the same industries. On the other hand, by 1992 this considerably deteriorated the efficiency of non-private enterprises measured in unit labor cost.

It is difficult to identify the causes of this development. The data weakly support the hypothesis that the private sector was less affected by the structural and demand shocks since they concentrated mainly in trade and services. But at the same time they also grew fast in manufacturing

Table 11.14. Unit labor cost by ownership class across industries in percent.

	1989	1990	1991	1992
Total enterprises	13.2	13.1	13.3	16.1
Private enterprises	13.9	11.4	9.6	13.8
Agriculture, hunting, forestry, fishing	13.5	11.6	7.1	11.2
Mining, quarrying	18.5	9.1	16.3	20.0
Manufacturing	14.1	11.9	11.7	12.3
Electricity, gas, water	6.1	11.8	8.6	9.8
Construction	20.9	18.8	14.5	16.6
Wholesale/retail trade, restaurants, hotels	7.9	7.6	5.0	15.4
Transport, storage, communication	13.1	10.0	8.4	13.4
Finance, insurance, real estate, business services	13.6	12.0	11.3	15.7
Community, social, personal services	18.0	17.8	15.3	16.7
Non-private enterprises	13.1	13.5	14.8	17.9
Agriculture, hunting, forestry, fishing	15.9	16.7	17.3	19.9
Mining, quarrying	14.6	15.6	22.3	26.7
Manufacturing	9.6	10.0	11.9	12.4
Electricity, gas, water	7.5	7.6	7.3	9.9
Construction	18.8	21.8	23.3	24.5
Wholesale/retail trade, restaurants, hotels	17.5	18.0	20.3	27.8
Transport, storage, communication	22.4	23.8	23.8	26.5
Finance, insurance, real estate, business services	13.8	13.1	13.6	53.0
Community, social, personal services	23.9	23.4	19.9	19.8

Source: Author's calculations.

which was heavily affected by these shocks. The data may also suggest that the private sector adjusted faster to the shocks than the non-private one.

The data on unit labor cost show higher efficiency in the private sector than in the non-private one. *Table 11.15* and *Table 11.16* give the after-tax return on equity in the different ownership classes and industries. According to these figures, private enterprises perform clearly better than non-private ones. The worsening figures of the private enterprises with FDI might have been brought about by two factors. First, these enterprises invested heavily in the 1989–1992 period which may have worsened their current profitability but will increase their future one. Second, these enterprises usually realize their profit outside the borders of Hungary due to the high Hungarian tax burden. Another fact indicated by *Table 11.15* and *Table 11.16* is that the performance of non-private enterprises worsened dramatically in 1992.

Table 11.15. After-tax return on equity by ownership class in percent.

	1989	1990	1991	1992
Total enterprises	4.6	2.8	1.7	2.1
Private enterprises	5.3	3.7	1.8	4.1
Private enterprises with FDI	4.0	1.2	0.4	−2.2
Private enterprises without FDI	5.7	4.8	2.5	6.7
Non-private enterprises	5.0	3.8	2.0	−2.6
State-owned enterprises	4.7	4.4	2.7	0.2
Cooperatives	5.1	3.1	0.7	−6.5

Source: Author's calculations.

Table 11.16. After-tax return on equity by ownership class across industries in percent.

	1989	1990	1991	1992
Total enterprises	4.6	2.8	1.7	2.1
Private enterprises	5.6	3.5	2.0	6.5
Agriculture, hunting, forestry, fishing	2.6	0.9	0.4	−1.9
Mining, quarrying	1.1	1.6	3.6	52.9
Manufacturing	6.2	3.1	2.6	4.4
Electricity, gas, water	2.7	3.2	2.9	28.0
Construction	24.1	9.4	9.2	17.7
Wholesale/retail trade, restaurants, hotels	2.6	3.0	1.2	3.6
Transport, storage, communication	6.5	2.7	4.2	13.2
Finance, insurance, real estate, business services	8.1	2.1	3.0	11.8
Community, social, personal services	7.2	2.6	0.7	−0.5
Non-private enterprises	4.7	3.7	1.6	−3.7
Agriculture, hunting, forestry, fishing	3.4	2.5	0.3	−9.8
Mining, quarrying	0.1	1.7	0.7	−0.8
Manufacturing	5.7	4.6	1.9	−3.3
Electricity, gas, water	2.1	1.3	0.7	−0.1
Construction	3.7	2.7	1.1	−2.5
Wholesale/retail trade, restaurants, hotels	6.2	8.0	2.7	−0.7
Transport, storage, communication	1.1	2.0	2.0	−0.8
Finance, insurance, real estate, business services	4.3	2.3	1.8	−1.2
Community, social, personal services	5.4	4.1	1.6	−0.2

Source: Author's calculations.

The performance of private enterprises shows some stability. This implies that privatization is one of the most important ways to recover. However, one might argue that the state sector cannot be privatized much faster since Hungary did not choose give-away privatization schemes. Under these conditions the bad performance of non-private enterprises could have had an adverse effect on the performance of private ones. Two different channels are possible. First, since the budget constraint of non-private enterprises cannot be regarded as hard the competition in real wages between the two sectors can worsen the efficiency of the private enterprises.[10] The possibility of this occurring in the future is suggested by the wage development in 1991–1992. Second, the declining activity of non-private enterprises can lower the demand for trade and other business services. In addition to the possible negative effect on private activities, unemployment can grow further if non-private enterprises try to lower their unit labor costs by laying off workers. This reasoning indicates that to achieve a general recovery the governance of the state-owned enterprises should also be improved.

It should be emphasized that this analysis is still preliminary. Further theoretical and empirical research is required to explain enterprise performance in the transition period.

Notes

[1] Kornai 1993 emphasizes the special characteristic of this recession, which he calls "transformational" recession.

[2] Roughly speaking, Tukey's estimation gives higher weight to an individual figure if it is closer to the median and lower weight to those which are far from the median.

[3] For simplicity, I use only the term GDP. In this sense it means GDP at basic prices, that is, net of commodity taxes. The real growth rate of GDP also refers to the real growth rate of GDP at basic prices.

[4] Private sector consists of private enterprises, small businesses, and the economic activity of households.

[5] The category of small businesses is used by the Hungarian Central Statistical Office and includes the activities of self-employed, not incorporated, businesses.

[6] Although private enterprises did not operate in the agriculture, this does not mean that the private activity as small businesses and as households did not play an important role in this sector.

[7] In the term "real wage rate," real means from the point of view of households since the nominal indices are divided by the consumer price index.

[8] When looking at the figures on mining and quarrying in 1992, it is hard to believe that almost 40% of the employees worked in private enterprises. A distorting factor could have been that the most important state-owned enterprises

went bankrupt in 1992 and their end-of-period data were not included in the data set.

[9] It should be noted that the transport and telecommunications industries and business services operate under special circumstances. Despite the fact that the many small transport companies were established by private agents between 1989 and 1992, the aggregate data are still dominated by two very large Hungarian companies: Hungarian Telecom and Hungarian Railroads. Their presence might explain the relative stability of the unit labor cost in these sectors. According to the table in business services the unit labor cost deteriorated in 1992. This explanation requires further investigation, but the most likely reason is the very weak performance of the financial and insurance enterprises.

[10] Coricelli and Milesi-Ferretti (1993) point out the possible incentive for "predatory wage" behavior if the uncertainty about the future is high enough.

References

Coricelli, F., and Milesi-Ferretti, G.M., 1993, On the credibility of "Big Bang" programs, *European Economic Review*, **37**:387–395.

Kornai, J., 1993, *Transformational Recession: A General Phenomenon Examined Through the Example of Hungary's Development*, Discussion Paper, No. 1, Collegium Budapest, Institute for Advanced Study, Budapest, Hungary.

Chapter 12

Output Decline and the Dynamics of Privatization in the Czech Republic

Aleš Čapek

12.1 The Economic Decline

The beginning of economic reforms in the Czech Republic led to a sharp decline of output in the economy (*Table 12.1*). It is estimated that between 1989 and 1992 the Czech GDP in real terms declined by more than 20%; almost two-thirds of this economic decline occurred in 1991. In 1992 and especially early 1993 we can observe a slowdown of this overall decline and even signs of recovery in certain sectors of the economy. These latter sectors include construction and transportation of goods, which experienced a very sharp decline in 1991 but some real growth in 1992; in construction this growth was evident on a yearly basis, while in transportation growth was observed on a quarterly basis. The pattern of economic decline is more alarming within industry and agriculture. Here we can observe, in 1992 and the first half of 1993, continuing steady decline, reflecting the fact that restructuring within these sectors will be a longer and more painful process.

There is certain clear diversification of the economic decline within the industry itself. On the one hand, a major economic decline can be observed within the machinery complex (machinery, electrotechnical and electronics industry, optical instruments, metal working), in the production of consumer goods (textile, apparel, furniture), as well as in manufacturing of chemicals

R. Holzmann et al. (eds.), Output Decline in Eastern Europe, 285-300.

Table 12.1. Real economic growth in the Czech Republic in 1990, 1991, and 1992 in percent (1989 = 100).

	1990	1991	1992
GDP	98.8	84.8	78.8
Gross industrial output[a]	96.6	73.0	63.0
Gross output in construction	94.2	63.7	66.8
Gross agricultural output	97.7	89.0	78.5
Transportation of goods (based on ton km)[b]	88.0	68.6	68.0

[a]In 1990 and 1991 enterprises with more than 100 employees; in 1992 enterprises with more than 25 employees.
[b]Public road and rail transport.
Source: Author's calculations using Czech Statistical Office data.

and noniron metallurgy. On the other hand, only a minor decline took place within the energy and fuels complex and also in manufacturing of food and tobacco products.

Output decline has many sources, both external and internal. In another study, Buchtíková and Čapek (1992) show that the loss of Eastern markets can explain only a minor part of the overall decline in output in the Czech Republic. However, since the loss of Eastern markets took place in a period of sluggish economic growth in Western countries, territorial reorientation of external trade of the Czech Republic was not easy. The shrinkage of domestic demand due to restrictive fiscal and monetary policies applied in a situation of internal disequilibrium and inflationary bias is another major demand-side explanation of the economic decline.

On the supply side the impact of the process of privatization is crucial. Uncertainties connected with privatization led to certain pre-privatization rigidity in the behavior of the big state-owned enterprises (SOEs), characterized by lower investment activity, growing indebtedness, and decline in output accompanied by a surprisingly low rate of unemployment.

The restrictive policies should be seen in the context of old ownership relations. It was reasonable to apply macroeconomic restriction in a non-privatized monopolized economy with distorted price relations where additional demand would have only spilled over into higher prices and would have led to inefficient allocation of resources.

12.2 The Dynamics of Privatization

Privatization is a major factor affecting the dynamics of output and employment. The speed at which the private sector is evolving in the Czech Republic

Table 12.2. Number of registered entrepreneurs between 1989 and the first quarter of 1993, at the end of the period.

1989	1990	1991	1992	1993
65,200	370,000	1,058,500	1,205,900	1,030,100[a]

[a]Decline in the number of entrepreneurs in the first quarter of 1993 was due to the obligation to re-register in January 1993.
Source: Czech Statistical Office.

Table 12.3. The dynamics of small privatization, at the end of the period.

	6/91	12/91	6/92	12/92	6/93
Number of privatized units	4,700	14,200	20,000	22,500	23,100
Value of privatized property (bill. current Czech koruna)	2.7	14.5	25.3	29.5	30.0

Source: Czech Statistical Office.

is influenced by the role which this sector played before economic reforms started. One specific feature of this country (and of former Czechoslovakia) is that in the beginning of the transformation process the private sector was nearly nonexistent. In 1989 the share of state sector in GDP was 97% in former Czechoslovakia, compared with about 70% in Poland and 86% in Hungary (Chavance, 1993, p. 49).

Since 1990 the share of private sector in the Czech economy has steadily grown. Between 1990 and 1992 the growth of the private sector was mostly the result of privatization of the small business sector in the economy. *Tables 12.2* and *12.3* show the growth of the registered private entrepreneurs and the dynamics of the "small" privatization within which mostly parts of the service sector (retail trade, catering, repair shops, parts of public transportation) have been privatized. Only a few big enterprises were privatized during this period.

The increase in the dynamics of the privatization process that took place in 1993 was due to progress in the privatization of big businesses – especially through the voucher method as well as "ownership transformation" of the agricultural cooperatives. As a result, the growth of the private sector dramatically accelerated in 1993.

In the first half of 1993 the share of the private sector is estimated to have reached 77.5% in gross agricultural output, 60.2% in construction, and 75.0% of the volume in retail trade. In industry the share of the private sector was still only 17.6%, and the effect of voucher privatization is yet to

Table 12.4. Share of the private sector in the economy in percent.

	1990	1991	1992	1993[a]
Total GDP	4.0	11.0	19.5	44.2
Industry		8.9	14.1	17.6
Agriculture and forestry		13.2	18.9	
Construction		26.8	48.4	60.2
Transport and communications		0.6	3.1	
Trade		12.6	33.3	
Services		10.5	28.3	

[a]First half of 1993.
Source: Czech Statistical Office.

Table 12.5. Number of employees in firms with more than 25 employees by type of ownership in 1992.

Type of ownership	Number of employees	Growth: 1991=100
Total	3,709,699	89.8
State	2,999,425	88.1
Nonagricultural coops	156,734	75.8
Private	166,288	139.3
Municipal	65,953	103.6
Social organizations	27,598	86.5
International (joint ventures)	41,701	129.4
Foreign owned	4,440	322.4
Mixed ownership	8,485	105.7
Agricultural coops	238,863	77.6
Other	222	403.6

Source: Czech Statistical Office.

be felt in the future. In total in the first half of 1993 about 44% of GDP originated in the private sector (*Table 12.4*).

Similar trends have been observed in employment, perhaps with the difference that the initial concentration of the expanding private sector in the labor-intensive economic activities have led to a higher share of the private sector in total employment compared with its share in GDP. If we take the data from *Table 12.5*, add the estimated 1 million individual entrepreneurs, and include the transformed cooperatives and the international, foreign and mixed enterprises in the private sector, we end up with about 42% of total employment in the private sector in the economy at the end of the first quarter of 1993 (this number inevitably involves double or triple counting the same individuals in different activities).

Table 12.6. The size distribution of firms in industry, in number of firms and percent.

No. of employees	December 1990 No. of firms	December 1990 Distribution in %	December 1991 No. of firms	December 1991 Distribution in %	December 1992 No. of firms	December 1992 Distribution in %	April 1993[a] No. of firms	April 1993[a] Distribution in %
25–99	n.a.		n.a.		658	27.2	998	35.5
100–149	105	9.1	179	13.7	244	10.1	n.a.[a]	
150–299	185	16.1	249	19.0	543	22.5		
300–599	228	19.8	283	21.6	410	17.0		
600–1199	213	18.5	252	19.2	264	10.9		
1200–2499	241	20.9	210	16.0	190	7.9		
2500–4999	122	10.6	95	7.3	79	3.3		
>5000	57	5.0	42	3.2	28	1.2	22	0.8
Total	1151	100.0	1310	100.0	2416	100.0	2809	100.0

[a]Size-distribution categories in 1993 of enterprises with more than 100 and fewer than 5,000 employees are not comparable with previous years.

Source: Czech Statistical Office.

Table 12.7. The size distribution of firms in the construction sector, in number of firms and percent.

	December 1991		December 1992		May 1993	
No. of employees	No. of firms	Distribution in %	No. of firms	Distribution in %	No. of firms	Distribution in %
25–49	n.a.		174	22.1	330	29.5
50–99	n.a.		165	20.9	307	27.4
100–199	73	18.6	147	18.7	202	18.0
200–399	111	28.3	157	19.9	162	14.5
400–599	94	24.0	73	9.3		
600–799	57	14.5	38	4.8	102[c]	9.1[c]
800–999	24	6.1	13	1.6		
1000–1499	13	3.3	8	1.0	17[b]	1.5
1500–5000	17	4.3	13[a]	1.6		
>5000	3	0.8				
Total	392	100.0	788	100.0	1120	100.0

[a]More than 1,500 employees.
[b]More than 1,000 employees.
[c]Covers firms with 400–999 employees.
Source: Czech Statistical Office.

Privatization as well as organizational restructuring in state-owned enterprises (SOEs) has led to changes in the size distribution of firms. The Czech economy, once dominated by large state conglomerates, is gradually moving toward an economy with a strong small-business sector. The average size of the state enterprises has decreased considerably as well. This overall tendency can be illustrated by the data on industry and construction in *Tables 12.6* and *12.7*.

12.3 The Economic Trends in the Nationalized (Large) and Private (Small) Sectors

12.3.1 Output and employment

Different size categories of firms – independent of ownership type – have played different roles in the economic transformation in the Czech Republic (*Table 12.8*).

Between 1990 and 1991 a number of new small businesses were established and began operating. After hesitant growth during these years, the

Table 12.8. Changes in production and employment in industrial firms by number of employees (indices[a]: previous period = 100).

No. of employees	Production 1991	Production 1992	Production First quarter 1993/ First quarter 1992	Employment 1991	Employment 1992	Employment First quarter 1993/ First quarter 1992[c]
<25[b]		400.0	124.0		110.0	100.7
25–99		118.0	126.6		121.5	123.3
100–149	64.0	94.0	92.1	83.9	91.2	97.3
150–299	71.7	89.8	92.1	87.1	88.5	97.3
300–599	70.0	85.0		88.4	84.9	
600–1199	72.4	84.3		86.4	85.2	
1200–2499	74.1	81.0		87.1	86.6	
2500–4999	74.1	86.6		88.1	89.2	
>5000	82.0	87.7	92.1	90.7	89.8	92.4

[a]For the calculation of indices the same enterprises were taken into account for every two periods compared.
[b]Estimate.
[c]Classification of firms with more than 300 and fewer than 5,000 employees is not comparable with previous years.
Source: Czech Statistical Office.

small-business sector experienced a period of rapid expansion in both output and employment in 1992.

This trend continued in the beginning of 1993, mainly in the category of firms with between 25 and 99 employees. Toward the end of 1992 the privatization process of the very small economic units with less than 25 employees was nearly completed, and the growth of employment in the firms of this size decelerated. Nevertheless, the growth of output in this category was still well above average.

During this period output and employment in firms with more than 100 employees continued to decline. One general feature of this overall decline mainly for the year 1991 is that the decrease in real output was more dramatic than the decline in employment. One standard explanation of this phenomenon is that for obvious reasons (institutional rigidities) fluctuations in employment lag behind fluctuations in output.

There are, however, some additional reasons for this employment lag in the Czech economy. One is the lack of experience with reductions of employment and layoffs at the enterprise level and the hesitations on the part of managers to fire employees. Another reason is the uncertainty about the future and the expectations that perhaps the decline in both domestic demand and foreign demand is only temporary. The third explanation is that in the situation of transformation uncertainties and during the reshaping of the different power groups in the economy, employees and managers became natural allies in their struggle against the "privatizers" and the reformers in the center. Accordingly, the managers were very cautious in their employment policies.

Finally, perhaps the most important explanation for output and employment trends at the beginning of the economic reform was the kind of wage regulation that was applied. The basic idea of wage regulation in 1991 was not to regulate the amount of wages paid by the SOEs but to control the average nominal wage rate (see Buchtíková and Flek, 1993). Certain official limits on quarterly nominal wage rate growth were agreed upon in the tripartite body and these limits were related to the rate of inflation – namely, the CPI. The wage regulation thus put pressure on the development of nominal and real wages but not on employment. Even in 1992, in spite of some modifications, the wage regulation was still very liberal toward overemployment (*Table 12.9*).

These general trends in output and employment in firms with more than 100 employees are to some extent differentiated among different size categories of these firms. In 1991 the decline in output in the small and medium-sized firms (firms with 100–600 employees) was deeper, and the

Table 12.9. Growth of average wage in firms (previous period = 100).

No. of employees	1991	1992	First quarter 1993
25–99	n.a.	120.4	123.8
100–149	112.0	122.0	122.5[a]
150–299	115.3	119.8	121.0[b]
300–599	115.7	121.1	122.9[c]
600–1199	115.8	118.1	122.2[d]
1200–2499	116.1	118.6	123.5[e]
2500–4999	116.9	118.8	120.0[f]
>5000	118.6	120.5	123.6

Firms employing between [a]100 and 299, [b]300 and 499, [c]500 and 999, [d]1000 and 1999, [e]2000 and 2999, [f]3000 and 4999.
Source: Czech Statistical Office.

decline in employment in these firms lagged behind their output drop to a greater extent than in the bigger firms. As a result the decline in productivity in the big firms was less dramatic, and the large industrial firms looked like the more successful ones (*Table 12.10*).

In 1992 this difference disappeared, and the trends became even slightly reversed. The output decline was more dramatic in the big firms, and it was accompanied by less than proportional decline in employment. The more radical reduction in employment in the group of firms with between 100 and 600 employees resulted in real productivity growth in these firms.

In a further analysis we could not find any significant relation between wage increases, the growth in productivity, and the size of firms. On the other hand, if we structure the firms by type of ownership we find some regularities (*Table 12.11*). There are significant differences in the growth of wages and their absolute levels between different categories of firms, with foreign and international firms having the highest wages and the most dynamic growth and the various cooperatives, municipal firms, and social organizations exhibiting the lowest absolute wage levels. Wages are not regulated in private firms. While these wages are quite high in absolute terms, surprisingly they are growing only modestly. The data, however, cover only firms with more than 25 employees and do not show the dynamics of remuneration of individual entrepreneurs.

At the beginning of 1993 the relatively clear pattern of trends experienced in the previous years with respect to output and employment in firms of different sizes becomes blurred. The only clear trend is the persistent high dynamics of the smallest industrial firms.

Table 12.10. Labor productivity in industrial firms.

	Labor productivity total industry = 1			Change in labor productivity in %, previous period = 100		
No. of employees	1991	1992	First 4 months of 1993	1991	1992	First quarter 1993/ First quarter 1992[a]
25–99		0.9	0.9		97.1	102.6
100–149	0.9	0.9	0.9	76.3	103.1	94.7
150–299	1.2	1.0	0.9	82.3	101.4	94.7
300–599	1.1	1.0		79.2	100.1	
600–1199	1.0	0.9		83.7	99.0	
1200–2499	0.9	0.9		85.1	93.4	
2500–4999	0.9	0.9		84.1	97.1	
>5000	1.1	1.3	1.4	90.4	97.7	99.7

[a]Classification of size of firms with more than 300 and fewer than 5,000 employees is not comparable with previous years.
Source: Czech Statistical Office.

Table 12.11. Average wage in firms by type of ownership in 1992.

Type of ownership	Average wage total = 1	Growth 1991 = 100
Total	1.0	122.1
State	1.0	121.5
Nonagricultural coops	0.8	121.7
Private	1.1	119.0
Municipal	0.9	120.7
Social organization	0.9	122.7
International (joint venture)	1.3	137.0
Foreign owned	1.4	123.1
Mixed ownership	1.0	127.5
Agricultural coops	0.7	98.7
Other	1.0	114.9

Source: Czech Statistical Office.

Labor productivity in absolute terms is understandably highest in the big, capital-intensive firms and low but increasing in the small firms. At the same time in the group of "second largest" firms, with between 1200 and 5000 employees, the absolute level of productivity is low and declining. These are the typical Czech industrial firms which in the past formed the core of the Czech economy and are now experiencing the most difficult process of restructuring. Their situation is reflected in *Tables 12.10* and *12.12*, the latter showing the percentage of firms in different size categories with declining output. The above-mentioned "second largest" firms have the

Table 12.12. Share of industrial firms with declining output, in percent.

No. of employees	1991	1992	1993[a]
25–99		36.8	36.3
100–149	51.4	54.1	55.7
150–299	82.3	68.1	55.7
300–599	88.7	74.6	
600–1199	93.3	76.9	
1200–2499	89.5	82.6	
2500–4999	94.7	81.0	
>5000	85.7	78.6	63.6

[a]The classification of firms with more than 300 and fewer than 5,000 employees is not comparable with previous years.
Source: Czech Statistical Office.

worst results in this respect. On the other hand, the best results are in the category of small firms.

Basically trends similar to those in industry, i.e., rapid growth of output and employment in small firms and the steepest declining performance in the "second largest firms," can be observed in the construction sector. The statistical data for construction distinguish between different types of ownership, illustrating the rapid economic growth of private construction firms and the decline of state firms (*Table 12.13*).

12.3.2 Financial results

The financial results of firms by type of ownership differ with regard to both their levels and change.

The basic conclusion that can be drawn from *Table 12.14* is that in 1992 international firms had the best results. If we exclude municipal firms, which play only a negligible role in the economy, profitability of the international firms grew rapidly between 1991 and 1992.

The high productivity of the international firms is reflected in the high share of material costs and low share of wage costs in total costs. Thus in international firms, wage cost inflation, in spite of the relatively high level of wages in these firms, is not a serious problem. The growing financial costs are counterbalanced by growing profitability.

The financial results of all other major categories of firms are less favorable. Profitability in both private and state firms decreased in 1991–1992 in spite of the monopoly profits achieved by many of the firms in both sectors.

Table 12.13. Output and employment trends in construction firms by type of ownership (previous period = 100).[a]

Type of ownership	Growth of output, percent 1991	1992	First 5 months 1993/ First 5 months 1992	Growth of employment, percent 1991	1992	First 5 months 1993/ First 5 months 1992
State	66.7	91.0	71.0	82.5	79.1	83.7
Cooperative	58.8	90.4	70.3	84.5	83.5	84.4
Private	278.0	169.1	133.6	265.8	139.0	165.8
Other	89.3	113.8	105.6	93.2	95.8	123.4

[a]The same enterprises were taken into account for every two periods compared.
Source: Czech Statistical Office.

Table 12.14. Selected financial indicators for firms by type of ownership in 1991 and 1992.

	State firms	Coops	Small priv. firms[a]	Private firms[b]	Municipal firms	Internat. firms
Profitability[c]						
1991	12.0	−2.3	4.3	10.7	9.0	3.1
1992	8.8	−5.9	n.a.	6.8	23.1	10.1
Shares of costs in total output						
Material costs						
1991	62.4	58.2	59.0	65.1	57.5	79.1
1992	63.1	61.3	n.a.	59.3	51.1	71.7
Wage costs						
1991	10.3	17.5	7.1	8.8	19.9	5.3
1992	11.4	17.5	n.a.	8.9	13.4	5.8
Financial costs						
1991	12.9	20.4	10.7	13.5	11.6	9.0
1992	12.8	20.0	n.a.	17.1	26.7	12.3
Share of the individual categories of firms in total output[d]						
1991	84.8	6.8	5.2	1.1	0.0	2.2
1992	85.5	7.1	n.a.	2.4	0.0	5.1

[a]Includes individual entrepreneurs and small partnerships.
[b]Includes private firms with more than 25 employees.
[c]Profits/total cost in percent.
[d]Total output is the sum of output of the above categories of firms. In 1992 without small private firms.
Source: Author's calculations using CSO data.

The cooperatives even experienced net losses in both years, and their losses have continued to grow.

The increase in the financial costs (including interest payments) in the private firms is an alarming development in view of their decreasing profitability. In 1992 the share of financial costs stabilized in the state sector and in the cooperatives, in fact at a very high level.

The good financial performance of firms with the participation of foreign capital is further reflected in the role bad debts as well as "bad" accounts receivable play in their financial balances. As can be seen from *Table 12.15* the financial performance of both the foreign and international firms is much better than the performance of domestic firms. The large share of bad assets in private domestic firms' accounts receivable and the bad debts in their accounts payable is quite alarming, especially considering the short time period they had to accumulate these assets.

Table 12.15. Accounts receivable (AR) and accounts payable (AP) in firms of selected[a] types of ownership in 1992.

	AR			AP[b]		
Type of ownership	Total	Bad AR	Share of bad AR in total AR	Total	Bad AP	Share of bad AP in total AP
Total	100.0	100.0	51.0	100.0	100.0	33.5
State	85.8	88.4	52.5	81.7	86.9	35.6
Coops	4.1	4.3	52.6	4.1	6.0	48.6
Private	2.1	2.9	61.3	3.8	3.2	28.8
Internat. (jt. ventures)	5.5	3.2	29.2	6.1	2.1	11.4
Foreign owned	1.4	0.5	18.5	3.4	0.8	7.5

[a]Only major ownership-type categories are included. Thus, the percentages do not add up to 100.
[b]Includes wages and taxes payable.
Source: Author's calculations based on the CSO data.

From other sources we know that within the state sector the absolute amount of bad assets and debts was decreasing during 1992, even though in absolute terms it still played a dominant role in the total amount of bad assets and bad debts in the economy.

These data indicate at least two major policy issues. First, the sector of private domestic firms, though growing rapidly, faces some financial problems and thus may represent a less stabilizing force in the economy than expected. Perhaps surprisingly, but in compliance with the above data, three out of four bankrupt firms in the first phase of bankruptcies in 1993 were private firms. This fact reflects low financial discipline in many of the new private firms and some natural weaknesses of the new firms (lack of capital, lack of skills, limited access to the markets dominated by the SOEs, and so on). These latter chracteristics of the private sector, for whatever reasons, confirm the idea that privatization itself without complementary government policies will not solve the restructuring problem in a satisfactory way.

Second, the data show that the firms with foreign capital participation represent the most prospective and promising sector in the economy even though at present growing from a very low level. These firms are characterized by both high growth dynamics and a healthy financial situation.

From this perspective the inflow of foreign capital is highly desirable not only because it is a source of financial funds and technical or managerial know-how, but also because it brings financial discipline and supports sound financial growth.

12.3.3 Bank credit

Between February 1992 and September 1993 the share of SOEs in the total credit to the nonfinancial sector declined from 85% to 56% while the shares of domestic and foreign private firms increased from 14% to 40% and from 0% to 3%, respectively. This dramatic restructuring of the credit market was accompanied by specific development of the interest rates. During the observed period the interest rates on credits to private firms were clearly above those of the SOEs.

The developments in the market of bank credit reflect the pragmatic attitudes of the commercial banks in the first phases of economic transformation. The few big domestic banks which dominate the market have quite naturally been connected with the big SOEs in the past. Many of these enterprises now face serious financial problems and the chain effect of bankruptcies could have an adverse impact on the banks. In this situation the credit conditions provided by the big banks are more favorable to their traditional customers than to their new private clients. This tendency was evident especially during the beginning of the privatization process when the new private firms represented unknown entities to the banks. It is expected that as the private sector stabilizes, the conditions under which the private firms are provided with credit will be brought nearer to the SOEs' credit conditions. The financial results of the private firms, however, so far do not create the preconditions for more significant changes in the current interest rate policy.

The influence of the developments in the bank credit market on the financial situation of the firms should not be overestimated. In the absence of strict bankruptcy procedures and in a situation of high interest rates, the firms – both the state-owned and private-owned – chose the strategy of growing mutual indebtedness as a way of obtaining "credits with zero interest rates."

12.4 Conclusions

The statistics available have enabled only a partial analysis of the output trends in the economy. The data have described the rapid growth of the private sector together with a changing size distribution of firms. In spite of these "restructuring" processes the real volume of output is still significantly below the pre-reform levels. During 1992 and 1993 there were only partial signs of recovery in different parts of the economy.

The pre-privatization rigidity and lack of restructuring efforts, with regard to both allocative and internal inefficiencies, in the big SOEs during a period of severe structural shocks contributed substantially to the economic decline. Among the SOEs a particularly problematic group is the group of "second biggest firms." The first biggest firms belong to a special category, not only because they are often better equipped with technology or capital from the past but also because the government pays special attention to their privatization and even undertakes certain restructuring efforts.

The disproportion between the decline in output and employment at the beginning of economic reform is the result of a hesitant approach toward reducing the employed work force in a situation of uncertainties about future output prospects, rising new coalitions in the economy, and applying new wage regulations.

In spite of the great dynamics of the private sector and its growing contribution to the total output, even this sector is characterized by some financial problems. Lack of financial discipline, the spillover of the debt problem from the state sector, and the unfavorable credit policy are the causes of financial instability in many of the small private firms. As expected the best economic results are achieved by firms with foreign capital.

Uncertainty still remains concerning the performance of the new large and medium-sized firms that have been established in the course of the two waves of voucher privatization. They represent the decisive part of the economy, and their performance will have the greatest impact on future economic growth in the Czech Republic.

References

Buchtíková, A., and Flek, V., 1993, *Income Policy and Wage Development in the Czech Republic*, Czech National Bank, Institute of Economics, Prague, Czech Republic.

Buchtíková, A., and Čapek, A., 1992, The split of the Czechoslovak economy and the specific features of the Slovak economy, *Revue Obchodu Prumislu a Ekonomiky* (The Revue of Trade, Industry, and the Economy), **8** [in Czech].

Chavance, B., 1993, The mixed economy in the period of post-socialist transformation, *Cahiers du CEFRES*, **3**.

Comments on the Papers by Ákos Valentinyi and Aleš Čapek

Michal Rutkowski

The general framework of the two papers is clear. On the one hand, a once dominant state sector is being steadily eroded. State firms are shedding labor, some are closing, others are being restructured. A new private sector is emerging and growing. Unemployment is a result of the reallocation process.

Even though the framework is clear, the details result in a blurry picture. As far as *the state sector* is concerned there is heterogeneity of performance across industries, enterprises, and, even more importantly, over time (Valentinyi, *Table 11.4*). The state firms do not necessarily behave as perverse labor-managed firms, maximizing income per worker and disregarding employment and output effects of such actions. In fact, although employment fell significantly, real wage decline was even steeper.

As far as *the private sector* is concerned, the characteristics are also different across sectors (again Valentinyi, *Table 11.14*). Moreover, there are two distinct streams in the private sector. The first stream consists of hundreds of thousands of self-employed individuals or small enterprises with a few employees. The second stream comprises joint stock companies with a high rate of employment.

Therefore, it is easier to compare the state and the private sector than to make comparisons inside sectors. In this paper, I comment extensively on the behavior of output, employment, and wages in the state sector, and then I comment on the employment and wages in the private sector in the Czech Republic, Hungary, and Poland. My examples refer mostly to Poland.

The State Sector: Output and Employment

Output performance is transparent, and both authors use similar facts and arrive at similar conclusions about huge contraction. Employment performance poses more questions. Why did employment fell much less than output? The authors tend to indicate the time lag as a reason for this (see Čapek, Section 12.3). This view is understandable. Just prior to 1990 the East European economies were experiencing some "shortageflation" (more in Poland than in other countries) due to excess aggregate demand ("overheating" typical of socialist economies) with a widespread lack of financial discipline including a budget deficit and loose control of the money supply. Open unemployment did not exist, but many vacancies were advertised, and so the U/V (unemployment/vacancy) coefficient was much less than one. Instead of open unemployment substantial labor hoarding existed, estimated at up to 15%–25% of the labor force. There were signs of increasing mismatch: having included labor hoarding in the overall rate of unemployment the Beveridge curve was shifting outward. Under these circumstances, one could obviously expect a drop in employment commensurate with a drop in output. If this has not happened yet, the time lag explains the difference. Let us try to challenge this view.

First, there is no reason to expect that a fall in output would bring a fully commensurate fall in employment, because productivity – no matter how it is measured – is procyclical. It is difficult to estimate precisely how procyclical it might have been in Central and Eastern Europe during 1990–1991, but evidence from other countries shows that, on average, output rises (falls) by about 1.25% when man-hours employed rise (falls) by 1%. Ignoring differences between the labor input measured by man-hours and the number of employees, let us assume that in the Central and East European case this coefficient was really 1.25. This means that during a 1% drop in output we might have expected a 0.8% drop in employment. [The coefficient for Eastern Europe may be even higher then 1.25 due to labor hoarding at the starting point. Rotemberg and Summers (1990) show that firms, or industries, that hoard more labor also have more procyclical productivity. The reason is that firms that hoard large quantities of labor have lower marginal costs than those that do not. Hence the wedge between price and marginal cost is larger, and productivity is more procyclical.]

Second, putting aside sectoral aspects, a demand shock is going to produce a drop in employment due to the demand deficiency resulting from a fall in real wages. This is the macro effect. But, at the same time, falling real wages can be expected to produce an increase in labor demand through the substitution of labor for capital – that is, in the short run, the use of more labor with a fixed capital stock. This is the micro effect. Both are well known and described extensively in the literature: the macro effect is a typical Keynes–Kalecki effect, while the micro effect is described in every microeconomic textbook. The net outcome thus depends on the relative strength of the macro and micro effects.

What happened in Central and Eastern Europe in 1990–1991? Real wages dropped significantly, increasing the share of profits and negatively affecting aggregate demand. At the same time, a drop in real wages encouraged firms to hire more labor. Might these factors alone have offset the macro effect and explain why employment dropped much less than output did, with existing labor hoarding at the outset?

This reason explains the situation only partially. What matters is certainly the elasticity of labor demand. In Eastern Europe, the fraction of total costs that are payments to labor is low, below 20%. Assuming an elasticity in the range of 0.15–0.2, and taking into account the proportions between a drop in output and a drop in real wages, an increase in labor demand due to the micro effect could not have been more than 0.20–0.25% for a 1% drop in output. This, however, does not completely explain actual events.

Let us now look at some findings of the shortage phenomenon. It may offer some insights on the gap we seek to fill.

The basic problem is as follows: What is the effect on actual employment of a decrease in capacity utilization, if at the starting point this capacity utilization exceeds the "welfare optimum?" There should be no doubt that before 1990 the Polish economy was "overheated," that is, the attempted capacity utilization was above the "tolerance limit" defined as a point where the marginal social cost begins to exceed the marginal social benefit. "Overheating" has many dimensions. For the labor market, the following two are the most important:

1. An attempt to maximize capacity utilization creates (in a socialist economy) a famous coexistence of shortage and slack. Striving to achieve the maximum capacity utilization can increase measurable output and productivity; but, at the same time, it leads to bottlenecks, a forced substitution of inputs, a forced intertemporal reallocation of labor, a decrease in quality, and widespread shortages. The more frequent and intensive the shortage, including labor shortage, the greater the internal slack, including labor slack, will be.
2. Capacity utilization above the "welfare optimum," due to bottlenecks, increases the demand for finance, particularly for working capital. This is, in particular, the case in countries where capital markets are far from perfect, where the availability of cash or savings within the firms becomes critical. It decreases investment and therefore actual labor utilization.

The demand shock that took place in Eastern Europe sharply decreased the degree of capacity utilization. Exact data are not known; however, given the high degree of monopolization, when firms applied the mark-up pricing rule and as the mark-up increased, the degree of capital utilization fell. My hypothesis is that a part of this fall produced an *increase* in actual employment and thus generated an effect working in the opposite direction to the standard macro effect of falling demand. How great this effect was depends on the previous "overheating" – that is, the capacity utilization above the "welfare optimum." Disappearance of shortage implies that employees (who used to be alternately overworked and idle in short intervals due to widespread bottlenecks and forced substitution in the pre-reformed economy) have actually become better utilized after the demand shock and so a decrease in capacity utilization has occurred. Their work has become better organized. Both labor slack and on-the-job unemployment have decreased since shortage and "overheating" disappeared.

Certainly this perverse effect could have been working only in a small portion of capacity utilization fall above the "welfare optimum." The size of the portion is extremely difficult to estimate since due to measurement problems we know very little about the slack created by shortage in the "overheated" economy. Roughly, assuming that $n\%$ rate of shortage creates $n/4\,\%$ "rate of slack" (on the basis of some micro-observations about behavior of raw materials' stocks in state enterprises), we need to know estimates of the rate of shortages to perform the calculations. Such an estimate for Eastern Europe was done in 1986 on the basis of forced savings and arrived at the result of about 6% (Kolodko and McMahon, 1987). This suggests results ranging between 1% and 1.5% of the decrease in labor slack, explaining 0.05%–0.075% of increase in labor demand during the 1% output drop.

Finally, in a shortage economy, vacancies constituted an important part of labor demand. Hence, we have to take into account the sharp drop in vacancies advertised – from 250,000 in December 1990 to 50,000 a year later in the case of Poland, similar to the situation in other East European countries. This drop allows us to account

Table C.2. Results of estimates.

Actual effect of a 1% drop in output on a fall in employment – empirical evidence from Poland, Czech and Slovak republics, and Hungary	0.5%
Why employment did not fall more:	
• Procyclical behavior of productivity (coefficient 1.25 assumed)	0.2%
• Increase in the demand for labor due to the fall in real wages (standard micro effect, elasticity 0.15–0.2 assumed)	0.20–0.25%
• Decrease in labor slack due to the fall in capacity utilization (Kornai's shortage removal effect)	0.05–0.075%
• Decrease in vacancies	0.05%
Total	1.00–1.075%

Source: Author's estimates.

for 0.05% of the fall in employment which should have occurred otherwise and which almost fills the gap.

Table C.2 provides results of the rough estimates. They rest on arbitrary assumptions, but they illustrate important phenomena for understanding labor market adjustment in the post-shortage economy. The basic message is that the adjustment in Central and Eastern Europe is consistent with expectations based on theory, especially if some less frequently discussed issues are taken into account.

Some factors that are not taken into account in *Table C.2* could also matter. The first one is sectoral shifts. The anticipated effect of adjustment to the labor market would be a reallocation of employment from nontradables to tradables, which would result from devaluation and tight monetary policy and force firms to find new sales outlets. If we take into account that labor intensity in Eastern Europe is higher in the tradables sector than in the nontradables sector, we may expect that wage-driven sectoral shifts toward tradables offset the standard macro effect and can explain why employment decreases by a small fraction. The problem is that the data do not seem to confirm the above hypothesis; at least in Poland, the decline in employment in exporting sectors was not smaller than elsewhere.

Two remaining factors that may also explain differences are not yet verifiable: time lag and workers' heterogeneity in terms of quality. In the first case we may expect a retarded effect in Eastern Europe soon; the second case would mean that the best-qualified workers, with above average individual labor productivity, have been lost.

The Private Sector: Employment and Wages

As far as private-sector development is concerned, the authors give a very good account of heterogeneity inside the private sector and of different growth across subsectors. They point to a rapid increase both in output and in employment, indicating that initially employment in the private sector was very often parallel to the employment in the state sector. The most interesting finding of the authors is that the growth of wages in the domestic private firms lags behind the growth of wages in the state sector and in foreign and international firms (Valentinyi, Section 11.3; Čapek, Section 12.3).

The finding about the level and change of wages calls for further research, in particular looking at the hiring and firing practices of the private sector. Two hypotheses seem plausible:

1. Having the first job in the public sector and the second job in the private sector is widespread. Therefore, employees get only part of their remuneration from the private sector. If their marginal productivity in the private sector exceeds the productivity in the public sector, while the wage is growing faster in the public sector, there is a move toward subsidization of the private sector by the public sector. It might not be bad for the economy as a whole, even if it is not favorable for the public sector.
2. Wages in the private sector, the growth of which lags behind the state sector, indicate increasing dualism in the labor market of East European countries with a unionized state sector and a secondary private sector. Given binding floors on minimum wage in the state sector, this may improve job matching in the labor market and increase flexibility.

Hypotheses (1) and (2) together may indicate that it is possible to restructure the economy without high levels of open unemployment. The authors implicitly indicate that job-to-job flows appeared to dominate labor market restructuring and open unemployment has not reflected a process of "creative destruction" in which unemployment is a necessary condition and supporting factor for economic growth. This suggestion is consistent with other papers that find a very low level of flows from unemployment to jobs in Eastern Europe (Blanchard *et al.*, 1993).

References

Blanchard, O., Commander, S., and Coricelli, F., 1993, Unemployment and Restructuring in Eastern Europe, Paper prepared for the World Bank Conference, October 7–8, World Bank, Washington, DC, USA.

Kolodko, W.G.W., and McMahon, W., 1987, Stagflation and shortageflation: A comparative approach, *Kyklos*, **40**(2):176–197.

Rotemberg, J.J., and Summers, L.H., 1990, Inflexible prices and procyclical productivity, *Quarterly Journal of Economics*, **105**(4):851–874.

Part III

Policy Issues of Output Decline

1 Einleitung

2. Einige relevante Merkmale der ZW Wirtschaft (kurz)
- Zentrale Planung des Outputs
- zentr. Vorgabe der Preise
- „soft-budget-constr." für die Un ~~bei den Firmen~~
- Geldüberhang

3. Mögliche Erklärungen des Outputrückganges im Laufe des Transf.prozesses (Liberalisierung, Privatisierung, Stabilisierung)

3.1. „Klassische" Erkl. des Outpr. (durch NF u Angebotsschocks (Bofinger, 199_)

3.2. Erkl. durch die Rolle des Kredits (restr. Geld- u. Kr. pol.) (Calvo & Cor, __) Kap. 5. 1905

3.3. Institutionelle Erkl. des Outputrückgangs (Aktive Rolle des Staats auf den Fin.märkten) (keine zentr. Planung, banking system) (M. Raiser, P. Nunnenkamp).

4. Trade-off-Situation in Rußland in 1996-97: Infl-n vs. Wachstum.

5. Mögl. Wege der Problemlösung

„Outputrückgang als Anpassungsproblem ~~im Laufe~~ der Transf-n in Rußland"

Chapter 13

Output Decline and Recovery in Central and Eastern Europe: The Role of Incentives

Martin Raiser and Peter Nunnenkamp

Since the demise of socialism, policy makers in Central and Eastern Europe have been bombarded with advice from the West on how to stabilize, privatize, and liberalize their economies. Reform programs centered on these three catchwords had proved quite successful in highly distorted developing economies, such as Chile since the mid-1970s and, more recently, Mexico and Argentina. So, why shouldn't this panacea work in countries struggling with the legacies of central planning to guarantee their smooth transition to market economies? Euphoric expectations have been frustrated by the depth and the length of the transition crisis. The ongoing debate on the nature of this crisis clearly suggests that not only did policy makers have to learn their lessons, but so did external advisers, whose cookbook remedies turned out to be insufficient.

This paper argues that early neglect of incentive problems during transition to a market economy figures prominently among the deficiencies of traditional policy prescriptions. In Western-style economic reforms, even heavily distorted economies could build on existing basic institutions and familiar mechanisms of economic policy design. This framework limited the uncertainty of economic agents. By contrast, economic transformation in Central and Eastern Europe is complicated by the simultaneous complete

R. Holzmann et al. (eds.), Output Decline in Eastern Europe, 309-334.

redesign of institutional arrangements, including the entire body of laws, regulations, and conventions under which economic agents operate (Schmieding, 1993).

Until this institutional void is overcome, producers and investors are confronted with an unprecedented degree of uncertainty. Unsettled issues relating to the new division of labor, the allocation of property rights, and the system of coordination create microeconomically perverse incentives, resulting in wait-and-see attitudes of private entrepreneurs, end games played by managers in state-owned enterprises (SOEs), and myopia of employees. This chapter presents an analytical framework for analyzing such incentive problems by referring to the well-known concept of soft budget constraints (Section 13.1).

The empirical analysis concentrates on the Czech and Slovak republics (Czechoslovakia before 1991), Hungary, and Poland as the most advanced economies in transition. Section 13.2, which provides an institutional interpretation of the common output decline in these countries, shows that serious incentive problems prevailed during the early phases of transition. To improve the chances for economic recovery, removing perverse incentives is crucial. In this respect, significant differences have recently emerged among the post-socialist economies (Section 13.3). Adjustment incentives are shown to depend critically on institutional arrangements and policy interventions that encourage discipline in the financial sector, shape the process of wage formation, and prevent a persistent struggle over the distribution of property rights (Section 13.4). The analysis suggests that the Czech Republic has governed the transition more efficiently than have nearby countries in transition.

13.1 Incentive Problems of Soft Budget Constraints

The concept of soft budget constraints has been developed by Kornai (1980) to explain inefficiency in centrally planned economies. Evidently, the incentives for enterprises to strive for a cost-minimizing use of scarce resources are seriously impaired when input and output prices are determined by political bargaining rather than by market forces, when tax obligations are negotiated in a discretionary way, when subsidies are easily available, and when preferential access to credit is guaranteed. Prices in factor and goods markets are deprived of their signaling role, with detrimental effects on allocative efficiency (Raiser, 1993b). The macroeconomic spillovers of budget softness at the enterprise level are twofold (Hofman and Koop, 1990). First, microeconomic inefficiency translates into macroeconomic instability to the extent that SOEs absorb public resources to maintain inefficient operations. Second, the lack of competitive market forces weakens the incentives for process and product innovations, which is likely to result in lower growth of the economy.

Budget constraints of enterprises are not perfectly hard in any other system of economic coordination, but they are definitely much harder in a market economy than in a centrally planned economy. The replacement of paternalistic government protection of inefficient SOEs with market relations can reasonably be expected to ultimately result in an incentive structure of enterprises that is conducive to efficiency and economic growth. Privatization, liberalization, and stabilization are indispensable for this transformation to succeed. However, deficient incentive structures cannot be removed overnight by a reform program encompassing these three elements. Transitional problems stem from the interrelations between policy measures, each of which takes time to become effective. Policy inconsistencies are thus difficult to avoid, and incentive problems due to uncertainty are likely to persist during the transition period.

Taking into consideration the inefficiency of the institutional framework in socialist economies, budget softness may become even more pervasive in the early phases of transition, i.e., once the central plan is abolished. Economic reformers' desire to dissociate themselves firmly from the past led to a rapid dismantling of traditional coordination mechanisms that were still functional prior to the start of economic transformation. By contrast, it takes time to establish new mechanisms for coordinating the division of labor. Behavioral modes must become ingrained in economic agents, legal codes must be set up, and administrators must be trained to apply new and less cost-intensive decision algorithms. The slow process of institutional change may result in an "institutional void" in the interim (Schmieding, 1993), with uncertainty and a short-term attitude dominating the behavior of economic agents. When binding commitments that ensure the honoring of exchange contracts do not exist and when third-party enforcement is absent or not credible, transaction costs rise and the benefits from the division of labor are reduced. Price liberalization and profit orientation serve as a "carrot" only if the "stick" of financial discipline is in place, too. As long as the costs of adapting can be socialized, enterprises still have insufficient incentives to cover their costs out of revenues, to pay for the goods they buy, to honor their debt contracts, and to meet their tax obligations (Kornai, 1993). The persistence of soft budget constraints may be reflected in payment delays and inter-enterprise credits (Raiser, 1992). Non-performing bank assets are their counterpart in the financial sector.[1] Furthermore, wage increases that are not in line with the development of labor productivity point to collusion of managers and workers in depleting the assets of enterprises that are still owned, but are no longer effectively controlled, by the state (Schmieding, 1993, p. 239).

Given that institutional change is inherently slow, the primary task of reducing the costs of transition rests with the governments of emerging market economies (EMEs). The crucial question is how to fill the institutional void left in the ruins of the centrally planned economy. The concept of soft budget constraints suggests that each government's principal role is to monitor the behavior of SOEs until privatization is completed and a market-based incentive structure conducive to minimal friction in industrial adjustment has been established. The different aspects of budget softness indicate various ways that governments can influence the incentive structures of economic agents during the transition period. Lower transaction costs are to be expected if governments succeed at the following:

- Enforcing tax obligations and cutting subsidies.
- Overcoming the inherited problem of bad debts and improving financial discipline with regard to the extension and allocation of new credits.
- Preventing inter-enterprise debt from becoming an alternative source of easy financing.
- Ensuring wage flexibility in the absence of well-functioning labor markets.
- Enforcing market exit of permanent loss-making enterprises.
- Designing privatization strategies so that a persistent struggle over the distribution of property rights is avoided.

To oversee the transition to a market economy, governments must be strong enough to act "against the interests of groups usually able to organize against the imposition of austerities" (Haggard and Kaufman, 1989, p. 236). The remainder of this chapter seeks empirical evidence to support this proposition. First, more-or-less-common incentive problems at the beginning of economic and institutional transformation are stressed. Second, emerging differences in the reform strategies of those EMEs already well into the second stage of transformation are discussed, and the consequences of such differences for overcoming perverse incentive structures are analyzed.

13.2 Incentive Problems Before Privatization: An Institutional Explanation of Output Decline

In the Central and East European economies, the first two years of transition were marked by unexpectedly large output declines and gradually rising unemployment. Furthermore, in Hungary, Poland, and recently Slovakia, sizable fiscal deficits re-emerged after initial budgetary consolidation, and persistent moderate inflation followed the adaptive price shock. Our central argument is that increased uncertainty and the institutional void characteristic of the initial phase of economic transition are the main factors behind the common output decline in all EMEs.[2] The rise in transaction costs can be modeled as a supply shock affecting all firms, regardless of their market potential. Only managers who expect personal gain in the long run will take the risk of investing in new customer networks, marketing skills, and demand-oriented product innovation; this is why growth remains concentrated in the embryonic private sector. Managers of SOEs, by contrast, economize on input purchases, reduce output, and collude with workers in depleting the assets of their firms. Falling SOE profitability depresses fiscal revenues, while the reliance of SOEs on monetary substitutes, such as inter-enterprise credits to finance wage increases in excess of labor productivity growth, undermines price stability. Relatively low post-stabilization inflation, sustained fiscal consolidation, and the absence of large-scale unemployment in the Czech Republic may then be related to a more favorable institutional policy design at an early stage.[3]

The severity of the transformation crisis in all EMEs can be attributed to three policy inconsistencies in the institutional realm (the remaining paragraphs in this section draw substantially on Schmieding, 1993). First, the coordination mechanism in EMEs becomes decentralized at an early stage, while economic actors have as yet no long-term perspective guiding their decisions due to the delay in privatization. Insiders in SOEs and the state-owned banking sector cannot be sure they will remain in place once their firms or banks have been privatized. The prevailing uncertainty in the economy and the inheritance of financial legacies that bear little or no relation to an enterprise's market potential make any evaluation of performance extremely difficult. However, if good behavior is not likely to be rewarded in the future and monitoring of present transactions is weak, the incentives to play end games are great. One manifestation is the consumption of SOE assets by managers.[4] Another consequence is the spread of inter-enterprise credits in Poland, Hungary, and Czechoslovakia (*Table 13.1*).[5] If the managers of an SOE have little stake in its future, they can afford to accumulate debt in the form of unpaid bills, and they will not enforce payment contracts on their own customers. Inter-enterprise credits are thus one crucial element of budget softness for SOEs, once official bank credit has been tightened (Bofinger, 1992; Raiser, 1992; Kornai, 1993).

The second element of initial policy inconsistency is found in financial deregulation under the conditions of little competition and a lack of supervision in the banking sector. The commercial banks, cut out of the old state monobank, typically inherited highly concentrated and fundamentally weak portfolios (Buch and Schmieding, 1992). Enforcing debt repayment by old customers could cause the financial collapse of these customers, which would ultimately threaten the survival of the banks themselves. The assessment of creditworthiness requires skills that are rare. As long as the state remains the owner of the newly founded commercial banks and private competitors are few, bank officials have little incentive for prudent capital management. Rather, a wait-and-see attitude is adopted toward corporate clients in the public sector and non-performing loans are rolled over. Such a strategy may undermine the stability of the entire financial system if, as in EMEs, the banking sector's capital base is weak. In 1992, it was estimated that of all bank loans to the enterprise sector, 11% of those in the Czech Republic, 25% to 35% of those in Hungary, and 26% of those in Poland were non-performing (Buch *et al.*, 1994, p. 94).[6] This is the second crucial element of budget softness, and it makes the control of credit volumes by indirect monetary instruments largely elusive. Early government action to sever old credit lines and recapitalize the banking system may be crucial for ensuring financial stability. Arguably, Czechoslovakia was more successful than Hungary and Poland in this matter, explaining its better performance in containing inflation.

The third inconsistency concerns the premature liberalization of wages. When governments of EMEs are reluctant to enforce existing bankruptcy regulations and sanctions for cost-overruns are absent, SOE workers have very few incentives to keep wage demands in line with labor productivity. To ensure worker cooperation in depleting a firm's assets, SOE managers yield to worker demands, thus exacerbating the profitability crisis in the public sector and ultimately worsening fiscal problems for the government. *Figures 13.1* to *13.3* show that only in Czechoslovakia was a rise in unit labor costs largely avoided, which has enabled the Czech Republic to limit unemployment and avoid a fiscal crisis during its transition thus far. By contrast, Hungary and especially Poland registered real product wage increases substantially above

Table 13.1. Inter-enterprise credit in Czechoslovakia, Hungary, and Poland, 1990–1992, quarterly.

	1990				1991				1992			
	I	II	III	IV	I	II	III	IV	I	II	III	IV
Czechoslovakia												
Billion koruna			–		88.6	113.0	147.1	174.3	170.2	–	154.4	–
% of bank credit			10.1[a]		13.4	17.0	21.2	23.0	22.8	–	18.6	–
Hungary												
Billion forint			90.5[a]				159.8[a]		197.0	–	–	104.0
% of bank credit			14.2[a]				20.8[a]		26.5	–	–	13.4
Poland[b]												
Trillion zloty	75.1	81.5	77.3	103.0	109.1	126.1	143.0	153.3	177.0	190.6	197.5	217.3
% of bank credit	234	207	167	184	140	138	135	145	130	127	125	117

[a]Year-end figures.

[b]Dues and claims resulting from the delivery of goods and services (receivables).

Czechoslovakia: 1990, Buch and Schmieding (1992); 1991–1992, Czech Ministry of Finance, unpublished data.

Hungary: Kornai (1993); NBH (1993).

Poland: GUS (various issues).

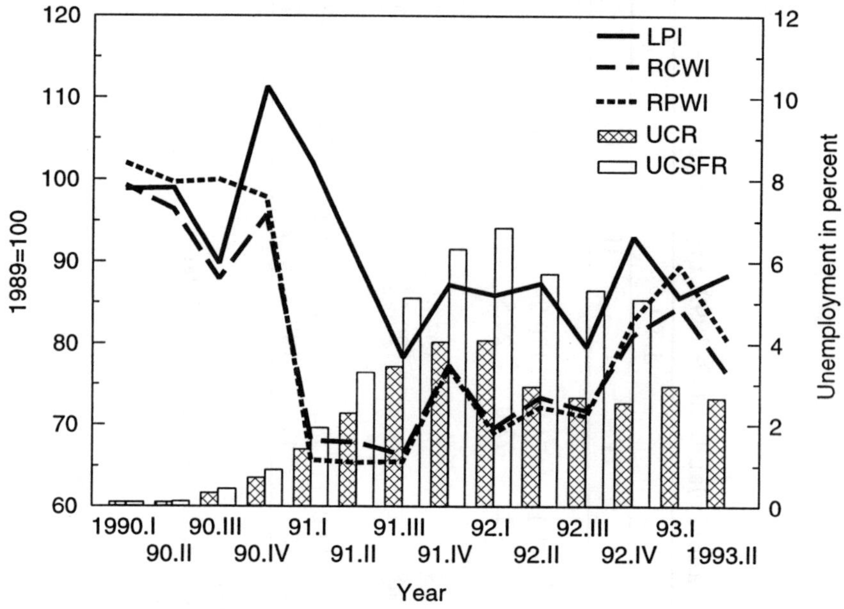

Labor productivity index in industry (LPI): IMF, 1993; PlanEcon, 1993.
Real average wage index in industry calculated with the use of consumer price index (RCWI): PlanEcon, 1993.
Real average wage index in industry calculated with the use of producer price index (RPWI): PlanEcon, 1993.
Unemployment rate Czech Republic (UCR): PlanEcon, 1993.
Unemployment rate CSFR (UCSFR): Statisticke Prehledy, 1993.

Figure 13.1. Labor productivity, real wages, and unemployment in the Czech Republic (for 1991 and 1992 labor productivity data refer to the CSFR).

labor productivity growth (see also Estrin *et al.*, 1992b). The underlying reasons for these divergent developments are addressed in Section 13.3.

13.3 Government Monitoring and Adjustment Incentives During Privatization

13.3.1 Institutional reforms: An overview

All EMEs considered in this chapter enacted a number of significant institutional reforms in capital and labor markets simultaneously with, or even before, price liberalization and macroeconomic stabilization (for a more detailed presentation, see EBRD, 1993b). In the capital market, all three

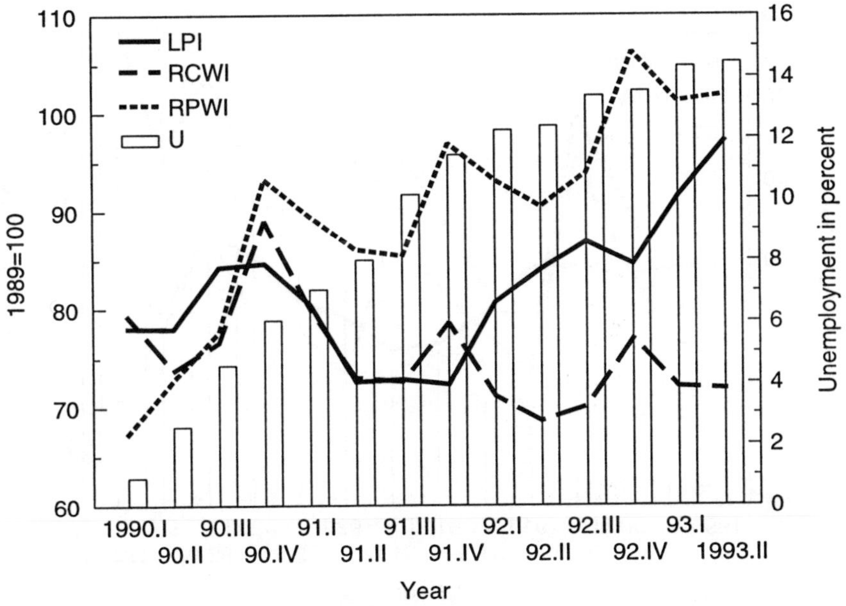

Labor productivity index in industry (LPI): PlanEcon, 1993.
Real average wage index in industry calculated with the use of consumer price index (RCWI): PlanEcon, 1993.
Real average wage index in industry calculated with the use of producer price index (RPWI): PlanEcon, 1993.
Unemployment rate (U): PlanEcon, 1993.

Figure 13.2. Labor productivity, real wages, and unemployment in Poland.

countries created a two-tier banking system as a crucial precondition for the efficiency of capital allocation. Hungary got a head start, with four commercial banks operating by 1987. Poland followed in 1988, and Czechoslovakia started its banking reforms only in 1990. However, Hungary's and Poland's relatively early starts were severely hampered by the failure to introduce banking regulation at an early stage and by the legacy of a highly concentrated loan portfolio. In response to the monopoly of state-owned commercial banks, Czechoslovakia and Poland used credit ceilings and controls over interest rates to monitor the growth and distribution of credits. In Hungary, no credit market controls were effectively operated and real credit to enterprises contracted sharply only in response to the introduction of accounting and bankruptcy legislation in December 1991.

In the mid-stages of transition, the development of a well-functioning capital market in EMEs hinges fundamentally on recapitalizing the commercial banking sector, overcoming the bad-loans problem, and introducing

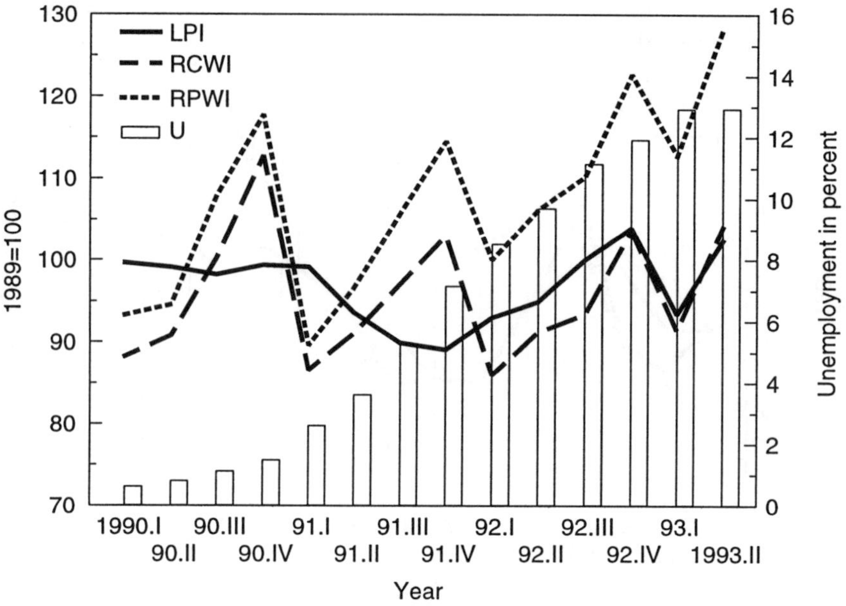

Labor productivity index in industry (LPI): PlanEcon, 1993; Statisztikai Havi Közlemények, 1991.
Real average wage index in industry calculated with the use of consumer price index (RCWI): PlanEcon, 1993; Statisztikai Havi Közlemények, 1991; IMF, 1993.
Real average wage index in industry calculated with the use of producer price index (RPWI): PlanEcon, 1993; Statisztikai Havi Közlemények, 1991; IMF, 1993.
Unemployment rate (U): KOPINT-DATORG, 1992; PlanEcon, 1993.

Figure 13.3. Labor productivity, real wages, and unemployment in Hungary.

financial discipline by strengthening bank competition, enforcing supervisory legislation, and enabling creditors to enact bankruptcy procedures (see also Begg and Portes, 1992; Buch and Schmieding, 1992). This process is now going on in all Central and East European countries. Czechoslovakia was rather quick in introducing banking regulations and has taken significant steps toward the recapitalization and privatization of banks. Moreover, a new bankruptcy law has been in effect since April 1993, but restructuring is favored over liquidation (CBU, 1993, p. 391). Hungary pioneered the strict enforcement of bankruptcy legislation in 1992, but at tremendous costs for its industrial sector. In Poland, existing bankruptcy legislation remained largely unenforced until the second half of 1992. In the area of banking competition, Hungary and Poland seem more advanced than Czechoslovakia (Buch *et al.*, 1994).[7]

In the labor market Czechoslovakia has been most interventionist. Tight wage controls remained in place until December 1992, and re-emerged in the Czech Republic in July 1993. In Poland, the tax-based incomes policy (TIP) was initially nonbinding and later ineffective. The main reason was the relaxation of monetary policy in mid-1990, which provided SOEs with the resources for large nominal wage increases (*Figure 13.2*; see also Raiser, 1992). The TIP in Hungary has not attempted a reduction in real wages.[8] Hungary offers the most generous social-security system, particularly to its unemployed, while the Czech Republic shows the largest activity in the realm of creating new employment (Burda, 1993).

Evidently, significant policy differences have emerged. Specific interventions in capital and labor markets may have enabled the Czech Republic to create an incentive structure that limits the friction in the transition to a market economy. These are considered in more detail in the following section. It should be noted, however, that the Czech government has been comparatively less constrained by powerful interest groups and its policy stance may not be applicable in other EMEs.

13.3.2 Capital market reforms: How to discontinue financial laxity

As long as banks are not privatized and competition in the banking sector is weak, there is little incentive for creditors to discontinue financial laxity. As a result, enterprises with soft budget constraints fail to undertake the necessary adjustments to new relative prices, and the friction in economic transition increases. Thus, the first step for the government is to limit public banks' discretion in extending credit lines to their traditional customers.

Czechoslovakia has been the most resolute in limiting the access of SOEs to credits (Raiser, 1993a). Real credit to SOEs declined in both 1991 and 1992. At the same time, the private sector benefited from real credit expansion. In the Czech Republic, the private sector's share in total loans from the banking sector increased to 26.4% in 1992 from a level below 1% two years earlier.[9] Significantly, this share was higher than the private sector's estimated contribution to GDP. By contrast, new private enterprises faced obstacles to obtaining bank credit in Poland and Hungary.[10] According to recent estimates, Polish SOEs still absorbed 65% to 75% of total credit in 1992, while the private sector had grown to 45% to 50% of GDP (Buch *et al.*, 1994).[11] Hungary's early start with banking reform did not materialize into a more healthy capital market. The significant contributions to fiscal revenues of bank profits from corporate lending at high real interest rates, in the absence of bank regulation, blinded the government to the serious problem of non-performing assets building up in the banking sector (Ábel and Bonin, 1992). Until the end of 1991, the political will to enforce financial discipline of large SOEs was largely absent (Estrin *et al.*, 1992a, p. 797).

The enforcement of tight credit controls is, of course, only a makeshift replacement for an incentive structure conducive to efficient capital allocation. An appropriate regulatory framework in the banking sector is essential if banks are to improve their capital base and adopt prudent lending policies. At the enterprise level, sanctions have to be enforced through bankruptcy legislation. However, these "sticks" rely on the complementary existence of positive rewards. These rewards include debt consolidation schemes that support the banks' efforts to recapitalize themselves and the option of debt-equity swaps if banks are willing to provide the necessary finance for enterprise restructuring.

Progress in this matter has been extremely slow in Poland. In September 1991, a law on the restructuring of SOEs opened the possibility of liquidation if a firm delayed tax payments for more than three months. However, the number of forced liquidations has remained rather limited. In mid-1992, out of 708 cases only 78 had been concluded (Heinrich, 1992). Moreover, tax deferments have accounted for a rising share of budget deficits since 1991 (Raiser, 1992, p. 41). A decentralized, market-based program on the financial restructuring of banks and SOEs became effective only in March 1993.[12] Due to this delay, interest margins have been rather high since 1990 (*Figure 13.4*). The fragility of Poland's banking system may still send a destabilizing blow to its recovering economy, and it is open to question whether the gradual approach to bank recapitalization is sufficient to overcome the problem of bad debt, which is most significant in Poland.

Hungary introduced virtually the entire package of regulations and sanctions at once in December 1991. As a result, the number of bankruptcies is huge (over 4,200 filings in 1992 alone) and unemployment has doubled, while inter-enterprise credits have fallen dramatically and bad debts have stopped accumulating. Unfortunately, Hungary's government disregarded the "carrots" in the process. Thus, corporate lending was curtailed sharply, which, due to the indiscriminate bank behavior affected the whole economy (OECD, 1993b, pp. 135ff.). Until recently, banks were not supported in their attempt to reach the new capital requirements. In December 1992, a consolidation scheme was introduced and bad loans in the banking sector fell to 12% of total corporate lending (Buch *et al.*, 1994). However, the write-off element in Hungary's consolidation program may not have been sufficient (Ábel and

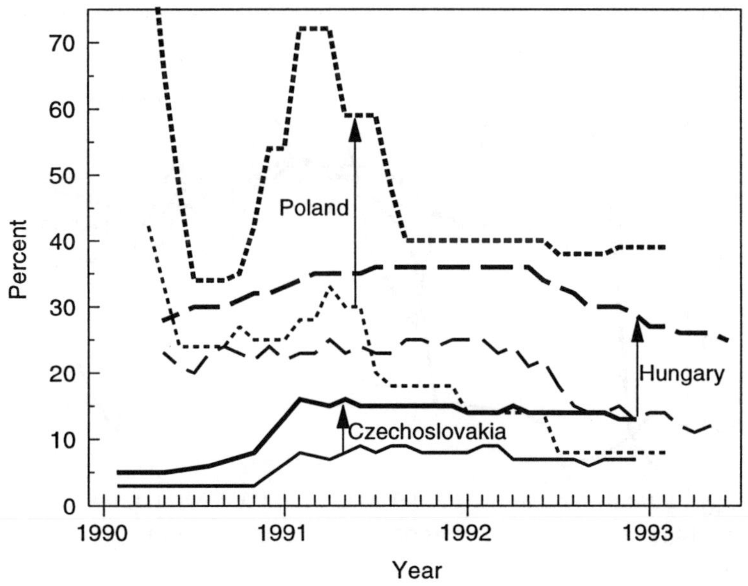

Spread Poland: Lending rate on credits with lowest risk rates (one to six months) minus one-month deposit rate (NBP, 1993, various issues).
Spread Hungary: Lending rate by commercial banks (weighted average, maturing within one year) minus deposit rate by commercial banks (weighted average, fixed for less than one month) (NBH, 1993, various issues).
Spread Czechoslovakia: Average nominal lending rate to enterprises minus average nominal deposit rate to enterprises (PlanEcon, 1993, various issues).

Figure 13.4. Nominal interest rate spread in Czechoslovakia, Hungary, and Poland.

Bonin, 1993).[13] Thus, interest margins have been rising since 1991 and huge budget deficits continue to push up the real cost of credit (*Figures 13.4* and *13.5*). Finally, because conflicts among creditors were looming large, a significant number of enterprises found themselves in court proceedings over who was to shoulder the burden of restructuring (Szanyi, 1993).

In contrast to Poland's hands-off approach and Hungary's legislated shock therapy, Czechoslovakia and, recently, the Czech Republic have attempted to complement tight monitoring of public banks and enterprises with well-dosed capital injections. Only three months after price liberalization, the Consolidation Bank was founded to take over Kcs 110 billion of inherited long-term credits from the banking sector. In October 1991, a further Kcs 50-billion bond issue by the National Property Funds of the Czech Republic and Slovakia allowed commercial banks to rid themselves of non-performing assets at a 50% to 80% discount. At the same time,

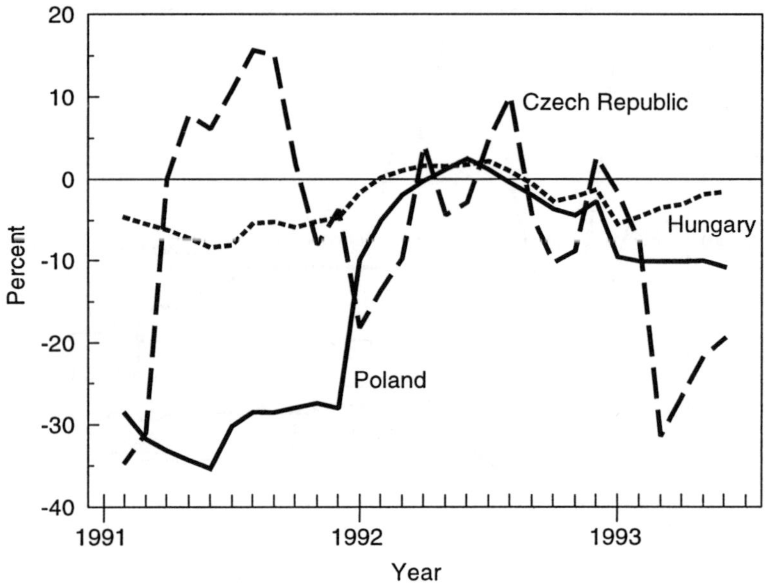

Poland: Refinancing credit interest rate deflated by three-month backward-looking moving average of the monthly consumer price index (NBP, 1993, various issues).
Hungary: Short-term refinancing rate (period between rediscounting and maturity less than 60 days) deflated by consumer price index (corresponding period of previous year = 100) (NBH, 1993, various issues).
Czechoslovakia: Discount rate deflated by consumer price index (corresponding period of previous year = 100) (SBC, 1992, various issues).

Figure 13.5. Real refinancing rate in Czechoslovakia, Hungary, and Poland.

the government was careful not to administer too large a shock to its few and fragile banks. A schedule for capital adequacy ratios was announced in March 1991.[14] The central bank's refinancing rate was kept low in real terms to allow recapitalization, but there was a ceiling on maximum interest margins. As *Figure 13.4* reveals, this has enabled Czechoslovakia to avoid the explosion of interest margins characteristic of financial liberalization in an environment of fragile capital markets and monopolistic supply structures. Consequently, the chances for bank lending to finance investments were relatively favorable.[15] Moreover, the substantial equity stake acquired during the first wave of privatization by some of the main commercial creditors should enhance their monitoring role in the restructuring of enterprises.

13.3.3 Incentive effects of incomes and labor market policies

Possibly the most important real effect of different incentive structures in capital markets is their impact on adjustment in the labor market. If budget constraints remain soft, managers have scope for wage increases in excess of labor productivity growth. This, in turn, depresses profitability in the state-owned sector, while raising the wage level for private firms. Hence, large unemployment becomes an unavoidable by-product of economic transformation. The ensuing social and fiscal costs may threaten the sustainability of economic reforms. In this respect the Czech Republic's extraordinarily low level of unemployment warrants special attention.

The development of real wages and labor productivity, as shown in *Figures 13.1* to *13.3*, indicates that the relatively low unit-labor costs in Czechoslovakia allowed more labor-intensive production and thus limited unemployment. The underlying dynamics are crucial here. Czechoslovak industry shed labor at a pace roughly similar to Poland's, but only in Slovakia were these redundant workers not absorbed by the labor market.[16] In the Czech Republic the unemployment/vacancy ratio has remained extremely low (Burda, 1993, p. 38). This suggests that low unit-labor costs not only limited the profitability crisis in SOEs (thus stabilizing fiscal revenues), but also lowered entry barriers for new private firms.[17]

The competitiveness of Czech industry is reflected in its dynamic export performance. Remarkably, the Czech Republic increased exports to Germany by more than 50% in the first quarter of 1993, compared with the same period a year earlier, and this in the midst of a severe recession in Germany (PlanEcon, 1993). By contrast, Poland and Hungary have recently moved into trade deficits with Western countries. Again, it may be argued that low unit-labor costs have allowed the Czech Republic to make the most of its export potential. At the same time, the Czech koruna has remained fixed against a basket of foreign currencies since January 1991, while the exchange rates of the forint and the zloty have recently come under new pressure.

The most important government intervention in the Czech labor market has been a tightly enforced incomes policy. The determination to prevent SOEs from fueling a wage-price spiral has recently been demonstrated with the re-introduction of wage controls in July 1993. Wage control had already been applied in the first full year of transition: over 1991 a decline in real wages of 12% was agreed on with trade unions. When inflation overshot the expected target, nominal wage indexing was unilaterally abolished by the federal government (Myant, 1992, p. 195), and the overall decline in real wages reached 24% at the end of 1991.

Another aspect of Czech labor-market policies is the combination of an extremely tight unemployment benefit system with substantial active employment creation. Burda (1993) provides scores for the disincentive effects of the unemployment benefit package for EMEs. The Czech Republic ranks most favorably, while fiscal problems in Hungary are clearly related to the generosity of its social policies. Total labor market programs in the Czech Republic were limited to 0.51% of GDP in 1992 (OECD, 1993a, p. 78) compared with 2.78% in Hungary and 2.51% in Poland; however, active employment measures were more than 60% of total outlays compared with 14% in Hungary and 11% in Poland (Burda, 1993).

It is the combination of wage controls and tight social-security policies that has helped Czech labor market adjustments thus far. As in the case of capital market reforms, the government has intervened where markets were absent. Crucially, controls have been nondiscretionary so that the scope for rent-seeking has been contained in the Czech Republic. The government's ability to impose its agenda on different interest groups is evidenced in its approach to privatization, as well.

13.3.4 Privatization strategies: Corporate governance, vested interests, and the struggle for property rights

After the rationale of central planning had been increasingly undermined by principal-agent problems, i.e., the lack of effective control of SOE managers by the state, the solution was initially thought to be greater autonomy of SOEs. However, as long as there was no alternative monitoring system, incentive problems could not be overcome by the retreat of the state in Hungary (particularly since the New Economic Mechanism of 1968) or in Poland (since 1981). Since the demise of the socialist regime, privatization has been assigned the main task of introducing a rational structure of corporate governance, thereby creating incentives for cost efficiency and structural adjustment. These objectives were relatively easy to achieve in small enterprises in services, trade, and industry. Small-scale privatization is almost complete in Hungary, Poland, and the former Czechoslovakia (EBRD, 1993b). Principal-agent problems are largely absent as most of these enterprises are managed by their owners. By contrast, progress proved much more difficult with respect to large industrial SOEs, and it remains heavily debated which methods of large-scale privatization best ensure effective corporate governance.[18]

The speed of privatization determines the length of the interim period, during which economic coordination in EMEs has already been decentralized, and economic agents still have no long-term perspective guiding their decisions (see Section 13.2). Incentive problems resulting from an uncertain future distribution of property rights persist in all EMEs. Large-scale privatization is probably the reform area that has seen the least progress; it is generally taking much longer than expected (AMEX, 1993; UN ECE, 1993, p. 41). Nevertheless, significant differences have emerged among the countries considered in this chapter:

- The process of ownership transformation appears to be most advanced in the Czech Republic (EBRD, 1993b, p. 40), although it took a long time to decide on the voucher scheme and, thereby, to overcome "the pre-privatization rigidity in the behavior of the big SOEs" (Čapek, Chapter 12). The first phase of mass privatization (involving 1,500 SOEs) was completed in December 1992, and another wave is under way (AMEX, 1993, p. 6).[19]
- Hungary has adhered to gradual privatization. The State Property Agency, founded in 1990, accepted initiatives for SOE transformations from insiders and from outside investors, but retained the right to make case-by-case decisions. Apparently, the privatization process has subsided somewhat. Although about 15% of Hungary's larger SOEs had been privatized by mid-1992 (Heinrich, 1992), this share increased only to around 20% by mid-1993 (AMEX, 1993, p. 6).
- Large-scale privatization in Poland has been sluggish, even by East European standards (Winiecki, 1992a). The mass privatization program, which has been discussed since late 1989, has failed to get off the ground (Heinrich, 1993, pp. 9f.). The establishment of investment funds, which were to assume control over several hundred SOEs and were to be managed by international management firms and banks, was seriously delayed.

While the reasons for the different speeds of privatization are manifold, the struggle between the state and various interest groups, particularly SOE managers and workers, over the distribution of property rights stands out from the point of view of incentives (see also EBRD, 1993b). The evidence suggests that the delay of privatization depends on the severity of such conflicts and on whether vested interests in the form of customary property rights, were taken into account when designing privatization strategies (the remaining paragraphs in this section draw heavily on Heinrich, 1993).

The costs of postponed microeconomic adjustment resulting from protracted struggles for property rights are probably highest in Poland. The substantial decentralization of economic coordination established in 1981 resulted in a system of self-management, by which employee councils were empowered with far-reaching *de facto* property rights.[20] The central authorities increasingly lost control over SOE operations. Consequently, a rather weak state had to deal with entrenched insider interests after the political revolution in 1989. The mass privatization program was a futile attempt to regain state control by abolishing the employee councils before the shares were transferred to investment funds.

This program met with the strong resistance of SOE insiders, whose customary property rights were threatened. Paradoxically, the managers and workers of SOEs were legally enabled "to block any practical privatization move" (Winiecki, 1992b, p. 80), as ownership transformation was made contingent on prior approval of the respective employee council. Potential outside investors were discouraged from incurring the costs of formulating an adjustment strategy, and most SOEs were kept in a state of limbo. Survey results reveal that the struggle for control resulted in wait-and-see attitudes, insufficient efforts at technological and organizational adaptation, and deteriorating profitability (Dabrowski *et al.*, 1992). Given this lack of government control, a more promising privatization strategy would probably have been "to buy off the resistance of insiders by recognizing customary property rights and officially granting insiders substantial ownership rights in their firms" (Heinrich, 1993, p. 3). This proposition is supported by the observation that adjustment efforts were more pronounced in firms under "voluntary liquidation," most of which were ultimately owned or leased by SOE insiders.

Decentralization of SOE decision making had an even longer tradition in Hungary. State control had been weakened in 1985, when enterprise councils were empowered with authority that resembled their counterparts in Poland. Top-down privatization strategies suffered from the same constraints, i.e., a weak state confronted with powerful insider interests. The situation was complicated by the passivity of commercial banks, which had neither an interest in concluding cases of SOE liquidation nor sufficiently strong incentives to invest money for restructuring potentially healthy firms (see Section 13.3.2). The foundation of the State Property Agency indicates that Hungary, too, attempted to reinforce state control over the privatization process. Nonetheless, the Hungarian government respected the customary property rights of SOE managers, thereby containing adjustment disincentives due to persistent uncertainty about the outcome of conflicts between the government and the enterprises. The slow pace of privatization led to a return to more decentralized methods (OECD, 1993b, pp. 68ff.). Decisions on the privatization procedure by the State Property Agency are not binding for self-managed enterprises, and small and medium-sized enterprises have been allowed to perform their own privatization without direct government involvement since late 1991.

In contrast to Poland and Hungary, SOEs in Czechoslovakia had been tightly controlled by the state until the regime change of late 1989. Consequently, the new government was in a relatively strong position to pursue privatization strategies of its own design, without being constrained by customary property rights of SOE insiders (for an overview on ownership transformations in the Czech Republic, see Ceska, 1993). The government grasped this opportunity: although the voucher scheme "involved neither a preferential treatment of managers or workers in the auction process nor any up-front concessions to induce enterprises to participate" (Heinrich, 1993, p. 9), ownership transformation is progressing rather smoothly and rapidly. This suggests that the costs to a strong government of breaking insider resistance to privatization are comparatively low.

However, a new ownership structure of former SOEs is conducive to cost efficiency and restructuring only if privatization results in a strong property-rights regime (Williamson, 1992; Frydman and Rapaczynski, 1992). In particular, the voucher system runs the risk of extreme fragmentation of ownership, so that shareholders would lack the incentive and ability to exercise effective control over management. The problem of insufficient corporate governance has been contained in the Czech case, because investment funds play a crucial intermediating role in the voucher system (EBRD, 1993b), though this is by spontaneous development rather than by deliberate policy design. The large majority of individual investors opted to place their vouchers with these funds rather than buy shares of particular enterprises.[21] The impact of privatization on managerial efforts for efficiency and restructuring thus depends on the behavior of investment funds.

It is still too early to judge whether investment funds in the Czech Republic have sufficient incentives for effective monitoring. On the one hand, their incentives may have been weakened by requiring each fund to limit its share in one particular firm to 20% and to include at least 10 firms in its portfolio. On the other hand, first indications are that some investment funds have already been active in controlling the enterprises in which they have significant stakes (CERGE, 1993).[22] Moreover, compared with their Hungarian counterparts, Czech commercial banks are better prepared to play a positive role in enterprise restructuring. They participated significantly in mass privatization.[23] The acquisition of significant equity stakes provides incentives to overcome bottlenecks to effective monitoring, such as the lack of expertise and deficient accounting systems, and strengthens the banks' interest in the solution of the problem of bad debt, which threatens to impair the value of their shares. Finally, the Czech recapitalization scheme encourages banks to use their leverage to initiate and supervise the restructuring of privatized firms.[24]

13.4 The Governments' Retreat: Incentive Compatibility After Privatization

We have argued that governments bear considerable responsibility for reducing the costs of transition from socialism to a market economy and for improving the chances for economic recovery. The question for policy makers in EMEs is not whether to intervene at all, but how to fill the institutional void typically prevailing in the early phases of transition and how to contain incentive problems stemming from uncertainty of economic agents and temporary policy inconsistencies. The degree of transitional friction depends on the strength of the government, i.e., its ability to effectively monitor the transformation process and resist rent-seeking by pressure groups (especially SOE insiders). A strong government is less prone to erratic policy shifts and better prepared to create predictable and strict conditions for enterprises and banks. The higher the government's credibility and reputation of unconditional commitment to reform, the easier it will be to enforce direct controls and to prevent later moral hazard problems.

The experience of the frontrunners in economic transition suggests three major areas where governments in latecomer EMEs could contribute to lowering transition costs. First, the lack of competitive capital markets requires government action to discontinue financial laxity. Second, government intervention is required to shape the process of wage formation in the absence of well-functioning labor markets. Third, the speed of large-scale privatization determines the length of the interim period, during which incentive problems result from ill-defined and unprotected property rights.

Direct interventions cannot remain forever. The progress made with privatization and the extent to which redundant labor may easily be absorbed by the growing private sector determine the appropriate timing for the government's retreat (Burda, 1993). In this respect, the Czech example suggests that the more effective direct controls have been, the earlier they can be replaced by indirect measures. For example, the volume of credit in the Czech Republic is now controlled by interest-rate policy. The need for an incomes policy to avoid a second-round wage push is reduced to the extent that a booming private sector accounts for a rising share in GDP.

Some incentive problems may persist even once privatization is complete. The crucial question remains whether the change in ownership results in a strong or a weak property-rights regime. Only a strong property-rights regime would minimize principal-agent problems and create sufficient incentives for cost efficiency and restructuring. The debate on alternative systems of corporate control in advanced market economies suggests that a clearly superior model, which might be copied by EMEs, does not exist. Nonetheless, there is some evidence suggesting ways to strengthen corporate control after privatization, or at least how to circumvent major pitfalls.

It is important to avoid extreme fragmentation of ownership. As a promising avenue to effective monitoring, investment funds might be put in a controlling position in important parts of the economy. If commercial banks are actively involved in the management of these funds, the incentives for banks to acquire the skills necessary for monitoring of, and sound lending to, enterprises would be strengthened. At the same time, the chances for profit for banks having a strong say in enterprise restructuring can be expected to induce more competition in the financial sector of EMEs. This would help in overcoming the chicken-and-egg problem (EBRD, 1993b, p. 18) – namely, that a viable banking sector is required for sustained economic growth, but new banks are unlikely to consider market entry unless the economy is reviving. Universal banking may thus become the hallmark of investment-led growth in EMEs.

Furthermore, the positive incentive effects of privatization depend on whether the government strictly adheres to a hands-off approach after the change in ownership. The failure of large-scale privatization in Chile in the 1970s is telling in this respect (Agarwal and Nunnenkamp, 1992). The new private owners had easy access to public loans for financing the acquisition of firms and could reasonably expect to be bailed out once financial problems emerged. Recent plans in Hungary to establish an interest-free credit facility accessible to citizens for buying company shares have similar flaws. The privatization investment facility leaves the government holding the downside risk, and most likely the ultimate ownership, as the shares can be sold back to the government at their face value (OECD, 1993b, pp. 78ff.). Under such conditions, perverse incentives persist and budget constraints remain soft. Asset stripping by investors, who can keep all dividends, is encouraged, while the deterioration of the market value of the shares is borne by the government.

Moral hazards can only be contained if privatization definitely releases the state from entrepreneurial risks. This may be easier to achieve if privatization goes along with decentralization, as huge industrial conglomerates have significant political leverage irrespective of whether ownership is public or private. Ultimately the success of privatization hinges on the government's ability to organize its own retreat once and for all.

Notes

[1] These phenomena may replace more traditional fiscal aspects of budget softness, such as loose tax enforcement and subsidies.

[2] This position contrasts structuralist and demand-led interpretations of output decline (Berg, Chapter 5; Gomulka, 1991). Also, it does not support the credit-crunch hypothesis (Calvo and Coricelli, 1992). For a critical review of these alternative arguments and a defense of the institutionalist position see Raiser (1993a) and Schmieding (1993).

[3] During the IIASA Conference Jan Svejnar has alerted us to the fact that Slovakia displays all the crisis features observed in other EMEs, in spite of having benefited from the same institutional policy design as the Czech Republic. However, significant differences between the two republics of the CSFR emerged during 1992, in particular. Arguably, the uncertainty prevailing in Slovakia with respect to an anticipated split, leading to the loss of substantial fiscal transfers from the federal government, exacerbated the short-term orientation of economic actors.

[4] Some evidence suggests that asset depletion has been used as a method of insider privatization in Poland and Hungary (Heinrich, 1993; Pinto *et al.*, 1993). In Czechoslovakia the relatively advanced mass privatization and the close monitoring of SOE behavior, via credit and wage controls, has limited the scope for asset depletion.

[5] The ratio of inter-enterprise credit to bank credit is extraordinarily high in Poland. This is partly because the Polish banking system has played only a limited role as a financial intermediary so far (Buch *et al.*, 1994).

[6] In Hungary 85% of bad loans accumulated after 1989, and in Poland the high inflation of 1989 had all but wiped out inherited bad debts. Hence, rather than merely attributable to financial legacies, the problem of bad debt is at the heart of lacking financial discipline in these EMEs. Evidently, state-owned banks are most affected. In the Czech Republic, 15% of their loan portfolio is non-performing; in Poland state-owned banks carry up to 60% of bad debts (Buch *et al.*, 1994, p. 94; Gomulka, Chapter 9).

[7] The first Polish bank was privatized in 1992, but political resistance delayed further privatizations.

[8] Wage limits were not enforced in 1992, and excess wage taxation was abandoned altogether at the beginning of 1993 (OECD, 1993b, p. 25).

[9] According to Čapek (Chapter 12), the share of domestic private firms in total credit to the nonfinancial sector continued rising to 40% in September 1993.

[10] In Poland this has not prevented the private sector from booming. Self-financing through earnings and loans from family members has been dominant so far. In the longer run, however, unofficial curb markets are not a promising alternative to efficient financial intermediation if economic growth is to be sustained.

[11] For Hungary no comparable disaggregated figures are available.

[12] *Inter alia*, the program allowed for the trading of bank debt on secondary markets and debt-equity swaps; for details, see Buch *et al.* (1994).

[13] The government was planning a second program for 1993 that envisaged direct augmentation of bank capital (OECD, 1993b, p. 142).

[14] Capital requirements were raised gradually, from 4.5% of total assets (1991) to 6.25% by 1993 and to a projected 8% by 1996.

[15] Investment had increased to 120% of the 1989 level by the last quarter of 1992 (PlanEcon, 1993).

[16] For some exogenous factors that may have complemented the positive role of low unit-labor costs in the Czech Republic, see Raiser (1993a). It should be noted that historical, geographical, and structural differences, the absence of significant foreign capital inflows, and policy inconsistencies since the split account for the inability of Slovakia to capitalize on its competitiveness in labor-intensive production.

[17] Because these activities are concentrated in the services sector, they are typically characterized by very low labor productivity and initially are unrecorded by official statistics (EBRD, 1993b). Hence, the significant increase in private-sector activities is not yet reflected in a rise in GDP.

[18] This is not surprising because no unanimous model of corporate governance in advanced market economies exists that might have guided privatization strategies in EMEs (Frydman and Rapaczynski, 1992).

[19] Slovakia has given up the voucher system of mass privatization in favor of a wider variety of methods of sales.

[20] Their authority included the hiring and firing of managers, wage setting, and profit allocation.

[21] Seventy-two percent of vouchers have been invested by investment funds on behalf of individuals (EBRD, 1993b, p. 40). The 13 largest investment groups, some of which had established several funds, took control of 77% of all voucher points given to funds (Mládek, 1993, Table 6).

[22] Mládek (1993) notes that SOE managers are trying to escape from voucher privatization in the current second wave, after their earlier assumption, that dispersed ownership would render monitoring elusive, proved wrong.

[23] Three of the largest four investment funds are run by banks. These three banks account for 13% of the total book value of firms approved for privatization (PlanEcon, 1993).

[24] Given that the sum of bond issues by the Consolidation Bank was fixed in advance, banks might be expected to select firms considered potentially healthy

for write-offs of inherited debts. Effective monitoring is a prerequisite for such a decision.

References

Ábel, I., and Bonin, J., 1992, Crippled Monetary Policy: Hungary's Financial Legacies, Wesleyan University, Middletown, CT, USA [mimeo].

Ábel, I., and Bonin, J., 1993, Hungary's Loan Consolidation Programme: Gradualism Returns, Wesleyan University, Middletown, CT, USA [mimeo].

Agarwal, J.P., and Nunnenkamp, P., 1992, Methods and Sequencing of Privatization: What Post-socialist Countries Can Learn from Chile, Kiel Working Paper, No. 527, Institute of World Economics, Kiel, Germany.

AMEX (American Express Bank), 1993, Central and East Europe: Myths and realities, *The AMEX Bank Review*, **6** (19 July).

Begg, D., and Portes, R., 1992, *Enterprise Debt and Economic Transformation: Financial Restructuring of the State Sector in Central and Eastern Europe*, Centre for Economic Policy Research, Discussion Paper, No. 695, London, UK.

Bofinger, P., 1992, The experience with monetary policy in an environment with strong microeconomic distortions, *Economic Systems*, **16**(2):247–268.

Buch, C., and Schmieding, H., 1992, *Better Banks for Eastern Europe*, Kiel Discussion Paper, No. 192, Institute of World Economics, Kiel, Germany.

Buch, C., Funke, N., Heinrich, R., and Raiser, M., 1994, *Overcoming Obstacles to Successful Reforms in Economies in Transition*, Kiel Studies, Institute of World Economics, Tübingen, Germany.

Burda, M., 1993, Unemployment, labor markets and structural change in Eastern Europe, *Economic Policy*, **8**(16):101–138.

Calvo, G., and Coricelli, F., 1992, Stagflationary effects of stabilisation programs in reforming socialist economies, *The World Bank Economic Review* **6**(1):71–90.

CBU (Czech Business Update), 1993, *Weekly Newsletter*, various issues, Prague, Czech Republic.

CERGE (Center for Economic Research and Graduate Education) 1993, *Investment Privatization Funds as New Owners of Privatized Enterprises*, Charles University, Prague, Czech Republic.

Ceska, R., 1993, Three years of privatization in the Czech and Slovak republics, *Privatization Newsletter of the Czech Republic and Slovakia*, **17**(June/July): 1–5.

Dabrowski, J., Federowicz, M., and Szomburg, J., 1992, Privatization of the Polish state-owned enterprises: The second report, *Economic Transformation*, No. 29, The Gdansk Institute for Market Economics, Gdansk, Poland.

EBRD (European Bank for Reconstruction and Development), 1993a, *Quarterly Economic Review*, April.

EBRD (European Bank for Reconstruction and Development), 1993b, *Annual Economic Outlook*, September.

Estrin, S., Hare, P., and Suranyi, M., 1992, Banking in transition: Development and current problems in Hungary, *Soviet Studies*, **44**(5):785–808.

Estrin, S., Schaffer, M., and Singh, I., 1992, Enterprise adjustment in transition economies, in M. Blejer, ed., *Eastern Europe in Transition: From Recession to Growth?* World Bank Discussion Paper, No. 196, Washington, DC, USA.

Frydman, R., and Rapaczynski, A., 1992, Privatization and corporate governance in Eastern Europe: Can a market economy be designed? in G. Winckler, ed., *Central and Eastern Europe: Roads to Growth*, Washington, DC, USA.

Gomulka, S., 1991, The causes of recession following stabilisation, *Comparative Economic Studies*, **2**:71–89.

GUS (Glowny Urzad Statystycny), 1993, *Binletyn Statystycny*, various issues, Warsaw, Poland.

Haggard, S., and Kaufman, R., 1989, The politics of stabilization and structural adjustment, in J.D. Sachs, ed., *Developing Country Debt and Economic Performance, Vol. 1: The International Financial System*, University of Chicago Press, Chicago, IL, USA.

Heinrich, R., 1992, Privatisierung in Polen, Ungarn und der CSFR: Eine Bestandsaufnahme, *Die Weltwirtschaft*, **3**:295–316.

Heinrich, R., 1993, *The Merits of Insider Privatization What Russia Can Learn from Eastern Europe*, Kiel Discussion Paper, No. 201, Institute of World Economics, Kiel, Germany.

Hofman, B., and Koop, M.J., 1990, Makroökonomische Aspekte der Reformen in Osteuropa, *Die Weltwirtschaft*, **1**:161–172.

IMF, 1993, *International Financial Statistics*, various issues, International Monetary Fund, Washington, DC, USA.

KOPINT-DATORG, 1992, *Economic Trends in Eastern Europe*, Vol. 1, No. 2, Budapest, Hungary.

Kornai, J., 1980, *The Economics of Shortage*, North-Holland Publishing, Amsterdam, The Netherlands.

Kornai, J., 1993, The evolution of financial discipline under the postsocialist system, *Kyklos*, **46**(3):315–336.

Mládek, J., 1993, Czech Privatization Process: Time for Corporate Governance, Paper presented at the Conference on Output Decline in Eastern Europe: Prospects for Recovery? International Institute for Applied Systems Analysis, Laxenburg, Austria. Revised verion forthcoming in *Empirica*, 1994.

Myant, M., 1992, *Transforming Socialist Economies: The Case of Poland and Czechoslovakia*, Edward Elgar, Aldershot, UK.

NBH, 1993, *Monthly Report*, various issues, National Bank of Hungary, Budapest, Hungary.

NBP, 1993, *Information Bulletin*, various issues, National Bank of Poland, Warsaw, Poland.

OECD, 1993a, *Employment Outlook*, Organisation for Economic Co-operation and Development, Paris, France.

OECD, 1993b, *Economic Surveys: Hungary 1993*, Organisation for Economic Co-operation and Development, Paris, France.

Pinto, B., Belka, M., and Krajewski, S., 1993, Transforming State Enterprises in Poland: Microeconomic Evidence on Adjustment, Country Department II, Policy Research Working Paper, No. 1101, World Bank, Washington, DC, USA.

PlanEcon, 1993, *Monthly Economic Monitor*, various issues, Washington, DC, USA.

Raiser, M., 1992, Soft Budget Constraints: An Institutional Interpretation of Stylised Facts in Economic Transformation in Central Eastern Europe, Kiel Working Paper, No. 549, Institute of World Economics, Kiel, Germany.

Raiser, M., 1993a, Governing the Transition to a Market Economy, Kiel Working Paper, No. 592, Institute of World Economics, Kiel, Germany.

Raiser, M., 1993b, The No-exit Economy: Soft Budget Constraints and the Causes for Success or Failure of Economic Reforms in Developing Countries, Kiel Working Paper, No. 581, Institute of World Economics, Kiel, Germany.

SBC, 1992, *Financial Statistical Information*, State Bank of Czechoslovakia, Prague, Czech Republic.

Schmieding, H., 1993, From plan to market: On the nature of the transformation crisis, *Weltwirtschaftliches Archiv*, **129**:216–253.

Statisticke Prehledy, 1993, *Monthly Statistics*, various issues, Czech Central Statistical Office, Prague, Czech Republic.

Statisztikai Havi Kozlemenyek, 1991, *Monthly Bulletin of Statistics*, Budapest, Hungary.

Szanyi, M., 1993, The Liquidity Crisis and Bankruptcy Procedures in Hungary, Institute of World Economics, Budapest, Hungary [mimeo].

UN ECE, 1993, *Economic Bulletin for Europe*, Vol. 44, United Nations, New York, NY, USA.

Williamson, O.E., 1992, Private ownership and the capital market, in H. Siebert, ed., *Privatization*, Institute of World Economics, Tübingen, Germany.

Winiecki, J., 1992a, *Privatization in Poland: A Comparative Perspective*, Kiel Studies, No. 248, Institute of World Economics, Tübingen, Germany.

Winiecki, J., 1992b, The political economy of privatization, in H. Siebert, ed., *Privatization*, Institute of World Economics, Tübingen, Germany.

Chapter 14

Opening Western Markets: The European Community's Response

Anne Bucher

Trade liberalization is a key ingredient of the reform programs in Central and Eastern Europe as there are very few channels in the initial stage of transition through which economies in transition can be exposed to market mechanisms. The six Central and East European countries (CEECs), namely, Bulgaria, the Czech and Slovak republics, Hungary, Poland, and Romania, have adopted comprehensive trade liberalization programs, which, combined with realistic exchange rate policies and steps toward currency convertibility, support a rapid adjustment of their prices to world levels. A substantial degree of competition in the CEECs' domestic markets has thus successfully been introduced. The question arises, however, whether Western markets are sufficiently open to meet the double objective of supporting the emergence of a profitable export sector in Eastern Europe and contributing to a possible export-led recovery, given the unavoidable negative impact of restructuring and stabilization in the first years of the transition process.

Products produced in Eastern Europe have been given increased market access in industrialized countries, with a preliminary step of extension of

This paper draws on research on relationships between the European Community and Central and East European countries carried out by the Directorate General for Economic and Financial Affairs of the European Commission, to be published in *European Economy* in 1994.

R. Holzmann et al. (eds.), Output Decline in Eastern Europe, 335-348.

the general system of preferences scheme (GSP) to the six CEECs granted by the main industrialized countries. The European Community (EC, now European Union) and the European Free Trade Association (EFTA) countries, which, for proximity reasons, are natural trade partners of Eastern Europe, have gone further and set up a long-term framework to develop their trade relationships with the region. The first move was made by the EC, with the signing of Association or Europe Agreements (EAs) with the CSFR, Hungary, and Poland in December 1991, of which the trade provisions entered into force on 1 March 1992. Agreements with Bulgaria and Romania were signed in November 1992 and March 1993, respectively. The interim agreements covering trade provisions for Romania and Bulgaria were implemented, respectively, on 1 May 1993 and 31 December 1993. In June 1993, at the EC Council in Copenhagen, a new trade liberalization package for all the associated countries was adopted and immediately put into effect. EFTA agreements with the same countries closely followed the conclusion of the EAs and became effective on 1 July 1992 for the CSFR, 1 March 1993 for Poland, 1 May 1993 for Romania, 1 June 1993 for Bulgaria, and 1 October 1993 for Hungary. The two sets of agreements are very similar, although the EFTA–CEEC agreements are more generous in scope and speed of liberalization for industrial products. They both aim at a progressive establishment of a free trade area by the beginning of the next century, except for agricultural products.

The EAs are too recent to be subject to a thorough evaluation. Their rapid conclusion *per se* reflects the strong political commitment of the Community to improve market access for Eastern products even if the agreements fall short of the goal of immediate and complete free trade. On the basis of available evidence, this chapter tries to assess the adequacy of the EC response to the requirements of the transition process in the CEECs. The first section reviews trade trends; the second section gives a brief description of the trade provisions of the EAs; and the third section assesses the impact of trade protection.

14.1 Developments in CEEC–EC Trade

14.1.1 General trends

Following the dismantling of the CMEA in 1990–1991 and far-reaching trade liberalization measures taken in all transition economies as first steps of the reform process, all associated countries have massively reoriented their trade toward Western markets. Trade statistics do not allow the size of the reorientation to be captured with accuracy. However, all statistical sources confirm the scale of the changes. As shown in *Table 14.1*, the former CMEA partners' share in both total imports and total exports of associated countries shrank by about 25 percentage points between 1988 and 1992. Symmetrically the share of industrialized countries increased by the same order of magnitude. Most of this trade expansion with the West was absorbed by the Community, whose share in CEECs' exports increased from about 23% in 1988 to 49% in 1992 and in imports, from 19% to 46% over the same period. EFTA countries also absorbed a moderate part of this expansion. The size and proximity of the Community market are the main factors underlying this faster integration between the Community and the CEECs. But one of the unexpected features of these developments is that EC–CEEC trade relationships intensified in both directions, while other industrialized countries increased their share in CEECs' imports with few or no gains for CEECs' exports.

On the Community side, although CEECs still represent a small share of Community imports and exports, in both cases less than 5%, trade is expanding fast: between 1989 and 1992, CEECs' share in Community trade doubled, increasing from 2.6% to 4.1% for EC exports and from 2.9% to 3.3% for EC imports. The growth of CEECs' exports to the Community accelerated from an annual growth rate of 11% over 1987–1989 to 16.3% over 1990–1992 and outperformed growth in trade with nearly all other Community partners (see *Figure 14.1*). For manufactured products, these changes are even sharper.

The massive expansion of EC–CEEC trade corresponds to an intensification of trade across the board, confirmed at a disaggregated sectoral level. At the NACE three-digit level, covering 107 industrial sectors, only six sectors recorded a negative growth rate over the period 1990–1992, representing 5.7% of CEECs' exports to the Community. This happened in a context of overall slowdown in Community imports and resulted in CEECs increasing their share of Community imports in all but 15 products, among which agricultural and food products have a significant weight. Romania is the only country which failed to improve its performance in the Community market.

14.1.2 The role of trade with the Community during transition

To evaluate the role of trade liberalization in transition and in particular the contribution of the Community, a more precise evaluation of the CEECs' export potential is needed. At this stage, we have only fragile and partial

Table 14.1. Breakdown of CEECs' trade in 1988, 1990, and 1992.[a]

	Exports			Imports		
	1988	1990	1992	1988	1990	1992
Bulgaria[b]						
World	100.0	100.0	100.0	100.0	100.0	100.0
Eastern Europe & NIS	66.8	63.1	31.5	62.3	57.5	37.2
Industrialized countries	12.4	17.1	36.7	23.7	17.7	44.8
of which						
EC countries	5.8	10.4	30.8	16.7	14.8	32.6
EFTA countries	0.7	1.6	2.9	3.0	1.9	6.2
USA	0.3	0.7	2.2	1.3	0.9	2.7
Japan	0.5	0.5	1.1	1.6	0.5	1.2
Rest of the world	20.7	19.8	31.9	14.0	24.8	18.1
Czechoslovakia (CSFR)[c]						
World	100.0	100.0	100.0	100.0	100.0	100.0
Eastern Europe	17.0	13.5	10.3	25.7	14.0	5.6
NIS	34.2	25.9	10.3	31.8	21.6	24.7
Industrialized countries	33.5	45.0	63.3	30.2	56.4	62.2
of which						
EC countries	24.2	32.0	49.5	17.7	32.1	42.0
EFTA countries	7.5	10.7	10.6	8.2	18.0	13.5
USA	0.6	0.6	1.9	0.3	0.4	3.3
Japan	0.6	0.8	0.8	0.3	0.3	1.1
Rest of the world	15.2	15.7	16.1	12.3	8.0	7.4
Hungary						
World	100.0	100.0	100.0	100.0	100.0	100.0
Eastern Europe	11.8	8.2	6.3	12.4	9.0	6.6
NIS	27.7	20.6	13.1	25.2	19.5	16.8
Industrialized countries	37.2	51.7	69.0	41.4	52.3	68.7
of which						
EC countries	22.5	34.2	49.5	25.2	31.5	42.4
EFTA countries	10.0	12.2	14.7	12.2	15.7	20.6
USA	3.0	3.6	3.2	2.2	2.7	2.9
Japan	1.0	1.2	0.9	1.4	2.1	2.4
Rest of the world	23.3	19.5	11.6	21.1	19.3	7.8
Poland[d]						
World	100.0	100.0	100.0	100.0	100.0	100.0
Eastern Europe	12.0	6.8	5.0	11.7	5.4	4.4
NIS	25.0	15.3	12.8	27.4	19.8	11.8
Industrialized countries	44.7	64.7	68.5	43.9	63.7	72.0
of which						
EC countries	30.3	46.8	55.6	27.2	42.5	53.1
EFTA countries	10.0	13.8	8.7	11.7	16.8	11.2
USA	2.7	2.8	2.6	2.0	1.6	3.6
Japan	1.1	0.8	1.0	1.5	2.3	1.3
Rest of the world	18.2	13.2	13.7	17.0	11.0	11.7

Table 14.1. Continued.

	Exports			Imports		
	1988	1990	1992	1988	1990	1992
Romania						
World	100.0	100.0	100.0	100.0	100.0	100.0
Eastern Europe	11.7	9.4	5.9	16.1	12.3	6.9
NIS	21.7	25.2	13.0	31.6	23.6	14.5
Industrialized countries	34.7	43.0	42.1	12.8	30.4	50.2
of which						
EC countries	24.0	31.4	32.5	6.2	19.6	37.5
EFTA countries	3.2	3.6	5.6	1.3	4.0	6.5
USA	4.9	5.8	2.0	2.7	4.6	3.8
Japan	1.3	1.6	1.4	0.7	0.8	1.3
Rest of the world	31.9	22.3	38.9	39.5	33.6	28.4
Total 5 countries[e]						
World	100.0	100.0	100.0	100.0	100.0	100.0
Eastern Europe & NIS	44.6	35.2	18.9	49.2	37.1	23.3
Industrialized countries	34.1	48.2	62.4	31.2	43.8	64.2
of which						
EC countries	22.7	33.8	48.5	19.2	27.8	44.7
EFTA countries	6.6	9.8	9.9	7.6	11.2	12.8
USA	2.4	2.5	2.5	1.6	2.0	3.6
Japan	0.9	0.9	0.9	0.8	1.1	1.6
Rest of the world	21.8	17.4	19.5	19.8	19.6	13.0

[a]Source: IMF – Direction of Trade Statistics (DoTs) unless otherwise specified. Eastern Europe = Albania, Bulgaria, Czechoslovakia, Hungary, Poland, Romania. Industrialized countries = OECD member states except Turkey. NIS = Newly independent states of the former Soviet Union, including the Baltic states.
[b]Source: PlanEcon except for flows with the EC; Eastern Europe includes former Yugoslavia.
[c]Import data from national customs statistics in koruna converted into dollars at current exchange rates.
[d]Import data for 1992 from PlanEcon.
[e]The various sources are not compatible. Totals for the regional and national trade balances are given for illustrative purposes only.

indications of possible developments at the product level. The reorientation of trade toward the West was not supported by a restructuring of CEECs' exports, and it is premature to predict the likely impact of the ongoing industrial restructuring on future comparative advantages of associated countries.

The product composition of CEECs' exports to the Community has proved to be remarkably stable over the past five years. *Table 14.2* gives indications of the main structural features of CEECs' industrial exports. The

Table 14.2. CEECs' export base in the Community market in 1987 and 1992. Product composition of CEECs' exports at NACE two-digit level, in percent of total.

Sectors	Bulgaria		CSFR		Hungary		Poland		Romania		CEECs	
	1987	1992	1987	1992	1987	1992	1987	1992	1987	1992	1987	1992
21 Extract., prep. metal ores	0.0	0.4	0.1	0.1	0.0	0.1	0.5	0.4	0.0	0.0	0.2	0.2
22 Prod., process., metals	20.9	15.3	12.8	13.7	9.9	6.5	14.6	15.9	9.7	9.0	12.4	12.7
23 Extract., nonmet./energy min.	0.2	0.5	1.6	1.2	0.1	0.1	0.1	0.9	0.0	0.0	0.5	0.7
24 Manu. nonmet. min. prod.	1.7	2.8	7.1	8.0	2.4	2.6	2.7	3.5	2.8	5.3	3.7	4.8
25 Chemical industry	16.7	11.2	12.7	9.6	12.5	10.8	11.6	8.5	8.0	5.9	11.6	9.2
26 Artificial fibers	1.0	0.7	1.0	1.0	0.4	0.4	0.2	0.4	1.7	0.9	0.8	0.6
31 Metal articles	1.2	2.0	2.4	7.0	3.4	5.1	3.2	6.6	2.9	2.9	2.9	5.9
32 Mechanical engineering	7.0	6.0	7.5	7.9	5.7	7.3	4.1	4.6	2.8	3.6	5.2	6.2
33 Office mach., data process	0.9	0.4	0.1	0.4	0.2	0.6	0.1	0.1	0.1	0.0	0.2	0.3
34 Electrical engineering	4.0	4.7	3.7	5.8	7.1	11.1	4.0	4.1	2.8	3.1	4.4	6.1
35 Motor vehicles, parts	0.4	0.6	3.9	7.4	0.7	3.3	4.7	4.4	3.6	1.0	3.2	4.7
36 Other means of transport.	0.1	0.3	0.7	1.2	0.1	0.2	2.3	1.5	1.9	1.4	1.2	1.1
37 Instrument engineering	0.2	0.4	0.5	0.5	0.5	0.7	0.4	0.3	0.2	0.2	0.4	0.5
41 Food, drink, tobacco	12.1	9.7	5.2	2.7	20.7	15.5	17.5	10.5	4.3	2.9	12.3	8.5
43 Textiles	8.3	8.6	7.5	5.8	6.5	5.7	4.3	3.5	9.2	8.3	6.7	5.3
44 Leather, leather goods	0.9	1.9	1.2	1.1	1.4	1.3	0.6	1.0	0.7	0.5	0.9	1.1
45 Footwear, clothing	9.9	22.6	8.0	9.5	17.2	17.8	14.4	17.0	22.1	33.5	14.9	16.4
46 Timber, wooden furniture	3.9	3.8	10.5	6.7	5.1	4.7	9.6	11.6	23.4	18.9	11.3	8.8
47 Paper, paper prod., printing	1.5	1.8	6.3	4.0	1.0	1.2	1.5	1.6	1.2	0.3	2.5	2.2
48 Rubber, plastics	1.4	2.8	3.0	3.1	2.3	2.8	1.1	1.6	1.7	1.4	2.0	2.3
49 Other manufacturing	7.6	3.8	4.2	3.3	2.8	2.1	2.0	2.4	0.8	1.0	2.7	2.5
	100.0	100.0	100.0	100.0	100.0	100.0	100.0	100.0	100.0	100.0	100.0	100.0

Source: Eurostat (Comext database).

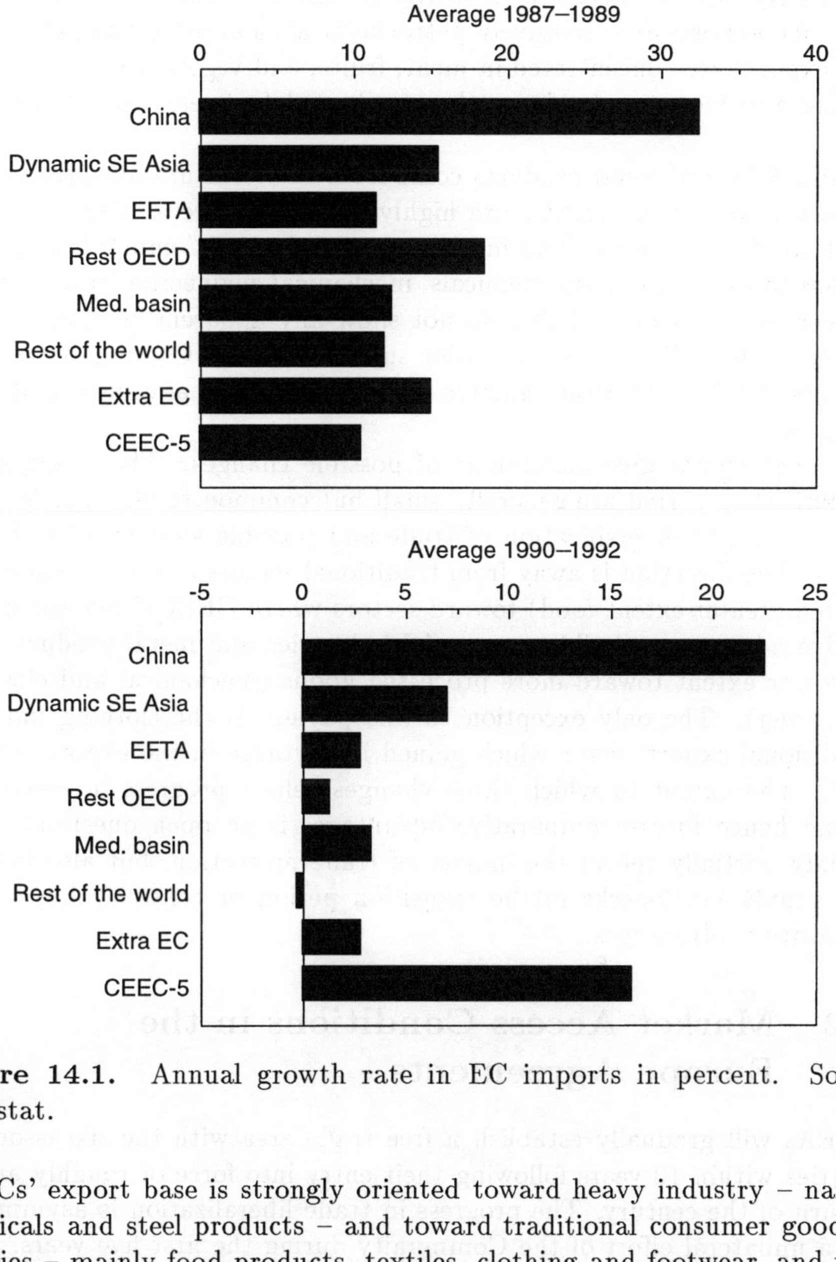

Figure 14.1. Annual growth rate in EC imports in percent. Source: Eurostat.

CEECs' export base is strongly oriented toward heavy industry – namely, chemicals and steel products – and toward traditional consumer goods industries – mainly food products, textiles, clothing and footwear, and wood products. Each of these sectors accounts for about 10% of the CEECs' exports to the Community. At the product level, the specialization is even more clear. Iron and steel products covered by the European Coal and Steel

Community (ECSC) account for nearly all exports of metal products. For chemicals, exports are exclusively petrochemicals and other basic chemicals. Food exports are concentrated in meat, fruits, and vegetables. Ready-made clothing and footwear dominate the textile and footwear and clothing sectors.

About 50% of wood products come from the furniture industry.

Sectors on which CEECs are highly dependent are also sectors where they have developed a strong market position in the Community. The exceptions to this pattern are chemicals, mechanical engineering, and electrical engineering, for which CEECs do not show any apparent comparative advantage. The CEECs are also major suppliers to the Community of some products which are more marginal in their exports, such as cement and metal products.

Recent trends give indications of possible changes. The changes over the 1987–1992 period are generally small but common to all CEECs. They indicate a slight diversification of trade and possible specialization in new sectors. The direction is away from traditional sectors (steel and chemicals, and to a greater extent food) toward sectors where CEECs have some comparative advantages (building material industries and metal products) and to a lesser extent toward more processed goods (mechanical and electrical engineering). The only exception to this pattern is the clothing industry, a traditional export sector which gained importance in the exports of each CEEC. The extent to which these changes reflect progress in restructuring and hence future comparative advantages is an open question. They certainly partially reflect the impact of trade protection, but also indicate some supply bottlenecks in the transition period or consolidation of past comparative advantages.

14.2 Market Access Conditions in the Europe Agreements

The EAs will gradually establish a free trade area with the six associated countries within 10 years following their entry into force or roughly around the turn of the century. The progress in trade liberalization is asymmetric, with a unilateral effort of the Community during the first five years. Most of the tariffs and quantitative restrictions (QRs) were removed upon entry into force of the agreements, with some notable exceptions for agriculture, textiles, and steel and coal products. The agreements also include provisions on rules of origin, antidumping, and safeguard clauses.

14.2.1 Agriculture

The EAs offer the most preferential regime given by the EC to its trade partners. They translate the GSP trade concessions into permanent tariff preferences and eliminate quantitative restrictions. However, the real issue is the competition with EC producers. In this respect, trade concessions represent only a very limited opening, the binding constraint being the system of levies and tariff ceilings applied within the common agricultural policy (CAP). Tariffs in agriculture are around 15%. However, when the various forms of protection and support to Community farmers are added and converted into *ad valorem* tariff equivalents, trade barriers about double the price of imported agricultural products.

14.2.2 Industrial products

Tariffs

For the majority of industrial products originating in associated countries, the EC has abolished customs duties upon entry into force of the agreements. Exempted from this rule are some basic products (Annexes IIa and IIb of the agreements), sensitive products (Annex III), some textile products (Protocol 1 on products covered by the Multi-Fibre Agreement, MFA), and certain steel and coal products (Protocol 2 on products covered by the ECSC). Following the package adopted at the Copenhagen Summit, duties on basic products will be abolished within a maximum of two years. They apply to products such as salt, sulfur, earth, and stones. The products listed in Annex III roughly correspond to the sensitive products within the GSP. These products vary in each EA and include the following items: minerals, chemical fertilizers, footwear, porcelain, furniture, cars, television, radio, numerous iron and steel products, glassware, leather products, and tires. These products are subject to tariff quotas, ceilings, or tariffs. Ceilings and quota levels are increased each year. By the third year of implementation, tariffs within or outside tariff quotas will have been progressively reduced and will then be abolished. Duties will be eliminated at the end of the fourth year for steel and coal products. The tariffs on textiles and clothing will also be progressively reduced and will reach zero at the beginning of the sixth year. Duties on reimports into the EC after processing or working in the associated countries were abolished on entry into force of the agreements. Only textile products are affected by substantial tariffs, in the range of 5% to 10% in the first year of implementation of the Europe Agreements.

Quantitative Restrictions (QRs)

All quantitative restrictions, except on coal and textile products, were abolished on the date of entry into force of the agreements. Whereas duties and QRs on coal will be completely abolished in 10 of the member states in 1994, Germany and Spain have been allowed to maintain national restrictions for another four years. Following the Uruguay Round Agreement, the QRs on textiles will be removed within the first five years of implementation of the agreements.

14.2.3 General trade provisions

Trade policy vis-à-vis CEECs is also defined in various articles on antidumping, safeguards, and rules of origin.

The safeguard provisions draw heavily on principles laid down in other Community trade agreements or regulations. The EAs have a general safeguard measure and specific ones for the textile, steel and coal, and agriculture protocols. With regard to serious disturbances or serious deterioration in the economic situation of a (Community) region, in the general safeguard clause the potential scope for safeguard applications is slightly larger than had been foreseen in the GATT provisions. Unlike GATT, which is a multilateral agreement based on the principle of nondiscrimination of trade partners, it allows regional measures to be taken. Judging by the use of safeguards within other Community trade agreements – in particular, the EC–EFTA agreement, which is very close in this respect – the safeguard clauses are rarely applied, but favor consultations between trading parties, leading to measures such as voluntary export restraints (VERs).

The only case of safeguard action undertaken by the Community so far concerns steel deliveries into France, Germany, and Italy coming from the Czech and Slovak republics. The selective import quotas introduced in late 1992 were decided under the provisions of the ECSC products protocol of the EAs.

In the past, CEECs were particularly penalized by the EC's antidumping policy. CEECs represented about 20% of EC antidumping actions. These applied mainly to chemicals and steel, and many past antidumping actions are still in force. This might explain why there is, so far, no case of application of antidumping under the EA regime. The main change introduced by the EAs is the switch for CEECs from the status of state-trading countries to market economies, implying that dumping is defined in reference to a "normal" price calculated according to established methods. However, in the transition, where monopolies will still dominate the production structure for some years, the calculation of a normal price raises technical difficulties, which might affect trade relationships with CEECs.

Rules of origin are defined for individual products at the Community level, and apply equally to all preferential trade partners (although the GSP regime is somewhat different). The only concession in favor of the CEECs is the possibility of cumulating, which has been given for goods incorporating imports or value added from the Community or from one of the associated countries. The low threshold for import content is often criticized, but the main difficulties are the technicalities of assessing empirically the origin of the goods. In practice, this has raised problems for application of the cumulation rule.

14.3 Evaluating the Degree of Market Opening in Europe Agreements

The EAs have been criticized for falling short of market opening on various counts. But apart from effective clear trade restrictions in some areas, mainly in textiles and agriculture, their effective impact depends on the interpretation and use of their provisions and instruments. It is too early to assess their impact, but some preliminary indications have shown, beyond the usual general criticisms of the agreements, which trade restrictions will likely be binding. The analysis in this section focuses on industrial products for which information is more readily available.

The immediate effect of the agreements is to consolidate trade preferences given through the GSP and to remove quantitative restrictions across the board. This means that 50% of CEECs' exports of industrial products benefit from a complete free trade regime in the Community. The other 50% fall into the category of "sensitive" sectors in a broad sense, for which trade concessions are limited to various degrees depending on the products. The sensitive products in Annex III, which represent between 20% and 25% of the Community's industrial imports from associated countries, remain subject to tariff quotas and ceilings, which will disappear two years following entry into force of the agreements. These temporary trade provisions are not seen as restrictive. In the case of ceilings, for instance, above which a tariff can be reimposed at the request of a member state, tariffs have not been reintroduced in practice or if they have been, it was done with considerable delays,

Table 14.3. Tariff concessions on industrial products in the Europe Agreements.[a]

	Bulgaria[b]			CSFR[b]			Hungary[b]		
	1992 MFN tariff	1993 EA tariff	Year of liberalization in EA	1992 MFN tariff	1992 EA tariff	Year of liberalization in EA	1992 MFN tariff	1992 EA tariff	Year of liberalization in EA
Basic products (Annex IIa)	3.9	1.9	1994	4.5	2.2	1993	5.0	2.5	1993
Basic products (Annex IIb)	6.2	5.0	1997	6.2	5.0	1996	6.0	4.8	1996
Sensitive products (Annex III)	9.0	2.9	1998	8.8	2.4	1997	8.8	2.1	1997
Textiles (Protocol 1)	12.8	9.2	1999	12.1	8.7	1998	12.5	9.0	1998
ECSC coal (Protocol 2)	8.3	8.3	1996	1.3	1.3	1993	0.5	0.5	1996
ECSC steel (Protocol 2)	3.9	3.1	1997	4.0	3.2	1997	3.5	2.8	1997
Other industrial products	4.8	0.0	1993	5.1	0.0	1992	5.1	0.0	1992
Total industrial products	7.2	3.0		6.8	2.1		7.5	2.5	

	Poland[b]			Romania[b]		
	1992 MFN tariff	1992 EA tariff	Year of liberalization in EA	1992 MFN tariff	1992 EA tariff	Year of liberalization in EA
Basic products (Annex IIa)	7.5	3.7	1993	4.3	2.2	1994
Basic products (Annex IIb)	3.7	3.0	1996	0.0	0.0	1997
Sensitive products (Annex III)	7.9	0.9	1997	6.1	2.3	1998
Textiles (Protocol 1)	13.3	9.5	1998	13.3	9.5	1999
ECSC coal (Protocol 2)	3.4	3.4	1993	0.4	0.4	1996
ECSC steel (Protocol 2)	3.3	2.6	1997	4.6	3.7	1998
Other industrial products	3.6	0.0	1992	6.7	0.0	1993
Total industrial products	6.4	2.4		8.9	4.4	

[a]Without taking into account the market-access package agreed upon at the Copenhagen Summit in June 1993.
[b]Tariff rates are defined in percent, weighted by the commodity structure of 1992 exports to the EC.
Source: Deutsche Institut für Wirtschaftsforschung (DIW) Berlin – Commission services.

Table 14.4. Weight[a] of nonagricultural "sensitive" products in CEECs' exports to the Community in 1992.

	Bulgaria	CSFR	Hungary	Poland	Romania
Sensitive products (Annex III)	5.3	26.2	19.9	23.3	24.4
Textiles (Protocol 1)	28.1	12.9	21.3	18.8	37.8
ECSC coal (Protocol 2)	0.2	2.4	0	7.2	0
ECSC steel (Protocol 2)	6.5	8.2	3.7	4.9	6.5

[a]In percentage of CEECs' exports of manufactured products to the Community.
Source: DIW – Commission Services.

and only when ceilings were already exceeded by large amounts. Moreover, for products in Annex III, tariff concessions are substantial, with a switch upon entry into force of the agreements from a most-favored-nation (MFN) rate of about 8%, on average, down to a tariff rate in the agreements of about 2% (see *Table 14.3*).

Restrictions in the textile sector are more substantial. Products covered by the Multi-Fibre Agreement represent a high share of CEECs' exports of industrial products to the Community, between 13% for the CSFR and 38% for Romania (see *Table 14.4*). Tariff concessions are limited, with an MFN rate of close to 12% and a first-year rate in the EAs of between 8% and 9%. In practice, quantitative restrictions affect only a subgroup of products. Except for the CSFR, utilization rates of quotas are usually low, and quota increases granted in the agreements are rather generous. This leaves room for large increases in textile imports from CEECs in the coming years, even though there is no long-term commitment to dismantle protection to support CEECs' industries. This applies mainly to direct imports. Constraints on outward-processing trade (OPT), which is the most dynamic component of CEECs' exports of textiles and nearly 80% of Hungary's and Poland's export earnings in the sector, are more binding.

The situation is substantially different in the steel and coal sectors. Before the implementation of the Europe Agreements, quotas were nearly systematically fully utilized. Tariffs on these products are low, below 5%. Thus the main benefit expected from the EAs is the removal of QRs. However, past antidumping actions remain, together with the threat of new antidumping proceedings under the regime of the EAs. As with textiles, this does not affect all countries equally: the Czech and Slovak republics, for which exports of steel represent nearly 10% of their exports of industrial products to the Community, and Poland, with a corresponding share of coal exports of 7%, are penalized more than the other three associated countries.

14.4 Conclusion

In short, the Europe Agreements provide for a rather fast liberalization of trade for the majority of industrial products. But they fall short of complete free-market access in three areas: agriculture, steel, and textiles. Trade restrictions might also arise from the application of antidumping clauses, but the other general trade provisions do not strongly threaten the pace of liberalization. It would be restrictive to assess the Community's response on the basis of these achievements only. The EAs are a first step of a long-term integration process, which has the accession of associated countries to the Community as its ultimate goal. Various measures and official commitments have been made to progress toward this goal.

The Community has admitted that more must be done to remove deadlocks in the sensitive sectors. This action might not take the form of trade concessions and is conditional on the outcome of other internal and external negotiations. Changes in textiles have been dealt with in the Uruguay Round Agreement. For agriculture, the tensions and constraints might become looser with the implementation of the reform of the Common Agricultural Policy. Other forms of partnerships or cooperation with CEECs are also being investigated in the area. Similarly, in the steel sector, an initiative aiming at consolidating EC and CEECs restructuring programs of the steel industry is being considered. Further developments might materialize soon in these areas.

In addition, the non-trade components of the Europe Agreements should not be underestimated. They might, in particular, improve the climate of cooperation and reduce trade disputes. When the full EAs come into force, priority will be given to the implementation of the provisions on competition and approximation of laws. One of the likely positive developments is that the adoption of EC competition regulations will mitigate the use of antidumping procedures, progressively moving toward a regime close to the EC–EFTA framework.

Finally, the commitment to enlargement made by the EC heads of state at the June 1993 Copenhagen Summit is a political commitment which rules out any setback in the implementation of the EAs and the cooperation of the Community with associated countries.

Comments on the Paper by Anne Bucher

Sándor Richter

Two papers presented at the IIASA Conference on Output Decline in Eastern Europe addressed the role of the CMEA collapse in output decline of the Central and East European countries (CEECs) while only one paper dealt with the role of the European Union's (formerly European Community) contribution to the anticipated recovery in this region. Considering, however, the data on the quick foreign trade reorientation from former CMEA areas toward Western Europe I think that at future conferences the ratio of papers on the respective topics will be the inverse.

Anne Bucher's data show that the CEECs have a growing market share in the European Union's imports. This fact deserves further research. Several questions must be considered. Which countries were the main losers of the CEECs' market share gains? Were the losers the same in each commodity group? Answers to these questions would be expedient when trying to identify CEECs' main non-EU competitors. Taking the total (imported and domestic) consumption in the European Union, is there still a market share gain for the CEECs' exporters? If yes, or in the commodity groups where the answer is yes, who were the losers of the CEECs' gains: countries (firms) inside the EU or countries (firms) outside the EU? The answers to these questions have several policy implications.

The author presents data on the composition of trade between the CEECs and the EU. I think we should restrain from formulating far-reaching assumptions from these data. Some 50% of trade is still restricted in some way. We do not know what composition of trade would have emerged if these restrictions had not been in place. Here I refer to the problem of market share gains. Market share gains can be considered genuine only when all restrictions have been removed. In the commodity groups with restrictions actual market shares do not reveal much about potential market shares.

The author writes that mechanical engineering and electrical engineering are the sectors where CEECs do not show comparative advantages. Is that statement really justified? Currently average wages are at least 10 times lower in the CEECs than in Western Europe. Average productivity is also lower by almost the same extent. But these averages are misleading. Western investors in an ever-growing number of firms in the CEECs have implanted new technology and management methods, and have integrated these firms into their own worldwide system. The wages paid by these firms may be somewhat higher than the average in the given country, but the gap between these somewhat higher wages and the Western wages still remains tremendous. The overnight improved performance and very low wages constitute a highly competitive mixture and can emerge in any commodity group, including nearly all high-tech branches. Parallel to these competitive enclaves the rest of the economy remains blocked by the low productivity, and this blockage results in a limited opportunity for using the wage differential in competing with Western firms.

An often-cited problem of the Association or Europe Agreements between the CEECs and the EU is the access of the firms in the CEECs to the EU markets. It is rarely mentioned that, even with a delay due to the built-in asymmetry, trade barriers restricting access of firms in the EU to markets in CEECs are being removed. I would like to raise the question whether it would be expedient to prolong (by two to three years) the period required to remove these trade barriers. My answer is yes for several reasons. First, the EU has had a huge trade surplus vis-à-vis the CEECs, further any forthcoming recovery in the CEECs will obviously induce a surge of imports, mostly from the EU regardless of the existing trade barriers. This means that the prolongation of the prevailing level of protection in CEECs by a few years would not really hurt EU interests. Second, although foreign trade liberalization was quite quick and across the board in the CEECs, we should not regard the present level of protection negligible. In Poland and Hungary the average tariff level is well above 10%, in the successor states of the CSFR the deeply undervalued (compared with purchasing power parity) national currency provides protection for the domestic market. Consequently these countries still have much to lose by removing the existing trade barriers imposed on imports from the EU. The purpose of the quick liberalization at the beginning of the transformation was to create the necessary competitive pressure on the CEECs' domestic market to replace the missing domestic competition which was the consequence of the inherited monopolistic and oligopolistic structures. This target was attained. The necessary pressure imposed by foreign competition is a reality in each CEEC. In the course of the quick liberalization the damage from lost domestic market shares and the recessionary impacts were not treated seriously. But these disadvantages must be reckoned with again when the new wave of import competition imposed by completely unrestricted imports of industrial products from the EU begins. This wave might damage the fragile stability of what the CEECs will have achieved by that time.

In summary, the possible prolongation of the still existing restrictions on imports from the EU by two to three years would likely benefit the CEECs by providing some extra time for adjustment for firms delivering to the domestic market and by contributing to the fight against recession. This delay in removing the trade barriers, however, would not cause any serious damage to the EU. The Copenhagen Summit brought concessions for the CEECs' exporters; another gesture could include strengthening the asymmetry between the CEECs' export and import sides.

Chapter 15

Disinflation Without Output Decline: Tales of Exchange-Rate-Based Stabilizations

Alberto F. Ades, Miguel A. Kiguel, and Nissan Liviatan

Central and East European countries experienced severe output declines during stabilization. To many this is not surprising, as reductions in the budget deficit and tight monetary and credit policies are usually recessionary. But the importance of stabilization in the output decline is still under debate because these programs were accompanied by major structural reforms to switch from centrally planned systems to market economies (see Blejer *et al.*, 1993; Bruno, 1993; Calvo and Coricelli, 1992; Lipton and Sachs, 1990). Curiously, the output declines were as severe in countries that made major strives to stabilize (for example, Poland and the CSFR) as in those where inflation was rampant and fiscal stabilization is still lagging (Russia and Romania).

This chapter contributes to the debate on the output decline by discussing experiences outside the region and drawing lessons from them. A first piece of evidence, discussed in Section 15.1, is that, paradoxically, a number of stabilization programs in Latin America were associated with an initial expansion in output (the empirical evidence is summarized in Kiguel and Liviatan, 1992). These episodes correspond to programs that used the

The views expressed in this paper do not necessarily reflect those of the World Bank or its affiliated institutions.

R. Holzmann et al. (eds.), Output Decline in Eastern Europe, 351-371.

exchange rate as the nominal anchor (exchange-rate-based stabilization or ERBS) in chronic high-inflation economies.[1] In a typical ERBS program the initial expansion is followed by a recession. In this paper we summarize previous findings and present new evidence from the recent Argentine convertibility plan on the business cycle in the high-inflation economies.

The second piece of evidence, examined in Section 15.2, describes experiences with money-based stabilization (MBS) programs in the high-inflation Latin American economies. Although MBSs are few and sparse in these economies, the facts strongly indicate that in contrast to ERBSs they are clearly recessionary. In this paper we briefly examine the MBS programs in Argentina and Peru in 1990, both aimed at stopping hyperinflation.

The third piece of evidence, presented in Section 15.3, comes from Western Europe. We argue that the phenomenon of expansionary exchange-rate-based stabilizations might not be confined to the high-inflation economies. An ERBS program launched in Denmark in the early 1980s to fight a low to moderate rate of inflation generated similar outcomes to those described above. Whether the pattern observed in Denmark is the rule or the exception remains an open question, as similar ERBSs in France and Ireland (with rates of inflation comparable with Denmark) were associated with an initial recession. The paper presents evidence on these episodes and reasons for the dissimilar outcomes.

The chapter concludes with a comparison of the various episodes presented and a discussion of how expectations of the possible success or failure of the program affect outcomes. The chapter closes with an examination of the plausibility of other theories, especially whether disinflations that expand credit can account for the expansionary or recessionary impact of stabilization programs (Calvo and Coricelli, 1992; De Gregorio *et al.*, 1992).

15.1 A Review of the Evidence on Expansionary Stabilizations in Latin America

The evidence presented in Kiguel and Liviatan (1992a) indicates that ERBS programs in the high-inflation economies of Latin America (as well as in Israel) do not follow the standard Phillips curve trade-off in the medium run. Stabilization programs in these countries are often associated with a "business cycle": after a small initial recessionary effect, or even with no effect of this kind, the reduction in inflation is associated with an initial expansion of output above the historical trend, and with a drop in unemployment. The expansionary phase may continue for a number of years ending in a recession.

The findings are robust in the sense that they apply to different types of ERBS programs undertaken over three decades in Argentina, Brazil, Chile, Mexico, Israel, and Uruguay.[2] Some programs relied on shock therapy (for example, the Austral plan in Argentina), while others followed a gradual approach (the so-called Tablitas); some were orthodox and relied entirely on market forces (the Southern Cone programs of the late 1970s), while others resorted to price and wage controls (for example, the so-called heterodox programs). The findings are also largely independent of the fiscal stance, indicating the business cycle in cases where the programs reduced the budget deficit as well as in those where the budget deficit did not change, or even increased.

A *typical* ERBS program in a high-inflation economy displays the following features:

- *Real Activity.* In general, economic expansion starts soon after the initiation of the stabilization program. Usually, the behavior of unemployment is compatible with GDP growth, that is, unemployment falls in the growth phase of the cycle. The fact that most ERBSs are preceded by a recessionary period relative to trend indicates that there is excess capacity, which may provide suitable conditions for the upswing.
- *The Balance of Payments.* ERBSs are usually associated with a deterioration of the trade balance in the course of the program. In a typical case the current account goes into the red during the expansionary phase. The capital inflows that finance these deficits are, as a rule, reversed at some advanced stage of the boom when the recessionary phase begins. The inability to finance the growing current account deficits is, in most cases, the immediate reason for halting the boom.
- *Relative Prices.* As a rule, real wages increase with the upswing of economic activity, but sometimes we observe a lag that can be due either to the fact that the real wage has been raised up front to take into account the anticipated erosion by the sluggish reduction in inflation (as in the Argentine stabilization from 1967 to 1970) or to the case that the real wage is deliberately kept, for some time, below its equilibrium level by income policies (as in Israel in 1985).
- *Consumption and Investment.* Most of the expansions of output are accompanied by a "consumption boom," as consumption grows faster than GDP (which is also growing). Investment played a dominant role in the Argentine program of the 1960s, much of it being directly induced by government policies. In the programs of the 1970s it was the Chilean ERBS which was driven by a continuous investment boom. The role

of investment was not significant in the 1980s, mainly because of the reduction in capital inflows following the debt crisis.

The main conclusion of Kiguel and Liviatan (1992a) is that the expansionary phase of ERBS programs can be explained as a speculative boom that builds on the expectation of future reversals of policy. The role that credibility plays is that of being absent. In their view, agents expect the stabilization to be only temporary and therefore shift future consumption and investment expenditures to the present.[3] This behavior soon leads to a real exchange-rate appreciation, current account deficits, and the collapse of the plan.

15.2 Money-Based Stabilizations

In contrast to the ERBSs, money-based stabilizations are typically recessionary. The Chilean stabilization of 1974–1975 represents a typical (and one of the few) money-based stabilization program in a high-inflation economy, as the government applied a fairly persistent monetary crunch in the face of accelerating inflation (this program is analyzed in Edwards and Edwards, 1987; Foxley, 1983; Ramos, 1986). Between September 1973 and June 1976 the danger of hyperinflation was averted, in this respect the tight money was effective. However, inflation, which exceeded 500% in 1973, did not fall below 200% (annualized) till the end of this period. This sluggishness of inflation was accompanied by a dramatic rise in unemployment (from 4.6% in 1973 to 16.8% in 1975) and negative growth, including a fall in GDP of 12.9% in 1975. The very early recessionary effect of these policies is unquestionable.

The recent stabilization programs in Argentina and Peru to stop hyperinflations provide additional evidence on the differences in outcomes associated with money- and exchange-rate-based stabilizations. Peru adopted a money-based stabilization in August 1990, and Argentina implemented one in March 1990 following a number of failed stabilization attempts.

In Peru, the program achieved a dramatic fall in inflation, but it stopped short of bringing the economy to low or moderate inflation levels (*Figure 15.1*). Monthly inflation declined from 400% in August to 9% in October and 5% in November; but after that it rebounded, reaching 23% in January 1991, and then stabilizing in the 5% to 8% range for the rest of the year. Tight money and fiscal discipline were more effective in stabilizing the exchange rate than in dealing with inflationary rigidities.[4]

The March 1990 program in Argentina showed the effectiveness of the tight money-fiscal combination in blocking hyperinflation (*Figure 15.1*).

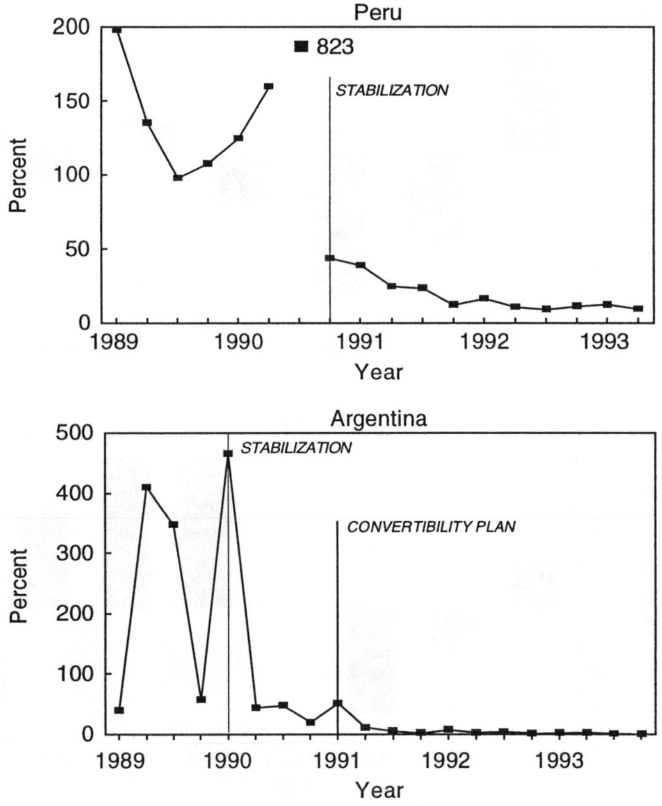

Figure 15.1. Quarterly inflation rates in Peru and Argentina from 1989 to 1993. Source: *International Financial Statistics*, various issues.

Inflation declined from 95% in March 1990 to just 11% in April. In the short run, the money-fiscal combination brought about an important reduction in inflation, but it failed to reduce it below a basic rate of 10% per month.

While the programs were successful on the inflation front, they were associated with a poor growth performance. As shown in *Figure 15.2*, Argentina did not grow in 1990 and, since the beginning of the stabilization, Peru has had problems in returning to positive rates of growth. In addition, as shown in *Figure 15.3*, there was a sharp appreciation in the real exchange rate (some 25% in Peru and 30% in Argentina). In Peru, the real appreciation was associated with a deterioration in the trade balance (*Figure 15.4*) but a surplus in the balance of payments throughout the period, as capital flew in. In contrast, Argentina ran a large and continuous surplus in the

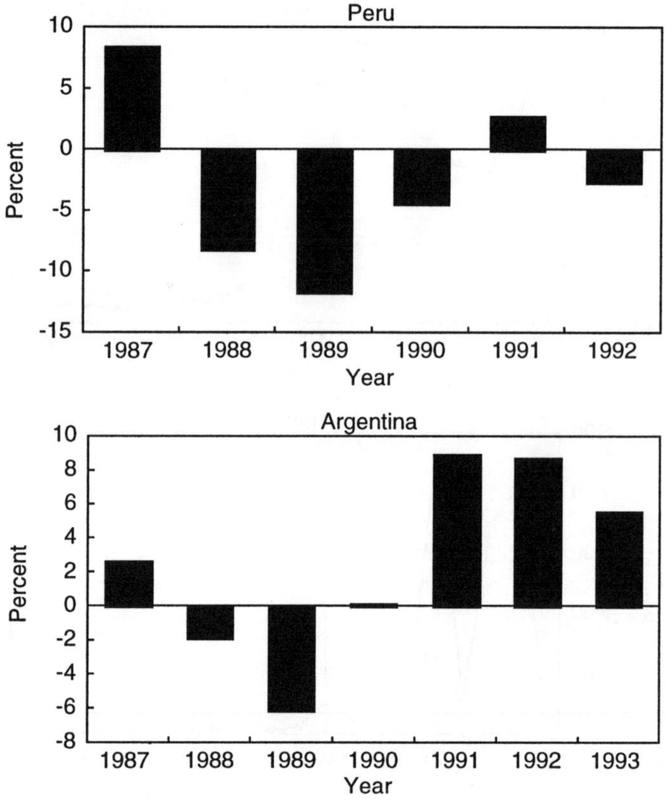

Figure 15.2. GDP growth rates in Peru and Argentina. Source: *International Financial Statistics*, various issues.

trade balance in spite of the real appreciation. The deep recession in economic activity (which started at the time of the hyperinflation) can partly explain the comfortable trade balance position.

The failure to fully tame inflation in Argentina induced the most recent and daring ERBS program, the convertibility plan, with outcomes similar to those discussed in Section 15.1. This program was far-reaching, as there was a major effort on the fiscal side, especially through higher revenues, while the new economic team went further and tied its own hands by adopting a so-called orthodox fixed exchange-rate system where the currency is fully convertible. In addition, the convertibility law imposed strict limits on the amount of central bank financing to the nonfinancial public sector, the requirement to hold enough international reserves to back the monetary

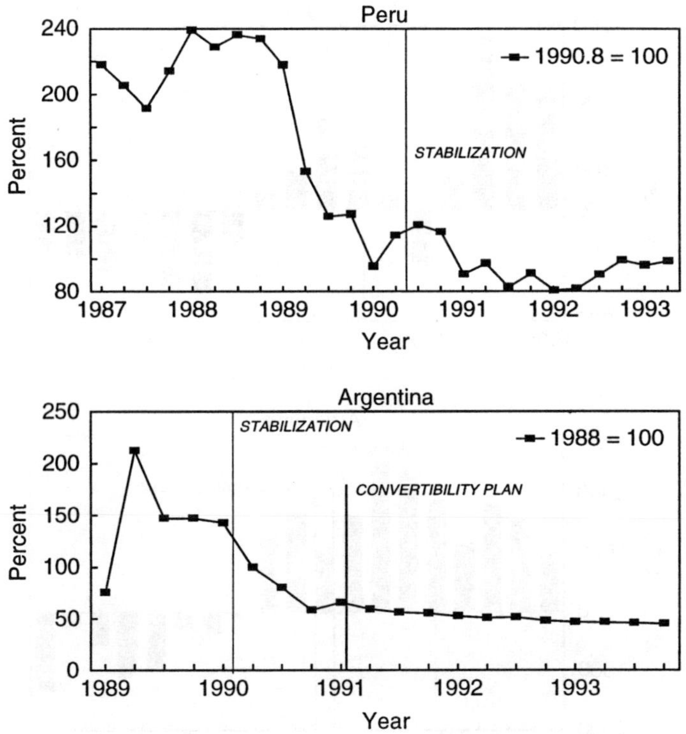

Figure 15.3. Real exchange rates in Peru and Argentina. Source: World Bank.

base, and the need for congressional approval for the central bank to effect a devaluation (for details on the convertibility program see Canavese, 1992).

The Argentine program has been extremely effective in bringing down inflation, as it has remained at the lowest levels in recent decades and only slightly higher than international rates (*Figure 15.1*). Annual inflation was just 8% in 1993. Other outcomes are similar to those described for other exchange-rate-based stabilizations (*Figure 15.2–15.4*). There was dramatic turnaround in growth, as GDP growth exceeded 8% in 1991 and 1992. Both investment and consumption increased significantly during this period. The real exchange rate continued to appreciate, as inflation did not converge quickly enough toward international levels. Finally, and not surprisingly, the trade balance deteriorated as a result of the real appreciation and the higher level of economic activity. There is a clear contrast between the two phases of the Argentine stabilization effort.

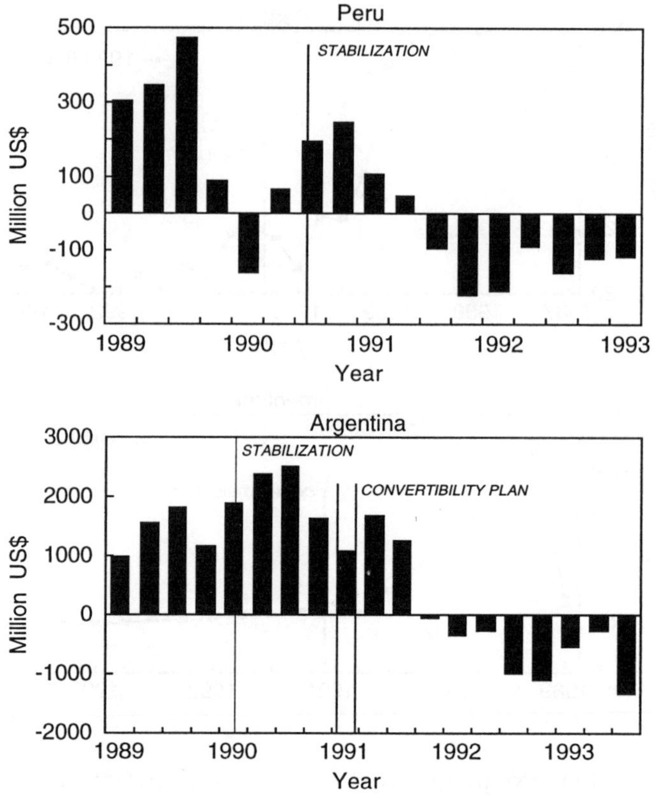

Figure 15.4. Quarterly trade balance in Peru and Argentina from 1989 to 1993. Source: *International Financial Statistics*, various issues.

15.3 Exchange-Rate-Based Stabilizations in Denmark, Ireland, and France

Denmark, Ireland, and France embarked on ERBS in the early 1980s.[5] While there was no explicit announcement about exchange-rate policy in these programs, the fixing of the central parity against the ECU (*Figures 15.5*) indicates that the exchange rate clearly functioned as a nominal anchor.

In contrast to the ERBS in Latin America, these three European programs were aiming at much lower rates of inflation (from the initial rates of 10% in Denmark, 20% in Ireland, and 12% in France). The outcomes of the three stabilizations in Europe do not always fit those of the Latin American ERBSs. While the stabilization in Denmark was associated with an initial

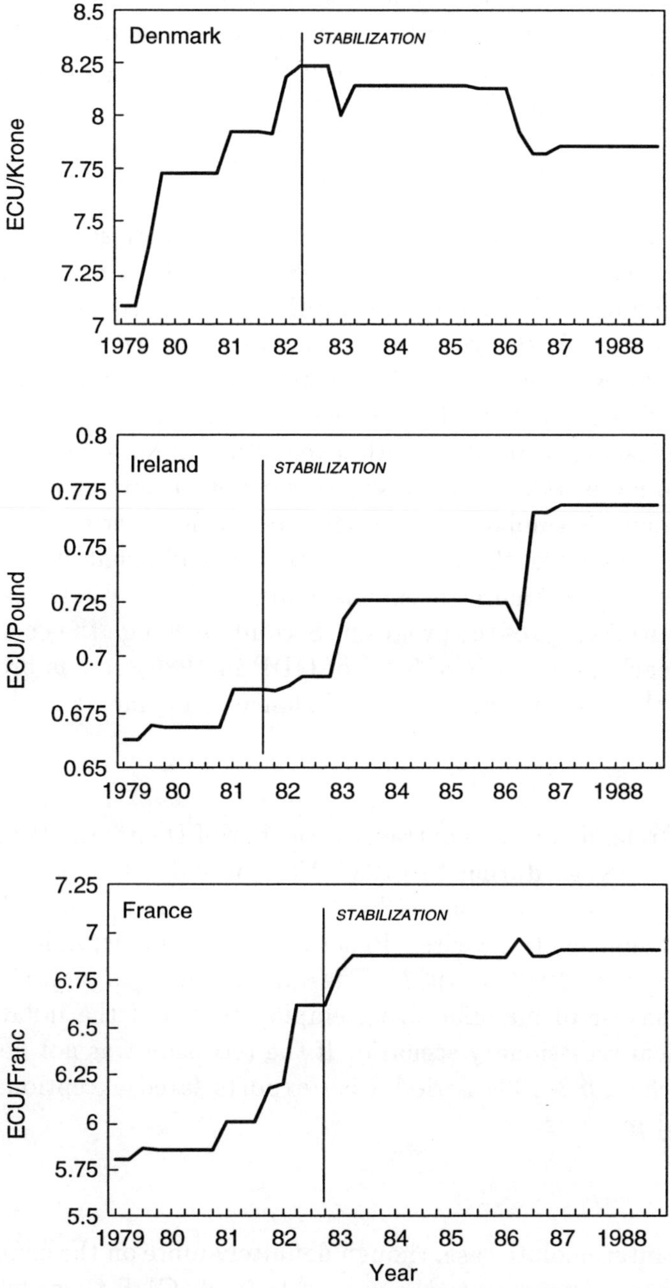

Figure 15.5. Central parity of domestic currency against the ECU for Denmark, Ireland, and France from 1979 to 1988. Source: *European Economy*, various issues.

expansion in output, consumption, and investment, this was not the case in France and Ireland, where the programs were recessionary. In this section we briefly examine the outcomes of the three programs, and compare the findings with other ERBSs.

Denmark

In Denmark disinflation was expansionary in the early stages with an average GDP growth rate of 3.7% between 1983 and 1986. Growth was driven by domestic demand, with private consumption growing (over the same period) at an average of 4.4% per year and business investment increasing at 13.1% (all data are drawn from OECD National Income Accounts). The top chart in *Figure 15.6* shows the spectacular behavior of manufacturing employment during stabilization, coinciding with a reduction of inflation.[6] The expansionary period was followed by a recessionary one (starting in 1987). In this respect the cycle is similar to the ERBSs in Latin America.

Two features make the Danish experience fundamentally different from that of many Latin American expansionary ERBSs. First, real wages fell during the initial stage of the program. Second, although the current account worsened (reaching a deficit of 5.4% of GDP in 1986), it was brought under control and the plan did not end in a balance of payments crisis.

Ireland

The case of Ireland sharply contrasts with that of Denmark. While GDP did not grow on average during the 1982–1984 period (after being negative in 1982 and 1983), consumption fell by 7.1% in 1982 and remained almost flat during the following two years. Business investment experienced negative growth rates from 1982 to 1987. The middle chart in *Figure 15.6* shows that the behavior of manufacturing employment and the inflation pattern fit the classical recessionary scenario. If the recession was not deeper, it was because in the 1982–1984 period Irish exports fared exceptionally well on international markets.

France

France is an intermediate case, though definitely more on the contraction side of the spectrum. Contrary to the case of Ireland, GDP never fell. However, its growth rates were considerably below those of the OECD average until 1986. Although consumption growth fell, it was business investment that suffered the most dramatic blow, falling an average of 3.1% per annum in the

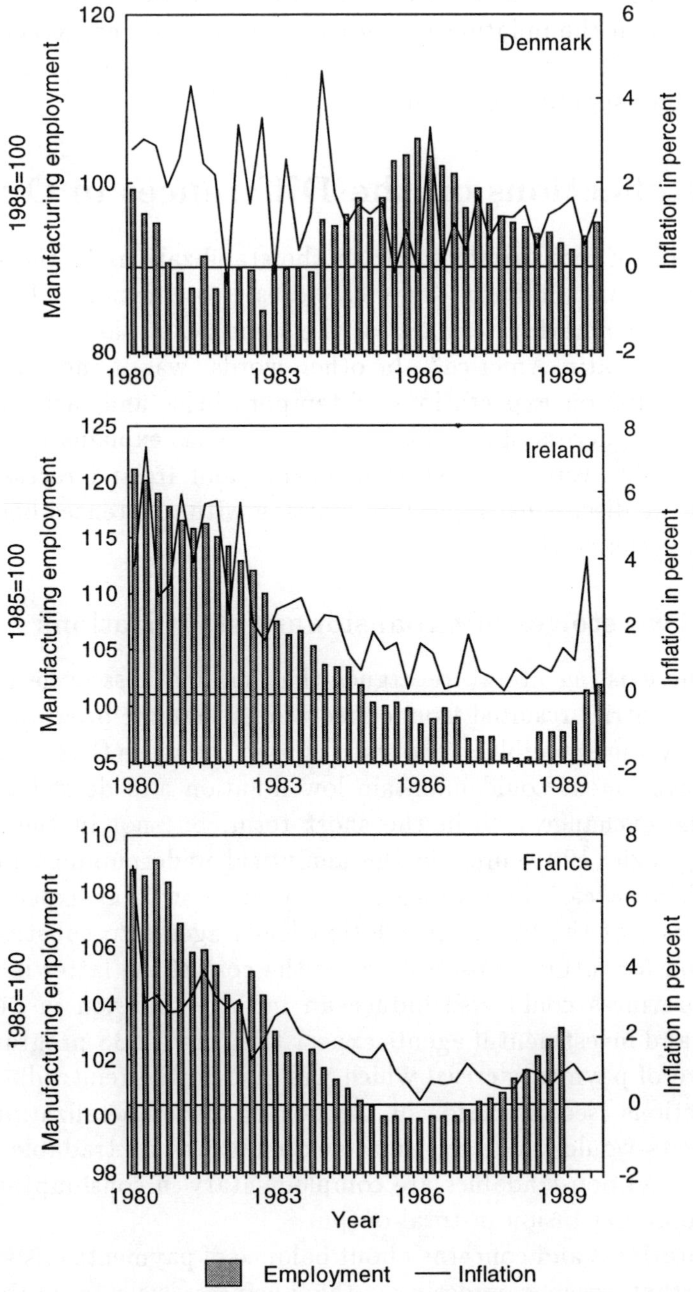

Figure 15.6. Manufacturing employment and inflation rates in Denmark, Ireland, and France from 1980 to 1989. Source: *International Financial Statistics*, various issues.

period 1983–1984. Again, *Figure 15.6* shows that the behavior of industrial employment and the inflation pattern fit the classical recessionary scenario. In contrast to Denmark there was an improvement in the current account and real wages slightly increased.

15.4 Reflections on the Differences in Outcomes

The evolution of real variables during the stabilizations in the three European countries and in Latin America raises two questions. First, was the expansion in Denmark after 1982 of the same nature as those observed in the ERBSs in Latin America? In other words, was it mostly speculative in nature, based on expectations of temporariness and lack of credibility about the final success of disinflation? If not, what explains it? The second question is, why were the ERBSs in France and Ireland recessionary? In this section we discuss each question starting with differences between Latin America and Denmark.

15.4.1 Two stories of expansionary stabilizations

Much of the existing literature argues that the business cycle in the Latin American countries resulted from expectations that the programs were temporary. They were credible in the short run, in the sense that people thought that the government could maintain low inflation and defend the commitment to the exchange rate in the short term, but not in the longer run. Calvo and Végh (1991) provide the analytical underpinnings for this conclusion. Using a cash-in-advance model they show that expectations of a future reversal of the initial disinflation leads agents to substitute present consumption for future consumption, as the cost of the latter is larger.

Temporariness could also induce an initial expansion in output, consumption, and investment if agents expect that the ERBS programs will end in a balance of payments crisis, which will lead to the reintroduction of import restrictions (see discussion on temporary trade liberalization in Calvo, 1986). Agents would try to anticipate expenditures on tradable goods; and if tradables and non-tradables are complementary in consumption, this will also lead to an expansion in total output.

Temporariness and concerns about balance of payments crisis were probably important reasons underlying the business cycle in Latin America. Reinhart and Végh (1993) find empirical evidence supporting the temporariness hypothesis for at least some of the ERBS programs in Latin America. But was the expansion in Denmark of a similar type?

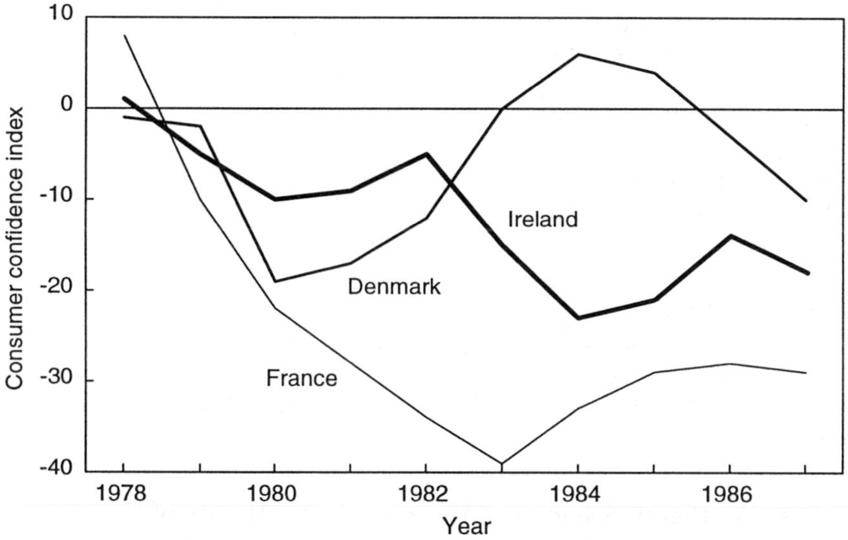

Figure 15.7. Consumer confidence index in Denmark, Ireland, and France from 1978 to 1987. Source: *European Economy*, various issues.

A brief look at the evidence suggests that in Denmark different factors were at work. The announcement of the disinflation program quickly led to overoptimistic expectations of future output and inflation developments. Optimism about lower future inflation resulted in a fall of real interest rates initially. In addition, the evolution of the index of consumer confidence (*Figure 15.7*) shows that the stabilization was accompanied by a marked change in consumer confidence. The program was favorably received, and this was expressed in an increase in private consumption.

The growth rates of the *shares* of private consumption and investment in GDP illustrate the differences in the nature of the expansions in Latin America and in Denmark. Demand booms based on the expectation of a future policy reversal are likely to be characterized by strong consumption effects. In contrast, fears of a future policy reversal lead to low investment rates in the private sector. As argued in Morales (1991), "The persistent weakness of public finances may awaken fears of future confiscatory measures against the private sector through exchange-rate manipulations, punitive taxes, or outright expropriation." We thus expect to observe different patterns in credible and non-credible expansionary stabilizations: in stabilizations of the first type, we expect to see investment playing a leading role in the demand boom; but, when expansions are of a speculative nature, consumption

Table 15.1. Average growth rate of share of private consumption and total investment in GDP during disinflation, in percent.

Sample	Private consumption	Investment
Latin America and Israel: 1960–1990	1.8	−0.24
Latin America and Israel: 1970–1990	2.22	−3.9
Latin America in the 1960s	0.5	2.9
Latin America during the Tablitas	1.2	−0.11
Latin America in the 1980s	1.6	0.32
Israel	3.7	−4.1
Denmark: 1983–1986	0.7	9.4

For Latin America, investment represents total investment. For Denmark, we used private, nonresidential capital formation.
Sources: For Latin America and Israel, Kiguel and Liviatan, 1992a; for Denmark, OECD National Income Accounts.

dominates. We therefore averaged the annual growth rate of the *share* of private consumption in GDP during the years of major stabilization programs in Latin America and Denmark. We did the same thing with investment. As shown in *Table 15.1*, the results are striking.

There are two major differences in the roles that private consumption and investment played during the stabilization booms between the Latin American chronic high-inflation countries and Denmark. First, in Latin America the share of private consumption typically increased more than the share of investment during stabilization. This is especially so if one takes only the stabilization plans of 1970–1990. For this subsample, the growth in the share of private consumption is almost 30% higher than in the whole sample. These results are consistent with the theory that expectations of future reversals of policy were based on previous failed stabilizations. This effect seems to have become more important since the 1970s.

The second major difference is that the roles of consumption and investment are drastically reversed in Denmark. The increase in the share of investment is almost 13 times as large as the one for consumption. Favorable expectations appear to have been an important force underlying the Danish boom.

Bruno and Meridor (1991), based on the Israeli experience after the 1985 stabilization program, argue that optimistic expectations about the success of stabilization programs to bring down inflation can explain an initial increase in consumption. They say that when "a stabilization program succeeds in correcting fundamental factors, there will be an increase in perceived permanent income and wealth, which in turn will manifest itself in an increase in both consumption and investment." The Danish episode certainly supports this view.

While consumer optimism provides an appealing explanation for the beginning of the boom in Denmark (and possibly Israel), it does not explain the ensuing recession. One would need to assume initial *overoptimism* about the program. A casual look at the confidence indices for Denmark suggests that overconfidence could have been a factor in the business cycle during the stabilization.

15.4.2 Why were France and Ireland recessionary?

The recession in France and Ireland does not support most of the evidence on ERBSs in the high-inflation economies and in Denmark. But, this should not be surprising. After all, didn't these programs follow the standard pattern predicted by the Phillips curve? And what explains the difference between these programs and other ERBSs that were expansionary?

First, in comparing Denmark with France and Ireland, it is clear that the overoptimism observed in the former was absent in the latter two countries. The indices of consumer confidence were declining in France and Ireland during the stabilization programs (as shown in *Figure 15.7*), but they were increasing in Denmark. In addition, indices depicting the general economic situation were pessimistic in France and Ireland. Expectations about the evolution of real variables were clearly not supporting an expansion in either France or Ireland.

This pessimism about economic performance seems to have been accompanied by adverse expectations about disinflation. Real wages rose during the disinflation in France and Ireland, an indication that workers' demands for wage increases remained above actual inflation. The fact that these wage demands were maintained at a time when agents were pessimistic about economic performance suggests that inflationary expectations were not in line with the program. These outcomes stand in sharp contrast with the results in Denmark, where real wages fell while economic activity was booming.

But why didn't lack of credibility resulted in an expansionary phase as in the high-inflation economies of Latin America? Two reasons are possible. First, lack of credibility, or temporariness, has different meanings during periods of low or moderate inflation. In the high-inflation economies, temporary ERBS programs are expected to bring down inflation rapidly early on, but this is followed by a reversal in which inflation creeps up to previous levels. Calvo and Végh (1991) explain that the reduction in interest rates provides a great incentive for increased consumption (and possibly investment). In addition, because the rekindling of inflation is expected to end in a balance of payments crisis, accompanied by capital outflows and the reintroduction of trade and foreign exchange controls, there is an incentive to anticipate consumption. In contrast, in low- and moderate-inflation economies nominal (and real) interest rates are likely to rise (or fall only slightly) eliminating one of the sources of the expansion. In both France and Ireland real interest rates, in fact, rose at the beginning of the stabilization program (but they fell in Denmark).

The second mechanism is also less important in the low-inflation economies, because agents usually do not expect a full reversal of the program. Instead, the concern appears to be about how much and how fast inflation is going to fall. In other words, there are doubts about the pace of disinflation – an idea that is implicit in the expectations-augmented Phillips curve. This type of adverse expectation is not likely to lead to an expansion in consumption or investment.

15.4.3 Credit in exchange-rate-based stabilizations

An alternative, more classic, explanation for the differences in outcomes would be to emphasize the role of credit. It has been argued that in Latin American countries the fall in nominal interest rates that followed the initial reduction in inflation was associated with an increase in credit. This idea is not inconsistent with the results of the cash-in-advance model, where the initial expansion results from an increase in wealth (Calvo and Végh, 1991). An alternative interpretation of that result is that lower interest rates increase the supply of credit and aggregate demand, as agents who were deprived from credit before obtain access to it in the new situation.

De Gregorio *et al.* (1992) indicate that bunching can have a role in explaining increases in consumption. In their paper they state that a sudden reduction in inflation generates a positive wealth effect which induces consumers to bring forward their purchases of durable goods, thus inducing an aggregate consumption boom. If the model were to be extended to credit, a sudden increase in the availability of credit (and/or its cost) would have a similar effect. Once again credit could have an important explanatory role.

A brief look at the European episodes (*Figure 15.8*) indicates that credit to the private sector (as its ratio to GDP) became tighter in Ireland. In Denmark, credit to the private sector was tight in the late 1970s and early 1980s but then it increased during the expansion. Credit in France was expanding throughout the period, so it is difficult to argue that tight credit underlay the poor growth performance at the outset. Credit to the private

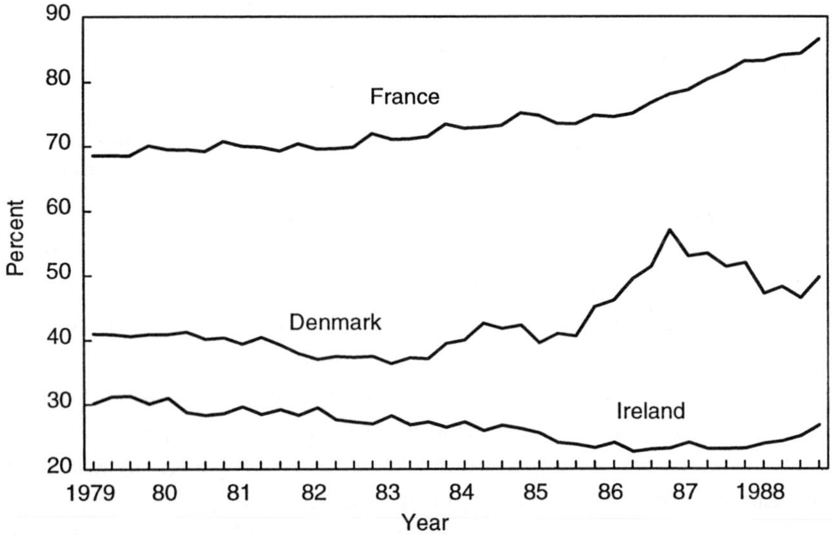

Figure 15.8. Domestic credit to the private sector as a ratio to GDP in Denmark, Ireland, and France from 1979 to 1989. Source: *International Financial Statistics*, various issues.

sector clearly expanded between 1985 and 1987 when growth increased in France. On the whole, it seems that credit policies mattered.

Although data for the Latin American countries are less reliable, it seems that credit expansions were important in Argentina and Chile during the expansions of the late 1970s.

15.4.4 Exchange-rate-based stabilizations in Eastern Europe

Among East European countries, Poland is the one that most resembled the high-inflation economies of Latin America.[7] It had high inflation for a couple of years, and it adopted an ERBS program to reduce inflation to manageable levels. Presumably, of all the stabilization programs implemented in Eastern Europe, the Polish program is the one that was most likely to face expectations of temporariness and speculative booms of the type observed in Latin America.

The Polish stabilization program, as discussed in Calvo and Coricelli (1992) and Lipton and Sachs (1990) among others, in fact went through the opposite cycle: it started with a severe recession and, according to most accounts, it is only now starting to get out of it. The cycle was more similar to that of France and Ireland than to the Latin American programs, though few would argue that the main issue was how much and how fast would inflation fall. It would have been difficult to rule out temporariness arguments at that time.

What explains the recession in Poland? Most would argue that a combination of factors were at work: systemic reforms, the collapse of the CMEA, and the stabilization effort. The key question, and one that we will not be able to answer, is whether the marginal contribution of the ERBS program was expansionary or contractionary.

Calvo and Coricelli (1992) argue that tight credit was a determining factor for the recession, and this effect dominated the possible expansionary effects from fixing the exchange rate. The evidence presented above indicates that tight credit was a factor in Ireland and to some extent in France.

Credit policies can partly explain why the ERBS program was recessionary in Poland in contrast to the experience of other high-inflation economies. Why could Poland maintain tight credit policies while adhering to the fixed exchange rate? Mainly because Poland did not have access to foreign loans to finance an expansion in consumption or investment. Otherwise, the fixed exchange rate would probably have added an expansionary bias to the program because the problem of lack of credibility in Poland was similar to that of the high-inflation Latin American countries.

15.5 Concluding Remarks

This chapter has provided new evidence from Latin America and Europe on the business cycle observed in stabilization programs. How relevant are the findings presented here regarding the output decline in Central and Eastern Europe? First, the evidence indicates that non-credible, temporary exchange-rate-based stabilizations are generally expansionary. Given that many of the stabilization programs in Central and Eastern Europe relied on a fixed exchange rate, and that the *ex ante* chances of success were probably assessed to be small (and hence were not credible), the effects should have been less recessionary than otherwise. In other words, fixing or announcing the path of the exchange rate in these countries in all likelihood reduced the costs of stabilization.

Second, the evidence in this paper indicates that tight credit and monetary policies mattered. Even in countries that used the exchange rate as a nominal anchor, when they managed to maintain tight credit policies, the outcome was an initial recession. Of course, this can only be done if there is relatively low capital mobility, as is the case in most countries in Central and Eastern Europe.

Finally, the evidence from Latin America indicates that the costs of disinflation even in countries that used money-based stabilizations have been much smaller than those observed in Central and Eastern Europe. Argentina and Peru, for instance, experienced stagnation (rather than a decline in GDP) during the MBS program, and only Chile suffered a severe output decline (of about 12%). But as in Eastern Europe, it is difficult to attribute the whole decline to the stabilization, as the country was also hit by a severe terms-of-trade shock and was undertaking major structural changes. In sum, although money-based stabilizations are recessionary, it is doubtful that they can explain a decline in output of 10% or more, as observed in Central and Eastern Europe.

Regarding the importance of credibility the chapter makes two points. First, expansionary stabilizations do occur, and they are mainly associated with overconfidence (as was the case in Denmark) or with temporariness and lack of credibility (as in the high-inflation economies of Latin America). Second, lack of credibility will not always lead to an expansion. In particular, it is not likely to happen if the programs are not expected to end in a balance of payments crisis. The experiences of France and Ireland, two low-inflation countries, which launched stabilizations programs that were not fully credible, illustrate that recessions are likely to happen when agents have pessimistic expectations about the pace of disinflation; this is reflected in the sluggish response of prices and wages to the programs.

Notes

[1] Chronic high-inflation economies are loosely defined as those where the median rate of inflation exceeds 30% per month for five years.

[2] The ERBS programs included in the study were those in Argentina in 1959, 1967, 1973, 1978, and 1985 (the Austral plan); in Brazil the 1964 program and the 1986 Cruzado plan; the 1976 Chilean program; the 1978 Uruguayan program; the 1985 Israeli program; and the Mexican program in 1988.

[3] Investment and durables consumption are the components of expenditures that are most affected by speculative activity. They are also both greatly affected by falls in real interest rates, such as the ones observed in the Tablita stabilizations during the late 1970s.

[4] Inflation receded somewhat in the final quarter of the year (to about 7% per month), when the exchange rate started to appreciate in nominal terms. However, this proved to be temporary, as inflation had a new big outburst in February 1991.

[5] Austria is another example, as it fixed the exchange rate to the German mark in 1974 (see Hochreiter and Winckler, 1993). A detailed discussion of the three programs is presented in Ades *et al.*, 1993. In addition, Sachs and Wyplosz (1986) examine the French stabilization; Giavazzi and Pagano (1990), the Danish program; and Dornbusch (1989), the Irish plan.

[6] For Denmark, the inflation series was smoothed using standard exponential smoothing techniques and a value of $\alpha = 0.3$.

[7] Yugoslavia prior to its breakup also closely resembled the high-inflation Latin American countries.

References

Ades, A., Kiguel, M., and Liviatan, N., 1993, *Exchange-rate-based Stabilization: Tales from Europe and Latin America*, Policy Research Paper, No. 1087, World Bank, Washington, DC, USA.

Blejer, M., Calvo, G., Coricelli, F., and Gelb, A., 1993, *Eastern Europe in Transition From Recession to Growth*, Discussion Paper, No. 196, World Bank, Washington, DC, USA.

Bruno, M., 1993, *Crisis, Stabilization and Economic Reform*, Oxford University Press, Oxford, UK.

Bruno M., and Meridor, L., 1991, The costly transition from stabilization to sustainable growth: Israel's case, in M. Bruno, S. Fischer, E. Helpmann, and N. Liviatan, eds., *Lessons of Economic Stabilization and Its Aftermath*, MIT Press, Cambridge, MA, USA.

Calvo, G., 1986, Temporary stabilization: Predetermined exchange rates, *Journal of Political Economy*, **94**(December):1319–1329.

Calvo, G., and Coricelli, F., 1992, Stabilizing a previously centrally planned economy: Poland 1990, *Economic Policy*, **14**(April):176–226.

Calvo, G., and Végh, C., 1991, Exchange Rate Based Stabilization under Imperfect Credibility, Working Paper 91/77, International Monetary Fund, Washington, DC, USA.

Canavese, A., 1992, Argentina's Convertibility Plan, Instituto Di Tella, Buenos Aires, Argentina [mimeo].

De Gregorio, J., Guidotti, P., and Végh, C., 1992, Inflation Stabilization and the Consumption of Durables, International Monetary Fund, Washington, DC, USA [mimeo].

Dornbusch, R., 1989, Ireland's disinflation, *Economic Policy*, **8**:173–209.

Edwards, S., and Edwards, A.C., 1987, *Monetarism and Liberalization: The Chilean Experience*, Ballinger Publishing Company, Cambridge, MA, USA.

European Economy, various issues, Commission of the European Communities, Brussels, Belgium.

Foxley, A., 1983, *Latin American Experiments in Neoconservative Economies*, University of California Press, Berkeley, CA, USA.

Giavazzi, F., and Pagano, M., 1990, Can severe fiscal contractions be expansionary? Tales of two small European countries, *NBER Macroeconomics Annual*:75–122.

Hochreiter, E., and Winckler, G., 1993, The Advantages of Tying Austria's Hands: The Success of the Hard Currency Strategy, Working Paper No. 9307, Department of Economics, University of Vienna, Austria.

International Financial Statistics, various issues, International Monetary Fund, Washington, DC, USA.

Kiguel, M., and Liviatan, N., 1992a, The business cycle associated with exchange-rate-based stabilization, *The World Bank Economic Review*, **6**(2):279–305.

Kiguel, M., and Liviatan, N., 1992b, Three Big Inflations: Argentina, Brazil and Peru, Policy Research Working Paper 999, World Bank, Washington, DC, USA.

Lipton, D., and Sachs, J., 1990, *Creating a Market Economy in Eastern Europe*, Brookings Paper on Economic Activity, Brookings Institution, Washington, DC, USA.

Morales, J., 1991, The transition from stabilization to sustained growth in Bolivia, in M. Bruno, S. Fischer, E. Helpmann, and N. Liviatan, eds., *Lessons of Economic Stabilization and Its Aftermath*, MIT Press, Cambridge, MA, USA.

Ramos, J., 1986, *Neoconservative Economics in the Southern Cone of Latin America: 1973–1983*, Johns Hopkins University Press, Baltimore, MD, USA.

Reinhart, C., and Végh, C., 1993, Nominal Interest Rates, Consumption Booms and Lack of Credibility: A Quantitative Examination, International Monetary Fund, Washington, DC, USA [mimeo].

Sachs, J., and Wyplosz, Ch., 1986, The economic consequences of President Mitterrand, *Economic Policy*:261–322.

Summary

Output Decline in Eastern Europe: Summing up the Debate

John Williamson

By the time the transition is over, I suspect that we may have quite a good understanding of how it could have been done properly, for the Conference on Output Decline in Eastern Europe, as well as the book, does suggest that some progress is being made in understanding what is going on.[1] In particular, we no longer seem totally fixated on making emotion-laden one-dimensional comparisons between virile/crude defenders of big-bang shock therapy versus supine/sophisticated defenders of gradualism.

We started by considering whether, and to what extent, the recorded decline in output in Eastern Europe could be a statistical artifact generated by factors such as the difference between gross domestic product (GDP) and net material product (NMP) or a failure to record the increasing output of the private sector. My priors were that such considerations reduced the extent of, and the need to worry about, the output decline, but that a real problem remains after all reasonable allowance is made for such factors as the fall in output of bads, the underrecording of the growth of the irregular economy, and the decline in hours worked (apparently of importance, at least in Romania; Earle, 1993). The session did not lead me to revise those priors greatly, although Dallago's chapter (Chapter 2) does demonstrate the possibility that the irregular economy[2] might be mitigating the recorded decline (e.g., because some sectors of unrecorded activity were decreasing) rather than necessarily exaggerating the decline. It was particularly disappointing

R. Holzmann et al. (eds.), Output Decline in Eastern Europe, 373-380.

that there was no analysis designed to probe the credibility of the recent downward revision of the extent of the Polish output decline (as well as to ask whether there might be a need for similar revisions in regard to other countries).

We then turned our attention to the causes of the output decline. One important result seems to have been established beyond reasonable doubt [see the chapters by Borensztein and Ostry (Chapter 4) and Berg (Chapter 5)], that the proximate cause of the output decline was principally a fall in demand rather than dislocation on the supply side.[3] The competing story that a credit crunch disrupted the purchase of inputs still does not look persuasive, despite the explosive growth of inter-enterprise credits documented in the Calvo and Coricelli chapter (Chapter 8). It is easy to convince oneself that coordination failures and the perverse incentive structures analyzed by Raiser and Nunnenkamp (Chapter 13) pose fundamental supply-side impediments to a rapid growth in output; however, they do not yield a compelling story to explain the falling output of state enterprises, which is the puzzle that we have to resolve.

Two sources of declining demand in the Keynesian sense are reasonably clear. One is the fall in demand from the former Soviet Union (FSU), which Rosati (Chapter 6) shows was primarily a consequence of the FSU recession and only secondarily due to the demise of the CMEA at the beginning of 1991. Gács (Chapter 7) shows that a surprisingly large part of that loss in demand was initially compensated by a successful switch in sales from the FSU to the West, although Hungary's recent export reduction has wiped out much of that offset. The other clear source of declining demand is related to inventories (Berg). In place of the chronic overaccumulation of inventories as almost the only store of value available to enterprises under the *ancien regime*, one had an *ex ante* inventory depletion prompted by the introduction of market incentives.

Nevertheless, it is implausible that Keynesian demand deficiency was the main part of the story.[4] First, the Chu and Schwartz chapter (Chapter 10) does not identify a squeeze on public expenditure (although it would certainly have been nice to have had some data for constant-employment deficits). Second, it is not obvious that either fiscal or monetary policy was particularly tight in some countries, for example, Romania or the FSU (excluding the Baltics). Finally, the rapidity with which a demand increase translated into an acceleration of inflation in Poland in July 1990 is difficult to reconcile with a Keynesian approach.

What, then, is the common factor that provides the primary explanation for the fall in demand in all the economies in transition? Berg suggests that it was demand shift despite his paradoxical finding that the output decline was largest in consumer goods. Borensztein and Ostry diagnose a supply shift rather than a demand shift, but the appropriateness of their framework has been severely criticized. It should be noted that when output declines because demand shifts from A to B in the absence of a capacity to increase the output of B, one can even argue about whether to classify that as a demand shock or a supply shock. To the firm producing A, however, it certainly looks like a shortage of demand.

One implication of accepting demand shift as the primary explanation of the output decline in Eastern Europe is that it would be a mistake for the region to lean too heavily on the Ades–Kiguel–Liviatan analysis (Chapter 15) of inflation stabilization in Latin America. In particular, using the exchange rate as a nominal anchor and delaying the recessionary cost of stabilization is simply not an option. The lessons that remain valid are that fundamentals such as fiscal discipline matter, that policy needs to be credible, and that Chile provides an excellent role model to demonstrate the advantages of following a real exchange-rate rule, provided that it is accompanied by an appropriate fiscal stance and something in the way of an incomes policy. However, rather than looking to recent Latin American experiences, we should perhaps recall a long-forgotten analysis of the late 1950s about how inflation could be initiated by demand shift (Schultze, 1959). Such inflation seems likely to be particularly stubborn – that is, the unemployment cost of stabilization seems likely to be particularly great.

Accepting demand shift as the main explanatory factor might lead one to seek insight from two-sector models. Although one might reasonably identify the contracting sector as consisting of large state firms and the expanding sector as composed of small private firms, the aggregates on which attention is focused in the chapters by Valentinyi (Chapter 11) and Čapek (Chapter 12), these do not provide much insight into the process of adjustment. To get such insight, one presumably needs to have something more in the way of a model that poses the critical questions. For example, it is not obvious, *a priori*, whether one should expect faster growth of the private sector to increase output in the state sector (because of positive income effects) or to decrease it (as resources are bid away). An analysis that focused on that question would have been highly constructive.

We then turned to a consideration of the prospects for, and the policies needed to promote, recovery. After the fall of the Berlin Wall, I recall telling journalists that the countries of Central and Eastern Europe could look forward to a long period of catch-up growth similar to that enjoyed by Western Europe in the 1950s. I suppose that if I had been pressed I would

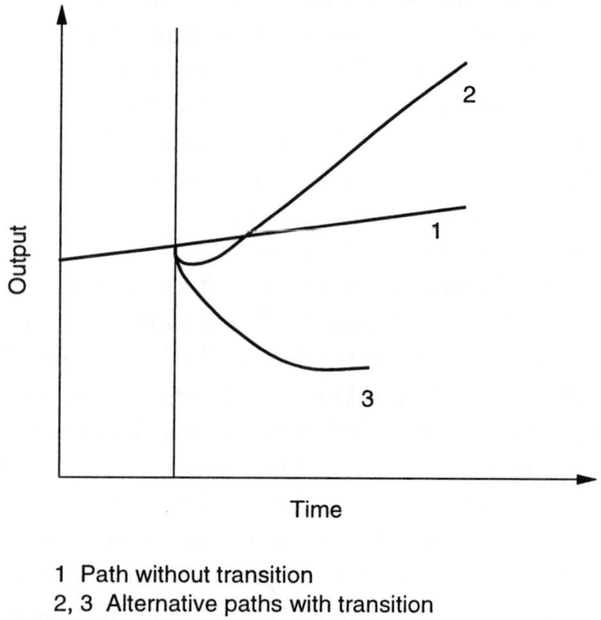

Figure S.1. Alternative paths of output.

have conceded the likelihood of an initial dip in output resulting from the switch from a sellers' market to a buyers' market in both labor and product markets; but the basic story would nonetheless have been one of output rapidly surpassing that of the no-reform path, as shown in *Figure S.1* by the crossing of path 1 by path 2 shortly after the start of the transition. We are now sadder and wiser, and we know that up to this point the transition has been marked by a deep and prolonged decline in output, as shown by path 3, with only the first hints of an upturn apparent in one or two countries, notably Poland. My expectation is still that Eastern Europe will in due course experience catch-up growth so that path 3 will head upward, parallel to path 2, and eventually overtake path 1. However, one has to admit that, at this stage, such expectations are based on faith and theory rather than experience and evidence.

To what extent can the disappointing experience to date be attributed to policy errors? A group of Washingtonians with interests in both Eastern Europe and Latin America recently discussed what lessons from experience in the former region we could draw on to advise Cuba on designing its transition, if and when such advice is asked for. Everyone agreed on one and only one point: the Cubans should avoid restitution like the plague. By introducing unnecessary and lengthy delays into the establishment of clear property rights, the insistence on restitution (rather than compensation) has set back the reform process and the revival of growth by months or even years.

A second general error is suggested by the diagnosis of demand shift as the cause of the recession and by the recognition that high unemployment involves sheer economic waste. The implication is that those who argued in favor of transitional protection (McKinnon, 1991; Flemming, 1993) were right. Output of low-value-added goods might not have fallen as much, prior to the investment necessary for the expansion of output in the new sectors, had the price changes resulting from liberalization been phased in gradually. The most efficient way of achieving such a gradual phase-in would not have been to delay price liberalization itself, but to provide temporary protection for the declining sectors ("senile-industry protection"). Those who have denied this conclusion seem to have argued implicitly from a model where the marginal product of labor in an industry is constant; under this assumption, one certainly wants to maximize the speed with which resources are redeployed from the low-productivity sector to the high-productivity sector. However the more realistic assumptions posited by Flemming (1993) involve putty-clay technology and short-run diminishing returns to labor, and under those conditions it is intuitively obvious that there are potential gains from temporary senile-industry protection.

Nonetheless, I fear that it is now too late to secure the benefits of transitional protection, at least in Central Europe. The last signal one wants to send to senile industries at this stage is to start trying to revive their output. Perhaps there is still some scope for senile-industry protection in the FSU, but Central Europe is going to have to rely on growth of the new sectors.

While there have surely been many other errors, my impression is that these have been country-specific rather than general. However, it is time to consider what policy changes might be able to accelerate the revival of growth.

A first obvious possibility to consider is Keynesian demand expansion. If any participant in the conference believed this to be an important part of the answer, he or she kept quiet about it.

Similarly, I cannot persuade myself that the growth in open unemployment is likely to help lubricate the flow of labor to the expanding sectors, and thus help revive growth – a view that seems to be held by those who take the models of labor search literally. It surely is not true that workers are precluded from searching for new jobs until they have lost their existing employment (certainly I never felt it necessary, or even advantageous, to postpone looking for a new slot until I had ceased my previous job). On the contrary, workers' skills atrophy rapidly once unemployed. Unemployment beyond the rate needed to bring, and keep, inflation under control is an unmitigated economic waste as well as a social evil.

A much more convincing line of reasoning is that expansion of the new sectors depends on filling the institutional and entrepreneurial void left by the collapse of central planning with the sorts of institutions and practices commended by Raiser and Nunnenkamp.

However, the most common supply-side advice is to speed up privatization. I have to say that the information presented does not provide much support for that thesis. On the basis of experiences in Poland, Szomburg (1993) concludes quite specifically that "the sale of a company to a strategic foreign investor is the only method that brings a radical and fast improvement in terms of better manufacturing and financial results." We endorsed Voszka's (1993) reservations regarding the specific preferential credit provided for privatization in Hungary, the so-called E-loans; I, at least, would echo her view that governments should shift the emphasis from selling enterprises to improving the business environment by codifying transparent and stable laws and regulations. In the future, we must spend more time discussing how those fine sentiments can be translated into concrete actions.

Mládek (1993) is more optimistic, but the jury is still out on whether voucher privatization as used in the Czech Republic (or, for that matter, Russian-style privatization, which gives effective control and most of the property rights to insiders) is going to resolve the principal-agent problem and generate an incentive to behave entrepreneurially. I confess to having my doubts: in Britain the primary gains from privatization came, not after privatization, but when state firms were being prepared for privatization, which has led me to muse that the ideal corporate form may be a state enterprise in the process of being privatized.[5] It also leads me to question whether it makes sense to put all the emphasis on achieving private ownership rapidly rather than on privatizing properly (which, above all, means using the process to achieve a competitive market) and reforming the public sector in the interim. The fascinating Czech experiment may cause me to revise my views.

My guess is, however, that the financial sanitization discussed by Gomulka (Chapter 9) is of greater importance. There seemed to be a general view that precedents suggest that it is a mistake to split the bad loans off into separate institutions. What is clear is that well-capitalized banks that are technically able to find creditworthy entrepreneurs and financially able to make loans to them, and that are able to deny credit to the industrial cripples, are of key importance in accelerating the growth of new sectors.

All postwar experience suggests that any sustained growth will have to be export-led. Continued access to Western markets and renewed expansion of those markets are, therefore, of key importance in reviving the economies of the region. We had a fair and frank review of the checkered record of the EC in this regard from Bucher (Chapter 14). Let us hope that the West will not fail the countries of Central and Eastern Europe by closing its markets in response to problems that, while difficult, do not compare with those of the transition.

As acknowledged above, the transition has so far proved much more difficult than most of us anticipated during the euphoria of late 1989. However, it is right to remember that the initial postwar recovery of Western Europe was much longer and more painful than had generally been expected in 1945. Indeed, it was only some five years later, in 1950, that recognition began to dawn that those trying years had been well-spent building the base for a long boom; and only years later did it become clear that catch-up growth would ultimately lead Western Europe to virtual parity in living standards with the USA. The difficult counsel that we need to offer to Central and Eastern Europe is to combine a patient resolution to get the fundamentals right and to avoid false panaceas with a constant search for policy changes that could indeed bring forward the longed-for day when it becomes clear that the region is on the path of catch-up growth.

Notes

[1] The Conference was held at IIASA, Laxenburg, Austria, on 18–20 November 1992. Comments are also made in this chapter on papers that were presented at the Conference but are not included in this book.

[2] Dallago's distinction between the "regular economy" (which operates within the framework of the law), the "irregular economy" (which pursues legitimate goals outside the law), the "criminal economy" (which pursues illegal goals), and the "informal economy" (non-monetized activity) struck me as quite useful; although one should note that, in Latin America, the term "informal sector" is widely used to describe Dallago's "irregular economy."

[3] This conclusion also emerges unambiguously from Table 4 in Kornai (1993). It is not clear, however, that the same would hold true of the former Soviet Union.

[4] Czechoslovakia still seems to provide a possible exception, for both fiscal and monetary policies were made quite tight by the excessive devaluation.

[5] I suspect the reason for the good performance of state enterprises in the process of privatization is precisely that the principal-agent problem is minimized,

provided the managers and workers know they have a stake in a successful privatization.

References

Earle, J.S., 1993, Output Decline and Labor Market Adjustments in Romanian Industry, Paper presented at the Conference on Output Decline in Eastern Europe: Prospects for Recovery? International Institute for Applied Systems Analysis, Laxenburg, Austria.

Flemming, J., 1993, *Relative Price Shocks and Unemployment: Arguments for Temporarily Reduced Payroll Taxes or Protection*, European Bank for Reconstruction and Development, London, UK [mimeo].

Kornai, J., 1993, *Transformational Recession*, Discussion Paper No. 1, Institute for Advanced Study, Collegium Budapest, Hungary.

Mládek, J., 1993, Czech Privatization Process: Time for Corporate Governance, Paper presented at the Conference on Output Decline in Eastern Europe: Prospects for Recovery? International Institute for Applied Systems Analysis, Laxenburg, Austria.

McKinnon, R.I., 1991, Liberalizing foreign trade in a socialist economy, in J. Williamson, ed., *Currency Convertibility in Eastern Europe*, Institute for International Economics, Washington, DC, USA.

Schultze, C.P., 1959, Recent Inflation in the United States, Paper presented to the Joint Economic Committee of the US Congress for a study on Employment, Growth, and Price Levels, Washington, DC, USA.

Szomburg, J., 1993, The Logic of Polish Privatization, Paper presented at the Conference on Output Decline in Eastern Europe: Prospects for Recovery? International Institute for Applied Systems Analysis, Laxenburg, Austria.

Voszka, É., 1993, An Attempt to Speed Up Privatization in Hungary: Experiences with the E-Loan, Paper presented at the Conference on Output Decline in Eastern Europe: Prospects for Recovery? International Institute for Applied Systems Analysis, Laxenburg, Austria.

International Studies in Economics and Econometrics

1. T. Harder: *Introduction to Mathematical Models in Market and Opinion Research.* With Practical Applications, Computing Procedures, and Estimates of Computing Requirements. Translated from German. 1969 ISBN 90-277-0096-6
2. A.R.G. Heesterman: *Forecasting Models for National Economic Planning.* 2nd rev. and ext. ed. 1972 ISBN 90-277-0224-1
3. A.R.G. Heesterman: *Allocation Models and Their Use in Economic Planning.* 1971 ISBN 90-277-0182-2
4. M. Durdağ: *Some Problems of Development Financing.* A Case Study of the Turkish First Five-Year Plan (1963-1967). 1973 ISBN 90-277-0267-5
5. J.M. Blin: *Patterns and Configurations in Economic Science.* 1973 ISBN 90-277-0203-7
6. A.H.Q.M. Merkies: *Selection of Models by Forecasting Intervals.* Translated from Dutch. 1973 ISBN 90-277-0342-6
7. H.C. Bos, M. Sanders and C. Secchi: *Private Foreign Investment in Developing Countries.* A Quantitative Study on the Evaluation of the Macro-Economic Effects. 1974 ISBN Hb 90-277-0410-4; Pb 90-277-0439-2
8. R. Frisch: *Economic Planning Studies.* A Collection of Essays. Selected, introduced and edited by Frank Long, with a Preface by Jan Tinbergen. 1976 ISBN Hb 90-277-0245-4; Pb 90-277-1194-1
9. K.L. Gupta and M. A. Islam: *Foreign Capital, Savings and Growth.* An International Cross-Section Study. 1983 ISBN 90-277-1449-5
10. C.A. van Bochove: *Imports and Economic Growth.* 1982 ISBN 90-247-3052-X
11. O. Bjerkholt and E. Offerdal (eds.): *Macroeconomic Prospects for a Small Oil Exporting Country.* 1985 ISBN 90-247-3183-6
12. D. Weiserbs (ed.): *Industrial Investment in Europe.* Economic Theory and Measurement. 1985 ISBN 90-247-3270-0
13. J.-M. Graf von der Schulenburg and G. Skogh (eds.): *Law and Economics & The Economics of Legal Regulation.* 1986 ISBN 90-247-3377-4
14. S. Pejovich (ed.): *Socialism: Institutional, Philosophical and Economic Issues.* 1987 ISBN 90-247-3487-8
15. R. Heijmans and H. Neudecker (eds.): *The Practice of Econometrics.* Studies on Demand, Forecasting, Money and Income. In Honor of Jan Salomon Cramer. 1987 ISBN 90-247-3502-5
16. A. Steinherr and D. Weiserbs (eds.): *Employment and Growth.* Issues for the 1980s. In Honor of Albert Kervyn de Lettenhove. 1987 ISBN 90-247-3514-9
17. M.J. Holler (ed.): *The Logic of Multiparty Systems.* 1987 ISBN 90-247-3515-7

18. J.M. van Brabant: *Regional Price Formation in Eastern Europe.* Theory and Practice of Trade Pricing. 1987 ISBN 90-247-3540-8
See also below under Volume 23
19. A.M. Wesselman: *The Population-Sample Decomposition Method.* A Distribution-Free Estimation Technique for Minimum Distance Parameters. 1987 ISBN 90-247-3603-X
20. P. Coffey (ed.): *Main Economic Policy Areas of the EEC - Toward 1992.* The Challenge to the Community's Economic Policies when the 'Real' Common Market is Created by the End of 1992. 3rd rev.ed., 1990 ISBN 0-7923-0810-7
21. A. Breton, G. Galeotti, P. Salmon and R. Wintrobe (eds.): *The Competitive State.* Villa Colombella Papers on Competitive Politics. 1991 ISBN 0-7923-0835-2
22. S. Pejovich: *The Economics of Property Rights.* Towards a Theory of Comparative Systems. 1990 ISBN 0-7923-0878-6
23. J.M. van Brabant: *Remaking Eastern Europe.* On the Political Economy of Transition. 1990 ISBN 0-7923-0955-3
24. J.M. van Brabant: *Privatizing Eastern Europe.* The Role of Markets and Ownership in the Transition. 1992 ISBN 0-7923-1861-7
25. J.M. van Brabant: *Integrating Eastern Europe into the Global Economy.* Convertibility through a Payments Union. 1991 ISBN 0-7923-1352-6
26. G.W. Kołodko, D. Gotz-Kozierkiewicz and E. Skrzeszewska-Paczek: *Hyperinflation and Stabilization in Postsocialist Economies.* 1992 ISBN 0-7923-9179-9
27. P. Mihályi: *Socialist Investment Cycles.* Analysis in Retrospect. 1992 ISBN 0-7923-1973-7
28. A. Breton, G. Galeotti, P. Salmon and R. Wintrobe (eds.): *Preferences and Democracy.* Villa Colombella Papers on Competitive Politics. 1993 ISBN 0-7923-9321-X
29. K.Z. Poznanski (ed.): *Stabilization and Privatization in Poland.* An Economic Evaluation of the Shock Therapy Program. 1993 ISBN 0-7923-9341-4
30. P. Coffey (ed.): *Main Economic Policy Areas of the EC-After 1992.* 4th Revised Edition. 1993 ISBN 0-7923-2375-0
31. J.M. van Brabant: *Industrial Policy in Eastern Europe.* Governing the Transition. 1993 ISBN 0-7923-2538-9
32. H.J. Blommestein and B. Steunenberg (eds.): *Government and Markets.* Establishing a Democratic Constitutional Order and a Market Economy in Former Socialist Countries. 1994 ISBN 0-7923-3059-5

33. S. Pejovich: *Economic Analysis of Institutions and Systems.* 1995
ISBN 0-7923-3214-8
34. R. Holzmann, J. Gács and G. Winckler (eds.): *Output Decline in Eastern Europe.* Unavoidable, External Influence or Homemade? 1995
ISBN 0-7923-3285-7

KLUWER ACADEMIC PUBLISHERS – DORDRECHT / BOSTON / LONDON